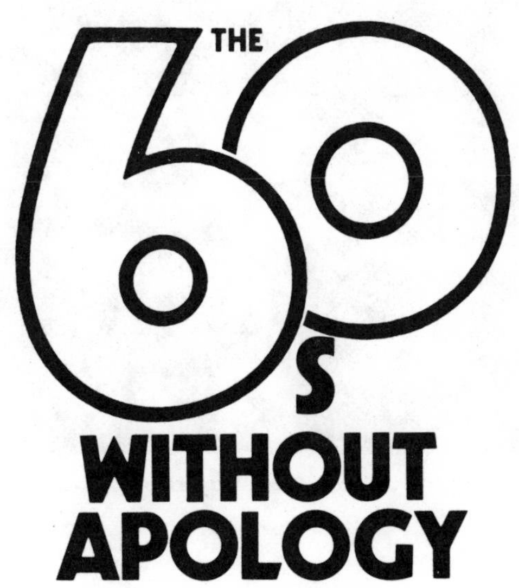
THE
60
S
WITHOUT
APOLOGY

WIN cover, November 1, 1969. Photo by Henry Gordillo, courtesy of the War Resisters League.

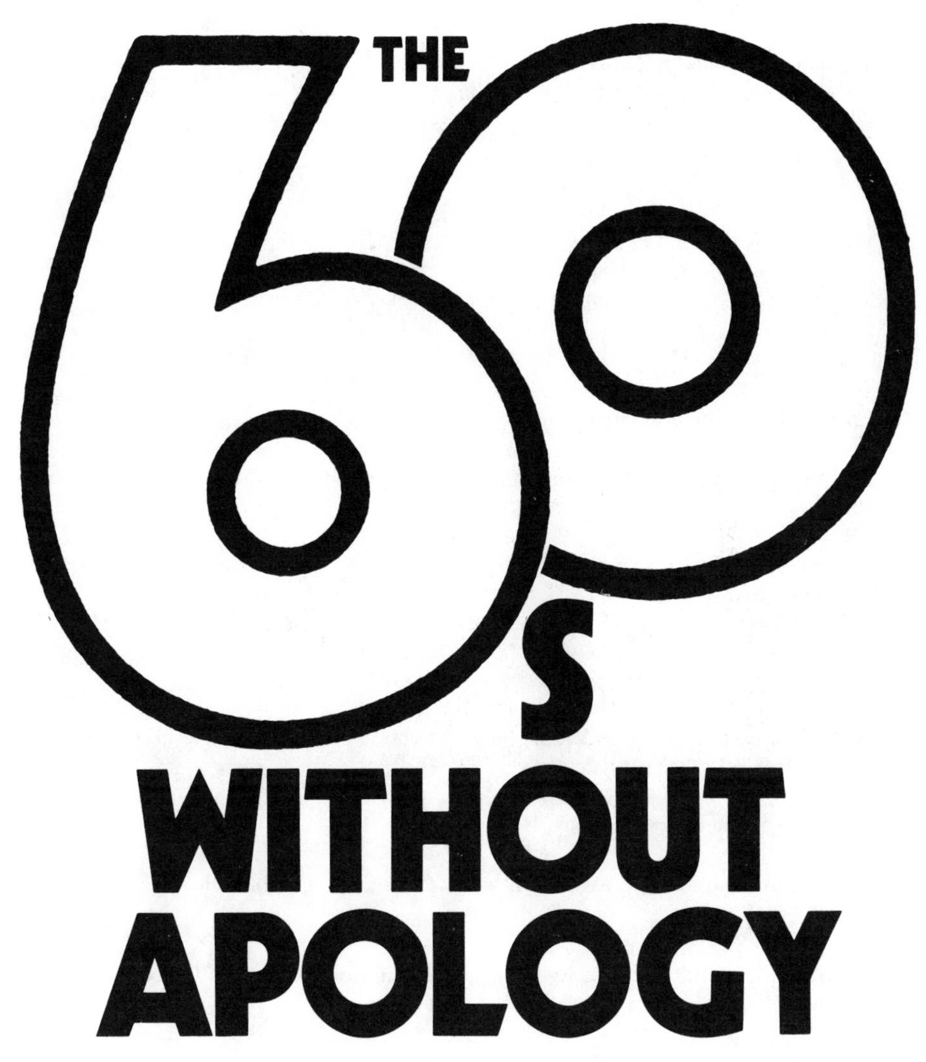

EDITED BY
SOHNYA SAYRES, ANDERS STEPHANSON,
STANLEY ARONOWITZ, FREDRIC JAMESON

UNIVERSITY OF MINNESOTA PRESS • MINNEAPOLIS
IN COOPERATION WITH SOCIAL TEXT

Published by the University of Minnesota Press
2037 University Avenue Southeast
Minneapolis MN 55414

The University of Minnesota is an equal-opportunity educator and employer.

Printed in the United States of America

This book corresponds to a special double issue of **Social Text** (Volume 3, no. 3 and Volume 4, no. 1, Spring-Summer 1984).

The **Social Text** editorial collective during the time of preparation: Nancy Anderson, Stanley Aronowitz, Serafina Bathrick, Rachel Bowlby, John Brenkman, Stephen Bronner, Michael Brown, Michael Denning, Jean Franco, Jeff Halley, Fredric Jameson, Sohnya Sayres, Loren Shumway, Anders Stephanson, Cornel West, Richard Wolff, George Yudice.

Special thanks to: Nancy Anderson, Finvola Drury, Peter Gourfain, Wendy Graham, Robert Roth and Daniela Salvioni.

Design and cover: Cynthia Carr.

Production: Stanley Aronowitz, Cynthia Carr, Daniela Salvioni, Sohnya Sayres, and Anders Stephanson.

All submissions and subscriptions to the journal **Social Text:** P.O. Box 450, 70 Greenwich St., New York, NY 10011

See page 391 for CIP data.

ISBN 0-8166-1366-2
0-8166-1337-0 (pbk.)

CONTENTS

ACKNOWLEDGMENTS

[RE]TAKES

"Christmas Cantata" by the Bread and Puppet Theater, a performance for the Angry Arts Against the War in Vietnam, January 25–February 5, 1967. Some 500 artists participated in that protest. Photo by Karl Bissinger.

INTRODUCTION

THE SOCIAL TEXT EDITORS

Not even the dead are safe if they *win* . . .
Walter Benjamin

The second and third movements of Luciano Berio's *Sinfonia* (1970) are emblematic of the 1960s. After a two-minute memorial to Martin Luther King, the third movement evokes the contrast between the exuberant past and the decentered present. Against the backdrop of the Scherzo movement of Mahler's second ("Resurrection") symphony, a continuous rendition which provides the only apparent structure, we hear bits of the 60s—fragments from May 1968, in France, conversations about art and music, references to other events, chatter.

Like Schoenberg, Berio has introduced the human voice as an instrument without the mediation of melody; the voice speaks but not in song. While Mahler's music reminds us of that tradition which, however dissonant and rambunctious, is still familiar as high art, Berio is not concerned to replace the late-romantic canon with a new one, not even one claiming modernity. Here there is no attempt at congruity: the movement hangs together only by its statement about the nonsynchronicity between the time when the symphonic form was strained by the breakup of the familiar narratives, and the contemporary moment when formal coherence is abandoned. The reference to Schoenberg is to the spoken words in *Ode to Napoleon Bonaparte* where even the serial musical voice of the earlier *Pierrot Lunaire* has been left behind. However, Schoenberg, forever seeking a new system, made no break with the story. Berio, on the other hand, presents the bits of our time, and the Mahler only reminds us that there is no resurrection of the past, for the referent is present but recedes as the noise of the everyday gains ground. He reminds us of discontinuous time and space, where the old distinctions between speech and poetry disappear, where narratives lose their endings as well as their origins. His "movement" has no development and the bits of conversation are left to the listener to decipher, even if one suspects that the bits are merely the code of anti-aesthetics.

Still, the composer has chosen not only to remind us of the "Resurrection," the utopian hope, but has also framed his set of ruptures in the familiar segments of classical symphony. The past is impossible but still present; the future can only be signified but is submerged in a present filled with Derridian "beings." After the third movement with its cacophony of past and present we want silence. But the composer gives us more sound.

The "60s" is merely the name we give to a disruption of late-capitalist ideological and political hegemony, to a disruption of the bourgeois dream of unproblematic production, of everyday life as the bureaucratic society of controlled consumption, of the end of history. Late capitalism signifies the end of time, and space as its replacement. In Mahler's time at the turn of the century, the question still concerned historical transformation, progress, development, all linked to the contradictions of capital accumulation. In the 60s, this had become a struggle over turf with the seizing of the streets, of the Sorbonne, of the ideological state apparatuses themselves.

In this sense it differed from the last great historical upsurge in the Western countries, that is, the worldwide fight in the 1930s and 40s against fascism, the rise of the unskilled American industrial workers, the formation of the welfare state itself, all of which was quintessentially the politics of protest. In Paris, London and New York, great demonstrations of the unemployed filled the streets with demands that the state provide food, jobs and income. These were movements for concessions from a still omnipotent ruling class: even when socialists, radicals and communists in France formed a popular-front government (1936), its program was little more than a New Deal. The class struggle of this time was geared towards forming the *interventionist* capitalist state, not towards forcing capital to share institutional power. Great masses marched on the symbol of state power, the capital, and presented petitions for economic and social justice.

The struggles of the 60s, on the other hand, brought popular intervention into the apparatuses themselves: students, workers, middle strata transgressed the boundaries of power, symbolically taking the streets. Demonstrations were not framed as marches *on* power. One occupied instead. Students took over buildings at the universities in Frankfurt, London and Berkeley. At Columbia University in New York, when the administration appropriated a public park in adjacent Harlem to build a gymnasium, the students not only seized buildings but began to hold their own classes. What had begun as a struggle over urban space quickly passed on to the issue of the "poverty of student life." Similarly, the civil rights movement, which started as a fight for the right to vote, to sit at lunch counters and to use public toilets, particularly in the South, soon became an urban movement to capture the ghetto from established political and economic institutions. The demand for black power, the preeminent slogan of the late 60s, translated in practice into a fight for urban space. Though the media focussed attention on the Black Panther Party's insistence on its right to bear arms, the political campaigns of the Panthers for "community control" over schools, police and other services, and their breakfast programs for children and poor, actually thematized the passage from assimilationist demands to ones of autonomy. The conventional integration program, meanwhile, was recovered by the liberal fraction of capital which, in alliance with the newly emerging black bourgeoisie, finally broke the backs of the Panthers through a combination of repression and carefully orchestrated discursive manipulation. The Panthers, isolated from all but a few white supporters (though their international stature was very great), nevertheless had created a sizable, if temporary, base within the black under and working class, and the rhetoric of community control and black power outlived its particular origins, becoming the property of diverse social movements well into the 1970s.

In a similar vein, the concept of decentralized government (bringing the state closer to the people) became a widespread political issue in many cities and towns, in Europe as well as in the United States. Every institution of transfer payments (such as health, education and transportation) suddenly was beset with "citizen's formations" asking for participation in the planning and administration, sometimes even in the budget process. Reluctant officials were frequently obliged to establish advisory planning or administrative boards which included ("consumers" as well as producers and bureaucrats. Virtually every ideological state apparatus thus became contested terrain and so it was that the trade unions experienced the new phenomenon of a rank-and-file movement demanding workers' control over the union in the name of democracy. The unions, too, were now subject to spatial contestation.

In this domain, however, things took an unforeseen turn at the end of the decade. While the struggle over the institutions continued, a new fight emerged: the demand among workers, some middle strata and youth for *freedom from* the institutions of the quotidian. Workers in Turin and Lordstown, citadels of the car industry, the characteristic signifier of late-capitalist consumerism, undertook what one might call an action critique of the assembly line, for in their view the prison factory was not worth running, only escaping. Zero work, unwork, the merging on the line of work and play, this signalled a new politics of labor. It also created new space, cleared by freeing time normally subordinated to capital. This is no longer the unemployment of the economic crisis: it is workers turning away from labor itself, abjuring the income ineluctably tied to it. As capital aims to fill all spaces in the day with activity that produces surplus value, labor aims to free itself from these spaces, to create its own space inside the workplace. In the 60s, the anti-work ethic was thus introduced. When unions and socialist parties gradually lost some of their authority over the workers, industrial discipline gave way to a politics of control not over the compulsive production line but over time. "Free time" replaced the pride of the craft upon which the trade union and laborist tradition had been built.

Imagination was never in power except for the fleeting moment of the "last general strike," May 68 in France. Like its progenitor, the Paris Commune nearly a century earlier, this strike halted all production and disrupted totally the ideological apparatuses but did not manage to create alternative institutions that could sustain the revolt against the still-powerful Gaullist repressive machine and its concomitant old-order parties, including that of the communists. "Imagination" did not always square with institution-building in the late 60s. Some technicians, journalists and artists did transform a variety of media into self-managed organs of the revolution, but the new "subjects" often refused to codify their gains in the fear of having the old everyday life creep in through the front door. The revolt was so radically decentered—marking the triumph of molecular politics over its arch rival, the central committee, the principal contradiction, the key sector—that organs of coordination were difficult to keep up, not only for technical reasons but also because they were ideologically suspect. So the rhetoric of "let the people decide," "all power to the imagination," "refuse authority" often turned into babble. The antimass became the countermyth to that of the proletariat.

The 60s also saw the emergence of new historical subjects, or at least groups that constituted themselves as subjects on the basis, for instance, of sex and race. Having formed social movements, these subjects contested institutional spaces but also declared a sort of counterhegemony to the dominant social and ideological power. The new feminism carried on the traditional struggle for equality of opportunity, for equal access to jobs, educational resources and other public institutions, but was in fact preeminently engaged in reinventing woman in the context of the discourse of *liberation.* This implied carrying the challenge to gender relations beyond the realm of the division of labor into the area of social relations as such. The women's movement played with the language of domination and imposed on American society a bi-gender pronoun convention (his/her) to replace the ordinary masculine usage; it tried to form autonomous women's communities, reinvented the small consciousness-raising group to provide a new public sphere for women's discourse, founded newspapers, journals and magazines, started bars and clubs, all of it independent of male initiative. Some of these spaces were linked to the rediscovery of lesbian sexuality as public discourse, but it would be a mistake to conflate the creation of a women's space with its sexual component; it reached far beyond that.

Blacks, as opposed to Negroes, were of course another new subject, constituted on the foundation of an older black nationalism. Marcus Garvey was resurrected, along with his pan-African successors Dubois, Padmore, Nkrumah and Malcolm X. A new vocabulary followed. Afro-American became the sign of militant identity, a statement of cultural autonomy and international racial solidarity with Africans, Caribbeans and people of color everywhere. In this respect, it was not surprising that Marxism-Leninism, the ideology of third-world revolutions in many parts of the world, would attract younger black intellectuals and activists seeking a fusion of nationalism and revolution. Marxist-Leninist discourse thus achieved a powerful, if not dominant, position within the new nationalist vocabulary, and one result was the formation of various black-led revolutionary communist organizations, which despite their sectlike character must be seen generally as a significant phenomenon among the generation born after 1940.

Here one must mention the figure of Harry Haywood, whose *Negro Liberation*, written shortly after World War II, became a source of inspiration for an entire generation of young black revolutionaries. Haywood expressed the communist position that the blacks of the southeastern United States constituted a nation and ought to have self-determination. He also argued, along the lines of the Communist International in the late 20s, against all alliances with social democrats and other reformists, a posture which gained force among younger blacks at a time marked by the breakup of the coalition of blacks and whites which had produced the most sweeping legislative and juridical rights for blacks since the reconstruction. None of the ensuing organizations ever achieved the weight of the Communist Party in Harlem and other ghettoes of the 1930s and 1940s. They were smaller in numbers, shunned coalitions and so remained isolated. Yet their cultural and ideological influence in the decade after Malcolm's murder should not be overlooked. Some of the most active black theorists have emerged out of revolutionary nationalism and no national black periodical can now ignore nationalist ideas or cultural signifiers. Nationalists played a leading role when black studies sought and gained academic recognition in the late 60s.

There was a profound transformation in cultural relations: deformalization of the dress code in public places, introduction of Anglo-Saxon expletives into ordinary middle-class speech and so on. This was in fact a process of appropriation from various popular cultures, outstandingly those of blacks and workers. Jeans, for instance, ceased to be a sign of social class. A particularly important appropriation and rearticulation in this sense took place in music. Rock and roll had been the urban music of the black migration after World War II, and like other popular forms it combined earlier types of music, many of which originated in African and rural American environments: blues, syncopated rhythms, riffs of early-20th-century jazz. The result was rhythm and blues, which then mutated through the refinements of Otis Redding, Ray Charles and the coterie of Motown artists such as Stevie Wonder, Smokey Robinson, Marvin Gaye, the Supremes and the Temptations. As for the white reworking, it showed interesting class differences. In Britain, black music was thus appropriated by the working-class youth culture, perhaps primarily through Chuck Berry's influence. In the American case, the white recoding took the form of, on the one hand, the country-rock intonations of Buddy Holly and Elvis Presley in the 1950s, in turn clearly linked to the migration of hillbillies and to the emerging urban South, and, on the other hand, the largely middle-class culture of the following decade. The Jefferson Airplane, Bob Dylan, the Band, Velvet Underground, and in another register, the Beach Boys—these were all situated on a very different class terrain from either Presley or the Rolling Stones.

Nevertheless, British rock, its two American counterparts and the various black forms, collectively signified the advent of youth rebellion in the 60s. Again, a powerful vocabulary was invented by the new cultural forces, as can be seen in the lexicon of the 60s included in this work. In the last instance it was the music and the attached dance forms that really created a new public sphere, even more than the various code violations in dress and speech. Dylan, the Beatles and the Stones gave to the generation of 1940 an account of its journey from the center to the opposition. Rock told it all: the exhilaration and fear of separation from the comforts of suburbia, the boredom of student life, the arrogance of power so fiercely castigated in early Dylan songs, and, in obviously encoded lyrics, the saga of the subterranean drug culture. It was here, too, that the new mysticism was born, outwardly manifested in flower power and, to some extent, in the preoccupation with body and health. Here, too, there was a rediscovery of communitarian ideals.

The new sense and perception was by no means identical with the new politics and culture of the generation as a whole: not everyone was obviously a "head." However, to think about the rock of the 60s without seeing its link with drugs on the one hand, and the deep passion for both community and individuality on the other, unforgettably inscribed in Dylan's generational anthem *Like a Rolling Stone*, is to miss the point. Although the political counterculture was often hostile to what we may call its new-age equivalent—not surprisingly, considering the latter's religious mysticism and romantic view of nature — the social perceptions of this second counterculture found a moment of their own in rock and in some ways achieved a universality that specific oppositional politics could not.

Nor was it right to condemn the "agrarians," the health-food enthusiasts and the communards as merely narcissistic and withdrawn from the larger struggles. While one cannot claim that the ecology movement stemmed directly from the counterculture, especially in light of the long fights of progressive conservationists dating back to the 19th century, it is nevertheless common knowledge that ecological consciousness was reconstituted in the 1960s largely through infusions from the counterculture; for the traditional preservation forces had been immensely weakened by the postwar rush to industrial and residential development. There was now a new insistence on linking struggles against nuclear weapons and energy with efforts to combat pollution everywhere, all of which resulted in a massive movement that in its essentials came to be supported by perhaps a majority of Americans in the 1970s. Yet the relation of this new ideology to traditional left-wing politics remains problematic.

The 60s, then, provided the ecology movement with a popular base and, equally important, a cadre for conducting political wars against certain forms of capital accumulation. Ecotopias have now replaced traditional economic utopias as well as the technological ones, most recently peddled by the prophets of computerization as the road to unwork. Ecotopias do not exclude aspects of the other perspectives, but the emphasis is not in the end on the provision of material plenty: it is instead on the rational rearticulation of human social relations and our collective relation to nature. Some ecologists, to be sure, argue for alternative technologies with a fervor equal to that of mainstream technological determinists of the left and right, and in this sense adhere to the idea of unmitigated benefits from the current techno-scientific revolution. This is not an ecology rooted in the 60s counterculture, which renounced the domination of nature and promulgated a program for its *reenchantment*. In place of basing economic policy on growth, one would hence think of technologico-scientific choices in terms of their effects on life and nature. Implied here was also a new *common sense* about capital accumulation and its relation to the environment.

These, admittedly, are first-world ideologies. Perhaps only in northern Europe and North America has this new common sense really found a mass constituency. In the other two worlds, the persistence of poverty, scarcity, hunger and disease severely limits its reach. Indeed, even in the "advanced" capitalist countries of the Mediterranean and the British Isles, ecological politics remain difficult. Governments there, whatever their character, celebrate the triumphs of nuclear energy and are prone to economic growth politics regardless of ecological imperatives. As for the third world and "actually existing socialist societies," ecological politics is virtually absent from the former and in the latter finds itself entirely subordinated to the relentless drive to dominate nature so as to allow these regimes at least a partial escape from the capitalist marketplace.

The 60s was also a time when new global perceptions permeated public discourse. It was the first time in this century that anti-imperialist protest came to *dominate* the overall political agenda of the nation; the global domination of capital was challenged from within on a more serious scale than ever before. This was the first time, too, that the forces, as well as the relations, of production were subjected to a withering critique; the first time the prevailing sexual division of labor was taken up by a popular feminist movement; the first time that discrimination based on circumstances of birth (such as race) became the object of political contestation on a global level. The new freedom movements were linked to the world underclass in a complex way which put into question not only the glaring fact of economic exploitation but also the whole system of cultural domination. "National liberation" was in this sense something more than political and economic independence: while stressing international solidarity, it was simultaneously a denunciation of homogeneity as such. Though the 1970s has seen the recuperation of US hegemony by means of economic power and military terror, it is obvious that this is domination which can achieve little more than a temporary respite from imperial disintegration, just as the consolidation of military rule in Poland did not perforce end the hostilities between population and ruling class. Despite ensuing setbacks, the anti-imperialist gains of the 1960s were real.

Trashing the 60s has become a strategic feature of the current struggle for hegemony. Attacks on "permissiveness," the defense of the old-fashioned nuclear family ("haven in a heartless world"), the return of "excellence" in the schools (the old structured curriculum and authoritarian teaching), short hair and a general turn away from the cultural "styles" of the 60s, strident antifeminism and anti-gay backlash, the rise of an "intellectual" racism with the new Klan, the almost uncontested acceptance of slogans about "fiscal responsibility" which signify the dismantlement of the welfare state, the financial "realism" brandished in order to bring, by persuasion and menace alike, labor to the appropriate "givebacks"—all of these things are practical political issues, on which stands and struggles must be made. But they are also parts of a whole ideological conflict, for which Gramsci's term hegemony remains the most convenient shorthand, a conflict which includes contests over interpretations of history, and above all of that crucial period both sides call "the 60s."

From one point of view, this is an academic matter: even intellectually, it might well be said, it would be better to debate each of these issues separately on its own merits, than to fuse them into some vague debate over "visions" of history. But visions of history play an enormous—if incalculable—role in people's political practice in the present: and this all the more when the interpretation in question is a matter, not of "attitudes" towards a bygone age like the era of the Wobblies or of the American Revolution, but rather of people's immediate past. What you finally decide to think the 60s was is one of the forms in which you affirm or repudiate a whole part of your own life.

So it is nothing short of astonishing that the trashing of the 60s in the media generally should be met with so little indignation or resistance. The number of Americans still living today who were involved or touched in at least one political demonstration in the course of the period must be immense. Where are all those people, and what has become of the radical political culture that might normally be expected to emerge from such a tremendous wave of collective experience?

The enemies of the 60s are, however, everywhere visible and vocal, making their pitch in forms which vary from the rewriting of the Maoist Cultural Revolution in terms of Stalin's Gulag, to seemingly harmless and nostalgic celebrations of the lost innocence of the Eisenhower era. A single example: Hilton Kramer's journal *The New Criterion*, symbolically named after T.S. Eliot's conservative organ of the 1920s. Its first issue was a kind of manifesto in which the irresponsibility and frivolity of contemporary visual art was roundly denounced in the name of the high moral seriousness of the great modernisms of the recent past, from Picasso to Abstract Expressionism. The root cause of this degeneration was then identified—as the reader will have guessed—as the universal politicization of the 60s, whose baleful influence in the art world is found no less pernicious than in the realms of education, morality and civic responsibility.

One ought not to overestimate the success of the new right in producing an ideology capable of "gripping the masses," for Kramer's journal is intellectually vacuous and even the supreme manifesto of the new conservatism, George Gilder's *Wealth and Poverty*, has nothing sexier to offer in the way of a vision of the future than a return to religion and the old-fashioned nuclear family. What is more disturbing is the tendency of the left to respond in essentially defensive and reactive ways to this apparent flood-tide of anti-60s propaganda, a tendency reinforced by the increasing, and perfectly proper, sense of the political and ideological errors of that period, which have seemed to call for self-critique rather than unbowed, unrepentant reaffirmation.

The essays, interviews and testimonies we present here are on the contrary an attempt to combine the affirmative with the critical, an attempt to salvage certain positions now under severe attack. We have selected those who write as if their history mattered in making their critique—partisans who have used the intervening years to locate the trends, contemplate what to save, reconsider what failed, who are able to measure, intellectually and with experience, the political practices and cultural acts that will hereafter carry the impress of the 60s. Beyond that, reflecting the radical displacement in those years of homogeneity itself, we make no claim that ours is a complete account. We put this work before the reader in the form of an intervention, and we do so without apology.

PART 1

March 26, 1966. Photo by Harvey Richards, courtesy of the *Guardian*.

WHEN THE NEW LEFT WAS NEW

STANLEY ARONOWITZ

My 60s did not begin until 1962. I had been living in a different now, the worlds of the trade union movement, Newark peace and community organizing, and reform Democratic politics. These were the "nows" of the late 50s, a time which saw the rise of a new southern-based civil rights movement, a northern struggle for black community empowerment, and a middle-class peace movement which was not unlike our current nuclear disarmament campaigns. The civil rights movement had just entered its civil disobedience stage (lunch-counter sit-ins and freedom rides) but was still five years away from "black power," despite the respected but largely ignored voice of Malcolm X.

The early years of the decade remained infused with the culture of the 1950s. Rock and roll, an urban adaptation of the music of the black migration from the South, had emerged, but Dylan was still playing acoustic guitar and the Beatles were barely visible in the tin pan alley. The "high" culture of the era continued to smell of modernist sincerity and literary intensity. For the most part the Beats who gathered at the Cedar, White Horse and other bars in Greenwich Village remained enraged suburbanites, their energy, too, flowing from the weariness often attributed to them. Columbia alumnus Allen Ginsberg fulminated against a society that could reduce the "best minds" of his generation to drugged impotence and the massively oedipalized Jack Kerouac, finding no home to replace Lowell, Mass., returned to his mother. Clellon Holmes produced *Go!* and promptly vanished into college teaching. Like so many of the literary landmarks of the late 50s, his work turned out to be a brief candle light rather than a sustained flame that could guide a movement. In fact, only Kerouac, Ginsberg and San Francisco poet Lawrence Ferlinghetti survived the Beat movement. Most of their comrades literally sat out the 60s; by the late 50s their rebellion had degenerated into the cynical affectation characteristic of all failed romantic politics and art.

For most intellectuals, *Partisan Review* was still the measure of critical thought, even though its representative figures had long since abandoned the journal and been replaced by writers like Susan Sontag, for whom the tradition spawned by Philip Rahv and William Phillips was already a vague memory. For the succeeding generation preferred the aestheticism of Lionel Trilling, whose thesis of "authenticity" and "sincerity" had already been torn from the soil of revolutionary commitment, from the political radicalism of the founders of the magazine.

Before 1962, I used to hang out at the White Horse, where I gazed at Delmore Schwartz dying at his corner table, laughed at Brendan Behan's drunken tales (not realizing that he too was about to expire), and listened to the earnest conversations of the refugees of the political intelligentsia who had remained in the cities despite the suburban exodus of the 50s. I was part of the group of young trade union organizers. Some of us worked for the Garment Workers Union, which was then trying to revive itself by importing intense young radicals into the movement. Gus Tyler, the former leader of the revolutionary faction of the Socialist Party and now the director of the union's Training Institute,knew then what labor leaders have still not learned: that rank-and-file mobilization is impossible when the members and the bureaucrats are too far apart. Tyler's experiment, in what might be called John L. Lewisism, failed under conditions of cold war liberalism. The radical agitators, many recent college graduates such as Gus Sedares, Ted Bloom and Bob Wolk, were simply unwilling to go along with the programs of top-down unionism unless the leadership permitted them to take the class struggle to the growing unorganized sector of the industry. What they failed to grasp was that collaboration had sunk deep roots into the psyche of the trade union bureaucracy, indeed that it had become a way of life, not just a set of practical measures to save a dying industry.

Sedares was frustrated in his efforts to push the sclerotic ILGWU towards a militant, aggressive organizing campaign, but he found an alternative outlet for his remarkable ability. He scandalized the old socialists who dominated the union not by mobilizing the rank and file, for the concept of an active membership had long since disappeared from the union's lexicon, but by organizing his fellow staffers into the first Federation of Union Representatives (FOUR). Sedares argued that if the union had lost its vision of class struggle, not to mention that of a new society, it could at least pay its cadre a decent wage, provide good benefits and tolerable working conditions. Today, the "union within a union" idea has gripped the masses of tired trade union functionaries. The staffs of many international unions have organized for collective bargaining. Of course, the Garment Workers remain an open shop. As far as their staff representatives are concerned, the house David Dubinsky built adheres to the principle of self-sacrifice.

The Training Institute is disbanded but an important truth survives it: that unions cannot hope to become a major force in American life once again until they attract the most dedicated among young radicals. On the other hand, it may be argued that the new social movements emerging in the 60s were defined by their departure (in a double sense) from what C. Wright Mills called the labor metaphysic. The generation of the 50s still saw the labor movement as the lightning rod of global social transformation; their hopes were framed within the heroic visions of the struggle against capital, by the romantic idea of the self-emancipation of the toilers.

The McCarthy era, the obvious deterioration of the labor movement's militancy, the advent of consumer society—nothing could daunt the small band of radicals who downed gallons of beer every Friday at the White Horse. How appropriate it was that they should jostle in that packed room with the Beats and the veterans of an already eclipsed literary radicalism, a literary radicalism which had not been destroyed by the anti-Soviet denouement of the 30s alone. Its final resting place, of course, turned out to be the graveyard known as the Congress for Cultural Freedom and its journal *Encounter*, if it wasn't *Commentary* or the *Partisan Review* of the 50s. Max Eastman, perhaps the greatest of all radical journalists and editors, ended up writing for the ultra-conservative *Reader's Digest.*

There were exceptions to the rightward drift, some attempts to keep a distance from the Irving Kristols and the Sidney Hooks and other people for whom Stalin's betrayal had proved once and for all the superiority of liberal democracy over any possible revolutionary socialism. There was, for instance, the small group around *Dissent*, which had been founded by Irving Howe and Lewis Coser in 1952, and the even smaller group following *New Politics*, Julius Jacobson's attempt to preserve an independent Marxist presence in intellectual life. From one perspective, Howe's position resembled that of the emerging conservative/liberal majority among the formerly radical intellectuals. He concurred with Rahv's judgment that however egregiously awful capitalism remained, Stalinism and, by extension, Eastern Europe and China represented a worse alternative. Nonetheless, Howe retained his faith that democratic socialism could provide a realistic alternative to the antinomies of liberal exploitation and totalitarianism, while his peers lost faith altogether in the visions of an organized left.

The American Communist Party had broken apart following the post-Stalin crisis within the world communist movement, a crisis which had become acute with Khrushchev's famous report to the 20th Soviet Party Congress in 1956. Most young radicals, however, were relatively unaffected by this development since the American CP had virtually gone underground in the 50s on the assumption that the political repression at the time was a dress rehearsal for fascism. Some, including myself, were sympathetic to the party but remained troubled by its conservatism and caution. We were moved by the internal party debates and the concomitant information about Stalin's crimes, and taken aback by the clear errors of the party left. Our desire for some kind of radical affiliation was considerable, but it made no sense to join the decimated CP then, especially since the "right wing" of the party was already attracted to the pacifist A.J. Muste's call for regroupment among democratically minded leftists. Several evenings in 1957 and 1958, I journeyed across the Hudson river to hear leftists from various Trotskyist sects, so-called "right-wing" CP leaders and Muste himself debate prospects for a "new" left. They discussed the necessity of independence from the Soviet Union and the US, of unremitting commitment to democratic rights under socialist rule, of renewed efforts to revitalize the labor movement on the basis of rank-and-file militancy, of a strong intervention into the burgeoning peace movement, which had shown considerable strength since Adlai Stevenson's adoption of the nuclear test ban plank in his losing 1956 campaign.

Once the alliance between William Z. Foster's conservative faction and General Secretary Eugene Dennis's "centrist" group had foreclosed any hope of renovating the Communist Party along democratic lines, there began a debate among democratic socialists regarding possible affiliation with the reform-minded minority communists. At the same time, in 1959, the socialist-influenced League for Industrial Democracy decided that the moment had come to resuscitate its nearly moribund student group and invited the University of Michigan chapter to take charge of this task. It was symptomatic of the times that the concept of "industrial democracy" had lost entirely its meaning as a unifying slogan. The leading student figures Al Haber and Tom Hayden insisted, accordingly, that the name of the organization's student affiliate be changed to Students for a Democratic Society. Haber and Hayden shared the political perspective of LID's chairman, Michael Harrington, but abhorred the more conservative position of most of its board members. I first met Harrington at the White Horse during his literary neo-Trotskyist period, when he was better known for his literary criticism than the political writings. He was closer to Jacobson's *New Politics* than to the more staid *Dissent* in that he considered himself a revolutionary democratic socialist who believed in the formation of a labor party built around a strong labor–civil rights alliance. He supported the broad "third camp" position of his organization, the Independent Socialist League, rather than the pro-western line of *Dissent*.

As a trade unionist and Democratic party activist influenced by the old Popular Front politics, I debated Harrington and other Trotskyists in the early 60s precisely on the issue that was to mark the break between SDS and the Harrington-Howe wing of the socialist movement a few years later: I argued that working people and trade unionists had no choice but to seek change within the Democratic Party, that the multiplicity of movements to reform party procedures and platforms which had arisen out of the anti-corruption, peace and civil rights movements of the late 50s prefigured the chance for a new alliance that could at least mount an effective challenge to the most conservative wing of the party. Harrington at the time took the classic third-party position that noncommunist socialists have adopted since the turn of the century. Later in the decade Harrington changed his mind, but then found that there were new radicals who had picked up where he and Howe had left off.

Because New York City was a Democratic stronghold, New York Democrats were more concerned with the leadership question within the party than with beating the Republicans. Ideology and power were contested in the primaries, not in the general elections. The Liberal Party, composed of some trade unionists, mostly from the apparel trades, and ambitious lawyers, had long since lost its role as the balance of power and had become more or less harmless. The more "left-wing" American Labor Party had disappeared after its disastrous performance in the 1954 election and some of its activists were now part of the Reform Democrats. In this situation, the main issue for the Democratic Party was whether it could become a mass liberal party, that is, whether it could mobilize the new postwar professional constituencies in the shaping of party policy.

These were the last years of the political machine, a form of cultural as well as more narrowly constructed political power. The machine was founded on the institutions of patronage already weakened by the introduction of the civil service system of public employment and the professionalization of the service as a whole. Moreover, the immediate postwar period had witnessed the suburbanization of the working class and the lower-middle strata, the electoral base of the machine. When I had dinner in the early 60s at Cannon's, an old-time Irish bar on Broadway and 108th Street, I found Japanese food being served with the Guinness stout, a sure sign of incipient gentrification on the Upper West Side. Likewise, Greenwich Village, which was no longer a haven for artists, housed the coming leaders of the Democratic reform movement: Stanley Geller, who owned a gorgeous townhouse on 12th Street; Ed Gold, a journalist for Fairchild publications; Ed Koch, a lawyer with unbounded political ambition; and Sara Schoenkopf, a young professional politician whom I had first met during the Stevenson campaign when I was a leader of Young Democrats in New Jersey's Essex County.

Yorkville, once the neighborhood of German machinists, Hungarian laborers, and factories like American Cystoscope, where I had worked in the early 50s, was fast becoming the fashionable East Side. The district had been represented in Congress by a succession of moderately liberal Rockefeller Republicans, but the area still contained a strong local Democratic machine with a working-class constituency. To these precincts there came a young left-wing lawyer who together with the Yorkville leader and erstwhile party regular John Harrington attached himself to the reform movement. Mark Lane had been a criminal lawyer specializing in hopeless criminal cases in behalf of blacks and latinos. He possessed a talent singularly conducive to a successful political career, an unerring sense of publicity, a sixth sense for what would capture the public's political imagination.

He was not, however, endowed with a particularly vibrant or charismatic personality. Shy of personal encounters, his fiery social messages were delivered exclusively to larger audiences. He rented a small apartment in a slum building on Lexington Avenue in Yorkville, a sort of place that has all but disappeared now. He was also recently separated from his wife, the actress and folk singer Martha Schlamme. We were introduced by his brother-in-law Bill Nuchow, a Teamster official whose one moment of glory had been the presidency of an ill-fated taxi drivers' union in the late 50s. He might in fact have become a major figure in New York labor, had the Teamsters not abandoned the unionization campaign, but now he was a business agent for a Teamster local. Nuchow asked me to join the effort to elect Lane to the state assembly, and even though I was living in Newark, N.J., I agreed. The position of the incumbent Democrat was less entrenched than usual, mainly because East Harlem's Puerto Rican voters, subordinate to the Irish and Italian machine politicians after the passing of Vito Mercantonio's left-wing machine, were beginning to strike out on their own, and Mark Lane had gained prominence by representing poor Puerto Rican clients.

Lane's subsequent stay in the legislature was luminous, controversial and brief. His great achievement was the exposure of an illicit scheme between Republican Assembly Speaker Joseph Carlino and a coterie of businessmen to build fallout shelters, a scandal which led to Carlino's defeat in the next election and to instant stardom for Mark among the "clean government" types and the peace movement activists. By late 1961, he was calling small meetings of supporters, myself included, to determine if he should seek the nomination of the reform Democrats for the 19th congressional district, a horseshoe which came down the West Side and then curved around the Battery, ending up on the Lower East Side. Its representative was Leonard Farbstein, a product of the still powerful Democratic machine led by the almost legendary Carmine De Sapio. Farbstein was no worse than most others among the New York congressional delegation. His political base outside the machine lay primarily in the substantial orthodox Jewish community of the Lower East Side, but this once formidable socio-political force was now losing some of its weight because of the exodus to the suburbs and to Brooklyn, and because of the influx of Puerto Ricans. In 1960, the reformers had succeeded in beating De Sapio himself, winning control over most West Side clubs for the first time. Other strong challenges were mounted in Chelsea, where the new ILGWU-sponsored cooperative housing was replacing longshore slums. In order to take on Farbstein, Lane first had to get past the reform movement; although he was by far the best-known reform legislator in Albany, he was not a resident of the district and other reformers wanted the nomination too.

Early in 1962, Mark asked me to become his campaign manager. We got together a rather high powered inner circle that included Michael Harrington, who didn't see the campaign through; Susan Brownmiller, who had sparked his assembly campaign; and Ed Wallerstein, who was an old captain of the Vito Mercantonio organization and now active in the Yorkville Democratic Club. From the start, Lane was accused of being an outsider and of surrounding himself with carpetbaggers. But his campaign suffered from another and perhaps more crucial weakness: he fought on substantive issues before a group for whom such questions were subordinate, if not entirely irrelevant. For the reform movement was a loose antimachine coalition whose main concern was to eliminate corruption from the Democratic Party, by which was chiefly meant patronage. In short, "reform" entailed procedural renovation and a kind of civil service for professionals, making sure that elected officials were democratically chosen and that the most merited would get the jobs. Lane paid lip service to these issues but in fact could not have cared less who selected the candidates. He ran on public issues, although he was obliged to use the theme of anti-corruption extensively in his initial assembly campaign. In the spring of 1962, we tried to take the reformers by storm by raising such issues as the increasing US intervention in Vietnam, the growing concern over poverty, and the importance of better housing and jobs for residents of the district. Indeed, by the end of the designation campaign all the candidates were echoing Lane's platform down to the obscure and anomalous issue of Vietnam. Yet these were side issues as far as the movement was concerned. The reform Democrats of New York, Illinois, California and elsewhere were plainly on the liberal wing of the party, but their chief interest lay in the question of control, for which purpose the issues of Vietnam, nuclear weapons and civil rights had little relevance. Lane, on the other hand, considered Congress a place for national policy; procedural questions made him impatient.

The reform movement was an early expression of a new style in American politics. Large numbers of professional middle strata and small businessmen had participated in the Stevenson campaign, which raised the possibility that the Democratic Party for the first time could become a mass organization, something beyond a leadership coalition between labor, blacks, professional politicians and a fraction of capital. The focus here lay on clean government and popular democracy rather than on peace, civil rights and economic justice, though unquestionably the movement could become the vehicle for these traditional concerns. In fact, the greatest and last triumph of this new political "class" was the presidential nomination of its epitome, George McGovern, a history professor turned politician, from South Dakota.

Lane lost the designation fight and quit the assembly seat shortly thereafter. His politics, grounded in the primacy of questions of economic justice, was rapidly fading from the scene. Later, he was to reenter the discourse of the 60s in a rather peculiar way by his relentless conspiracy investigations of the John F. Kennedy assassination.

I entered the 60s myself through my friendship with Evelyn Leopold, who, at the time of Lane's campaign, was running Ed Koch's losing primary fight for the assembly; Koch ran on behalf of the Village Independent Democrats. Evelyn was living on W. 21st Street with several SDS leaders. She had met them in 1960 when editing the Douglass College paper. Hayden was then the editor of the *Michigan Daily* and was organizing college newspaper editors for civil rights. The first time I came to the 21st Street house, I was greeted by Al Haber, a resident and also the current head of SDS. Characteristically, he was drenched in mimeograph ink. Mike Harrington was still regarded by the SDS, in late spring 1962, as the closest thing to a mentor. Hayden, who lived in the apartment with his wife Casey, was like Harrington a middle-class midwesterner of Irish Catholic background. Like Harrington, he exemplified the adage "you can take the boy out of the church but you can't take the church out of the boy."

Tom and Al were then preparing for the first national conference of this relatively new and very small organization. It was to be held in June at Port Huron, Michigan. Tom was responsible for writing the organization's political manifesto. He had returned recently from a trip to the South where he had gotten a fairly well publicized beating during a civil rights demonstration. This had established his credentials as one who would put his body on the line. As the first SDS President, he was clearly its best known and probably most influential leader, but by no means the only one. He embodied the spiritual and intellectual energy of this small movement of no more than 200 members, most of whom could be found on major campuses like Michigan, Harvard and Chicago. SDS held national meetings at Christmas and in the summer. The rest of the time people kept in touch by mail, telephone and through campus visits by the two national leaders. The SDS became highly visible because some of its members were also key activists in the then powerful National Students Association, and leading politicians and editors on some very important campuses. Despite its numerical insignificance, SDS thus organized an effective caucus for civil rights at the 1961 and 1962 NSA conventions. It became a veritable tribune for the growing movement for university reform, particularly the fight for a student voice in campus policy-making. It was also a catalyst in the student peace movement, helping to found the Student Peace Union.

I may have misunderstood the Democratic reform movement at the time, but I could not have mistaken the primacy of the *moral* in SDS. It was the most articulate expression of what became the leading theme of the ideology of the 60s: the attempt to infuse life with a secular spiritual and moral content, to fill the quotidian with personal meaning and purpose.

The reform Democrats and SDS shared the belief that they themselves were the new historical subjects. The spurious doctrines of the student as "nigger" or as a new class were merely clumsy ways for this generation to separate itself from the old labor metaphysic, to declare itself competent to name the system that oppressed humanity. The *Port Huron Statement*, written by Hayden but collected from many sources, retained the outline of a liberal argument: its pages resound with the rhetoric of economic and social justice. But the subtext concerned the generation after Ginsberg's, a generation which not only prided itself on having the best minds but also claimed its own subjectivity.

"Participatory democracy," fighting for "the people" to have "control over their own lives,"—this goal reflected self-interest as much as anything else. The students, who were too young and too far removed from direct power to be concerned with the electoral issues of reform Democrats, inveighed on the contrary against the institutions themselves. It was a matter of replacing the old institutions of control—control over their own lives—with other structures. In this sense reform was only useful to the extent it demobilized existing political power.

By June, I was practically living on 21st Street with Evelyn and the SDS staff. They came home from the office and I from my union, and we would immediately plunge into long discussions about the labor movement, civil rights, the Democratic Party and the Kennedy Administration. As a relatively weak political movement, they recognized the need to find allies in all of these arenas. Hayden was trying to pry some money from Walter Reuther and the UAW and went to Detroit to meet with him. Yet, despite playing "student organization" for the adult counterparts, Hayden, Haber, Tod Gitlin from Harvard, Bob Ross and others, did not ingratiate themselves with trade union and liberal leaders because they believed that the labor-liberal coalition had no future in American politics. They were indeed deeply convinced that these were forces of the past which ought to be scrapped. While making compromises and seeking temporary alliances, they were actually looking for an alternative formula with which to transform the United States into a democratic utopia.

In this sense, the *Port Huron Statement* was remarkable for its continuity with traditional American ideas of popular self-government, egalitarian ethics and social justice, and refused socialist discourse. It broke with the old left by ignoring entirely the question of the Soviet Union, Marxism and communism. Not since Earl Browder's slogan "Communism is 20th-century Americanism" in the 30s had there been such an attempt to invent an indigenous radical discourse. There was no "socialism," "revolution" or "workers' control" here, but "participatory democracy" instead, the tradition of Mills and Thorstein Veblen, the refusal of explicitly Marxist categories.

It was not the Cold War alone which had brought this about. It was the passion for a fundamental break with the radical past, with the sectarian debates, foreign subcultures and sterile programs. The communist and socialist past was not repugnant, it was just irrelevant for contemporary purposes. A new language to forge group solidarity was therefore necessary—and Tom Hayden and his friends understood that.

Historians of this "new left" have frequently mocked the SDS for spending the first half of any meeting adopting the agenda and defining the rules of debate, and even sympathetic observers have sometimes ascribed this strange ritual to inexperience or to the absence of a viable political culture. This criticism misunderstands the nature of the new left, summarized in a single word: process. It signalled an almost religious return to *experience* and a converse retreat from the abstractions of the red politics of yesterday. One worked out personal and procedural issues in great and often exhausting detail as a way of fusing the personal with the political, of creating a community not primarily of interest (political rationalism) but of *feeling*. So in some respects a national meeting of the SDS was an orgy of incantations. Rhetorical repetition, procedural debate, moral invocations to kindness and equality were all part of the process of community building, a psychopolitical experience in which duration played a purgative part in transforming traditional political interactions into what was described as "movement behavior." This style drove many left and liberal politicos to distraction.

From 1962 to 1965, I attended these meetings, having been coopted along with several others as an advisor. This job actually began on 21st Street, but my interest then was not enough to bring me to SDS meetings. I was drawn in by the unfortunate aftermath of the *Port Huron Statement*. A CP-led youth group, the DuBois Club, had sent an observer to the conference. He was a rather timid fellow called Marvin Markman and was regarded by the SDS people as harmless. But when the word reached the League for Industrial Democracy that a bona fide communist had been permitted to observe the SDS convention, the roof fell in on the students. During a meeting (that has become part of the lore of the new left), Harrington and other Board members excoriated the SDS leaders for political naiveté: having had the bitter experience of witnessing communist hegemony on the American left during the 30s and 40s, as staunch anti-Stalinists, the Board concluded that the CP was not merely wrong on a variety of political questions but that its presence was actually detrimental to the task of rebuilding the democratic left. It was not a question of political differences but of whether democracy and dictatorship, as they saw it, could coexist.

The incident would have blown over had the SDS leaders simply agreed to bar communists from future meetings, since there was never any proposal to admit them into the ranks, but SDS instead chose to treat the whole thing as a major issue between the old and new left. After this confrontation, SDS looked for other possible sources of contact with the mainstream of the labor and liberal communities. Ray Brown, a former union organizer and then an economist for the Federal Reserve Bank, myself and others, were asked to give talks at national meetings, hold workshops and be available for consultation. I was 29 years old at the time, Ray a little older. Most of the "students"—many were already in graduate school or working full time for some liberal or peace organization — were only between five or eight years younger, but had grown up under very different circumstances. We helped them because we shared their belief that a new movement was being born and that it would die if shackled to the past. I was convinced, like SDS, that the CP was little more than a nuisance, and I was also persuaded that anticommunism had been the scourge of the 50s, that the labor and progressive movements had been seriously crippled by their preoccupation with issues like the Soviet Union. With C. Wright Mills, James Weinstein, William Appleman Williams and others of *Studies on the Left*, I shared, too, the belief that a genuinely American movement could arise only by adopting the stance of leftist isolationism.

SDS had no sympathy for the American Communist Party or the Soviet Union, but this was a generation which had just emerged from the dark days of political repression and intellectual censorship commonly known as the McCarthy era. It was believed that the American CP was being persecuted not so much for its ties with the Soviet Union as for its dissent from the main drift of American foreign policy. In this way, SDS became an important repository of "anti" anticommunism: it held that the Cold War was responsible for the destruction of participatory possibilities, that it was a mask for central control and management of everyday life, a metaphor for the reduction of the American dream to rituals of conformity. In the pursuit of a new democratic ideal, of political redemption from the McCarthy terror, SDS was thus obliged to defend the rights of the CP. It also understood that the CP itself was no threat to democratic institutions, for the party was weak and in fact had to uphold these institutions in order to survive at all.

However, the new movement was determined to resist the examples of its elders. It chose neither the path of Marxist science as the historical equivalent of moral redemption after the capitulation by its political progenitors during the McCarthy era, nor the cold war liberalism of the disillusioned radical intellectuals of the 30s. Instead, SDS was the first organized expression of the postscarcity generation's new nationalism. Their idea was directed principally to the renewal of the atrophied institutions of American democracy, or more precisely, to the creation of new institutions of popular participation to replace existing bureaucratic structures. The problem was how to utilize the subversive possibilities that already existed in popular political culture. For the new left, the question of the Soviet legacy was simply irrelevant except negatively; the obsession among the various groups of the old left with the character of actually existing socialisms was regarded as a central reason for the demise of the left in American life. At the same time, the new left was deeply concerned with issues of race and third-world revolutions, regarding the civil rights and independence movements as correlates to democratic renewal, the support of which could assist the moral regeneration of the middle classes.

Much of the new left was guilty of a kind of collective amnesia, having rejected the idea that historical knowledge and living traditions could prevent repetition of past errors. Action/experience was to take precedence over history and memory. In this respect, one cannot but be impressed by the naiveté of the widely disseminated notion "Don't trust anybody over thirty," the proposition that older people are somehow a priori plagued by memories and beliefs, habits of thought and action, that ought to be buried.

Furthermore, there was an almost paranoid fear of what Sartre called the *practico-inert.* To admit, in other words, the limits of action was to court defeat. Undoubtedly, this delusion produced a series of disasters. So it was with the ill-fated community organizing efforts of SDS's Economic Research and Action Program (ERAP), an intervention in the black ghettoes and white underclass slums which generated much publicity but little benefit for the residents. Hayden and Carl Whitman had written a strategy paper in 1963 called *Toward an Interracial Movement of the Poor*, in which they argued for a multiracial alliance combining the research and organizing skills of students and other middle-class types with the authentic anticapitalist needs and demands of the poor, a "class" the authors believed to be distinct from the working class (big labor). These ideas were put into practice in the summer of 1964, which saw ERAP's entrance into Newark, Baltimore, Chicago and other northern cities. There was also the less radical but equally inspired efforts of the Northern Student Movement, which conducted literacy programs for black kids and assisted the Harlem rent strikes in the winter of 1964–65. However, the unstated concept was that whites could redeem themselves only by helping blacks to become free. It was the adoption of the concept of responsibility which is as old in the American tradition as abolitionism.

Community organizing, voter registration (primarily by the black Student Non–Violent Coordinating Committee [SNCC] in the South) and education projects challenged the liberal state and the institutions that supported it, thus providing an opening for mass participation. For student radicals the struggle for decent housing, for jobs and income, against rats and roaches, pointed clearly towards the authoritarian side of liberal democracy.

Most of these projects folded within a few years but they produced some interesting lessons. Take the Newark project for instance. I had played a fairly active role in helping ERAP and the New York rent strikes get moving and was, until 1963, the vice-chair of the Clinton Hill Neighborhood Council in Newark. This was an organization dedicated both to preserving the interracial character of the community and improving living conditions. From its inception in 1955, the Council distinguished itself by waging successful struggles against federally sponsored urban renewal, a project heralded by corporations and liberals alike as the key to the development of the decrepit inner cities. Although the Council became a political power in this rapidly changing city and was able to slow down the process of what we called "people removal," we were resisting large demographic and economic forces that proved too strong to withstand. When SDS decided to make a commitment to off-campus organizing, they turned to me, among others, for information as to what to do. I arranged for SDS to be invited to assist the Council; this was a match not made in heaven.

The SDS group called itself the Newark Community Union Project (NCUP) and formed its base in the city's South Ward. Conflicts soon arose between the student organizers and the Council, who counted among its members many black and white homeowners interested in code enforcement and other ways of preserving neighborhood and property values. The SDS group regarded these objectives as both limited and hopelessly middle class and broke with the Council, moving its territorial claims to the lower part of the Hill, where the people were poorer and the homes more dilapidated. Thereby they had not only defined a turf but also an ideological difference, arguing that poor and working-class residents often had divergent needs and demands. The working-class homeowners wanted to make the neighborhood safe, the schools better and the streets cleaner and better lit. In the view of the NCUP, the poor welfare recipients of the dilapidated areas, with their ill-clothed and ill-fed children, wanted political power in order to improve their conditions. A "union" rather than a council was therefore the appropriate form for this desperate constituency. Analogously, while the Council was mired in electoral politics, NCUP favored direct action, especially since most of its underclass members were not registered to vote. It was not a question, then, of finding the least common denominator which could unite the greatest number of residents (the policy of the Council), but of sharpening the differences between the poor and the wealthy, the people and the state. Later, NCUP was nonetheless forced to defend its gains through electoral politics, and they entered conventional coalitions around specific issues, candidates and programs. But the group had defined a new politics of community organizing that went beyond single issue coalitions. A union was no longer conceived in terms of "trade" or "craft" but as "community," a site of popular fusion formed apart from, and in opposition to, the established interests.

This innovation was remarkable both for its sectarianism and its political originality. We need not linger, in this context, on Hayden's—by 1964 he had become the leader of NCUP—unfortunate tendency to factionalism and personal power politics. What made NCUP interesting, on the contrary, was its creative fusion of traditional symbols such as "community" and "union," and the recognition of the need for self-representation among the poor. Even more important, in retrospect, was the fact that SDS, SNCC and other movements of this generation, provided a model for others to challenge the prevailing modes of representation. It was not the organization they built that defined the new left in American politics, but the deconstruction of the common conflations of aggregation and democracy, of interest and community, of voting and participation: a deconstruction which indeed created an ideological space for the multilayered movements of the late 1960s.

These were movements of a generation, not of a class, a race or specific interests or issues. It was a generation shaped by its parental predecessor, by the postwar migration to the suburbs and professional communities adjacent to the big cities, where happiness had become synonymous with economic security and maximum consumption. As a reaction, the new generation tried to create more than a different sort of politics; it tried to create a utopian community and indeed one may argue that the new politics was a product of this communitarian impulse. Some sought this community in southern rural slums and others in the ghettoes of northern cities. A small but important segment created a counterculture within the core cities—art in the East Village, agriculture in Virginia, California and Vermont, craft in Minnesota and upstate New York. These avant-garde movements were not marked so much by their formal innovations as much as by their conviction that efforts to reform the system were doomed to be absorbed by the antagonists. Hence the critique of liberal society took the forms it did, from the attempt to sustain an alternate economy based upon subsistence farming and small-scale production to that of finding the link between art and life in the combination of working, living and sexual space.

It might be objected that communitarian movements were naive, that their success depended on the longstanding affluence of the United States in general and the economic buoyancy generated by the Vietnam war in particular. And surely the notions of "participatory democracy," of the beloved community, of the counterculture are overdetermined and historically specific. However, to reduce their character to class origin, or to dismiss their social and political significance as narcissism or something worse, is to see the whole thing from the perspective of social conservatism.

There were really two countercultures in the 60s. My connection was mainly to the political counterculture, those who engaged in the politics of direct democracy, who organized traditional constituencies in new ways. The second were the cultural radicals, the artists, writers and, above all, the rock musicians and their audience, for whom the erotic revolution was a political movement. It is important to recognize the differences between these two tendencies. Even though there was some overlap, there was also considerable hostility between them. The cultural radicals believed the struggle within the state and its institutions hopeless and beside the point. For them the important question was freedom to be different, in political terms, freedom from the state. This doctrine did not foreclose political action, but its forms were different: smoke-ins and be-ins in Central Park and other places where ostensible law-breaking could visibly show defiance; building art and cultural communities on the Lower East Side, the

Haight in San Francisco and other cities; coffee houses where poetry and stories were recited; new dress codes, new sexual norms, concerts and so on where dope was passed around in an otherwise dark stadium or club.

It does not matter that such slogans as "sex, drugs and rock and roll" failed to encompass the many layers of social reality of the 60s, or that economic countercultures, communes and various other communities ultimately succumbed to interpersonal squabbles, external economic pressures, or the provocations of government agents and the like. What survives in memory is not the megalomania of this generation, which mistook its demographic proliferation for political power, nor the arrogance of those who invested themselves with magical powers; these excesses were merely symptoms of the affliction of historical amnesia. America's past is as mystified and weighs as heavily on the living as that of any other country. The difference is that widespread perception that only the glorious part constitutes our legacy and that to be American is to overcome all adversity. The new left was thus American in a double sense: it tried to invent a new past that served the present rather than the "truth" of the past, and, in a sort of Nietzschean way, it proclaimed the triumph of the will, the limitless capacity to shape the future in its own images. This magical quality marked the cultural politics of the 60s and distinguishes it from virtually every European counterpart except the French, where the slogan "All power to the imagination" replaced every traditional concern.

At the time, many older friends of the student and youth movements were amazed by the hubris of the new activists. We attributed their disregard for political and social boundaries to their inexperience, arrogance and megalomania. Of course, much of this was accurate. Hayden was impervious to criticism; Carl Wittman, the person who really started the Newark project, was moralistic to the point of absurdity; and others were similarly afflicted with delusions about the omnipotence of their movement. These very qualities were the source of antagonism between SDS and other movements, like SNCC, the West Coast free-speech and antiwar activists, and the Northern Student Movement. On the other hand, the same confidence and sense of purpose brought about results, among them the magnificent SDS March on Washington in April 1965 against the Vietnam war. Nevertheless, it was symptomatic that the organization did not follow up on this event, which had been so skeptically regarded by an assortment of social democrats and radicals on the outside. Instead, others like A.J. Muste, Staughton Lynd, Jerry Rubin and myself had to provide the links between the April demonstration and the growing antiwar movement. Astonishingly, the SDS leadership was still convinced that the future lay in local organizing among the poor and marginal groups. The chief promulgator of this view was Tom Hayden, later to become a very public antiwar activist.

II

Sometime in 1964 Jim Weinstein brought himself and the four-year-old *Studies on the Left* to New York from its birthplace in Madison, Wisconsin. The journal was started by students under the auspices of William Appleman Williams, a Wisconsin history professor who is now generally accredited with having spearheaded the school of American historical writing called "revisionism." Williams, together with C. Wright Mills, openly urged the generation of young intellectuals and political activists to break with all of the codes of traditional radicalism, especially the doctrines according to which the working class was anointed with sacred historical powers, and the Bolshevik Revolution was the transcendentally significant event for the fate of the American left.

In the late 50s Williams collected a large coterie of students, some of whom were refugees from the youth sections of the Communist Party. Among these were Jim Weinstein, Dave Eakins, Marty Sklar, Michael Leibowitz and Ron Radosh. He added some of the more promising younger historians, many of them too young to have been part of the organized left in the 50s but yet sympathetic to radical politics. Taken as a whole, this was probably the most resourceful and brilliant cohort that any American university possessed in that period. *Studies* was founded to provide the intellectual grist for the development of a new left. In its first issue, which appeared at the dawn of the new decade, it ran Mills's *Letter to the New Left*, a short document which served as the manifesto of this *intellectual* vanguard (but nonmovement) until the *Port Huron Statement*. It was Mills who first systematically laid out the doctrine of the American new left: abandon the labor metaphysic, don't get bogged down politically and emotionally in the controversies regarding the Soviet Union, China or anyplace besides the United States, rediscover American traditions, particularly the promise of a democratic society, equality and community, oppose the domination of large corporations over all aspects of American life, support national liberation movements abroad, but avoid endorsing their particular form of government—these were the succinct imperatives, and they became the creed of *Studies*.

The project throughout its seven-year history thus became a concrete investigation of American history and contemporary politics from the outlined perspective. Weinstein assumed the leadership, partly because he raised almost all of the necessary money for the journal and partly because he among the many editors was the most dedicated to the major principles prescribed by Williams and Mills. In his own field, the history of American socialism, he applied these ideas to the issues that united and divided the historical left: electoral versus direct action, the question of the Soviet Union, class versus sectoral politics, socialist campaigns versus reform struggles within the Democratic Party, the mass party versus the vanguard party. Despite his communist past, or perhaps because of it, he came down squarely on the side of the old prewar socialists, finding that the betrayal of Debs's party by both left and right led to the demise of the American left. Indeed, from its inception, *Studies* aimed to reconstruct a multi-tendency socialist movement in the United States, one that could successfully contest electoral offices, provide room for education and cultural development, and play an important part in the peace, civil rights and other social movements of the day. In the context of the 60s, when the American left divided between those wanting simply to resurrect and humanize Leninism and those who thought socialism archaic and wished to replace it with "democracy" pure and simple, the Williams-Mills-Weinstein position seemed to be a serious and reasonable alternative.

In the early issues, Sklar wrote some wonderful papers on the Wilson era in which he traced the origins of what became known as "corporate liberalism." Sklar argued that such "reforms" as regulation of corporate economic activities were anything but expressions of popular power over capital, their being on the contrary signs of a new integration of state and big business. The Interstate Commerce Commission, railroad commissions, and other governmental agencies developed by all national administrations after the 1890s, were means to rationalize competition, to accelerate the process of monopolization of leading sectors, and resulted not in more popular power over government, but in less.

Writers like Williams himself, Gabriel Kolko and Weinstein, whose book the *Corporate Ideal and the Liberal State* (1966) extended Sklar's argument to social welfare policy, shaped a new vision of the 20th century in America; "corporate liberalism" became probably the most influential doctrine of American historiography in the 1960s. In the bargain, 20th-century populist, trade union, social liberal and other movements were dismissed as either objectively corporatist, regardless of intention, or as grievously misguided in their refusal to choose an explicitly socialist alternative to corporate power. By showing that the corporations themselves wanted reform—though this has since proved somewhat of an exaggeration—the new left historians also hoped to demonstrate the futility of popular front politics according to which communists believed the Democratic Party to be a viable political arena for socialists. For if the New Deal, for instance, was little more than a brilliant and effective way of derailing radicalism, the success of the Communist Party in the 30s was merely the left face of corporate liberalism. Sklar and Williams provided a powerful counterweight to the conventional left wisdom that the CP was a heroic and strong force for social progress until the Cold War destroyed it or, as in the anticommunist left version, until the CP was mortally wounded by Stalinism. They argued that even the communist contribution to the building of industrial unions could be discounted, if it were true that industrial unionism, whatever its benefits from the point of view of the workers, was irrelevant from a socialist perspective. *Studies* did not go as far as to denounce the labor metaphysic, since most of its editors still believed in the leading role of the working class. But it did hold that American trade unions were part of the corporate/liberal consensus and not its opponent, regardless of the frequent strikes and disputes with individual employers.

Since many of the editors remained in Wisconsin or scattered to various American and Canadian universities when Weinstein moved east, he, Lee Baxandall and Helen Kramer began to look for some new editors. Shortly after they arrived, *Studies* held a party to which I was invited. I had known Weinstein from my days as a high school organizer in New York in the late 1940s. I was an international representative for the Oil, Chemical and Atomic Workers based in the northeast region. He asked me to join the *Studies* board and I agreed. For the next three years, till its demise, I was an active member of the board. Gene Genovese was also recruited, and within a year so was Norm Fruchter, an American writer who had been on the editorial committee of the *New Left Review* while living in England; Alan Cheuse, Fruchter's college friend and also a writer and a critic; Tom Hayden, now ensconced in Newark; and historian Staughton Lynd, who was ending his career at Yale.

The board divided along ideological lines from the start. It would be excessive to see the split as one between intellectuals and activists, but every meeting after 1965 reflected some aspect of this sort of dispute. Most salient was the issue of how important the new social movements of the decade were, and how they should be treated. Weinstein and Genovese could barely disguise their contempt for the mindlessness of the student, countercultural and, to a lesser extent, civil rights movements. At best these were to be regarded with benevolent condescension. The main task was to provide consistent socialist analysis of the main political struggles of the time and an evaluation of the American past from the point of view of an undogmatic but incisive Marxism. I generally sided with the Weinstein faction concerning the politics of the journal, insisting that socialism was the determinate negation of corporate capitalism and that the journal had to place itself within a specifically socialist ideological tradition of American radicalism. At the same time, as a participant in many of the new movements, I was fearful that Genovese's old leftism would destroy the journal's receptivity to their originality. Unfortunately, as with many other debates on the American left, the controversies were too often framed as antinomies: either the new social movements or ideological politics (albeit one sharply critical of old leftist positions).

In the end, it was agreed to subject the movements to critical reportage and inquiry. My only signed articles for *Studies* were pieces on the labor movement and community organizing, written from the perspective of the corporate liberal theme: the idea was always to show the reformist nature of apparently radical organizations and movements which did not adopt an explicitly socialist or even anticorporate view. Lynd and Hayden, often supported by Fruchter, argued that the movements were everything. Though Lynd had been a Trotskyist in the 1950s and came from a distinguished left-wing academic family, he was deeply influenced by Muste's version of radical pacifism. It is worthwhile to review some of Muste's activities in the 1950s and early 60s since the importance of his ideas, and of the groups he guided, has been strangely underestimated by historians.

In his early career, Muste was a Methodist minister of the social-gospel variety, but in the 30s he became a revolutionary Marxist, organizing the American Workers Party. This group played a key role in the famous Toledo auto strike of 1934, one of the three struggles that paved the way for the CIO. After a disastrous and sobering experience attempting to merge with the Trotskyists, Muste took a half-step back towards the religious left. From the late 1930s to his death in 1968, he organized and led a series of pacifist groups, most notably the Fellowship on Reconciliation, the War Resisters League, and the Congress of Racial Equality (CORE). During World War II he advised conscientious objection to some draftees, including Dave Dellinger, who was later to become his successor at the helm of the pacifist wing of the peace movement. In the 1950s and 60s he helped to articulate the aims of the nuclear disarmament campaigns and the resistance to the draft. Shortly before his death, he was fighting to establish the principle of nonexclusion within the antiwar coalitions so that communists, Trotskyists and other radicals could work with independent leftists, liberals and even some social democrats: no one was to be excluded in principle.

By the 50s, Muste had become a kind of Christian socialist but he was also a radical organizer of unusual ability. His vision was fundamentally at variance with both communist and democratic-socialist views. Although he respected and worked with progressive legislators on specific issues, he worked hardest on promoting direct, nonviolent resistance as the best and most morally defensible means to achieve social change. He was probably the preeminent exponent of Ghandism in the United States, but at the same time he adopted a unique version of Leninism, geared to the reality of radical American politics, exclusively as an organizational device. On the surface, Muste ran or advised a floating crap game of organizations that intervened on every major issue: peace, civil rights, African Freedom, religious and political liberty. He established informal relations with important figures of the developing movements on the strength of his personal stature: his quiet, firm way of speaking, his obvious political sophistication and enormous intelligence drew younger people to him, especially radicals seeking alternatives to social-liberal and sectarian left politics. He spoke a different tongue from the tired leftism of the 50s. For him, direct action was not merely a dramatic tactic to achieve specific ends, it was a way of life. If you sat at a lunch-counter, you were doing more than integrating a public facility and breaking Jim Crow practices, you were bearing witness to human inequality and to the possibility of creating the beloved community. Lynd was deeply influenced by Muste and so was I.

Muste had his own implicit theory of the student/middle-class professional as a historical agent. The working class had demonstrated its passion for both economic justice and social conformity, and Muste was therefore always looking for others who would be prepared to put themselves on the line to save humanity, to call attention to injustice, to initiate change. Hence the middle-class nature of his entourage, some of whom become public figures — notably Dellinger and Bayard Rustin. Most of his comrades, however, remained anonymous, creative apparatchiks willing to work long hours at low pay for idealistic reasons.

When Muste died, his co-workers scattered in different ideological directions. Bob Gilmore of Turn Toward Peace moved steadily to the right of the peace movement, became increasingly anticommunist and mainstream both in style and aspiration. Bayard Rustin, after brilliantly organizing the March on Washington together with Martin Luther King and a group of New York radicals, became President of the A. Phillip Randolph Institute, which, as time went by, came to oppose the militant wing of the black freedom movement. Rustin was always torn between his radical pacifism and his fierce loyalty to a neo-Trotskyist version of the United Front which in the end led him to a strong alliance with the mainstream labor unions. Dellinger stayed on the left and modified his pacifist beliefs in the wake of the national liberation movements of the 1960s. He succeeded Muste as the leading pacifist activist but lacked the latter's authority and talent for compromise, both necessary qualities to keep an ideologically diverse group together.

I had first met Muste in 1963 when I was chair for the Committee for Miners. I was seeking "notables" for our effort to defend some Kentucky miners who were on trial for conspiracy, having staged a wildcat strike against both the companies and their own corrupt union. Muste, a respected figure in some religious circles, agreed to help reach others, including former minister and Socialist Party leader Norman Thomas, who was now a fairly crotchety old warrior. However, not until the early days of the antiwar movement did I get to know Muste well. We sat together on coordinating committees that began to gain momentum in the summer of 1965, following the boldly conducted SDS March on Washington. We lived in the same Upper West Side neighborhood, so I frequently drove him home to his west 90s apartment after meetings. I learned that the popular image of a saintly yet slightly irascible fighter was only part of the truth. Muste was a strategic thinker. By the last year of his life, he was absolutely convinced that the struggle against the American intervention was the key to mass radicalization and urged that view upon me.

Subsequently, I become part of the Labor for Peace network that Sid Lens, Tony Mazzocchi and David Livingston of District 65 were organizing under the benign sponsorship of Pat Gorman of the Meatcutters, Frank

Rosenblum of the Clothing Workers, and Emil Mazey of the UAW. Mazzocchi, a member of the Board of the Oil and Chemical Workers, was clearly the most talented rank-and-file activist in labor's wing of the antiwar movement. I was critical at the time of his cautious, even conservative approach to the war, but he had his ear to the ground. Given the deep-seated anticommunism of American workers and their conviction that war work was needed for full employment, given George Meany's open hostility to any criticism of U.S. foreign policy from within the AFL-CIO, Mazzocchi stepped just far enough out on the limb to keep his legs intact. I, of course, got mine cut off because by 1966 I had gone public in my antiwar activities inside and outside the trade unions.

Lynd, under Muste's influence, organized a conference in Washington in August 1965 for the purpose of providing a forum for the many new movements which were trying to mobilize poor people, students and blacks. The *Congress of Unrepresented People*, as it was called, was intended as a protest against the hypocrisy of representative government, as a demonstration that direct action rather than traditional political participation was the only way to achieve justice. One of the by-results of the *Congress* was the first national coordinating committee for the new antiwar movement, a committee put together by Jerry Rubin, Frank Empspak and myself.

Lynd and Hayden disagreed with the old left less on the specific issues than on the reliance of the latter on state action, legislative methods, bureaucratic organization and the like. Furthermore, like many other new radicals, they were more interested in novel cultural and social relations than in reorganizing the principle of economic ownership as such. In this, they were early proponents of political and economic decentralization, the creation of nonbureaucratic forms which would "let the people decide" the questions affecting their lives, and the substitution of "community" for "society" (thus following Tönnies's famous distinction). The state was regarded not as an instrument of social justice and equality, but as an arena in which community, peace and other issues of the "people" could be fought out. The ultimate object, however, was to dismantle as much of the state's power as possible.

The *Studies* board in 1965–66 was not split along personality lines—though Lynd's slow, pacific and moral discourse was sometimes maddening to the New Yorkers—but on deep-rooted divergencies on the question of what the basis of a new left was supposed to be. Weinstein and Genovese may have broken with the Communist Party on political grounds, but they were, root and branch, socialists of the Second and Third Internationals, respectively. Hayden and Lynd, on the other hand, had a deeply religious conception of the "movement." Their argument that *Studies* should report the activities of the emerging social movements was well received by other board members. The battle ensued over the problem as to whether the journal had the right and responsibility to provide a critique of these movements. Hayden was particularly insistent that intellectuals on the outside should confine themselves to publicity for them, at the very most asserting their centrality to contemporary political discourse and situating them in the general liberation movement.

This cut to the heart of the role of the journal. In these years, *Studies* was perhaps the most influential and widely read of the growing band of new left periodicals. Despite its relatively modest circulation, its articles were widely discussed. Its editors were national figures in the movement, and its ideas were considered advanced. Weinstein, Genovese and myself saw the journal as a theoretical organ of a putative new socialist party that would gradually gain hegemony among the key activists in the movements. Having abandoned the old left organizations did not for us signify the absence of any hope for a mass socialist party, which could run its own candidates for public office, constitute the leading cadre of the movements, and eventually find means of building influence within the trade unions and other working-class organizations. Hayden, Lynd and Fruchter argued that these perspectives were far removed from reality. They, and the new radical generation, did not aspire to act within the confines of mainstream politics. They were searching, on the contrary, for a way to authenticate their own social and personal existence through action, for a way to construct a new moral order based on popular democracy as the antithesis of representation.

One can see in these debates the germ of what was to become the cause of the breakup of the movement in the later 1960s. Weinstein argued that movements without a political vehicle would inevitably collapse. But his often accurate criticisms failed to come to grips with the fundamental assumptions of Hayden and Lynd. For them, the issues had to be fought in order to build the movement, which was by no means intended to change the existing society but to presage an alternative one. Weinstein had replaced the palpably erroneous economic determinism of the old left with the primacy of the political; Hayden and Lynd challenged politics itself as a form of domination infinitely more oppressive than economic exploitation.

We socialists on the board also missed a second principle of the new radicalism: the aspiration to absolute sovereignty for the individual, whose power had been systematically undercut by representative government, trade union bureaucracies and large, impersonal institutions. The new left intended to restore power to the *person* (which is not to be confused, as it often was, with "power to the people," a formulation of the black civil rights movement where the individual was subordinated to group interest). Hayden and Lynd were, in this respect, early critics of what Gilles Deleuze and Felix Guattari were later to castigate as aggregate politics. Against the traditional macropolitics evinced by Weinstein, Genovese and myself, Hayden and Lynd advocated a micropolitics of liberation.

Weinstein was finally also involved in the politics of *interest*, the underpinning of such notions as class struggle, corporate liberalism and conventional conceptions of socialist revolution. Lynd, while not adopting Muste's reconciliatory stance, was less interested at this point in the political strategies deriving from rationalist assumptions, i.e., alliances, coalitions and blocs, than he was in movements stemming from individuality, spiritual renewal and love. The revolution would restore our humanity, bring us back to ourselves, and, in Marx's words, recreate our "species-being." The movement had to founded on the dignity of its subjects or it would inevitably degenerate into traditional interest group politics. The inspiration here was the early Marx and the left traditions of Protestant humanism, not revolutionary Marxism. Lynd's fundamental view was expressed in a book he wrote later with Alice Lynd, *Rank and File*, in which workers spoke for themselves about their work, their struggles and their hopes for the future.

The differences within the board were too wide. Lynd, Hayden and Fruchter finally resigned when they understood the intractability of Weinstein's position. Weinstein then disbanded the journal in 1967 and moved to the West where, three years later, he founded *Socialist Revolution* (now *Socialist Review*), a political journal seeking a new party. In 1972, Lynd and Weinstein came together again to form the New American Movement, a democratic-socialist organization which embodied the principles of both the communitarian and the traditional radical politics. From its inception, NAM was much closer to the ethos of the social movements of its time than to parliamentary politics. Its somewhat more conservative counterpart, the Democratic Socialist Organizing Committee, founded by Michael Harrington, Irving Howe and others in the same year, was in fact more attuned to Weinstein's original stance than his own organization.

Lynd and Hayden, like Weinstein and Genovese, were serious intellectuals. Both groups were profoundly persuaded that the left had to be, in the first place, an *American* movement. This left isolationism did not affect their shared hatred of imperialism and global American corporate interests, or their admiration for national liberation movements abroad. The idea was to build the movement on American traditions. The trouble was that each of them discovered antagonistic traditions. Lynd admired Thoreau and Hayden wrote his master's thesis at Michigan on C. Wright Mills. Although Weinstein drew much from Mills's *Power Elite* and followed his political writings with interest, he was more of a Marxist. As for Genovese, he remained an unreconstructed Leninist of the Italian variety, which meant that he believed in a polycentric world communist movement, admired Gramsci, but he was also interested in building an American Marxist party that could one day contest state power. In 1964, he became a national figure by declaring, while still a junior history professor at Rutgers, that he favored victory for the National Liberation Front in Vietnam.

However, Lynd and Hayden became, as the 60s wore on, more political activists than intellectuals. Like so many others, they were unable to break down the growing division between the two aspects of the radical movement, and ultimately came close to sharing the pervasive anti-intellectualism of the period. We, on the other side, increasingly defined the issue in terms of the need for *theory*. For Hayden, theory was a devaluation of concrete experience. On the other hand, what we meant by theory was not clear. Weinstein was hardly a theorist and Genovese's idea of theoretical discourse was mostly too traditional to be taken seriously by the other side. In fact, most of the writers of *Studies* were empirical historians. The journal did publish genuine contributions to theory. James O'Connor's two articles on community unions as a new form of social struggle advanced our collective understanding of the processes at hand very considerably; Harold Cruse produced a brilliant, if one-sided, historical critique of the role of the CP among blacks; and Martin Sklar, though no longer involved in the daily activities of the journal, succeeded in his few contributions to expand the historical perspective on corporate liberalism.

III

The antiwar struggle, in its first years an important but still sectoral movement, gradually came to consume almost the entire new left, including Hayden, Lynd, and for a time myself. This transformation was due mainly to the escalation in the war and the attention it drew in American political life. As the 1968 election approached and the size of the movement increased, antiwar leaders like Hayden, Dellinger, Rubin and Abbie Hoffman inevitably turned their attention to the Democratic Party convention in Chicago that summer. Many of them could not have cared less about the actual nomination, though others certainly were attracted to electoral politics after seeing how profoundly the protests had shaken the Democratic Party. Yet the coordinators of the movement, the majority of them either Muste's offspring, old SDS leaders, like Rennie Davis, or cultural radicals such as Hoffman, were still guided by communitarian ideas. Protest and confrontation would purge the sins of our culture: the antiwar movement was yet another occasion to exercise the popular will, to expose the sham of electoral representation, to mobilize the millions for control over their lives. Only a minority perceived the movement as a means to change power relations within the state or to create new alliances against imperialism.

The war, then, was seen largely as a symptom of the degeneration of our civilization, of the futility of bourgeois rationality, which had become the same as technological rationality. Antiwar protest, direct confrontation, was a politics of redemption. However, even as thousands of young people were battling with police in Chicago, the youth movement was beginning to fall apart. SDS, now a mass student organization with thousands of members all over the country, was beset by sectarian squabbles, squabbles which had begun in 1967 with the entry of a Maoist sect, Progressive Labor, into the movement. PL was formed in 1960 as a late spinoff from the Communist Party, partly as a product of the Sino-Soviet split, partly because the dissenters considered the CP hopelessly reformist. By the mid-60s, PL had discovered that the student movement was more than an amusement for upper-middle-class kids and indeed worthy of political intervention.

PL forced the usually laconic SDS leadership into intense ideological struggle. For the first time, members were forced to declare their "politics" beyond the ordinary combination of vague democratic radicalism and strong antiwar position. PL pushed its own, fully worked-out Marxist-Leninist perspective from which it was never prepared to deviate upon an organization which was somewhat of an ideological vacuum at the time. For SDS had grown much faster than its political and administrative resources could handle. A good number of the first generation of student activists had already graduated into antiwar work, trade union and community organizing, academia or, occasionally, "mainstream" liberal politics and the professions. Many of the old new leftists had gone to the media. It was a new leadership, then, that had to come up with a response to PL. For a time, they tried to rework the implicit ideology of their predecessors: "youth" became a class, a historical subject and the vanguard agent of change.

The early SDS leaders would never have seen their generation as "agent," "vanguard" or historical subject. For them it was always "the people," the poor, the blacks—in short, someone else. They had rejected the old left, but hesitated to go further than arguing for an antimass, antielite, antistate position. Their successors had no choice but to engage in ideological combat, faced as they were with a competent and determined PL cadre. In addition one could not deny the importance of Maoism and the Cuban Revolution in the context of mobilizing the political opposition. Maoism, as distinct from the actual achievements of the Chinese revolution, deeply influenced feminism and radicalized many youth, especially blacks. It also became a refuge for the multitude of radicals who abjured reformism but could not bear to support the Soviet Union.

The debate within SDS epitomized what was going on everywhere: it was just more visible because the discussion was open, had immediate organizational consequences and took place in the most highly respected new left outfit. The Trotskyist Socialist Workers Party, which had made a substantial contribution to the antiwar movement since 1965, was now challenging it to limit itself to minimalist slogans and leave broad ideological politics to the Leninist vanguard (like themselves)—a policy, incidentally, directly opposite that of the European Trotskyists. Other sects intervened too. By the end of the decade, the entire independent left was debating whether to transform its various organizations into preparty formations, and, if so, what one ought to do next. SDS split into four major factions, corresponding to the wider splits in the radical movement.

The first tendency, the Revolutionary Youth Movement, immediately became two. RYM 1, which was later to metamorphose into the Weather Underground, Prairie Fire, etc., argued that the United States was in a prerevolutionary situation, an old concept designating imminent armed struggle for political power. The perceived agents of this revolutionary upsurge were the oppressed black masses and the alienated, already countercultural youth. This alliance, forged through exemplary acts of violence against the symbols of white ruling-class power, would thus eventually topple the system. Now, critics have often labeled the Weather movement as nihilistic, juvenile, irresponsible and paranoid; it has also been blamed in pulp magazines for sexual experimentation, elitism and general zaniness. Yet one should be aware that the Weather people were an extension of the communitarian anarchic impulses of their entire generation. They misread American politics and the depth of the cultural rebellion. Like other isolated groups, they overestimated the repressive side of the state and of the large corporations, prophesying for a time the advent of fascism. As a result they engaged in some dubious acts of symbolic violence to show the vulnerability of the system and their own power. Yet these sometimes grotesque actions were not out of sync with the ideal of a total reconstruction of the human community: these "action critiques" of an apparently closed universe of liberal discourse can be defended if one accepts the premise that pluralism is simply another authoritarian form.

A total critique of the existing society, one which finds nothing redeeming in it, requires a broad political consensus in the population at large. Such was the case in Chiang's China, Batista's Cuba, Somoza's Nicaragua. The tragedy of the Weather Underground did not consist so much in the nature of its deeds as in the complete misunderstanding that the United States was another one of these cases. The question, then, is how they could fall into such an egregious error. Part of the answer lies in the nature of community building. Like other sects, they created a discourse for themselves which reinforced the self-imposed demand that political work necessarily had to be a "family" expression. Just as the family generates a series of behavioral rules, values and assumptions, so the Weather people insisted that its members endure rituals of initiation, tight security as to their comings and goings, and a strict system in which loyalty to the family was everything. The community in effect created a new reality to fit the mode of intervention. The Weather Underground inherited the hubris of the new left and added their own form of solipsism. Their feelings, perceptions and ideas were not represented to others as their own. They had become tribunes of the masses of revolutionary youth waiting in the high schools and the streets for the detonator to set them off in struggle—the new Weather vanguard. All others, especially leftists, were hopelessly mired in the culture and politics of liberal reform, inherently unable to make a real contribution to history because they had been coopted. The violence of the Weather faction was most acute in its language rather than the isolated acts of revolutionary deeds such as bank bombings. These capers were informed by a deep sense of righteousness. After a while, it was reinforced by blatant substitutionism. The masses had yielded to their masters and the Weather family had to awaken their revolutionary temper by the deed.

The other RYM faction was a throwback to the 1930s. The notion of youth as the vanguard was supplanted with an emphasis on working-class and black youth. Led by SDS vice-president Carl Davidson, Michael Klonsky and Bob Avakian, this group renounced the American perspective of the new left, replacing it with the figures of Mao and/or Stalin and the policies of the Third Period of the Communist International, that is to say, confrontation with social democrats and left liberals. The party form of organization followed its course. It was the complete antithesis of the early new left and the mirror image of PL. There was nothing libertarian or anarchist about it; it was deliberately mundane, glorifying the plodding and dogmatic style of the old left. For a time we witnessed a remake of an old film, but like all replays it suffered from having lost its original context.

The second tendency, the "mainstreamers," already in existence by the time of the split in 1969, gradually reverted to left-liberal politics though they retained its new left ideology, at first. These were the community organizers: Mike Ansara, who was later to form MASS Fair Share; Paul and Heather Booth, who founded the Midwest Academy as a training institute for community and "citizens action" organizers; and policy-oriented activists like Lee Webb, a leader in the Vermont Citizens Action Network and later the founder of the Conference for Alternative State and Local Politics; and, of course, Hayden himself.

Seen historically, this group was old left in the sense of the popular front. Their task was to bring new constituents like environmentalists and working-class neighborhood movements into the faltering labor-liberal coalition and to put new issues on the national political agenda. One of the latter, the struggle for safe, clean and cheap energy, became a central focus for coalition politics in the 1970s under Heather Booth's direction. The Citizens Labor Energy Coalition is perhaps the quintessential formation of this mainstream tendency. It combines energy and utility organizations, trade unions and citizens' groups in anticorporate campaigns against big utilities that are responsible for advocating and producing nuclear energy, raising gas and electric rates to pay for it and pressuring legislatures to give in. CLEC is a locally and nationally based model for this new citizens movement that pretty much denies any specific ideological politics except the anticorporate rubric. In recent years, citizens' action networks and coalitions have reentered local Democratic politics in behalf of liberal candidates and have reproduced the older orientation of progressive politics of the 30s and 40s. Yet at the outset, electoral politics had been subordinate to extraparliamentary legislative and street activity. Although the mainstreamers came out of the 60s, they have left it behind, taking their place in the left wing of the Democratic Party.

Third and perhaps most important was the formation of the new feminist movement about which much substantive has been said. Here I wish to emphasize that the socialist-feminist wing and a major segment of the radical feminists formed in opposition to the sexism of the male new left. SDS, antiwar organizations and countercultural movements of various kinds shared one major characteristic: women were mimeo-operators, coffee- and meal-makers and convenient bedmates for male leaders. I cannot recall a single major woman figure in the early SDS, although women comprised a large proportion of the membership. When the movement entered community organizing or mass antiwar activity, women assumed responsible roles in the actual work, but were rarely, if ever, considered leaders. Upon reflection, I remember the exceptions: Casey Hayden in Chicago's North Side organizing white welfare mothers; Betty Garman on the West Coast and Jill Hamburg in Newark. I am sure there were more women leaders in the mid-60s, but I am equally certain that they took a great deal of abuse and suffered humiliation. We were, simply, a male elite, on the *Studies* board, the leading antiwar coalitions, the counterculture affinity groups. The feminist movement became more than the property of a generation; it represented, mobilized, and embodied a large fraction of women as gender.

The fourth tendency was a small but not unimportant group which maintained the deep-seated beliefs of the new left, i.e., its reverence for decentralization, communitarian goals and democratic renovation of American society. Jeremy Brecher, Bruce and Kathy Brown, Paul Breines, Stu and Liz Ewen and many others became writers and publicists of a new type of libertarian socialism, which was not exactly anarchist in ideological orientation but certainly antistatist and antibureaucratic. At the end of the 60s, it was my tendency. For us the twin tragedy of the new left was the Leninist intervention and the left-liberal cooptation. For the most part, we went back to the Marxism of Georg Lukács, Rosa Luxemburg, Karl Korsch or the later Sartre, a Marxism without the sterile party politics and dogmatism of the new communist movement. At the same time, we tried to preserve the antiparliamentary or at least extraparliamentary perspective of the workers' councils. We celebrated the wildcat strikes of the late 60s in Italy and derived much inspiration from the May 68 events in France.

This tendency was not a movement, but many of the new journals shared the general perspective (*Telos, Liberation, Root and Branch*, one part of *Socialist Revolution*, particularly Carl Boggs and James O'Connor). Some local organizing efforts were informed by it. Eventually, this neo-Marxism also spurred a major Marxist revival in the universities. The "tendency" faded but survives as a current of cultural Marxism among radicals within a wide spectrum of activities today.

IV

I left the trade unions in the 1960s determined to break with my own political and occupational past. My activities in formal new left organizations terminated with enforced exile to Puerto Rico in 1966 when I was accused of being a leader of the "communist antiwar conspiracy in the labor movement." While sympathetic in the main, the President of the Oil, Chemical and Atomic Workers Union responded to right-wing pressure by sending me off on an organizing assignment in the Caribbean, thus avoiding having to dismiss me. Eventually, I took a leave of absence to write *False Promises*, and then, while I was on a trip back to the mainland, Russ Nixon, a Columbia professor, advised me to see some people in the New York City antipoverty program. I was hired subsequently by Bob Schrank, a former trade unionist and machinist, who had become assistant Commissioner of the Job Agency. I welcomed this. I was tired of traveling and living in motels, tired of trade union routine. Although the unions remained for me an important part of any possible movement for social transformation, the life of a labor functionary was not for me anymore.

After a year as program developer, I became director of a Lower East Side jobs program, spending the next two years as a community activist and administrator. My road was an alternate one to that of those radicals enamored of party or union building. The Lower East Side could not be organized along the same lines as citizens' action, most of which had been formed among white middle- and working-class constituencies. When we fought David Rockefeller's lower Manhattan expressway, when we tried to start coop housing movements in the slums and battled police in one of the several hot summers in the late 60s, when we struggled to obtain more jobs for youth than the city or the federal government were willing to yield, then the movement was based on poor and working-class Puerto Ricans in alliance with the remaining Italians. The organizers were recruited from the many social agencies that dotted the community. For these were the golden years of community action, the time that prompted Daniel Patrick Moynihan to address the problem of disruption and underclass organizing by devising for Nixon a guaranteed-income program for the poor as an alternative to the sprawling activities that marked Johnson's antipoverty crusade.

Moynihan's *Maximum Feasible Misunderstanding* referred to a panel at the Socialist Scholars Conference in 1970 where Michael Harrington and I participated in a debate about the value of the antipoverty program. I had asserted somewhat casually that its best feature was the employment of some good organizers, and Moynihan took this as evidence that the program was hopelessly misdirected. In retrospect, I think the hodgepodge of programs directed to the needs of the poor was one of the most interesting features of the entire decade. These programs provided support for SDS community organizing (the first welfare rights movements since the Depression), helped stop urban "renewal" dead in its tracks, and, equally important, trained a generation of organizers who together with some in the civil rights, anti-war and student movements came close to revitalizing the labor movement through farm workers' struggles and the still unfinished organization of the public sector.

These community organizers avoided the Maoist and Trotskyist alternatives for two reasons. First, both positions struck them, and me, as authoritarian ideologies opposed to the ideas of a self-managed society. Second, to many of us, Marxism was the necessary but insufficient condition for understanding our situation, while Leninism, despite the major contributions of Lenin himself, was not at all appropriate to the building of our movement: we believed that an American socialism had to be internationalist, especially in regard to national liberation struggles in the third world, but we were even more convinced that it had to build on specifically American traditions. While we were among the most active opponents of the war and fully grasped the danger of isolationist populism, we were more impressed by the perils of trying to relive the history of the American communists.

The "new communists" invaded the factories to constitute a workers' vanguard. Most of the time they fell on their faces, though locally they made intermittent gains. They produced weighty manifestoes proclaiming the imminence of the socialist revolution and elaborated strategies for defeating the liberals and social democrats (for which read ourselves) who would, just as in 1919, betray the workers at the brink of revolution. They talked the language of violence as much to purge themselves of their deep-rooted pacific feelings as to symbolically annihilate the enemy.

The various Trotskyist sects were considerably more sensible. For one thing, they refused violence and did not prophesy imminent fascism or revolutionary socialism. But they were no less workerist and vanguardist. Their trade union work was more successful because they supported the "most progressive" rank-and-file insurgencies in the Teamsters, Steelworkers and Communication workers' unions, and kept their leftism in the background. Yet, they found themselves in reform struggles against the most conservative bureaucrats along with other militants who were not socialist and for whom an honest contract and a democratic union was the limit; and that also tended to be the limit of this kind of entryism as such.

In the 1970s, an important fraction of the left "disappeared" into neighborhood activism, fights about nuclear power and opposition to the utilities which controlled it, feminist struggles for social autonomy and economic equality, and, of course, the academy where Marxism had secured some beachheads in various disciplines, notably economics and sociology. Often, we lost our distinct political identity as radicals, an identity that was not constituted by the sects, by the leftist journals, by the several socialist schools that survived the breakup of the new left. Many independent radicals felt that the time had passed when national movements were possible or even desirable. Nor did the left constitute a definite ideological tendency; it had become a subculture, a strain of American life that still resonated among intellectuals and activists but had lost its specific constituency elsewhere.

I had become, in the late 60s, a columnist for the *Guardian*, which was then the leading new left weekly, the place where activists and intellectuals debated radical strategies. It was clear to me that the task was to broaden the left public sphere created by the mass movements and that the press was probably the best way to do it. I wrote two kinds of pieces: analyses of current politics and labor developments, and a series that tried to bring a sense of history and social theory to my readers. I wrote on Marcuse's philosophy, the debate about fascism, the fate of the trade unions, the state of the American left and so on. I remained active, meanwhile, in the fight for urban space on the Lower East Side.

For me, the 60s ended when a group of Guardian staffers seized the means of production in protest against the stance of the paper on one of the factions of the new communist movement, RYM 2. The insurgents were sympathizers of the Weather Underground or antiauthoritarian independents. I abandoned my column in March 1970 with a piece in the *Liberated Guardian*, the shortlived alternative paper set up by the "rank-and-file" movement; I condemned both factions for sectarianism and that was for me the end of the new left.

By spring 1970, I was part of a project to start an alternative public high school in East Harlem, perhaps the first major institutionalization of the free school movement. We tried taking the long march through the bureaucracies, fighting for space inside the structure of prevailing power, waiting perhaps for the next conjuncture. Those dizzy years of building an institution would not erase the sense that this was a defensive struggle. We were now engaged in preserving our gains of the 60s in bits and pieces. I knew it was going to get worse before it would get better.

The Depression of the 1930s would certainly not have produced a mass popular left if capital had not reneged on its promise of the good life to both immigrant and native youth. For the American dream was synonymous with economic security. Capital had thus broken the social contract by closing the frontier of economic opportunity. Of course, young workers fared better than their older comrades who were consigned to the bread lines and Hoovervilles. But if one was lucky to have a job it did not mean dignity: wage labor in these times was self-evident humilation. By 1933, mass organizing among the unskilled and semi-skilled, most of them young, brought millions into both new industrial unions and old AFL craft unions.

The 60s revolt was caused by another kind of broken contract, one generated by the very success of the system during the New Deal in reconstituting the American dream. The generation born around 1940 and after never experienced the culture of deprivation and this opened the possibility of seeing the injustice of American foreign policy, racial discrimination and poverty as signs of the moral decay of late capitalism. These concerns were in fact mirror images of the middle-class discomfort with the banality of everyday life in the suburbs. Consumer society obliged its white, middle-class beneficiaries to accept the end of history as the price of economic security. For the new historical subjects this was too steep a price to pay: a euphoria grounded in mediocrity.

The end of the war removed the one universal issue from the public eye. When activists were forced back into single, often locally based, issue movements, or into trying to recapture the initiative by forming national organizations that substituted somebody else's revolution for our own, the era had ended. Some years ago, Peter Clecak told me that the enduring achievement of the 60s was the cultural changes it brought about, particularly the codification of a new morality in sex, gender and race. The strategic failure of the left to create new institutions of conventional political power can be forgiven. There was a time when the movement could have created a viable independent electorate in many states, though not on the national level. These formations would surely have cut the losses we have sustained during the recent conservative onslaught. Yet, despite the right-wing victories in the 1980s, the betrayal by a whole generation of liberals of their most cherished beliefs, the disintegration of the progressive coalition within the Democratic Party, imagination had succeeded in creating both institutional and ideological practices resistant to reversal. Certainly, as Brecht wrote referring to the rise of fascism, we live in dark ages; our justice system is once more suffused with the doctrine of retribution and it is once more possible for a President to defend holding a billion tons of butter in government vats instead of feeding the hungry and thus presumably destabilizing farm prices. But, Grenada notwithstanding, the administration cannot successfully invoke the Monroe Doctrine in Central America. The "halls of Montezuma" are no longer welcome to the Marines and the shores of Tripoli are out of bounds and the majority of Americans know it. Nevertheless, we must recognize that the conservatives are entrenched in political power and dominate the discourses of public policy to an extent not seen since the 20s. One important reason for this is that the upheavals of the 60s showed how tenuous are the ideologies and institutions that reproduce consent. Conservatives learned that tolerance is reserved for a secure system and that, while repression may not be necessary as yet, the real test is whether workers will accept their part in the system by sacrificing hard-won gains, whether the middle strata will remain oriented to career aspirations, and whether the minorities and the women will agree that they have been permanently defeated. Perhaps the other worlds that remain the indisputable legacy of the 60s will fade from memory like childhood itself. But if the new social movements are unlikely to play a central role in the near future, they persist in our own decade, reminding us that, contrary to the best efforts of reactionaries and to the most pessimistic prognoses of social theory, the future is not dead. It is just resting.

THE PARADOX OF THE AFRO-AMERICAN REBELLION

CORNEL WEST

The distinctive feature of Afro-American life in the 60s was the rise on the historical stage of a small yet determined petite bourgeoisie promoting liberal reforms, and the revolt of the masses, whose aspirations exceeded those of liberalism but whose containment was secured by political appeasement, cultural control and state repression. Afro-America encountered the modern American capitalist order (in its expansionist phase)—as urban dwellers, industrial workers and franchised citizens—on a broad scale for the first time. This essay will highlight the emergence of the black parvenu petite bourgeoisie — the new, relatively privileged, middle class—and its complex relations to the black working poor and underclass. I will try to show how the political strategies, ideological struggles and cultural anxieties of this predominantly white-collar stratum of the black working class both propelled the freedom movement in an unprecedented manner and circumscribed its vision, analysis and praxis within liberal capitalist perimeters.

For interpretive purposes, the 60s is not a chronological category which encompasses a decade, but rather a historical construct or heuristic rubric which renders noteworthy historical processes and events intelligible. The major historical processes that set the context for the first stage of the black freedom movement in the 60s were the modernization of southern agriculture, the judicial repudiation of certain forms of southern racism and the violent white backlash against perceived black progress. The modernization of southern agriculture made obsolete much of the traditional tenant labor force, thereby forcing large numbers of black rural folk into southern and northern urban centers in search of employment. The judicial repudiation of certain forms of southern racism, prompted by the gallant struggles of the National Association for the Advancement of Colored People (NAACP) and exemplified in the *Brown v. Board of Education* decision of 1954, was not only a legal blow against tax-supported school segregation; it also added historical momentum and political legitimacy to black struggles against racism. Yet, there quickly surfaced an often violent white reaction to this momentum and legitimacy. For example, Rev. George W. Lee was fatally shot in May 1955 for refusing to take his name off the voter registration list. Sixty-three year old Lamar Smith was killed in broad daylight in August 1955 for trying to get out the black vote in an upcoming primary election. And most notably, Emmett L. Till, a fourteen year-old lad from Chicago visiting his relatives, was murdered in late August 1955. These wanton acts of violence against black people in Mississippi, though part of the American southern way of life, reflected the conservative white reaction to perceived black progress. In 1955, this white reaction was met with widespread black resistance.

The greatness of Rev. Dr. Martin Luther King, Jr.—the major American prophet of this century and black leader in the 60s—was his ability to mobilize and organize this southern resistance such that the delicate balance between the emerging "new" black petite bourgeoisie, black working poor and black underclass was maintained for a few years. The arrest of Rosa Parks on December 1, 1955 in Montgomery, Alabama—as a result of one of a series of black acts of civil disobedience against Montgomery's bus line that year—led to the creation of the Montgomery Improvement Association (MIA), the adoption of a city-wide black boycott and the placement of King at the head of the movement. After nearly a year of the boycott, the U.S. Supreme Court declared Alabama's state and local bus segregation laws unconstitutional. Judicial repudiation of southern racism again gave the black struggle for freedom momentum and legitimacy.

King is the exemplary figure of the first stage of the black freedom movement in the 60s not only because he was its gifted and courageous leader or simply because of his organizational achievements, but, more importantly, because he consolidated the most progressive potential available in the black southern community at that time: the cultural potency of prophetic black churches, the skills of engaged black preachers, trade-unionists and professionals, and the spirit of rebellion and resistance of the black working poor and underclass. In this sense, King was an organic intellectual of the first order—a highly educated and informed thinker with organic links to ordinary folk. Despite his petit bourgeois origins, his deep roots in the black church gave him direct access to the life-worlds of the majority of black southerners. In addition, his education at Morehouse College, Crozier Theological Seminary and Boston University provided him with opportunities to reflect upon various anticolonial struggles around the world, especially those in India and Ghana, and also entitled him to respect and admiration in the eyes of black people, including the "old" black middle class (composed primarily of teachers and preachers). Last, his Christian outlook and personal temperament facilitated relations with progressive nonblack people, thereby insuring openness to potential allies.

King institutionalized his sense of the social engagement of black churches, his Christian-informed techniques of nonviolence and his early liberal vision of America, with the founding in February, 1957 in New Orleans of the Southern Christian Leadership Conference (SCLC). This courageous group of prophetic black preachers from ten southern states served as the models for young black southern activists. I stress the adjective "southern" not simply because most black people in the USA at this time lived in the South, but also because the core of the first stage of the black freedom movement was a Church-led movement in the belly of the violent-prone, under-industrialized, colonylike southern USA. Of course, the North was quite active — especially Harlem's Rev. Adam Clayton Powell, Jr. in Congress and The Nation of Islam's Malcolm X in the streets—but activity in the North was not the major thrust of this first stage.

Like David against Goliath, black activists openly challenged the entrenched racist white status quo in the South. Widespread white economic sanctions and physical attacks on black people, fueled by the so-called "Southern Manifesto" promoted in 1956 by Senator J. Strom Thurmond of South Carolina along with over a hundred congressmen, rendered both the Democratic and Republican parties relatively silent regarding the civil rights issues affecting black people. Two diluted civil rights bills (in 1957 and 1960) limped through Congress, and the Supreme Court, owing to congressional pressure, took much of the bite out of its earlier Brown decision. Black resistance intensified.

Inspired by the praxis of King, MIA and SCLC—as well as the sit-in techniques employed by the Congress of Racial Equality (CORE) in the North — four black freshmen students at North Carolina Agricultural and Technical College in Greensboro staged a sit-in at the local Woolworth's on February 1, 1960. Within a week, their day-to-day sit-in had been joined by black and white students from The Women's College of the University of North Carolina, North Carolina College and Duke University. Within two weeks, the sit-in movement had spread to fifteen other cities in Virginia, Tennessee and South Carolina. Within two months, there were sit-ins in seventy-eight cities. By the end of 1960, over fifty thousand people throughout the South had participated in sit-in demonstrations, with over 25 percent of the black students in predominantly black colleges participating. In short, young black people (and some progressive white people) had taken seriously King's techniques of nonviolence and the spirit of resistance.

This spontaneous rebellion of young black people against the southern taboo of black and white people eating together in public places exemplified a major component in the first stage of the black freedom movement: the emergence of politicized black parvenu petit bourgeois students. These students, especially young preachers and Christian activists, prefigured the disposition and orientation of the vastly increasing number of black college students in the 60s: they would give first priority to social activism and justify their newly acquired privileges by personal risk and sacrifice. So the young black student movement was not simply a rejection of segregation in restaurants. It was also a revolt against the perceived complacency of the "old" black petite bourgeoisie. It is no accident that at the first general conference on student sit-in activity which began Good Friday (April 15) 1960, the two keynote speakers—Rev. James Lawson and Rev. Martin Luther King, Jr.—launched devastating critiques of the NAACP and other "old" black middle-class groups. King articulated this viewpoint when he characterized the sit-in movement as "a revolt against those Negroes in the middle class who have indulged themselves in big cars and ranch-style homes rather than in joining a movement for freedom." The organization which emerged from this gathering later in the year—the Student Nonviolent Coordinating Committee—(SNCC)—epitomized this revolt against the political reticence of the "old" black middle class.

The major achievement of SNCC was, in many ways, its very existence. SNCC initiated a new style and outlook among black students in particular and the "new" black petite bourgeoisie in general. Its activist, countercultural orientation even influenced disenchanted white students on elite university campuses. Yet SNCC's central shortcoming was discernible at its inception: if pushed far enough, the revolt against middle-class status and outlook would not only include their models but also themselves, given their privileged student status and probable upward social mobility.

The influence of SNCC's new style was seen when James Farmer departed from the program directorship of the NAACP to become National Director of CORE. Within six weeks, he announced that CORE would conduct "Freedom Rides"—modeled on the 1947 Journey of Reconciliation led by CORE — to challenge segregation in interstate bus depots and terminals. On May 4, 1961 seven black people and six white people left Washington, D.C. Within ten days, one of the buses had been burned to the ground and many riders had been viciously attacked in Birmingham and Montgomery. This "Freedom Ride" was disbanded in Montgomery on May 17. A second "Freedom Ride" was initiated by SNCC, led by Diane Nash, composed of white and black people from CORE and SNCC. Violence ensued again, with twenty-seven people arrested and given suspended two-month sentences and fines of $200. They refused to pay and were taken to Parchman Prison.

These two "Freedom Rides"—though responsible for the desegregation of bus and train stations on September 22, 1961, by the Interstate Commerce Commission—served as a portent of the two basic realities which would help bring the initial stage of the black freedom movement to a close: first, the slow but sure rift between SNCC and King, and second, the ambiguous attitude of Democratic Party liberals to the movement. Both aspects came to the fore at the crucial August 1961 staff meeting of SNCC at the Highlander Folk School in Tennessee. It was well known that the Kennedy administration had called for a "cooling off" period, motivated primarily by their fear of alienating powerful southern Democratic comrades in Congress. At the meeting, Tim Jenkins, a fellow traveller of the Democratic Party, proposed that SNCC drop its emphasis on direct action and focus on voter education and registration. The majority of the SNCC staff opposed Jenkins's project owing to its connections with the Kennedy administration and the open approval of it by King's SCLC. In the eyes of many SNCC members, the "Establishment" against which they were struggling began to encompass both the Democratic Party's liberals and the SCLC's black activist liberals. This slow rupture would result in some glaring defeats in the civil rights movement, most notably the Albany (Georgia) Movement in December 1961, and also led to the gradual breakaway of SNCC from the techniques of nonviolence.

Yet in 1963, the first stage of the black freedom movement would culminate in its most successful endeavors: Birmingham and the March on Washington. The televised confrontation between the civil rights marchers and The Commissioner of Public Safety, Eugene "Bull" Connor, as well as the dramatic arrest of King, gave the movement much sympathy and support throughout the country. And the use of hundreds of black children in the struggle reinforced this effective histrionic strategy. Despite the bombing of the black Gaston Hotel, of King's brother's home, and black spontaneous rebellions in Birmingham, the massive nonviolent direct action—including over 3,000 people imprisoned—proved successful. The city of Birmingham, often referred to as the "American Johannesburg," accepted the black demands for desegregation and black employment opportunities. Furthermore, President Kennedy responded to the Birmingham campaign with a televised address to the nation in which he pledged his support for a comprehensive civil rights bill. However, the assassination of Medgar Evers, state executive secretary of the Mississippi NAACP, only hours after Kennedy's speech cast an ominous shadow over the Birmingham victory.

The famous March on Washington in August 1963—the occasion for King's powerful and poignant "I-have-a-dream" speech—was not the zenith of the civil rights movement. The movement had peaked in Birmingham. Rather the March on Washington was the historic gathering of that coalition of liberal forces—white trade-unionists, Christians, Jews and civil rights activists—whose potency was declining, whose fragile cohesion was falling apart. The central dilemma of the first stage of the black freedom movement emerged: the existence and sustenance of the civil rights movement neither needed nor required white aid or allies, yet its *success* required white liberal support in the Democratic Party, Congress and the White House.

The March on Washington exemplified this debilitating limitation of the civil rights movement. With white liberal support, the movement would achieve limited success, but slowly lose its legitimacy in the eyes of the now more politicized black petit bourgeois students, working poor and underclass. Without white liberal support, the movement could raise more fundamental issues of concern to the black working poor and underclass, yet thereby render the movement marginal to mainstream American politics and hence risk severe repression. It comes as no surprise that the March on Washington witnessed both the most powerful rhetoric and the most salient reality of the civil rights movement: King's great speech and the Kennedy administration's supervision of the March.

In summary, the first stage of the black freedom movement in the 60s —the civil rights struggle—began as a black response to white violent attacks and took the form of a critique of everyday life in the American South. This critique primarily consisted of attacking everyday cultural folkways which insulted black dignity. It was generated, in part, from the multifarious effects of the economic transformation of dispossessed southern rural peasants into downtrodden industrial workers, maids and unemployed city dwellers within the racist American South. In this regard, the civil rights movement prefigured the fundamental concerns of the American new left: linking private troubles to public issues, accenting the relation of cultural hegemony to political control and economic exploitation.

The major achievements of the civil rights movement were noteworthy: the transformation of everyday life (especially the elimination of terror as a primary mode of social control) of central regions in the American South; the federal commitment to the civil and voting rights of Afro-Americans; and the sense of confidence among black people that effective mobilization and organization were not only possible but imperative if the struggle for freedom was to continue. The pressing challenges were immense: transforming the power relations in the American South and North, obtaining federal support for employment and economic rights of the underprivileged, sustaining black organizational potency in the face of increasing class differentiation within the black community, and taking seriously the long-overlooked specific needs and interests of black women. The first stage came to a close principally because the civil rights struggle achieved its liberal aims, namely, absorption into mainstream American politics, reputable interest-group status in the (soon to falter) liberal coalition of the Democratic Party.

The second stage centered primarily on the issue of the legitimacy and accountability of the black political leadership. Like the first stage, this historical moment was engendered by a sense of black resistance and rebellion, and led by black petit bourgeois figures. Yet these "new" black middle-class figures had been highly politicized and radicalized by the strengths and weaknesses of King's movement, by the rise of the new left movement among white privileged students and by the revolutionary anticolonial struggles in the Caribbean (Cuba), Africa (Ghana and Guinea), Latin America (Chile and Bolivia) and Southeast Asia (Vietnam). The transitional events were the Mississippi Freedom Summer in 1964, the Democratic National Convention in Atlantic City, late August 1964, and the Selma campaign of 1965. The Freedom Summer brought to the surface the deep cultural and personal problems of interracial political struggle in America: white attitudes of paternalism, guilt and sexual jealousy, and black sensibilities of one-upsmanship, manipulation and sexual adventure. The Atlantic City convention illustrated the self-serving machinery of the Democratic Party, whose support even King at this point solicited at the risk of white-controlled compromise. Finally, King's Selma campaign, initiated by SNCC years earlier, was sustained primarily by federal support, escort and legitimacy. In short, the bubble was about to burst: the vision, analysis and praxis of significant elements of the black freedom movement was to move beyond the perimeters of prevailing American bourgeois politics.

The Watts explosion in August 1965 revealed the depths of the problem of legitimacy and accountability of black political leadership. The rebellion and resistance (especially in northern urban centers) could no longer find an organizational form of expression. In the cities, it had become sheer anarchic energy and existential assertion without political direction and social vision. The Watts rebellion was a watershed event in the black freedom movement in that it drew the line of demarcation between those who would cling to liberal rhetoric, ties to the Democratic Party and middle class concerns, and those who would attempt to go beyond liberalism, expose the absorptive role and function of the Democratic Party and focus more on black proletarian and lumpenproletarian interests.

The pressing challenges of the second stage were taken up by Martin Luther King, Jr. His Chicago campaign in 1966—though rejected by most of his liberal black and white comrades in SCLC — pushed for the radical unionization of slum-dwellers against exploitative landlords. His aborted poor people's campaign of 1967–68, initiated after his break with President Johnson and the Democratic Party which had been precipitated by his fierce opposition to the Vietnam War, was even more attuned to black, Latino and white working poor and underclass concerns. Yet, despite his immense talent, energy and courage, it became clear that King lacked the organization and support to address these concerns. Notwithstanding his 1968 murder—preceded by intense FBI harassments and threats—the widespread ideological fragmentation and increased class and strata differentiation in Afro-America precluded King from effectively meeting the pressing challenges. His new focus on the urban poor led to black middle-class abandonment of his movement; his nonviolent approach perturbed black committed leftists who welcomed his new focus; his Christianity disturbed black secularists and Muslims already working in urban ghettoes; and his integrationist perspective met with staunch opposition from black nationalists who were quickly seizing hegemony over the black freedom movement. In other words, King was near death politically and organizationally before he was murdered, though he will never die in the hearts and minds of progressive people in the USA and abroad.

Ironically, King's later path was blazed by his early vociferous critic, Malcolm X. Even as a narrow black nationalist under the late Honourable Elijah Muhammad, Malcolm X rejected outright white liberal support and ties to the Democratic Party, and he highlighted the plight of urban black working poor and unemployed people. More than any other black figure during the first stage, Malcolm X articulated the underlying, almost visceral, feelings and sensibilities of black urban America — North and South, Christian and non-Christian, young and old. His early rhetoric was simply prescient: too honest, too candid, precisely the things black folk often felt but never said publicly due to fear of white retaliation, even in the early 60s. In fact, his piercing rhetoric had primarily a cathartic function for black people; it purged them of their deferential and defensive attitudes toward white people.

Although Malcolm X moved toward a more Marxist-informed humanist position just prior to his assassination by rival Black Muslims in February 1965, he became the major symbol for (and of) the second stage of the black freedom movement in the 60s. What was accented was neither his political successes nor his organizational achievements, but rather his rhetorical eloquence and homespun honesty. Malcolm X did not hesitate to tell black and white America "like it is," even if it resulted in little political and practical payoff. This eloquence and honesty was admired at a distance by the black working poor and underclass: it expressed their gut feelings and addressed their situation but provided little means or hope as to how to change their predicament. The "old" black middle class was horrified; they publicly and secretly tried to discredit him. The "new" black petite bourgeoisie, especially black students, welcomed Malcolm X's rhetoric and honesty with open arms. It resonated with their own newly acquired sense of political engagement and black pride; it also spoke to a more fundamental problem they faced—the problem of becoming black leaders and elites with organic, existential and rhetorical ties to the black community.

In a complex way, Malcolm X's candid talk both fueled more protracted black rebellion and provided a means to contain it. In short, his rhetoric was double-edged and functioned in contradictory ways. On the one hand, it served as an ideological pillar for revolutionary black nationalism. On the other hand, his rhetoric was employed by manipulative black petit bourgeois politicians, professionals, administrators and students to promote their own upward social mobility. The adulation of Malcolm X in the black community is profound. Yet an often overlooked component in this adulation among the "new" black middle class was (and is) their subtle use of his truth-telling for their narrow self-serving aims. The relative silence regarding his black sexist values and attitudes also reveals the deep patriarchal sensibilities in the black community.

The revolt of the black masses, with hundreds of rebellions throughout the country, set the framework for the second stage. The repressive state apparatus in American capitalist society jumped at this opportunity to express its contempt for black people. And the basic mechanism of pacifying the erupting black ghettoes—the drug industry—fundamentally changed the content and character of the black community. The drug industry, aided and abetted by underground capitalists, invaded black communities with intense force, police indifference and political silence. It accelerated black white-collar and solid blue-collar working-class suburban flight, and transformed black poor neighborhoods into terrains of human bondage to the commodity form, enslavement to the buying and selling of drugs. For the first time in Afro-American history, fear and trepidation among black folk toward one another became pervasive. As crime moved toward civil terrorism, black distrust of and distance from the black poor and underclass deepened. And, of course, black presence in jails and prisons rapidly increased.

The revolt of the black masses precipitated a deep crisis—with political, intellectual and existential forms — among the "new" black petite bourgeoisie. What should the appropriate black middle-class response be to such black working poor and underclass rebellions? This complex response is best seen in the internal dynamics of the Black Power movement. This movement, more than any other at the time, projected the aspirations and anxieties of the recently politicized and radicalized black petite bourgeoisie. From Adam Clayton Powell, Jr.'s Howard University baccalaureate address of 1966, through the Meredith March, to the Newark Black Power Conference, the message was clear: beneath the rhetoric of Black Power, black control and black self-determination was a budding "new" black middle class hungry for power and starving for status. Needless to say, most young black intellectuals were duped by this petit bourgeois rhetoric, primarily owing to their own identity-crisis and self-interest. In contrast, the "new" black business, professional and political elites heard the bourgeois melody behind the radical rhetoric and manipulated the movement for their own benefit. The rebellious black working poor and underclass often either became dependent on growing welfare support or seduced by the drug culture.

The second stage was primarily a black nationalist affair. The veneration of "black" symbols, rituals, styles, hairdos, values, sensibilities and flag escalated. The "Black is Beautiful" slogan was heard throughout the black community and James Brown's "Say It Loud, I'm Black and I'm Proud" became an exemplary — and healthy — expression of the cultural reversal of alienating Anglo-American ideals of beauty and behavior. Yet this cantankerous reversal (like the black rediscovery of jazz) was principally a "new" black middle-class phenomenon.

The working poor and underclass watched as the "new" black middle class visibly grappled with its new identity, social position and radical political rhetoric. For the most part, the black underclass continued to hustle, rebel when appropriate, get high and listen to romantic proletarian love songs produced by Detroit's Motown; they remained perplexed at their idolization by the "new" black middle class which they sometimes envied. The black working poor persisted in its weekly church attendance, struggled to make ends meet and waited to see what the beneficial results would be after all the bourgeois "hoopla" was over. In short, the black nationalist moment, despite its powerful and progressive critique of American cultural imperialism, was principally the activity of black petit bourgeois self-congratulation and self-justification upon reaching an anxiety-ridden middle-class status in racist American society.

To no surprise, the leading black petit bourgeois nationalist groups such as SNCC (after 1966), CORE, Ron Karenga's US and Imamu Amiri Baraka's Congress of African People were viewed by black proletarian and lumpenproletarian organizations as "porkchop nationalists" who confused superficial nation-talk with authentic cultural distinctiveness, middle-class guilt with working-class aspirations, and identity-crises with revolutionary situations. The late Honourable Elijah Muhammad's Nation of Islam, though petit bourgeois in intent, was staunchly working poor and underclass (and especially strong in American prisons) in composition. Devoid of leading black intellectuals yet full of eloquent spokesmen, The Nation of Islam put to shame the "porkchop nationalists," not only by being "blacker than thou" in both mythology and ideology, but also by producing discernible results in the personal, organizational and financial life of its members and the black community.

The Black Panther Party (founded in Oakland, California, 1966) was the leading black lumpenproletarian revolutionary party in the 60s. It thoroughly rejected and consistently struggled against petit bourgeois nationalism from a view point of strong black leftist internationalism. Yet it was overwhelmed by the undisciplined character of black underclass life, seduced by the histrionic enticements of mass media and crushed by state repression. The only other major national response of black progressives against black petit bourgeois nationalism was George Wiley's National Welfare Rights Organization (founded in August 1967). But it was unable to sustain broad membership, and thereby control encroaching bureaucratic leadership. The League of Revolutionary Black Workers (founded in Detroit, Michigan, 1969), though regional in scope, was the most important revolutionary group among black industrial workers in the country. It eventually split over the issue of the role of black nationalism in a Marxist organization.

The rift between black petit bourgeois nationalists and black revolutionary leftists was best illustrated in the American response to James Forman's historic Black Manifesto. Forman, a former executive director of

SNCC, ex-minister of Foreign Affairs of the Black Panther Party, and leader of the short-lived Black Workers' Congress, proposed at the National Black Economic Development Conference in Detroit and later, more dramatically, at New York City's Riverside Church's 11:00 p.m. service, reparation funds of $500 million from white Christian churches and Jewish synagogues in order to finance the black revolutionary overthrow of the U.S. government. This "revolution" would turn into an "armed, well-disciplined, black-controlled government."

This symbolic gesture represented the peak of the black nationalist moment in the 60s, though it was enacted by a black Marxist. It also signified liberal white America's absorption and domestication of black nationalism. Despite the Manifesto's Marxist critique and demand of American capitalist society — such as the call for a black revolutionary vanguard party and even the call for white progressive people to accept this black leadership — the most salient issue became that of reparations to existing black middle-class groups.

The white American response to these demands on the ecclesiastical, educational and corporate levels was widespread. Of course, the major funds were not given to Forman's group (though it received about $300,000), but rather to church agencies, denominational caucuses, minority-oriented programs and, above all, black businesses and banks. Regardless of Forman's naive revolutionary intent, the black petit bourgeois nationalists triumphed. Soon the federal government and even the Nixon administration would openly support such moves in the name of "black self-determination" and "black capitalism."

The hegemonic role of black petit bourgeois nationalism had four deleterious consequences for Afro-America. First, it isolated progressive black leftists such that orthodox Marxism became the primary refuge for those concerned with class struggle and internationalism. And even in these new Marxist formations the Black Nation Thesis—the claim that black people constitute a nation within the USA—once again became the widely accepted understanding of Afro-American oppression. Second, the machismo lifestyles of black nationalists (of the petit bourgeois and revolutionary varieties) marginalized black women so that the black feminist movement of the 70s and 80s was often forced to sever ties from black male-dominated groups, thereby encouraging an understandable but innocuous black feminist separatism. Third, black nationalism disarmed and delimited a large number of young black intellectuals by confining them to parochial black rhetoric, pockets of "internal dialogues," which resulted in posing almost insurmountable walls of separation between progressive white, brown, red, yellow and black intellectuals. Last, black nationalist rhetoric contributed greatly to the black freedom movement's loss of meaningful anchorage and organic ties to the black community, especially the churches. In short, besides the severe state repression and the pervasive drug invasion, the black petit bourgeois nationalist perspectives and practices were primarily responsible for the radically decentered state of the black freedom movement in the 70s and 80s. This was so principally because they undergirded the needs and interests of the "new" black middle class.

The 60s in Afro-American history witnessed an unforgettable appearance of the black masses on the historical stage but they are quickly dragged off—killed, maimed, strung-out, imprisoned or paid-off. Yet history continues and the growing black petite bourgeoisie still gropes for identity, direction and vision. This black middle class is "new" not simply because significant numbers of black people recently arrived in the world of higher education, comfortable living and professional occupations, but also because they achieved such status against the backdrop of undeniable political struggle, a struggle in which many of them participated. And the relation of their unprecedented opportunities and privileges to the revolt of the black masses is quite obvious to them. This is why the "new" black middle class will more than likely refuse to opt for political complacency. Its own position hangs on some form of political participation, on resisting subtle racist practices, housing policies and educational opportunities. Only persistent pressure can ensure a managerial job at IBM, partnership in a Wall Street firm, a home in Westchester or a slot at Harvard College, whereas in the past little resistance by the "old" black middle class was required to service the black community, live in the Gold Coast of Washington, D.C. or send the kid to Howard, Fisk or Morehouse. The roots of the "new" black middle class are in political struggle, in SCLC, SNCC, CORE, in the values and sensibilities these groups generated.

The major challenge of the "new" black petite bourgeoisie is no longer whether it will take politics seriously (as posed in E. Franklin Frazier's classic *Black Bourgeoisie* in 1957). Rather it is what kind of politics the "new" black middle class will promote in the present national context of austere economic policies, declining state support of black rights and escalating racist violence and the prevailing international context of the crisis of capitalism, the nuclear arms race and anti-imperialist struggles. Like any other petite bourgeoisie, the "new" black middle class will most likely pursue power-seeking life styles, promote black entrepreneurial growth, and perpetuate professional advancement. Yet the rampant racism in American society truncates such life styles, growth and advancement. The "new" black middle class can become only a "truncated" petite bourgeoisie in American society, far removed from real ownership and control over the crucial sectors of the economy and with intractable ceilings imposed upon their upward social mobility.

Presently, there are three major political options for this "truncated" black middle class: electoral politics in the bosom of the centrist Democratic Party or conservative Republican Party; social democratic and democratic socialist politics on the margin of the liberal wing of the Democratic Party (e.g. Democratic Socialists of America) and inside grassroots black leftist nationalist preparty formations (e.g. National Black United Front); or orthodox revolutionary politics far removed from both bourgeois American politics and black grassroots groupings. The effects of the second stage of the black freedom movement in the 60s—beneath and between the endless ideological debates about violence vs. nonviolence, the viability of black-white coalitions, reform vs. revolution — primarily consisted of an oscillation between the first and third options, between vulgar *Realpolitik* and antiquated orthodoxy, bourgeois politics and utopian rhetoric, with no mediating moment, hence little acknowledgement of the historical complexity of the prevailing Afro-American predicament.

The prospects of galvanizing and organizing renewed black resistance are open-ended. The major tasks are repoliticizing the black working poor and underclass, revitalizing progressive black proletarian and petit bourgeois organizations, retooling black organic and traditional intellectuals and forging meaningful alliances and beneficial fusions with progressive Latino, Asian, Native American and white groups.

Despite the historical limitations of the "new" black petite bourgeoisie, the Afro-American predicament dictates that this group play a crucial role in carrying out these tasks. This is principally because the black middle class—preachers, teachers, lawyers, doctors and politicians—possess the requisite skills and legitimacy in the eyes of the majority of Afro-Americans for the articulation of the needs and interests of Afro-America. This unfortunate but inescapable situation requires that the politicized progressive wing of the black petite bourgeoisie and stable working class incessantly push beyond the self-serving liberalism of major black leaders and raise issues of fundamental concern to the black working poor and underclass. In short, the "new" black middle class must not be prematurely abandoned or denigrated. Rather, black progressives must keep persistent pressure on, and radical fire under, their liberal reformism until more effective political mobilization and organization emerges among the black working poor and underclass.

The repoliticizing of the black working poor and underclass should focus primarily on the black cultural apparatus, especially the ideological form and content of black popular music. Afro-American life is permeated by black popular music. Since black musicians play such an important role in Afro-American life, they have a special mission and responsibility: to present beautiful music which both sustains and motivates black people and provides visions of what black people should aspire to. Despite the richness of the black musical tradition and the vitality of black contemporary music, most black musicians fall far short of this crucial mission and responsibility. There are exceptions—Gil Scott-Heron, Brian Jackson, Stevie Wonder, Kenneth Gamble and Leon Huff—but more political black popular music is needed. Jamaican reggae music and Nigeria's Fela Anikulapo Kuti can serve as inspiring models in this regard. The radical politicization of black popular music, recently surfacing in Grandmaster Flash and the Furious Five's "The Message" and "New York, New York" (despite their virulent sexism), is a necessary, though not sufficient, condition for the repoliticization of the black working poor and underclass. Black activists must make black musicians accountable in some way to the urgent needs and interests of the black community.

The major prerequisite for renewed organizational black resistance is the political revitalization of existing black groups—fraternities, sororities, lodges, trade-unions and, especially, black churches. Without black religious participation, there can be no widespread black resistance. The prophetic wing of the Black Church has always been at the center of the black freedom movement. Without a strong organizational base, with deep organic connections in the black community, there can be no effective renewed black resistance. Only the political revitalization of black prophetic churches can provide this broad organizational base — as Rev. Herbert Daughtry's African Peoples' Christian Organization and other such groups are attempting to do.

The role of black intellectuals—organic ones closely affiliated with the everyday operations of black organizations or traditional ones nesting in comfortable places geared toward theoretical and historical analyses, social visions and practical conclusions—is crucial for renewed black resistance. Without vision, the black freedom movement is devoid of hope. Without analysis, it lacks direction. Without protracted struggle, it ossifies. Yet the vision must be guided by profound, not provincial, conceptions of what it is to be a human being, an African human being in predominantly white postindustrial capitalist America, and of how human potential can be best realized in an overcoming of existing economic exploitation, racial and sexual oppression. Likewise, the analysis must be informed by the most sophisticated and cultivated, not self-serving and cathartic, tools available in order to grasp the complexity and specificity of the prevailing Afro-American predicament on the local, regional, national and international levels. Last, the political praxis, though motivated by social vision and guided by keen analysis, must be grounded in moral convictions. Personal integrity is as important as correct analysis or desirable vision. It should be noted that while black intellectuals deserve no special privilege and treatment in the black freedom movement, the services they provide should be respected and encouraged.

It should be obvious that Afro-Americans cannot fundamentally transform capitalist, patriarchal, racist America by themselves. If renewed black resistance is to achieve its aim, alliances and coalitions with other progressive peoples are inescapable. Without such alliances and coalitions, Afro-Americans are doomed to unfreedom. Yet, the more consolidated the black resistance, the better the chance for meaningful and effective alliances and coalitions with others. Of course, each alliance and coalition must be made in light of the specific circumstances and the particular contexts. The important point here is that any serious form of black resistance must be open to such alliances and coalitions with progressive Latino, Asian, Native American and white peoples.

In conclusion, the legacy of the black freedom movement in the 60s still haunts us. In its positive form, it flows through our veins as blood to be spilt if necessary for the cause of human freedom and in the visions, analyses and practices that build on, yet go beyond, those in the 60s. In its negative form, it reminds us of the tenuous status of the "new" black petite bourgeoisie — its progressive potential and its self-serving interests, its capacity to transcend its parochial past and its present white subordination. The challenge of the black freedom movement in the 80s is neither a discovery of another Rev. Dr. Martin Luther King, Jr.—though it would not hurt; nor a leap of faith in a messianic black working class or underclass—though the role of both is crucial. Rather the challenge is a fusing and transforming of indigenous forms of American radicalism—of which black resistance is a central expression—into a major movement which promotes workers' self-management, cultural heterogeneity (including nonracist and nonsexist ways of life) and individual liberties.

ROCK AND THE POLITICS OF MEMORY

SIMON FRITH

In Britain as well as the USA, the 60s have a bad reputation. They're the leading target of Tory demonology; for Margaret Thatcher and her colleagues the 60s were when Britain went bad. And this is not just a party-political point. The Labour governments of 1964–70 were, it's claimed, as much an effect as a cause of the general malaise. Britain's 60s sickness was cultural; it was most clearly articulated by the cult of permissiveness—public license, private indulgence, pleasure without consequence. From the Tory perspective the consequences were, in fact, appalling: the *cement* of society (the authority of age and family, church and class, culture and nation) was corroded. British social democracy turned out to mean a soft, do-gooding, "welfare" state used (like the pill) as a way of avoiding any moral accounting system, blurring the disciplinary role of the marketplace.

There's an oddly Gramscian ring to such assaults on the 60s. Tory thinkers are as aware as socialist thinkers of the political importance of ideas, culture, common sense, and they're equally concerned with the class role of intellectuals. They thus explain the effects of permissiveness by reference to a systematic *trahison des clercs*: at the heart of the rot were all those teachers, lawyers, clerics, artists, critics, politicians, academics leaping on board the pop culture bandwagon, gorging themselves on immediate sensation, fawning upon youth. And it was the reversal of proper age relations that marked Britain's long-term loss of discipline and enterprise. For all their export earnings, the Beatles became national heroes because of their frivolity, because their sound of chirpy optimism concealed a loss of national will.

To read these arguments now is to be overcome with nostalgia—the Tory claims as to what happened so exactly echo what I thought would and should happen at the time—and the irony is that this (backhanded) celebration of the 60s should come from the right—from my current left perspective, the theory of counterculture seems like dippy idealism (the greening of America!) and the theory of the Revolutionary Youth Movement simply a romantic gesture at politics. But nostalgia works on feelings, not arguments, and what I suddenly remember is the feeling that music matters, that records, sounds, songs, rhythms *can* have all these consequences.

Take one of the 60s' key symbols, the Beatles' *Sgt. Pepper.* All we've got now is a collection of well-mannered pop songs in a fading pop art sleeve, but at the time the record was an event, the most orchestrated event, indeed, that pop had ever known. It was, according to its producer George Martin, "the watershed which changed the recording art from something that merely made amusing sounds into something which will stand the test of time as a valid art form: sculpture in music, if you like." This was, wrote Ken Tynan, "a decisive moment in the history of Western Civilisation." The Lonely Hearts Club Band represented a new movement of youth—classless and ageless too. Pop had a new purpose: to make out of pleasure a politics of optimism, to turn passive consumption into an active culture. Such ambition derived from the Beatles' authority as superstars—not just skilled pop musicians but skilled pop artists, self-conscious, calculating their entertaining effects. *Sgt. Pepper* was more than just another LP. In making their own style out of the street sounds of 1967, the Beatles gave these sounds a shape, an aesthetic form; they made the optimism concrete and so gave pop fans something to judge the moment by. The Beatles were not the leaders of a cultural movement but its symbols—they were as keen as everyone else to be followers of fashion. Their importance was to use their public position to *legitimate* Britain's nascent hippie ideology.

Sgt. Pepper wasn't the first rock LP (Bob Dylan had made that in 1965) but it marked most clearly the pop to rock move, the shift in the terms in which mass music was explained. The key word was "progress." The Beatles' own career—from homespun rock'n'rollers and hit ditty makers to subtle melodists, acute lyricists—was the model of such progress. It was obvious that "A Day in the Life" *mattered* more than "She Loves You," addressed issues other than teenage fun. Rock, in other words, described a more ambitious music than pop, in terms of form, content and impact. Rock ideologues (in *Rolling Stone*, for example) wrote about records' political and poetic significance; rock musicians both represented a subversive community (making the public sounds of the youth counterculture) and realized complex private dreams and feeling. Rock was presented to its audience as something to work on and commit oneself to as well as a sensation to be immediately consumed.

This ideology turned out to be a wonderful source of sales rhetoric—rock commitment meant buying lots of records, rock belief in progress sent people out to buy new releases even more reliably than the pop concern for trends and fashion. But that didn't come clear to me till later. What was most obvious at the time (1967, 1968) was that rock was "progressive" politically too. The rock sensibility—the combination of aesthetic and social assumptions people took to their musical choices, used to account for their tastes—had at its cutting edge a critique of mass culture which drew implicitly (and, via Marcuse, sometimes explicitly) on Frankfurt School positions. Rock arguments focused on the problem of commercial cooptation, on the transformation of culture into commodity ("selling out"), the music's relationship to organized political struggles, to protest. Rock's artistic claims were inextricable from its political claims (hence its central role in the counterculture)—there was a moment when even the most mindless groups (the Bee Gees, say) had to present themselves as something other than "entertainers."

This was a brief moment (from Woodstock to Altamont?). By the end of the 60s I recall the British left taking for granted the failure of rock to realize its countercultural claims (though, ironically, the most straightforwardly political rock records were still to come). In Britain, at any rate, there was an obvious migration from the Underground to Trotskyism, from age to class politics. Sex and drugs and rock'n'roll were dismissed as middle-class, male indulgences, while the few commentators who paused to wonder what had gone wrong pointed to the incorporation of rock into the leisure business on the one hand, to the fragmentation of the rock audience on the other. In short, rock's claims to be different from pop, to evade the logic of mass culture, turned out to be baseless. Rock was tied inevitably into the process of commodity production: the rock community was simply an easily manipulated consumer group.

This conclusion—a kind of traditional left told-you-so—has had a debilitating effect on subsequent Marxist analyses of rock (of 60s rock, in particular). For example, it has reinforced the sour Frankfurt view. The music which at the time was experienced as a challenge to notions of passive consumption is now cited as confirmation of them, and concepts of traditional left analysis (authenticity, realism) discredited in debates about other cultural forms, remain central to discussions of pop and rock. Thus in 1976–77 the British left had its interest in music revived by punk, which was interpreted as an attempt to seize the means of record production, as a rank-and-file expression of class interest, and lost that interest the moment punk was "coopted," the moment its audience "fragmented." And so pop is still defined as "escapism"—as if such a description precludes the need for further attention—just as it was in the 60s. What happened to music then appears to account for nothing at all in contemporary critiques of mass culture.

One reason for this is that rock ideologists' own claims (which, as I've suggested, anyway drew on the Marxist account of mass culture) are taken at their face value (the idea of progress, for example) so that their failure is easily shown. What is not considered is whether such claims made sense of the politics of pop in the first place, and this means a peculiar denial of people's 60s memories. The exhilaration, the sense of change and purpose, the emotional underpinnings of the *experience* of liberation are dismissed as fraudulent because of what happened next—just as the genuinely disruptive, ideological effects of our drug use in the 60s are concealed by blanket references to drugs' "inevitable" evil consequences. The "failure" of rock thus becomes equally inevitable — which makes it impossible to explain why we were all deluded in the first place. This is particularly a problem now because of the current ideological role of history and myth and memory. The Thatcherist attack on the 60s feeds into an attempt to reconstruct British common sense, and the left's muted response is therefore damaging. There may be good reasons why socialists and feminists are wary of permissiveness, reluctant to *celebrate* the 60s, but not to present some positive account of them is to cede an argument unnecessarily, to deny the 60s' continuing effects. Hippie ideology, hippie music, may be discredited but it survives in important interstices of youth and leisure culture and, if anything, increases in importance as we move from struggles in the workplace to struggles on the unemployment line. Put it this way: Rastafarian gigs in the 1980s are the closest thing to Grateful Dead concerts in the 1960s.

My own critique of the 60s is that they left us a legacy of good music but bad theory—I don't doubt rock's achievements but its claims. The problem is not that rock failed to break out of the pop form but that its ideologists misunderstood the significance of that form in the first place. By rock ideologists I don't mean rock critics but the people who articulate rock's common sense, the musicians, journalists, promo departments, disc jockeys, A-and-R men and record producers, who turn a sales process into a cultural process, who provide the terms in which producers and consumers alike explain their choices. Rock criticism, as such, developed as a critique of this ideology as much as of the music itself. And indeed, by the end of the 1960s the most acute critics in both the USA and the UK seemed marginal to rock culture, their position cutting across the usual rock discourse in its refusal to accept the pop-rock distinction.

This became clearer in the 1976–77 debates on punk I've already mentioned. Critics welcomed punk precisely because of its contempt for rock sensibility. "Rock," indeed, was much more clearly the punk enemy than capitalism—the "old farts" under attack worked in record companies and radio stations and music papers—and by the end of the 1970s "rockist" was a regular term of abuse, a shorthand way of dismissing records and performers. "Rockist" referred not just to a sound (the guitar-based "progressive" blues of the late 60s supergroups was the basic reference point) but also to an attitude, to the use of pop music as a sign of sincerity, a mark of community, a form of cultural opposition. Though from the post-punk perspective *any* musical claims to expressiveness, collectivity or anti-commercialism were obviously false, the response was not to dismiss the music but rather to reject its claims. Musicians who present their performances as "authentic" are evading the interesting issues of pop politics—the ways in which musics and meanings, performers and listeners are constructed *artificially*. It is precisely pop's artifice that allows it be a site of conflict.

The problem is not culture *versus* commodity but the contradictions of the culture of the commodity.

From this perspective, 60s rock people seem remarkably naive. I cringe at my own remembered belief in "the natural" (whether applied to music or sex or desire generally), which stands in pathetic contrast to the knowing postpunk assumption that *everything* is constructed (can be deconstructed), desires too, that there is nothing to be found *in* music, only the pleasure of being defined *by* it. Pop, it now seems, must be momentary (can't be progressive), represents nothing but itself (not youth, not class, not subculture) and this must be the starting point of any discussion of how it has effects. This certainly casts new light on the 60s. *Sgt. Pepper*, for example, gives me pleasure not because it was the first hippie art work but because it was the final triumph of mod. It is Swinging London music, a shopping style, the sound of consumption (male boutiques, sitar echoes and incense blurring in the traffic noises of Carnaby Street, the Kings Road, Saturday afternoons in the shopping center).

I realize now that *all* my favorite 60s songs were mod songs—play as hard work, work as just a chore—smart, restless songs from the Kinks, the Small Faces, the Stones. The roots of the postpunk pop sensibility lie in these ironic, distanced records, in their use of form as content. The game was to apply pop rules to any subject—mining disasters as well as love disorders. Pop songs about pop songs—the theorists had arrived (David Bowie was beginning his career as a would-be mod pop star, Bryan Ferry was studying pop art with Richard Hamilton).

The best of Britain's 60s pop bands was the Who because Pete Townshend was the smartest theorist. *The Who Sell Out* (note the title) was a buoyant, funny record with a much sharper concept than *Sgt. Pepper* and a much clearer sense of how pop worked—Townshend's songs were about music *as commodity*. The group took their links and jingles from a real station, the pirate Radio London, and wrote their own linking ads—Odorono! Medac!—but the point was that the "real" songs could just as well have been ads too—"Welcome to my life, tattoo!" *The Who Sell Out* was a pop art LP, a mocking presentation of the group as product which by drawing attention to this truth (the group *was* a product) seemed to deny it; by providing their own commercial setting the Who distanced themselves from it. But Townshend's argument was that teenage solidarity and excitement derived precisely from pop's commercial presence, and the real irony of *The Who Sell Out*, from his point of view, was that the teenage rebellion had been won. The mod generation hadn't gotten old but had taken pop over (hence Radio London) and as mod pop was routinized so disputes over definitions of pleasure shifted ground: mods went mainstream, stylists went hippie, and pop went psychedelic.

Psychedelic pop had the mod concern for looking smart, but the shift of drugs, from speed to grass and acid, meant a shift of aesthetic. Pleasure became more laid back, sensual space mattered more than emotional immediacy, and dance floor action no longer involved the mods' intense absorption in their own bodies but a more abstract absorption into a sound. Psychedelia was essentially elitist, but the joy of psychedelic pop was that it invited everyone to join the elite—the music was friendly, its mysteries still framed by hooks and an easy beat.

There was a tension involved, though, as there is in all pop movements—on the one hand the push to democracy, the attempt to please everyone; on the other hand the push to exclusivity, to make consumption a matter of individual difference. And psychedelic pop (partly because of its drug base) developed much more formally than previous movements its own musical language, its own coded sets of references and attitudes, its own journals. Such articulateness, the sheer weight of hippie words, turned a pop cult into an explicit counterculture, and counterculture meant artistic self-consciousness, not in terms of money-making but in terms of creativity. Hippie musicians began to identify with romantic artists generally—writers, painters, poets; they began to assume a culturally well educated audience even while proclaiming their own superiority to it. As musicians like Jimi Hendrix and Cream (named to stress their elite status) displayed their technical skills in lengthy improvisations, complex harmonies, opened-up rhythms that had never been dreamt of in three-minute pop songs, pop stars began to move from show-biz to bohemia, and bohemians seized on pop music as one more means of self-expression.

It was this self-definition of pop musicians as artists which really marked the ideological shift from pop to rock. At issue was the purpose of musicmaking—to please and put together a mass audience or to please and put together a coterie, and, ironically, it was therefore precisely at the moment when musicians presented themselves as political (because autonomous, serious) that they ceased to address the only political issues on which popular music has any bite—issues of pleasure, escape, banality.

The same sort of shift of attitude lies at the core of the history of pop in the USA. There mod pop was based in Los Angeles, which in the mid-60s functioned as London's twin town—in its boutiques and clubs, on its radio shows and records, the latest Anglo-styles were posed and sold. LA's great 60s hit, Buffalo Springfield's "For What It's Worth," seemed less to protest the youth-police battles along Sunset Strip than to celebrate them as style wars.

Buffalo Springfield's songwriters and singers, Steve Stills and Neil Young, began their musical lives as folk singers, and their move into pop was an example of the Beatles' most important effect on American music: thousands of disillusioned rock'n'roll fans (from Bob Dylan on down) who'd abandoned teenage music at the end of the 1950s for the "adult" concerns of folk, were convinced by the British sound that rock and roll was still an exciting form, and American Beatlemania further suggested that it was precisely its vast popular appeal that made rock and roll (compared to folk) an urgent, relevant, political medium. As Bob Dylan soon discovered, there's no greater musical power than a number one AM radio hit, and by 1967 American towns were filled once more with would-be pop stars, teenage garage bands, punks, making their own version of post-Beatle, post-Byrd, post-Yardbird psychedelic pop — fuzz tones, electric twelve strings, screamed vocals.

The problem was that at the same time (on campuses, in clubs) protest singers and poets were using the new rock sounds without wanting to be associated with pop at all. The folk use of rock increasingly meant taking over the pop form while denying the pop context, and the pop-to-rock move in the USA meant a triumph of bohemia—the American rock arguments came most clearly from San Francisco, a self-consciously anti-pop, anticommercial community. I remember being sold San Francisco in songs (Scott McKenzie's "San Francisco," the Flowerpot Men's "Let's Go To San Francisco," Eric Burdon's "San Francisco Nights") as if it were a natural product, like sunshine and flowers, but available, like all pop, only to the young at heart. I duly set off and was deeply shocked by my first concert, the Grateful Dead in Berkeley—to my mod pop tastes they looked and sounded so scruffy. The basis of the San Francisco community, it turned out, was not pop but art. San Francisco music was made out of nonpop forms, blues and folk and jazz, and addressed nonpop issues; the San Francisco sound was the sound of Beatniks.

The Beats' post-Beatles discovery was that they could read poetry to a rock and roll beat much more easily than they could to the more intellectual sounds of contemporary jazz. If Britain's hippie movement sometimes felt like a rerun of the 1950s self-discovery of teenagers by more affluent, more pretentious youth, the USA hippie movement felt to me like a rerun of the 1950s beat fantasy by more affluent, less guilty youth. In the resulting countercultural terms, what mattered most about the San Francisco sound was not its content (loosely meaningful lyrics went with loosely meaningful music) but its form. The music the bands made met the needs of acid-dropping audiences. It was rambling, loud, multitextured and raw; it used simple melodies and beat, but electronically distorted, to sound more difficult. The SF bands always seemed to have a relentless determination to exhaust their listeners; our aim on the floor was to follow one theme, one sound, through the haze.

This was a new sort of popular music which defined a new sort of popular audience, reflected a new organization of popular leisure. Hippie ideology itself stressed the music's bohemianism, its independence of the usual commercial practices of American pop, but what emerged from San Francisco most obviously was a new style of commercialism itself. The most significant people in the Bay Area turned out to be not musicians but entrepreneurs—Tom Donahue, the disc jockey who pioneered FM rock radio; promoter Bill Graham, who laid down the rules of the stadium rock show; Jann Wenner, who started *Rolling Stone*. The most important rock'n'roll impresarios previously had been outsiders, seizing on stars opportunistically (like Colonel Parker on Elvis Presley). The San Francisco operators, in contrast, emerged from within the new audience itself, and so disguised the exploitation involved in the rock marketplace in the name of "the rock community." The political significance of this was not that rock was coopted, but that the terms of its cooptation were concealed. Pop commercialism was so blatant that pop fans could never forget their consumer status; rock fans, by contrast, could treat record-buying as an act of solidarity.

The ultimate expression of this idea was the rock festival. Unlike the traditional pop package show, put together *for* the fans out there, the rock festival—in its length, its size, its setting, its reference to a folk tradition—was an attempt to provide materially the experience of community that the music expressed symbolically. This put a new sort of burden on the stars: they had to make themselves "known" to their audiences directly. Thus Janis Joplin was probably the most remarkable festival performer I saw because of her ability to use her emotions (which touched on self-loathing) to bind her listeners together. What came across from the stage (on record Joplin's technical and imaginative weaknesses are more obvious) was the feeling that she so trusted us that she was holding nothing back. Rock performance, in short, came to mean not pleasing an audience (pop style) nor representing it (folk style) but, rather, displaying desires and feelings rawly, as if to a lover or friend. The appeal of the other great festival performer, Jimi Hendrix, rested on the sense that his apparently uninhibited pursuit of pleasures was on show, for all of us to see and share.

Joplin and Hendrix set the intensive norm for rock shows, fed the rock audience's need for the emotional charge that confirmed they'd been at a "real" event. The questions they posed were central to rock: how to guarantee the emotional impact of their performances night after night after night (the answer lay in technology, volume, a gradually evolved repertoire of rock signs of emotion); how to relate public and private life when rock audiences expected no distinction (the answer was to ignore the audience, to deny that there was such a thing as a separate public persona—musicians soon found that they could make lots of money by apparently playing only to please themselves).

This sense of self-importance was most obvious in the singer-songwriters inspired by Bob Dylan. There had always been perfomers who wrote their own songs but they had not previously been regarded as distinctive popmakers. Paul Anka's "Diana," for example, had never been thought to express his own experience except in terms of clichés so general that they could be used by everyone (the point of pop). What Dylan and his successors brought into pop, then, was the concept of authenticity. Folk singers had always been contrasted to pop singers because they wrote and sang about the "real" world—the real world of politics, the real world of personal feeling—and it was this convention of reality that singer-songwriters brought to rock. The ramifications were immediate. Singer-songwriters' confessional mode, the appeal of their supposed "transparency," introduced a kind of moralism into rock—faking an emotion (which in postpunk ideology is the whole point and joy of pop performance) became an aesthetic crime; musicians were judged for their openness, their honesty, their sensitivity, were judged, that is, as real, knowable people (think of that pompous rock fixture, the *Rolling Stone* interview). Once again, the problem was not that performers sold out the rock community by becoming stars but that they presented themselves as if they weren't. And so avoided a central pop issue.

There was a similar evasion of pop responsibility in attitudes to fans, in the arguments about what it meant to be popular. The most obvious example of this was the Doors, the most militant exponents of the counterculture's romantic individualism. Jim Morrison's self-image as a poet referred not just to his lyrics but also to his personality, to his obsession with his own perceptions. He seized on the romantic ideal of decadence—it was *Morrison's* experience of rock performance that mattered, not his audience's. Given the right musical form Morrison's narcissism could indeed be compelling, but the rock audience became increasingly unimportant to him as a source of sensation. In the end, his legacy to rock was a style of contempt, the Californian version of the old bohemian argument that the pain of one "artist" is worth the boredom of any number of "ordinary" people.

Jim Morrison is a representative 60s figure (and remains one of the key models for young British rock performers) precisely because of his self-importance. He stood for the claim that rock became an art form through its pursuit of the extraordinary and the extreme, through the very process of self-indulgence. The Doors' music was actually pretty banal (which is why it sometimes worked) and my point is that the banality of groups like the Doors remains a more interesting aspect of the 60s than their pretensions (though as Jim Morrison continues to be mythologized this distinction gets harder to make—his pretensions have been fed into the pop parade as a sort of bohemian kitsch).

The 60s still stand ideologically as a moment of great musical significance, but it worked at the time as a series of moments of more or less triviality. Rock was certainly centrally important to my life then, but to my private life not my public one. Rock didn't cause me to be political but rather confirmed my politics as background music, as a permanent sound track of anger and hope and joy—the rock "community" was a community of feeling. Music mattered to 60s politics for its openness, its ambiguity. It was possible, for example, for some performers (the Doors, Jimi Hendrix, the

Stones, the Dead) to be a source of solidarity and enthusiasm for both the antiwar movement and the American soldiers in Vietnam. The politics of pop lie in what people do with it, how they use it to seize a moment, define a time, cull meaning around official knowledge. If pop offers private grief for public use, it also offers public words for private use. Its effects depend on its ability to resonate through different circumstances. Rock theorists got the public-private interplay all wrong, claiming the music as a publicly important phenomenon early on, giving musicians (John Lennon is the obvious example) a misleading sense of their own significance. Rock became a sort of official culture, lost its furtiveness; songs which should have worked as a fleeting subversion of moods became too didactic to be used by anyone. The political issues that popular music can explore—the ways in which people's "private" lives are public constructions—were dropped for the delusions of a rock "movement."

The songs that shaped my 60s worked not because of their "authenticity" but because of their playfulness—it was the sheer silliness of Scott McKenzie's "San Francisco" that made the hippie life seem so appealing. Songs that took it for granted that they didn't matter registered much more precisely than progressive rock the essential mood of the 60s, the sense of change and possibility. The 60s music that affected me made me laugh, implied a certain carelessness — Phil Spector's and the Beach Boys' soap operas, Bob Dylan's move into rock which made available a new tone of voice, the Stones' *Beggars' Banquet*, ironic commentary from the political sidelines. And above all, Motown music, soul, which lay at the heart of British musical experience in the 60s even if it doesn't fit the category "60s music." Soul music mattered to me more than anything else because I understood my desires and fantasies by reference to it—falling in love wasn't accompanied by Otis Redding's "My Girl" but defined by it.

What I'm describing here is the use and meaning of pop music now just as much as in the 60s (or in the 30s, come to that). What made the 60s different was not that this use of music changed, but that such pop meanings were in competition with the lightning raids of the self-styled artists, bohemians, folkies and hippies who claimed to do something with rock altogether different. I didn't really believe them but there's no doubt their activities heightened music's importance. What was misleading was the suggestion that this involved "progress" — pop isn't a form that progresses anyway and the suggestion that rock somehow went beyond pop, did things it couldn't do, concealed the way in which rock too was really a music of transitory private pleasures.

This is not to say that music has fixed meanings or values. Like all mass media it depends for its effects on its context, the response of active audiences, and more obviously than the other media, it also depends on memory. Music is such a powerful trigger of remembered emotion that it is probably more widely used for nostalgic reasons than for anything else. The politics of musical memory—the struggle to determine what the music meant then, why that matters now—is complicated by its double setting: to play *Sgt. Pepper* is to hear it as music now (in the context of corporate rock and postpunk pop) and as music then (memories, good in my case, of the summer of '67). Then *Sgt. Pepper* seemed to express most joyously the sense that we were on the move. Now (after the 1970s, the Sex Pistols, the new aggression of the right) I can't help thinking the move hit a dead end, and the 60s record I listen to all the time is *The Velvet Underground and Nico*, a record I don't even remember hearing at the time.

San Francisco ideologist Ralph Gleason once wrote after a Velvet Underground performance in the city that "Andy Warhol's Plastic Inevitable, upon examination turns out to be nothing more than a bad condensation of all the bum trips of the Trips Festivals." Warhol's offense was that he wasn't concerned to inspire or represent a community but simply wanted to stir people up and see what happened—he'd been drawn to the Velvets because they made such an unbearable din. For him they were not a rock group but a commentary on a rock group and the miracle (not Warhol's doing) was that their music was remarkable anyway. Lou Reed's songs picked at the underside of bohemia—drugs as sickness and money, sex as jealousy and pain. John Cale had an avant-garde obsession with textural repetition, with the impact on monotony of the slightest dissonance. The Velvets' sound was harsh, loud, unpleasant in its use of feedback and screeching; the Velvets' music was made not out of melodies, hooks and choruses but out of riffs, repeated phrases that built up their effects in layers, made their rhythmic and harmonic impact simultaneously. Each Velvet Underground song used a small cluster of notes that battered and battered against each other until feedback, a screech, was the only logical place to go.

The Velvet Underground's music, unlike most other 60s sounds, offered no escape. It was indubitably present, unavoidable, which is why it became such a profound influence on the 1970s development of a critical pop sensibility, a sensibility concerned with the politics of *form*—the Velvets still stand for the idea that the politics of music involves the struggle to make meanings in the first place, to define something stable in the ever-shifting play of pop signifiers. The Velvet Underground's first LP, then, like *Sgt. Pepper*, offered new arguments about what popular music could do, but where the Beatles' message was that everything was possible, the Velvets' was that everything was in doubt.

It's paradoxical to rethink the 60s with such pessimism (though I'd guess that the Velvet Underground's music is played these days as much as anything else from then) but in retrospect the point is that the Rock Revolution was far too easy. It proclaimed a utopia without struggle; it invoked disorder when the politics of pop really involves (did then too, which is what we must recall) the day-to-day, commonplace attempt to grasp reassurance from the realization that everything—love, sex, pleasure, power—is in doubt.

A 60s MOVEMENT IN THE 80s

INTERVIEW WITH DAVID APTER*

David Apter: What I find interesting about this Narita Airport movement is that it represents a coalition between farmers, who started out defending their private property and who became radicalized against the state, and militants, mostly people who started out as students, who were part of the new left, who left universities, sometimes high schools, and went into trade unionism and generally were heavily involved in Vietnam war demonstrations. The movement has now lasted almost a generation—almost twenty years.

Social Text: We were speculating on the originality of this Japanese movement in the sense that most other new lefts were never really able to hook up with a social base of this kind; and the only equivalent that comes close would be the ecological movement in Europe, but that also really came too late to make such connections. . .

DA: That's a central point. Exactly that kind of social base marks the beginnings of the left in Japan. So were what we call today environmental or ecological or pollution matters. This "coalition" left goes back to the turn of the century, to the Ashio Copper Mine strikes. The first socialist and Marxist parties in Japan saw the class struggle in terms of such issues as pollution and damage to the lives of miners (as a result of contemporary techniques of smelting copper). Neither government nor industry accepted that the injuries and deaths associated with copper mining were their responsibility. Hence, the Ashio Riots that took place around 1906/7 served in a sense to crystallize the left in Japan. It starts on that sort of basis, plus a strand of radical Christianity, a Protestantism that came in a bit earlier and which gradually shifted from evangelical proselytizing to social issues. There are some very famous people associated with that movement, some of whom shifted texts, from religious ones to Marxist. A few began to read Lenin. But mainly, the political left in Japan began with concrete issues.

**Conducted in New Haven, Connecticut in Spring 1982 by Michael Denning and Fredric Jameson*

Even though the movement was derivative, in the sense that the ideas used to mobilize were brought in from abroad, there was a real authenticity to the left because of the issues and participants—miners, fishermen, farmers, workers, and coalitions among them and militant students. The latter were important right from the start. Another important feature was radicalization of farm tenants. Both the Communist Party and the Socialist Party were strong in certain rural areas even before World War II. One obstacle to radical mobilization is this: in order to organize such movements in Japan, the problem always has been how to deal with the prior commitments of people and their loyalty to small groups, whatever group they already find satisfying. Loyalty may take precedence over militancy so that what we call trade unions are mostly company unions; there are very few radical unions in Japan and very little of what we would call horizontal unionization. If you are a trade unionist in Japan you are likely to be all in favor of your company (Honda or whatever). Working for that company, your chief antagonist is going to be Toyota, say, and not your own bosses. So the tremendous frustration of the left turns around how to identify an authentic class struggle in terms which the Japanese themselves can recognize. Landlord-tenant conflict is one. Marginalization of farmers is another. But working against both is a tradition of group affiliation in Japan associated in the past with something called the *gumi*: men went to work, went to war, went to school, in five-man teams, an intimate grouping of males which to some extent still survives. This tradition of groupness is the despair of the notion of class. One could be radical in the sense of antilandlord and antibourgeois but also in favor of the rural community—a sort of early radical right.

ST: Where does this kind of group come from? From a single village?

DA: From a village, or from a school, for example. It is very age graded. The group persists over time, and is reinforced by obligation. One of the most crucial things—and the Japanese are very ceremonial in their relationships, even among the left—is the way in which language itself defines people in terms of age, occupation and place, and status generally. For example, if somebody who was senior to you in school turns out to be junior to you in a company or whatever, there's a different way of addressing that person than if he were really a junior; and there will be a considerable discussion over the proper way to address the junior person, who may come up and slap the more senior person on the back to remind him that he is really inferior in terms of this other kind of age status. So it's a country in which all these minutiae of status and age and so forth are embedded in the language and that makes it more difficult for the left.

Nevertheless, there's a very authentic left history and there was a great boost to the left that came right after the first World War in the formation of the Japanese Communist Party.

ST: *Was that a split from an older socialist party as in Europe or the U.S.?*

DA: A split, but it also brought in as new recruits people who had been much more individual in their preoccupation with Marxism—scholars, literati, but previously joiners. The movement of Marxists at least from about 1906 to about 1926 starts at Tokyo University, the most prestigious university in Japan, then known as Tokyo Imperial University, which gave it a certain cachet. People met in intimate groups, developed safe houses, places where they could meet. It was a conspiratorial thing, since the police were always after them. . .

ST: *Was the Communist Party illegal in those days?*

DA: The JCP was illegal until after World War II but the phenomenon of secrecy largely predates the formation of communist parties as such. This earlier pattern established a sense of intimacy, a unique kind of intellectualism, centering particularly around the study of texts. They used to buy vast quantities of books from Charles Kerr in Chicago. Some had travelled in the United States. By the time the Communist Party was founded, these earlier groups of Marxists had already established a special left tradition which is very Japanese. You can go into even the most militant kinds of organizations—I've been working with radical sects, which occasionally kill each other, and a few of which come close to what's called terrorism—but within those groups you find a tremendous sense of awareness of the needs of other persons; there's almost a delicate sense of deference to that person's problems, needs, pressures. For the Japanese new left this gets generalized into a sense of resentment against the authoritarianism of the Communist Party. But there was always opposition to the authoritarianism of the Party even in the 30s and 40s especially when it insisted they follow the Moscow line. The Japanese party always had this double identity—part of the Comintern and so forth, but also these other very reluctant tendencies and to a greater extent than any other Communist Party I'm familiar with. One reason that's important is that most important figures remained Marxists after they split in opposition to the party line, providing a nucleus for the new left.

ST: *Now you're talking in particular about the postwar period.*

DA: Yes.

ST: *What about the Socialist Party or parties during that period?*

DA: Well, here you have to remember that the Japan Socialist Party has always been a more Marxist party than the ordinary social democratic party. The actual present day social democratic party is very recent and resulted from a split in the older Japan Socialist Party. This last still exists and has a left wing which is much more radical than the Communist Party and a right wing which is somewhat more social democratic but not as much as the Democratic Socialist Party, which split off around 1957 and which is much more what we would think of as a classical social democratic party.

ST: Do they specifically use a term equivalent to our expression "new left"?

DA: Oh yes, but to understand that you have to go back. The Communist Party founded a youth league, which was called the Gakuren; and when the Communist Party was reconstituted around 1947 or so, it established something called the Zengakuren, which was an all-Japan student organization. It operated along more democratic lines than the party itself. It had representatives from all the universities, and they met in congresses which essentially followed democratic principles, the key groups however being the various cells of the party itself within the universities.

ST: Just as a kind of sociological parenthesis, did these cells bear any relationship to the gumi *system you talked about before?*

DA: I don't know; I suspect there was a kind of metaphorical relationship at least, given the closeness of the male relationship on an age-grade system. People really go into the party cells, or into the new left sects, almost by chance, on the basis of close relationships or perhaps chance meetings; an old friend asks someone to come along to a meeting, and that will be the party or the cell or the sect they join; and to leave that is to *split*, which is an even more exaggerated phenomenon on the Japanese left than anywhere else.

There were many reasons why Zengakuren became disenchanted with the Communist Party after 1956; Hungary, the 20th Party Congress and revelations about Stalinism. There were also specific Japanese issues they wanted to pursue—for example, Koreans have always been discriminated against and that has always been a major issue for the new left. Other major targets were discrimination of the Ainu, but that's a very small minority; and what is called the Burakumin—the leatherworkers, really a kind of caste of untouchables. They can't pass because everybody knows who they are, everybody knows everybody else, everybody is Japanese; this is something very difficult to eliminate, even the language retains what you are. These issues were very low in the list of JCP priorities.

But perhaps the most important reason why the Zengakuren split was that at that point the Japan Communist Party decided to become a legalist party, a parliamentary party which they had not been until then. The Socialist Party had been more essentially parliamentary, the Communist Party had been underground although with an above-ground dimension. The new left was founded when the JCP decided to repudiate clandestine activities and to contest local elections, becoming the third or fourth largest party in the Diet.

Zengakuren decided that this was not sufficiently revolutionary. It would not adequately address the problems of class struggle: the party had sold out in every way, bureaucracy, on the level of intellectual content, etc., and so they split off in 1958 and took an initiative that was very important. In the past the great trade unions equivalent to the AFL-CIO Sōhyō had tried to mount popular demonstrations against American imperialism, against American controls, and so forth, but this was very difficult to do for several reasons. One was that the American occupation was on the whole fairly popular. It did a lot of things the Japanese wanted done and didn't really want to do themselves. It was popular with the (conservative) Liberal Democratic Party, because then they could say it wasn't any of their affair while gaining the benefits of power. The most important MacArthur reforms, for my purposes, involved two very significant land reforms which abolished the landlord-tenant system. That happened in ways that no Japanese government could have ever done. It broke up landed estates, it gave status to tenants who had been very militant, very peasant-oriented, some of them members of the Japan Communist Party, some of them extreme reactionaries, semi-fascists with romantic, nostalgic, antistate bias—not the personalized kind of thing we now associate with Mishima but more in the tradition of the peasant warrior—the true household at the base, with the Imperial household at the top, and no notion of state in between but rather a hierarchy of households . . . and these family worlds remained intact, tenant or nontenant. Finally those differences were broken down with the land reform and the government sponsored heavy investments in rural credit because the country was starving after the war (I'm saying all this because I'm going to be coming back to it later on). . . . Some of these peasants had become radicalized and joined the Japan Socialist Party or the Japan Communist Party but even these at one throw stopped being peasants and became rural entrepreneurs, all the while the family structure remaining very much intact. So here was one reason it was very hard to focus antagonism against the American authorities until you get to the next generation, and that was the generation of the radical militants of the Zengakuren, who saw the American presence in terms of military occupation and control of the airways that crisscrossed and dominated the sky above, while the land below, having gradually been turned over to the people themselves, began to disappear as industrialization (and pollution) spread into rural areas. In 1960—the Japanese constitution calls for the revision of the U.S.-Japan treaty every 10 years—the new left in Japan really begins around the issue of treaty revision. The students mobilized thousands and thousands of people, many more than the trade unions ever managed to do, and in mass confrontations they surrounded the Japanese Diet, they forced Prime Minister Ishi to resign. It was the first successful "citizens' participation movement"—meaning the linking up of trade unions, neighborhood movements, a movement called the Kitafuji movement which began in 1947 and which was a movement of mothers demonstrating against a U.S. airbase on the slopes of Mount Fuji—a whole series of smaller movements which finally all linked up in 1960 in a mass mobilization of literally over a million people called AMPO, the anti-U.S.-Japan-Security-treaty demonstration. And this is the real opposition in Japan. Still relatively primitive in form, it is this which the Sanrizuka farmers movement recapitulated and developed in the late 60s and 70s. This is the kind of *rassemblement* that the left had in mind, not some putative version of the Paris Commune. The new left in Japan begins in 1958/1960, particularly after AMPO 1960.

The Zengakuren, in turn, contained various tendencies. Two were most important. One was called Bundu, a name borrowed from the old radical German Bund, and the other was the Revolutionary Marxists. These now began to operate outside the framework of the Zengakuren, setting up their own. Eventually there were three Zengakuren. Also, since these were groups that didn't see themselves exclusively as students any more but also as professional revolutionary bodies, they defined the left as clandestine, militant and violent. The Bundu, which was heavily Trotskyist, promptly split into ten different sects—like religious sects which is where something like the *gumi* business comes in. These are extremely small, involve very intimate association with one another and a tremendous sense of passionate commitment. They operate within the world of class struggle. But since class struggle goes on all the time, just as no victory is ever decisive, so no failure is ever really a failure. They live on the minutiae of day-to-day tactics. The Revolutionary Marxists split into two as well as declaring war on each other, one calling itself Chukaku-ha and the other the Kakumaru-ha. An issue organized by the one is declared a fascist issue by the other. Tactics are quickly elevated into principles. The principles can be identified, say, as Leninism versus Trotskyism, grand strategic principles into which these small day-to-day tactical issues are transformed. So struggles which nobody else has ever heard of will be given a name; the May 22nd Struggle, for instance, which becomes the signifier for a huge doctrinal issue but won't work until there is some "disjunctive" event—violence. When somebody is killed that person becomes a martyr of the May 22 Struggle, etc. Then the whole thing becomes terribly iconographic and there's a lot of explicit manipulation of tactical symbolism as the basis for conceiving the struggle in terms of history or of daily events.

Now this dynamic characterizes all these groups (and also Maoism). Certain groups, like the Revolutionary Marxists—as opposed to the Bundu—are explicitly Leninist (without being anti-Trotsky, whom they retrieve from desecration by the JCP). Leninism means you need to go back to *What Is To Be Done* to understand the "true" nature of the clandestine party. They call themselves "true Leninists" to distinguish themselves from terrorists, people who split off from all these groups to join the Japanese Red Army, (of which there are again three sects). The most extreme and violent part of the Japanese Red Army was a small group called the United Red Army. Hunted, holed up in the mountains, it actually killed fourteen of its own members in attempts to "purify" their commitments by starving, beating, demanding self-criticism, etc. (about 1971). It is regarded by the

Revolutionary Marxists as terrorist, that is people who use indiscriminate violence, as against Lenin's conception. And this is very important, because the whole definition of what constitutes legitimate struggle, as opposed to indiscriminate use of violence against innocent people, informs the sects and most particularly that branch of the Revolutionary Marxists known as Chukaku-ha. It is a real distinction and not just a rhetorical one, since it involves very different kinds of attitudes and a sense of responsibilities, and it also allows the members of these sects to work today with radical farmers who wouldn't give the time of day to terrorists. They can be violent, but they believe they represent the antithesis of terrorist activity: they are against the state and can use violence against the state, but not the kind of indiscriminate violence against persons which we associate with terrorism.

The two really crucial groups which emerged from the splits in the Revolutionary Marxist, Chukaku-ha (Central Core) and Kakumaru-ha ("ha" meaning sect) (Revolutionary Marxists) declared war on each other. Chukaku-ha attacked Kakumaru-ha on the grounds that a social revolution has to settle its accounts with its radical sects before coming to power, otherwise it will become fascist (a lesson they thought they learned from the history of Nazi Germany). Kakumaru-ha killed the leader of Chukaku-ha in 1978 (appropriately named "Honda"), and Chukaku-ha has killed approximately thirty-four top leaders of Kakumaru-ha: all in all about seventy-seven people have been killed in these battles over an eleven year period. Kakumaru-ha has about four thousand members. Chukaku-ha has about fifty-five hundred. All these sects are organized outside the Sanrizuka movement. But because of this "war" Kakumaru-ha is not allowed on the site of the Sanrizuka antiairport movement. Today there are seventeen different sects on the site itself. Originally, in 1967 there were twenty-two. The Japan Communist Party, which originally supported the struggle of the farmers and the airport movement, was expelled by the farmers from the site in 1967. The Zengakuren was invited in by an ascetic Christian radical, an old man who was the leader of this antiairport league, a very interesting guy, a sculptor of some repute, and the owner of a farm implements shop, a man named Issaku Tomura. Here is the link I mentioned earlier, to an original Protestant radicalism. This man's father and grandfather were among the early Protestants and he came from an antiwar tradition. He was a very strong character whose equivalent would probably be less likely in American Protestantism than English dissent, muscular Christianity, methodism and the like. He invited the Zengakuren after being beaten up by the police. This meant outside support, most importantly the Chukaku-ha, but other sects as well. Each sect had to agree to abide by the rules laid down by the farmers, organized in a league, the antiairport league called the Hantai Domei. They built forts, solidarity huts, and then real fortresses to create a no-man's-land around the airport. The terrain became hostile, isolating the state, i.e., the airport, from the rest of the society. The class struggle then is society versus the state locked in a struggle in a "mobilization" space which is also a "semiotic" space. There are about thirty-three of these huts and fortresses. Some sects maintain several, manned and paid for by the sects from outside. Chukaku-ha is the most important, along with the Fourth International, which emerged from the Bundu, and these are the two leading, somewhat hostile, but nonetheless cooperative forces. The sects which are on the site cooperate to some extent. The Maoists have dissolved.

The conversion of this terrain into a semiotic space, a rallying ground for a variety of issues began when the decision to put the airport in this area was made in 1966, quite suddenly. The cabinet had planned originally to put it somewhere else but the farmers in the other area opposed the airport successfully. Within one week the government decided to shift the airport to Sanrizuka and for a variety of reasons. Sanrizuka was the site of an Imperial Horse Ranch where the Emperor had a small detached villa (and which is still there, falling into decay). Most of it is now airport runway. The Horse Ranch was beautiful, predating even the Tokugawa period. Many people in the area came originally as tenants on the Horse Ranch. The tiny crossroads at Sanrizuka was a place where visitors would stay, the roads going out from there to hamlets and villages. There was an old hotel where they could stay and beautiful magnolia and 15,000 cherry trees.

The government picked that site because it could gain access to land, like Crown land; but the local population was outraged. The farmers are all exsoldiers, some of them from the Manchurian campaign. Most were shocked at what they had done in the war, angry at having been taken in by the Emperor himself this way and vowed never so unthinkingly to accept authority. They were predisposed to resistance. This is why the family-world business is so important: by rejecting the past they rejected the primacy of the state as well. Their primary links to the state after the war were in the cooperative movement, which fixed the price of rice and provided agricultural support, and through the benefits afforded by the LDP government, which wanted to expand food production. So you have angry exsoldiers, angry because they've been had by the government and twice. All were *taishos*, i.e. from the generation of 1912–1926, a grandfather's generation for the militants, which is important because the young militants were "adopted," sometimes even squeezing out the children of the farmers themselves (which produced considerable internal tension). This "embrace" also provides a way for militants to drop out of the rigid age-graded system—if you don't go to this school, perform at this level, work in this factory and spend the rest of your life there, or in this ministry, or whatever, you're just not Japanese, there's no place for you in society. So highly monitored a society is it and with such incredible self-control that if the system breaks, or you drop out of it, then people become violent and angry. The tradition on the left, seeking a way to live a "sincere" life according to whatever one's beliefs are, can lead one to extreme isolation. It

Rally at Sanrizuka Park. Courtesy of *Asahi Shimbun*.

puts tremendous pressures on the individual. So by becoming adopted by these farmers the militants were somehow brought back into Japanese society, in a way that terrorists would never be accepted.

When this decision to shift the airport site was made in 1966, and the farmers first began to attack the government and to defend the site, to refuse to let surveyors come on the land, the women were the most militant. They chained themselves to the trees and to the bulldozers. Old women gathered buckets of human excrement and sprayed the police, tactics they learned from the mothers of the Kitafuji movement. Once this all began to hit the newspapers and the Zengakuren sent students out and the real violence began, the movement sent shock waves through Japanese society. To the militants the farmers were "peasants," like Vietnamese peasants. Here was the Vietnam war in Japan. Farmers stored potatoes deep down under the ground in concrete pits. Militants built bunkers underground expressing attachment to the soil. Militants also built their forts over bunkers constructed like the potato pits. When the bulldozers tried to knock down the forts, the hope was that they would sink into the pits, a tactic with parallels to the underground tunnels of the Vietnamese. This fitted in with the principles of the Hantai Domei. The reason for the new airport was that the old airport in Tokyo had filled up with American planes, supplies, troops. The new airport was located in Sanrizuka because this was the only place that wouldn't infringe on the already existing air routes, Blue-14 and the whole crisscrossing of the skies under American domination. The site was selected without proper consideration of the people who were already there. The basic struggle combined the Vietnam struggle, the class struggle, primitive accumulation and the creation of a double industrial reserve army, the farmers pushed off the land; peasants in Southeast Asia. The airport symbolized—and this is very important—a shift that took place when Ishi—the prime minister who resigned during the AMPO riots—was replaced by Ikeda, and Ikeda instituted a drastic change in government policy, shifting away support to agriculture to support for industry. What happened in the province where the airport site was located was characteristic of what was happening in the country at large, when petrochemicals came in. What had been beautiful farm land was now utterly polluted. The fish disappeared from the sea. The choice of the airport site now encroached on the last pockets of agriculture. So the airport became the symbol of the next stage of government policy, called the policy of income doubling, the deliberate aim of which was to treat the 1945–1960 period as the basis for a kind of primitive accumulation. Let farmers build up capital, then drive out all the weak farmers—and that included all of these small farmers, some of them from families farming there for a thousand years, others exsoldiers who came there after the war and brought marginal land up to reasonable levels of cultivation. So this policy was seen by farmers and militants as capitalism destroying Japan. All of these issues came together. You have the Minamata people working with the Hiroshima peace marchers. Everybody converged on the site. It's estimated that the militants in the fortresses—and the cadres who run these fortresses have links to the universities, the unions, and permanent citizen committees—were able according to police estimates (and the police are very accurate) to involve some 750,000 to a million people over the years: involvement meaning actually coming out and fighting the police, who used bulldozers and cranes against the fortresses, and helping farmers farm. The police wear steel helmets, almost medieval in type with mesh coming down to protect their necks. They wear heavy gauntlets and they carry huge curved shields which they use to smash in the faces of old women who chain themselves to the stockages or the trees. Particular events, like the last solitary tree of Komaino—an old village on the site where the first stage of the airport was—became iconographic. Several people chained themselves to this, the last pine tree that remained of the original forest. They were first sprayed with water cannons. Then a crane bent the tree and somebody came over with a chain saw and cut it down. Meanwhile, of course, pitched battles were fought. Thousands of people have been hurt and five people killed in this struggle. Episodes vary—one episode went on for five hundred days—and people came out and occupied the forts so the police couldn't destroy buildings and bulldoze the land.

ST: Now are the police still trying to destroy those forts today?

DA: Well, let me explain a little bit where things are today. The first violence broke out in 1967 when the government laid claim to the land and started to survey it. To do that they had to clear it, because a lot of it was forest. And the farmers immediately went in to stop this. First they had petitioned the government, and got no answer. Then the government decided to move in and make a show of force. At that point, the women acted, and remember that the Japanese woman is not exactly liberated; the farmers' wives are the workhorses of these small farms and do all the heavy work around the farm; well, they were the first ones to use militant tactics. And then gradually the Hantai Domei got organized, based on the villages, with one representative from each village; the villages being very jealous of their own prerogatives. If a village decides to sell its land to the airport corporation, it's very hard for anyone to do anything about it. But because the police were so violent—there are about twenty-seven villages in the area, seven or eight actually involved in the original site itself—most villages, even those initially divided over the airport, became pro-Hantai Domei. Part of the problem for the farmers is that they feel their obligation keenly, to family, village, etc. How much they commit themselves to the Hantai Domei is never an individual decision. In this sense, it is principle rather than political organization which counts. Farmers' lives are wholly different from militants. The militants who live in the fortresses recruit from all over the place. Theirs is invariably communal living. Life centers around a big kitchen, usually dirty, almost deliberately organic, so to speak, scattered about with all kinds of electronic equipment; helmets, bullhorns, sleeping pads for hundreds of people, great big pots for making rice—it's pretty primitive. The inside of the fortresses are constructed of heavy logs, with steel gates, and barbed wire—sometimes the nucleus was an old house, but mainly they are built around those tin huts which the Japanese use for construction, or else warehouses with struts on the outside and inside plywood. Usually there's one nice room where the leader lives where people take off their shoes when they come in. When it rains it's a sea of mud all over the place. A lot of the fighting takes place in the rainy season. The sects keep to themselves as sects; rarely will one sect mention another sect; the living inside is intense.

The police and the airport authorities have been successful in building the first stage of this airport; in the process of building this first stage, all these conflicts occurred. For example, at the 4000 meter mark, which is required by international law for jets to take off, the militants built an enormous steel tower on top of three stories of cement bunker with huge rooms inside. The bunker still exists, part of the tower still exists. When the police came in, in the early 70s, to take that tower down, you can imagine what it was like. There were thousands of people out there defending it. They collected rubber tires from all over Japan, poured gasoline on them and ignited them—threw Molotov cocktails and turned some of the police into human torches. Every time the police succeeded in tearing it down, it was rebuilt. There's still a good part of it there, and if you go up there, you can peer down the runway which is not quite 4000 meters. This is the world's most dangerous airport. Because the militants and farmers can fight at any moment without any warning, it's not only a terrible embarrassment to the government—international flights coming into this armed camp—it also forced the police and the government to build double lines of fences with huge watchtowers all around it, so it looks exactly like a concentration camp—searchlights, permanent houses on the tops, the police staring through their medieval outfits with binoculars. The fortresses completely circle the airport except for one side where there is a group of hotels.

And this for only the first stage of the airport. The second stage has not been built. The government has bought up a lot of land successfully from farmers, at tremendous prices, but there are twelve farmers, twelve apostles, who refuse to sell and who are holding up the second stage. And the job of the Hantai Domei is to see that there is enough familialism and villagism linked up to these twelve to prevent them from selling out to the government.

The intimacy of village life is the greatest strength of the Hantai-Domei. The intimacy of the fortress is the strength of the sects. Against this is the tremendous impersonality of bureaucracy, the machinery of government and all its accoutrements and mechanisms symbolized by an airport.

Actually Sanrizuka, the original crossroads on the imperial estate is itself still rather simple and very quiet. For a while, I lived at the top of the little church at the crossroads, Tomura's church. And I found that Sanrizuka has all the convenience of a rural small town even though it is truncated and cut off by the fence and by a big watchtower of the airport. Three points of the compass are boxed in by the militants whose solidarity huts and the fortresses with these big watchtowers peer into the watchtowers of the police on the other side. So the symbolism is superb. The militants wear helmets, white helmets for the Chukaku-ha, or red or black helmets for some others (who are sometimes regarded as anarchists on account of the color, but they're not really). You can tell what sect is involved by the color of the helmets.

ST: So the second stage area that remains to be built, that's the area that is occupied by the fortifications and the huts?

DA: That's right, they're scattered through there strategically. And the architecture is very interesting too, the more militant the sect, the more bristling the fortress; and very often, as with the Chukaku-ha, the militants are like soldiers, they've been posted there, they spend a certain number of years there and then they get posted to some other place.

ST: When was the first stage finished?

DA: The airport was opened in May 1978. It was supposed to open in March of that year (actually, the original projected date for the first stage was something like 1969) so you can imagine what the cost overrun must have been, just the cost of security alone is incredible. The militants, the Chukaku-ha in particular, have dominated the Chiba-doro, that is, the local prefecture branch of the locomotive engineers (the rest of it is dominated by the Kaku-maru). The airport depends on this union for fuel supplies. The Chiba branch (whose president I interviewed) is very pro-Hantai Domei. The militants also have maps of where a proposed fuel pipeline is supposed to be built. It has been impossible to build that pipeline. Everytime it is laid down somebody blows it up. All the fuel has to come in by tank car. With the locomotive engineers members of the Chiba branch of the union, Chukaku-ha can shut that airport down any time they want, in 48 hours; and they have on a number of occasions. There's a kind of unwritten agreement not to do it, though, as long as the government behaves itself and doesn't go too far against the militants.

ST: So all this time there hasn't been any loss of militancy or outside support in this movement, over all these years?

DA: Yes, there has, of course. It's interesting to speculate on the life cycle of a political movement of this kind—this one has certainly been going on much longer than anyone ever anticipated. To go back for a moment, though, to the opening, which was supposed to have been in March 1978, the Fourth International got a copy of the detailed plans for the airport from various adherents or supporters in the government, the office of

Women at the First Point in Komaino, fighting against riot police, February 25, 1971. Courtesy of *Asahi Shimbun*.

Sect members outside of airport, October 26, 1982. Photo by David Apter.

the architects (and don't forget, as the students grow up and "age-grade" themselves into positions of responsibility, they don't necessarily lose their sensitivity to the movement; so it's almost impossible to maintain security, and even though Japan is a very responsible and secretive society, with an extremely bright and loyal bureaucracy, it's penetrated at all these key points). Well, they got hold of these plans and a big rally was planned to protest the opening. This will just give you an example of how they work. Hantai Domei had mobilized five thousand supporters in Sanrizuka park near the imperial villa. It looked like it was going to get ugly. The Hantai Domei in itself has about 120 families, so it's very tiny, you see, but they mobilize all these supporting groups. The demonstration was encircled by police, overflown by police helicopters and so forth. Then the secretary general, who owns a kimono shop and is not a farmer but a very militant guy, got very tough. He took a group of supporters to the tower at the 4000 meter mark. The police were very upset by this tactic because you can practically touch the planes from there as they go overhead and you can peer right down the runway. So the police decided they couldn't let that happen, and sent reinforcements over. They beat up and arrested Kitahara, the secretary general. Another group of militants got flatbed trucks and smashed through the main gate which is the entryway to the airport, and on these trucks they had ten-gallon drums of gasoline which they ignited. But all these tactics were diversionary. The Fourth International, which organized all this, had the night before sent about 14 members down into the sewer system, the point being that it is unthinkable that Japanese would go down into a sewer; too unsanitary. Well they got into the sewers the night before and stayed there. When the confrontation began, they emerged from the sewers, went right to the main terminal, which had just been completed, took the elevator up to the top of the control tower, where they did millions of dollars worth of damage and hung red flags out; then they took the elevator back down and disappeared. I interviewed the guy who organized this, who is wanted by the police and who is the editor of a Trotskyist publishing house and he said, "Well, it wasn't very complicated, all we needed to do was to get the plans." The event was in retaliation for the police tearing down the 4000 meter mark tower but also of the storming of Tokyo University tower in 1969—a dual symbolism as the radicals saw it. It kept the airport from opening until the following May. Since that time there has been a kind of truce; there have been conflicts, of course, many people still get hurt, and some arrested, but this kind of massive *rassemblement* has tapered off. The government has been very anxious to avoid any more of these incidents.

So where it stands at the moment, then, is that there is a kind of truce. There are about 17 sects still left on the site. The Hantai Domei itself, the farmers' group, is getting divided and smaller. Mr. Issaku Tomura, who was really the unifying symbol for the whole thing, died of cancer. The secretary general, a very important person, has not really been able to fill the role the former president had. The person who took Tomura's place, a farmer, refused to become president officially, because he said nobody can really take his place. He's a real farmer, drinks sake until you can't stand up. He had members of the Weatherpeople and the Black Panthers come and visit him—an encounter it's almost impossible to visualize—and he says with relish that the Panthers never really understood the properties of Japanese sake, they all passed out. Anyway he's quite charming and enjoys talking about all this, with a certain amount of embellishment. . . . The general support in the area has declined, how much it's hard to say; for this movement has also taken its place as part of the Hiroshima antiwar movement and the antinuclear movement. In any important rally in Tokyo you're likely to find very rural farmers up on the platform with all kinds of other people. To give you an example, I attended a Chukaku-ha rally in Tokyo the day after interviewing several farmers. Two of those farmers were there to make speeches, one a woman who is the head of the women's league of the Hantai Domei, and the other was Mr. Shito, a very poor farmer, who found it difficult to reply to some of my questions, not because he didn't want to, but because he had just gotten back from a demonstration at Kita-fuji, where the mothers' movement is, and had drunk too much sake and left his false teeth on the bus. . . . On the same platform were representatives from almost all the other citizen protest groups in Japan. These are terribly impressive people, in all ways. And the sects also—I remember, having been in Berkeley during the 60s demonstrations, the incredible piety and simple-mindedness that was associated with a lot of the militancy, the screaming, the ego-centeredness and mutual manipulation—there's very little of that here. There's a tremendous emphasis on what things mean, on commitment. It's more old left in its austerity; the life in the fortresses is extremely austere, almost celibate. There are very few women, on the grounds that they introduce an element that can't be controlled, but there are some, and the women are very tough. The wives of the farmers are also very tough, and they can be bawdy and charming and jovial, especially when the men aren't around, but they still serve them just the same.

Now this movement is blending into a lot of others. It is no longer able to crystallize issues. In part, the problem is that basic government policy is popular in Japan. People have never been so rich. Farmers, even these farmers, have alternatives; they can be part-time farmers and also work in industry, if they want to; and you can really make a lot of money that way. So there's no ineluctable class struggle, no rural-peasant struggle. These farmers prefer full-time farming, are willing to take a lesser income as a result of it. For a time the movement was endowed with exceptional significance. There was a need for this physical space—to capture the state, to create a no-man's-land, to redefine the issues of militarism and industrialization. Underlying all these movements is the common belief that Japan's in-

Police shooting water at the Second Fortress, February 6, 1978. The day was below freezing, yet it took the police 15 hours to dislodge the demonstrators. Courtesy of *Asahi Shimbun*.

dustrial development simply amounts to reassuming the old project of the Southeast Asian Co-prosperity Sphere by peaceful means. They see as the underlying reality the renewal of Japan's old imperial "mission," which was put in military terms before, and is being put in economic terms now. That's the common denominator and it makes a lot of these people not only cynical of the governing party but also of parliamentary government generally. They are the other side of the coin, the other side of Japan as number one, which makes this particularly interesting, a permanent opposition that coalesces around all kinds of issues. The airport happened to be one of the most visible and symbolic of those with all sorts of subsymbols involved in it as well. It raised the questions of extra-institutional protest, issues which lots of people feel very strongly about and which are either too local or fragmented to get attention in parliament. Or from the government. Where you're dealing with large constituencies, large majority coalitions, paid off by the success of the regime, too many needs go unattended, too many are marginalized. And that's the big question: What are the limits of parliamentary and democratic institutions? I happen myself to be very doubtful about worker participation. I've worked on it in Yugoslavia, Chile and elsewhere and it is prone to becoming another bureaucratic device; to organize it is wonderful, to watch after it after five years is a disaster. But this community participation thing is different. It has a quality of spontaneity and a durability. It can occur at any time once the right issue is found and bring together these various movements which would otherwise be isolated, submerged and overwhelmed in any kind of ordinary parliamentary constituency, and which are not sufficiently powerful to act as interest groups. So that it's somewhere in between interest groups, workers' participation and extra-parliamentary opposition that you find the larger significance of this.

ST: Well, one of the further questions that arise is the analogies with the problems of the new left, the relationship between small groups like the Weatherpeople and the masses proper— something that never happened in the United States. . . . Is this movement organized differently?

DA: If you took the number of people involved in the Sanrizuka movement over the years, you're dealing with thousands of people who represent a pretty characteristic cross section of the children of fairly well established people. For example, people often asked me what I was doing in Japan. When I told them, they would recoil in horror as if I had some contagious disease. Then after a while, (it was usually the wife who would reopen the question) they would say, "You know, you ought to talk to my son or my nephew, or so and so." Everyone had or knew somebody involved. . . . Secondly, there were many other broad-based radical coalitions. One called Zen-kyoto was nonsect, involved a very large number of people. Tolerant of individual radical positions, the Zen-kyoto people tended to become planners and technocrats. They work in consulting firms, positions in government and so forth. They tend to keep their radicalism despite this and cherish their involvement in this movement. You can say that there is a large reservoir of people with radical experiences and sympathies out there, something more similar to the tradition in France. They are just as prone to be coopted, but they keep their radicalism. Their reasons for becoming radicals seem to be more permanent—so while they are functioning within society, they keep their own counsel.

ST: But you don't think that is because of the nationalism of this movement?

DA: No, I don't think it's nationalist, on the contrary it's antinationalist and anticapitalist. It's also anti-American. It is against industrialization, without necessarily being antimodernist: they're not nostalgic, they're not environmental romantics, not Sierra Club types. This larger group is somewhat different from the sects themselves, but all know people in the sects. Members of the sects come from the very same families and universities. Indeed, so do the civil servants—and many are of equivalent quality.

The new left movement in Japan is built on an old antagonism that a lot of people had against the state for different reasons. Even the conservative way was antibig business, antibureaucracy, anticapitalist, antibourgeois essentially, with some fascist elements in it, although it wasn't necessarily fascist. What's happening today is that the new right (the Mishima phenomenon, for example) has tended to become more powerful, the next generation of students—the present one—has tended to move towards the right on the basis of some of the same things that moved people to the left. The big difference is nationalism or remilitarization. There is a somewhat horrified reaction on the part of the older generation, including the parents of these new leftists, many of whom don't want to see that happen. There's a lot of antagonism to the extreme right, which is also antiparliamentary. So there is a sense in which, as it declines, the new left becomes more acceptable than it was in its own time. It has a more permanent characteristic. Its strength is independent of its popularity and the number of people joining the sects.

This has two further consequences. One is that it keeps the left away from terrorism. All three versions of the Japanese Red Army have literally been destroyed. Even those who went to Beirut, and that's the United Red Army in particular—their leading theorist has published a number of articles recently in Paris admitting to a lot of mistakes, that they were simpleminded in expecting to produce a revolution. This group, called the Japanese Arabs, can be pretty ferocious. They were the same ones who shot up the airport in Israel. I met some of those people. Today, I would say that they're embarrassed about their past and feel cut off from everything. The people who were holed up in the mountains are today almost all of them in jail if they aren't dead. In contrast, while the new left can be violent, it is not terrorist.

ST: The other basic question would have to do with consumerism and the coming of a certain Americanization of Japan, and to what degree that would lend itself to a media politics (terrorism has often been defined in those terms), and also to the degree to which this kind of movement is at all linked to a counterculture in the American or consumer-society sense.

DA: It's not really much like the American counterculture. I would describe it as a mixture of old left characteristics, with a tremendous sincerity and much greater degree of individual respect, plus the business of actually living communal lives: they give up a great deal to live collectively within the framework of specific causes, rather than simply hanging around and indulging in an orgy of criticism. There's almost no drug-taking for example, it's almost unheard of; very little drinking; if you drink at all in one of these solidarity huts, it has to be after an evening meal and meeting.

ST: How do they live on the cultural level? Do they listen to music, are they interested in political theater, etc.?

DA: No, very little. The intellectual leadership of the Fourth International is highly educated. Most others are less so. You must remember that they live under constant police surveillance, not exactly fugitives, but with the feeling that they are going to be harassed. They can be very cultivated and full of civility and willing to talk about cultural matters. They are very Japanese in the sense that they have no use whatever for what they would see as the randomization of social life, and in particular role-smashing characteristic of the American counterculture.

ST: But culture in the largest sense: are they interested in peasant culture, for example, since they're working with peasants, or are they simply not interested in culture at all?

DA: Very few, and not the real militants. Outsiders are interested, journalists, professional artists. For example, a superb film was made by the Ogawa Company. It runs for about four hours. It focuses on a single village, full of long shots, peasant faces, very stylized, almost a Noh drama. People take off their masks, so to speak. It is very well done, although it probably wouldn't appeal to American audiences since there are long mystifying silences and slow periods. Japanese become utterly involved. Among activists, however, there is very little preoccupation with culture as such; the journals I have had translated to me are more like trade union journals or like *Iskra*—they talk about practical things, marches, demonstrations, strikes, and there is almost nothing about the larger literary or cultural or even the historical dimensions of all this. As for the outside supporters, those people tend to live quite well and quite conventionally. Some have good print and record collections, know jazz, so they're cultivated in a sense. But they are certainly not interested in culture as new forms of language or in peasant beliefs or anything of that sort. In any case the farmers don't fit the peasant category. They are really small agro-businessmen.

ST: Then the related question would be about feminism and the role it plays in such movements in Japan.

DA: Well, of course that's very weak in Japan. There are individual feminists and strong women in these movements. But the feminist movement as such does not get much support and does not generate issues. What you do get is the mobilization of intellectuals generally, and there are many women teachers, professors, writers and activists in a variety of causes. The Sanrizuka movement has tried to rouse women and did inspire young militants.

RADICAL FEMINISM AND FEMINIST RADICALISM

ELLEN WILLIS

I was a radical feminist activist in the late 60s. Today I often have the odd feeling that this period, so vivid to me, occurred fifty years ago, not a mere fifteen. Much of the early history of the women's liberation movement, and especially of radical feminism (which was not synonymous with the w.l.m. but a specific political current within it) has been lost, misunderstood or distorted beyond recognition. The left, the right, and liberal feminists have all for their own reasons contributed to misrepresenting and trivializing radical feminist ideas. To add to the confusion, radical feminism in its original sense barely exists today. The great majority of women who presently call themselves "radical feminists" in fact subscribe to a politics more accurately labeled "cultural feminist." That is, they see the primary goal of feminism as freeing women from the imposition of so-called "male values," and creating an alternative culture based on "female values." Cultural feminism is essentially a moral, countercultural movement aimed at redeeming its participants, while radical feminism began as a political movement to end male supremacy in all areas of social and economic life, and rejected the whole idea of opposing male and female natures and values as a sexist idea, a basic part of what we were fighting. Though cultural feminism came out of the radical feminist movement, the premises of the two tendencies are antithetical. Yet on the left and elsewhere the distinction is rarely made.

Along with simply wanting to retrieve this history (my history), I think it's crucial for understanding what happened to the women's movement later, and what's happening now. In the first couple of years of its existence, radical feminism showed every sign of becoming a true mass movement. We had enormous energy and enthusiasm and used a variety of tactics—demonstrations and speakouts; tireless organizing among friends and coworkers, on street corners, in supermarkets and ladies' rooms; above all, a prodigious output of leaflets, pamphlets, journals, magazine articles, newspaper and radio and TV interviews. The movement exploded into public consciousness, pushed the National Organization for Women and other liberal feminist organizations way to the left, and grew so fast that existing groups didn't know what to do with the influx of new members. Organized radical feminist activism was most visible and prominent in New York City, Boston and Washington, D.C. and on the West Coast, but myriads of small groups inspired by radical feminist ideas sprang up all over the country.

It was radical feminism that put women's liberation on the map, that got sexual politics recognized as a public issue, that created the vocabulary ("consciousness-raising," "the personal is political," "sisterhood is powerful," etc.) with which the second wave of feminism entered popular culture. Radical feminists sparked the drive to legalize abortion and created the atmosphere of urgency in which liberal feminists were finally able to get the Equal Rights Amendment through Congress and most of the states. Radical feminists were also the first to demand total equality in the so-called private sphere—equal sharing of housework and child care, equal attention to our emotional and sexual needs. It's no exaggeration to say that the immense transformation in women's consciousness over the past fifteen years has been inspired by the issues radical feminists raised. One exasperating example of how easy it is to obliterate history is that Betty Friedan can now get away with the outrageous claim that radical feminist "extremism" turned women off and derailed the movement she built. Radical feminism turned women on, by the thousands.

Yet this movement collapsed as quickly as it had grown. By 1975 radical feminism had given way to cultural feminism. The women's liberation movement had become the women's movement, in which liberals were the dominant, not to say hegemonic force. Socialist and Marxist feminism, which had come out of other tendencies of the w.l.m. and segments of the left influenced by it, were theoretically confused and practically marginal.[1] Feminism had become a reformist politics, a countercultural community, and a network of self-help projects (rape crisis centers, battered women's shelters, women's health clinics, etc.).

How and why did this happen? Like other left social movements, feminism had to contend with the institutional and ideological power of American liberalism, which succeeded in marginalizing radical feminists while channeling the aspirations they aroused into demands for reform on the one hand, a cult of the individual "liberated woman" on the other. In addition, radical feminism had surfaced only a short time before the expansive prosperity and utopian optimism of the 60s succumbed to an era of economic limits and political backlash. The conservative retrenchment of the 70s had a critical negative impact, not only in strengthening political resistance to feminist demands but in constricting women's personal choices, making rebellion of any sort more difficult and risky, and undermining faith in the movement's more radical possibilities. Yet these external pressures, heavy as they were, do not wholly explain why radical feminism fell apart so easily and thoroughly. Contradictions within the movement, problems with its basic assumptions, played a crucial role.

I joined New York Radical Women, the first women's liberation group in New York City, in 1968, about a year after it had started meeting. By that time the group was deeply divided over what came to be called (by radical feminists) the "politico-feminist split." The "politicos'" primary commitment was to the new left. They saw capitalism as the source of women's oppression: the ruling class indoctrinated us with oppressive sex roles to promote consumerism and/or keep women a cheap reserve labor force and/or divide the workers; conventional masculine and feminine attitudes were matters of bourgeois conditioning from which we must all liberate ourselves. I sided with the "feminists," who at some point began calling themselves "radical feminists." We argued that male supremacy was in itself a systemic form of domination—a set of material, institutionalized relations, not just bad attitudes. Men had power and privilege and like any other ruling class would defend their interests; challenging that power required a revolutionary movement of women. And since the male-dominated left would inevitably resist understanding or opposing male power, the radical feminist movement must be autonomous, create its own theory and set its own priorities. Our model of course was black power—a number of the early radical feminists had been civil rights activists.

Though new leftists immediately accused the radical feminists of being bourgeois and antileft, in fact nearly all of us considered ourselves leftists of one kind or another—socialists, anarchists, pacifists, new leftists of various stripes. When I joined women's liberation I had no ongoing, organizational ties with the left and my politics were a somewhat confused blend of cultural radicalism, populism and Marxism, but I certainly thought of myself as a leftist. With few exceptions, those of us who first defined radical feminism took for granted that "radical" implied antiracist, anticapitalist, and anti-imperialist. We saw ourselves as radicalizing the left by expanding the definition of radical to include feminism. In accordance with that definition, we agreed that until the left embraced feminism, our movement should not work with leftist men or male-dominated left groups, except perhaps for ad hoc coalitions. Some feminists argued that it was also against women's interests to join left groups as individuals; others continued to work with men on various left issues and projects. Either way, we assumed that building an autonomous radical feminist power base would further the struggle for sexual equality in mixed left organizations, just as in other arenas. We took for granted the need for a radical, feminist left.

What we didn't do—at least not in any systematic way—was tackle the question of how to integrate a feminist perspective with an overall radical politics. At that stage of the movement it would have been premature. Our overriding priority was to argue, against pervasive resistance, that male-female relations were indeed a valid political issue, and to begin describing, analyzing and challenging those relations. We were really on uncharted territory, and trying to explore that territory while under very heavy pressure from the left and from the "politicos" in the w.l.m. to subordinate feminist questions to traditional leftist concerns. It's hard to convey to people who didn't go through that experience how radical, how unpopular and difficult and scary it was just to get up and say, "Men oppress women. Men have oppressed *me*. Men must take responsibility for their actions instead of blaming them on capitalism. And yes, that means *you*." We were laughed at, patronized, called frigid, emotionally disturbed man-haters and—worst insult of all on the left!—apolitical.

In retrospect I see that we were faced with an insoluble contradiction. To build a women's liberation movement we had to take male supremacy out of the context of social domination in general. Yet from the very beginning we ran into problems of theory and strategy that could only be resolved within a larger context. Radical feminists professed a radical skepticism toward existing political theories, directed as they were toward the study of "man," and emphasized "consciousness-raising"—the process of sharing and analyzing our own experience in a group—as the primary method of understanding women's condition. This process, so often misunderstood and disparaged as a form of therapy, uncovered an enormous amount of information about women's lives and insights into women's oppression, and was the movement's most successful organizing tool. Yet the emphasis on personal experience tended to obscure and mystify the fact that we all interpreted our experience through the filter of prior political and philosophical assumptions. (For that matter, the idea of basing one's theory on shared personal experience came from the Chinese revolution's "Speak pains to recall pains" via the black movement's "Tell it like it is.")

Many debates on feminist issues were really debates about differing overall world views. For example, when a group of radical feminists did consciousness-raising on sex, we discovered that most of the women who testified preferred monogamous relationships, and that pressure for more sexual freedom came mostly from men (at that point, heterosexuality was a more or less unchallenged assumption). There were a lot of arguments about how to interpret that material (did it represent these women's true desires, their objective interest given a sexist culture, or the psychology of the oppressed) and what to make of the minority who disagreed (was the difference in their situation or their emotional makeup, did they have false consciousness, or what). And to a large extent the differing positions that emerged depended on whether one viewed sexuality from a psychoanalytical perspective (my own ideas were very much influenced by Wilhelm Reich), a behaviorist perspective, a Simone de Beauvoirist existential humanist perspective, or an orthodox Marxist rejection of psychological categories as unmaterialist. Despite its oppositional stance toward the existing left, radical feminism was deeply influenced by Marxism. While many w.l.m. "politicos" tried to fit women's liberation into pre-existing Marxist categories, radical feminists appropriated certain Marxist ideas and assumptions (specifically, concepts of class interest, class struggle, and materialism) and applied them to male-female relations. Maoism, especially, was instrumental in shaping radical feminist ideas about the nature of power and oppression.

Though radical feminists did not deny being influenced by the ideas of other radical movements (on the contrary, we often pointed to those continuities as evidence of our own revolutionary commitment), we acted as if it were somehow possible for women to separate their ideas about feminism from their ideas about everything else. There was an unarticulated assumption that we could work out our differences solely within a feminist framework and ignore or agree to disagree on other political issues. Again, I think that assumption was necessary, in order to create a feminist framework to begin with, but it made for a very fragile kind of solidarity—and it also excluded large groups of women. The question of why the radical feminist movement was overwhelmingly white and mostly middle class is complex, but one reason is surely that most black and working-class women could not accept the abstraction of feminist issues from race and class issues, since the latter were so central to their lives.

At the same time, the narrowness of the movement's demographic base limited the value of generalizations about women and men based on feminists' personal experience. So another of the problems in interpreting data gleaned from consciousness-raising was, to what extent did it reveal patterns of male-female relations in general, and to what extent did it reflect the situation of women in particular social groups?

I don't want to be misunderstood—I think consciousness-raising did reveal a lot about male-female relations in general. In basic ways women's subordination crosses class, racial and cultural lines and it was a strength of radical feminism to insist on that reality. (We also insisted, rightly in my opinion, that male dominance had to be understood as a transhistorical phenomenon, though we didn't use that language. In effect we challenged historicism as an adequate conceptual framework for understanding politics—a challenge that's since arisen in other quarters.) I'll go further and claim that in accumulating detailed information about the interaction of men and women on a day-to-day level, the consciousness-raising process contributed important insights into the nature of power relations in general—not only sexism.

Still, our lack of attention to social differences among women did limit and distort both our analysis and our practice, and it's hard to see how that could have been avoided without reference to a politics about other forms of social domination. When the minority of radical feminists who were working class or from working-class backgrounds began to challenge class bias within the movement, the same problem arose: the movement had no agreed-on politics of class that we could refer to, beyond the assumption that class hierarchy was oppressive. And again the dilemma was that to turn our attention to building such a politics would conflict with the imperatives of the specifically feminist project that had just barely begun.

Very early in the game radical feminists tried to make an end run around this problem by advancing the thesis that women's oppression was not only the oldest and most universal form of domination but the primary form. We argued that other kinds of hierarchy grew out of and were modeled on male supremacy—were in effect specialized forms of male supremacy. This idea has a surface logic, given that all the hierarchical systems we know about have been ruled and shaped by men. But it's a false logic, I think, because it assumes that men in creating and maintaining these systems are acting purely *as men*, in accordance with peculiarly male characteristics or specifically male supremacist objectives. It implicitly denies that the impulse to dominate, or to use a more materialist formulation, an authoritarian response to certain conditions of life, could be a universal human characteristic that women share, even if they have mostly lacked the opportunity to exercise it. It's a logic that excludes women from history not only practically but ontologically, and it leads to an unrealistic view of women as a more or less undifferentiated underclass with no real stake in the power struggles of class, race, and so on that go on among groups of men.

This notion of women's oppression as the primary oppression was very appealing for several reasons. It was a way of countering the left's insistence that class oppression was primary and women's liberation at best a subsidiary struggle—we could claim that on the contrary, all previous revolutions were mere reformist preludes to the real thing. It allowed white middle-class women to minimize the ways in which women participated in and benefited from race and class privilege. Most important, I think, it seemed to offer a resolution to the contradiction I've been talking about: it held out the possibility that a feminist theory could also be a general theory of social transformation. For all these reasons I fairly uncritically bought this thesis—helped to sell it, in fact.

By 1969, radical feminists were beginning to meet in their own small groups. The first group to publicly espouse a radical feminist line was Redstockings, a spinoff from New York Radical Women, which Shulamith Firestone and I started early in 1969. Shortly after that, the October 17th Movement, a radical split-off from NOW led by Ti-Grace Atkinson, changed its name to The Feminists and proclaimed itself a radical feminist organization. These groups, which were both very influential in the movement, developed distinctive and opposing political stances.

Redstockings' dominant political tendency was a kind of neo-Maoist materialism. In addition to the belief in personal experience as the bedrock of feminist theory, this perspective was grounded in two basic principles. One was a view of sexual class struggle as the direct exercise of power by men, acting in their economic, social and sexual self-interest, over women. In this view institutions were merely tools of the oppressor and had no political significance in and of themselves. The idea that systems (like the family or capitalism) are in some sense autonomous, that they operate according to a logic that in certain ways constrains the rulers as well as the ruled, was rejected as a mystification and a way of letting men off the hook. To say, for instance, that the family oppressed women was to evade the fact that our husbands and fathers oppressed us; to say that men's sexist behavior was in any way dictated by social or familial norms was to deny that men oppressed women by choice, out of self-interest. The other principle was that women's behavior was always and only a rational, self-interested response to their immediate material conditions, i.e. their oppression by men. When women appeared to consent to their oppression, it was because they saw that individual resistance would not get them what they wanted, but only invite the oppressor's anger and punishment. As we built a movement capable of winning real change, more and more women would feel free to speak up and act collectively in their own behalf. The "pro-woman line," as this position was called, was absolutely antipsychological. It rejected as misogynist psychological explanations for feminine submissiveness or passivity, since they implied that women collaborated in or were responsible for their oppression. Psychological explanations of men's behavior were regarded as yet another way to avoid blaming men for male supremacy.

The most articulate and systematic exponents of these ideas were Kathie Sarachild and Carol Hanisch, both former SNCC activists and founding members of New York Radical Women, Irene Peslikis, who wrote the classic article "Resistances to Consciousness," and Pat Mainardi, author of "The Politics of Housework." I did not fully share these politics—I believed in the importance of the unconscious and thought the pro-woman line was simplistic—but I was profoundly influenced by them. They were quite effective in challenging my tendencies to over-psychologize everything when social explanations were staring me in the face, and to avoid confronting my painful personal relations with men by making abstract arguments about the system. The genius of the Redstockings brand of radical feminist materialism was its concreteness. It demanded that women examine their everyday lives and face the most immediate and direct sources of their pain and anger. For women who responded to that demand, the confrontations inspired a powerful and urgent desire to change things. Activism became a personal emotional necessity—always a more effective spur to organizing than abstract principle or moral sentiment—with specific and immediate as well as long-range goals. As a result the materialist version of radical feminism had by far the most impact on the larger society, in terms of changing women's view of themselves and the world and inspiring both individual rebellion and collective political action.

But the reductionism of the Redstockings line led to basic miscalculations. For one thing, it underestimated the difficulty of change. If, for instance, resistance to feminism or outright antifeminism among women comes solely from rational fears of the consequences of challenging male authority, then the way to combat it is simply to build a movement and convince women that sisterhood really is powerful—that organized and unified we can win. But suppose in addition to the rational fears and hopes, women suffer from deep unconscious convictions of their own powerlessness and worthlessness and the unlimited power of men? Suppose they unconsciously equate being a "good woman" in men's terms not only with survival but with redemption from utter degradation? If that's true, then the successes of a feminist movement may actually intensify women's fears along with their hopes, and provoke unbearable emotional conflict. And that can lead not only to various forms of female antifeminist backlash, but to feminists managing in various ways to sabotage their own movement—even to redefine feminism so that it embraces and glorifies traditional feminine values. Both these things have in fact happened, and are continuing to happen, and it's impossible to understand these developments or confront them politically without a psychological critique. I won't belabor the parallels with the overoptimism of classical Marxism and its inability to explain why large numbers of European workers supported fascism.

Similarly, the dismissal of institutions as "mere tools" was an obstacle to understanding how change takes place, or fails to. It became an excuse not to really study the institutions that affect women, especially the family. From Redstockings' perspective, the problem with the family was simply male supremacy: women were subordinated within marriage and at the same time forced to marry for economic security and social legitimacy; we were assigned the care of children, but denied control of our fertility. Left criticism of the family per se was dismissed as men's resistance to committing themselves to women and children, emotionally and financially.

This analysis was superficial. To begin with it ignored the way the fundamental premise of the family system—the definition of a man, a woman and their biological children as the basic social unit, with the corresponding assumption that the community as a whole has little if any responsibility for children—automatically puts women in an unequal position. Maternity is obvious; paternity must be acknowledged or proved in some formal way. So women in a familialist system need marriage to establish the father's social obligation to his children, and this in itself gives men power to set the terms of the marriage contract. When women seek to change those terms without challenging the family system itself, they run into a double bind. Women's demands for equality in the home come up against male resistance, and if they press their demands "too far," the probable result is not an equal marriage, but no marriage at all. (This is not abstract speculation; conflict over equality is clearly an element in today's high divorce rate.) Of course, the demands would not be possible in the first place if women had not already won enough economic and sexual independence to survive outside marriage. But for a women in a familialist society the price of freedom to live independently is all too likely to be "freedom" to support and rear children alone or be unwillingly childless. Furthermore, the economic inequality rooted in the patriarchal family system actually worsens as women are denied access to men's incomes and single motherhood itself becomes a barrier to economic advancement.

In short, feminism inevitably destabilizes the family, and so long as the family remains an unquestioned given of social relations, women are trapped into choosing between subordination and abandonment. This is the specter haunting contemporary sexual politics, as antifeminist women desperately try to restore the traditional bargain and feminists as desperately try to have it both ways. There's no way to understand, let alone resolve, this dilemma without an institutional analysis. The problem with our system of child rearing, which is absolutely basic to the oppression of women, is not only sexism but familialism—the equation of biological and social parenthood. Unless it's understood that way, the best we'll ever get is a jerry-built system of day-care centers designed to allow women to keep their shit jobs, and here and there the inspiring example of a "nurturing father" who expects the Medal of Honor for doing what mothers have always done.

But again, if it's impossible to understand women's condition without making a real critique of the family as an institution, the radical feminist strategy of isolating male supremacy from other forms of domination breaks down. The family has more than one political dimension: besides subordinating women, it's also a vehicle for getting children of both sexes to submit to social authority and actively embrace the values of the dominant culture. Among other things that means enlisting both women and men to uphold the family system and its sexual morality, in which sex for its own sake is bad and dangerous and must be subordinated to the "higher" purposes of heterosexual monogamous marriage and procreation. True, men have always had more license to be "bad" than women and have even been *required* to be "bad" to prove their manhood. But all this means is that men experience a conflict between their sexual desire and identity and their "higher" nature—not, as radical feminists have tended to assume, that men are free of sexual guilt and repression. This conflict and its manifestations—the perception of sex and love as separate or opposed, and sex as connected with violence—are integral to the patriarchal concept of masculinity, while femininity, on the other hand, requires the suppression of "bad" desires and a romanticized, spiritualized eroticism.

The sexual revolution loosened the grip of conservative sexual morality but did not basically change its psychic underpinnings. We all to some degree internalize familialist sexual ideology in its feminine or masculine version. To the extent that any of us rejects it, we are rejecting being a woman or a man as the culture defines it and defining ourselves as social, sexual deviants, with all the consequences that entails. We are all oppressed by having this ideology imposed on us, though some groups are particularly oppressed—women, youth, homosexuals and other sexual minorities. So there is a political fault line in the society dividing people who are in one way or another defending this ideology (and the practices that go with it) from people who are in one way or another rebelling against it. This line cuts across gender, and like class or racial difference creates real divisions among women that can't simply be subsumed in an antisexist politics. It also defies analysis strictly in terms of the "self-interest" of one class of people oppressing another. Ultimately the interest of sexual conservatives in suppressing sexual dissidence is their interest in obliterating possibilities they themselves have painfully relinquished. This interest is so powerful that there are few sexual dissidents—and I would call feminists and unapologetic gays dissidents by definition—who are not also conservative in some ways.

While ignoring all these complications, Redstockings' vision of direct confrontation between sexual classes put an enormous premium on unity among women. The idea was that if all women supported each other in demanding equality—if there were no women willing to "scab"—then men would have no choice but to accept the new order. This was the model of struggle put forward in *Fanshen,* William Hinton's account of revolution in a Chinese village, which circulated widely in the movement. It was inspiring reading, but America is not a Chinese village; Hinton's cast of characters, at least as he presented it, was divided by class, sex and age, but not by multiple ethnic and cultural antagonisms.[2] For all the reasons I've been laying out, I don't see universal sisterhood as a practical possibility. Fortunately, men are hardly a monolith—they are deeply divided along various social and political axes, disagree with each other on what "male self-interest" is, and don't necessarily support each other in the face of feminist demands. Feminist struggle will never be a matter of women as a united class confronting men as a united class, but rather of particular groups of women pressing on vulnerable points in the structure of male supremacy and taking advantage of divisions among men. Direct personal pressure on men to change their behavior will be more feasible in some communities than in others. Most early radical feminists operated in a social milieu that was middle-class, educated, culturally liberal and politically leftist. A degree of economic opportunity, access to birth control, and the decline of rigidly familialist mores—along with the fact that most of us were young and as yet uninterested in having children—allowed us a certain amount of independence, therefore power, in dealing with "our" men, and we were also in a position to appeal to their proclaimed belief in democracy and equality.

Even under the best conditions, though, direct confrontation has built-in limits, because it requires a level of day-to-day militance that's impossible to sustain over the long haul. After a while even the most passionate feminists get tired, especially when they see how slow the progress is. As soon as they ease the pressure, men take advantage of it and start a backlash, which then touches off a backlash by *women* who feel they've struggled too hard for not enough result. That's part of the story of the 70s. I'm not saying that personally confronting men is not worth doing, or that our doing it hasn't had lasting effects, because it has. But I think it is basically a minority tactic, and one that flourishes in the exceptional moment, rather than *the* model of revolutionary struggle.

When applied beyond the realm of direct personal combat to feminist demands for changes in public policy, the pure class struggle paradigm becomes much more problematic. These demands operate on two levels. They are aimed at men as a group in that they attack the sexist assumptions embedded in social and economic institutions. But they are also aimed more specifically at men (and the occasional woman) with institutional power—corporate, legal, medical, religious or whatever—who by virtue of their positions represent other interests and ideological commitments besides male privilege. Such interests and commitments may have priority over sexist imperatives or even conflict with them. Thus the alliances and oppositions that form around feminist demands are rarely based strictly on gender or sexual class interest.

For instance, although legal abortion reduces women's subordination and dependence on men, men as a class have not closed ranks against it. Rather, the active political opposition has come from sexually conservative familialists of both sexes (most but not all of whom are opposed to feminism across the board). Many men have supported legal abortion on civil liberties or sexual libertarian grounds. Others have supported it on racist grounds, as an antiwelfare or population control measure. Male politicians have more often than not based their position on abortion on one simple criterion: what would get them reelected. The medical establishment supports freedom for doctors to perform abortions while opposing feminist demands that paramedicals be allowed to perform them. And so on. Most men have at worst been indifferent to or ambivalent about the abortion issue; most women, on the other hand, *have* seen abortion rights as in their female self-interest. Without this asymmetry, it is doubtful that feminists could have won legal abortion or kept it in the face of heavy pressure from the right. As it is, our biggest defeat on this issue, the ban on Medicaid funds for abortion, has clearly involved other factors besides sexism. The new right took advantage of middle-class women's apathy toward the poor, while mobilizing antiwelfare sentiment among people outside the hard-core familialist antiabortion constituency. Often a combination of racist, antipoor and sexist feelings motivated men to opposition in a way sexism alone had not ("Let those irresponsible women have their abortions, but not at my expense"). Battles over measures to combat economic discrimination against women involve similar complexities. Some men, putting economic class loyalty or opposition to corporate power or commitment to economic equality above their specifically male self-interest, support such measures (especially if they hope to get feminist support for their economic agenda); some women oppose them, whether on familialist grounds or because of *their* economic class loyalty and/or ideological belief in a free market economy.

I use examples of struggles for reform because feminists have never yet been in a position to make an active fight for basic structural changes in institutions. Such a fight would be impossible for a feminist movement alone; to envision it presupposes the existence of a left capable of attacking state and corporate power. And in that context, the configuration of alliances and oppositions across gender lines would if anything be much more complicated than it is now.

The Feminists agreed with Redstockings that male domination was the primary oppression and that women and men were political classes. Beyond that the groups diverged. For one thing, The Feminists used the terms "sex role" and "sex class" interchangeably—they identified sexism with particular, complementary patterns of male and female behavior. Redstockings' view of sex roles, like its view of institutions, was that they reflected male power, but were not primary political categories. The Feminists' conflation of role and class provided a basis for rejecting the pro-woman line: if the female role, per se, defined women's oppression, then conforming to the role was upholding the oppression. The Feminists' attitude toward institutions was even more reductive than Redstockings', in the opposite direction. While Redstockings assumed that the sexist dimension of an institution could somehow be abstracted from the institution itself, The Feminists assumed that the primary institutions of women's oppression—which they identified as marriage and the family, prostitution, and heterosexuality—were entirely defined by sexism, that their sole purpose was to perpetuate the "sex-role system." Therefore, radical feminists must destroy them. (The Feminists had a penchant for words like "destroy" and "annihilate.") The Feminists also rejected consciousness-raising in favor of abstract theorizing, but never clearly laid out the philosophical or epistemological basis of their ideas.

For all the limitations of Redstockings' materialism, we at least knew that we had to base a feminist program on women's actual lives and feelings, and that the important thing was to understand women's behavior, not judge it from some utopian moral standpoint. The Feminists were idealist, voluntarist and moralistic in the extreme. They totally disregarded what other women said they wanted or felt, and their idea of organizing was to exhort women to stop submitting to oppression by being subservient or participating in sexist institutions like marriage. Once at an abortion demonstration in front of a legislative committee I had a huge argument with a member of the group who was yelling at the committee's female secretaries and clerks that they were traitors for not walking out on their jobs and joining us. The Feminists were the first radical feminist group to suggest that living or sleeping with men was collaborating with the system. They shocked the rest of the movement by making a rule that no more than a third of their membership could be married or living with a man.

The Feminists, and in particular their best-known theorist, Ti-Grace Atkinson, also developed a set of ideas about sex that will be familiar to anyone who has followed current movement debates. The first radical feminist to talk about heterosexual intercourse as an institution was probably Anne Koedt, a member of New York Radical Women who later joined The Feminists, in her essay "The Myth of the Vaginal Orgasm." Koedt was careful to distinguish between intercourse as an option and as an institutionalized practice defined as synonymous with "normal" sex. She also assumed that the point of sex was pleasure, the point of institutionalized intercourse was male pleasure, and the point of challenging that construct was equal pleasure and orgasm for women. Atkinson wrote an article elaborating on this idea of "the institution of sexual intercourse," but took it in a different direction. As she saw it the purpose of the institution was getting women to reproduce and the concept of sexual need or drive was mere ideology. What erotic pleasure was or whether it existed was unclear, especially in the present social context. In fact, heterosexual intercourse was so thoroughly corrupted by the sex-role system that it was hard to imagine a future for it even as an optional practice.

The Feminists' organizing manifesto condemned the institution of heterosexual sex very much in Atkinson's terms, and added that since sex was part of the marriage contract, marriage meant legalized rape. It also included the statement—tucked in inconspicuously, so it seemed a lot less significant than it does in retrospect—that in the context of freedom, physical relations between individuals of whatever sex would not necessarily emphasize genital contact. The implication was that any special interest in or desire for genital sex, heterosexual or otherwise, was a function of sexism. This was a mental leap that seems to me clearly grounded in unconscious acceptance of a traditional patriarchal assumption, namely that lust is male.

The Feminists' perspective on sex was a minority view within radical feminism, considered provocative but out on some weird edge. The predominant attitudes in Redstockings were more typical: we took for granted women's desire for genital sexual pleasure (the importance of fucking to that pleasure was a matter of debate) and focused our critique on the ways men repressed and frustrated women sexually. Though we theoretically defended women's right to be lesbian or celibate, there was a strong heterosexual presumption underlying Redstockings politics. It was tacitly assumed, and sometimes explicitly argued, that men's need for sexual love from women was our biggest weapon in both individual and collective struggle—and that our own need for *satisfying* sexual love from men was our greatest incentive for maintaining the kind of personal confrontation feminism required. We rejected sexual separatism as a political strategy, on materialist grounds—that simply refusing to be with men was impractical and unappealing for most women, and in itself did nothing to challenge male power. But beyond that we didn't really take it seriously as a personal choice, let alone an expression of militance. On the contrary, we thought of living without men as the bitter price we might have to pay for our militance in demanding equal relationships. Tension over these issues, among others, led an alienated minority to quit Redstockings and join The Feminists.

At that point lesbianism per se had not yet emerged as an issue, but there were pitfalls for lesbians in both groups' ideas. If you accepted Redstockings' assumption that the struggle for equality in heterosexual relationships was the nerve center of radical feminism, lesbians were by definition marginal to the movement. The Feminists offered a much more attractive prospect—by their logic lesbians were, simply by virtue of rejecting sexual relationships with men, a liberated vanguard. But there was a catch: the vanguard role was available only to lesbians willing to ignore or play down the element of sexual desire in their lesbian identity. As Alice Echols has pointed out, the convergence of homophobic and antisexual pressures from the movement eventually impelled the majority of lesbian feminists to accept this tradeoff and sanitize lesbianism by defining it as a political choice rather than an erotic one.[3] To complicate matters, many of the feminists who "converted" to lesbianism in the wake of lesbian separatism did so not to express a compelling sexual inclination but to embrace a political and cultural identity; some of these converts denied that lesbianism was in any sense a sexual definition, and equated their rejection of compulsory heterosexuality with "liberation" from sex itself, at least insofar as it was "genitally oriented." In this atmosphere, lesbians who see freedom to express their unconventional sexuality as an integral part of their feminism have had reason to wonder if the label "male identifier" is any improvement over "pervert."

Toward the end of 1969, Shulie Firestone and Anne Koedt started a third group, New York Radical Feminists, which rejected both the pro-woman line and The Feminists' arrogant vanguardism. Two of the group's theoretical principles have been important in the later history of the movement. One has to do with the meaning of male power. Most radical feminists assumed men wanted dominance for the sake of material benefits—by which they meant not only the economic, in the broad sense, benefits of the sexual division of labor, but the psychic benefits of having one's emotional needs catered to without any obligation to reciprocate. NYRF proposed in essence that men wanted to exercise power for its own sake—that it was intrinsically satisfying to the ego to dominate others. According to their formulation men do not defend their power in order to get services from women, but demand services from women in order to affirm their sense of power. The group's other important proposition was its entry in the ongoing debate about why women submit to their oppression. While Redstockings' answer was necessity and The Feminists' implicit answer was cowardice, NYRF insisted that feminine behavior was both enforced and internalized: women were trained from birth both to conform to the feminine role and to accept it as right and natural. This pass at an analysis of male and female behavior was incoherent, implicitly biologistic, and sexist. Besides suggesting that men, by virtue of their maleness, had an inherent predilection for power, NYRF's formulation gave men credit for being active agents while implicitly defining women as passive recipients of social indoctrination. The social-learning model, applied to women, also posed the same problem as all behaviorist psychologies—it could not account for resistance to the system. Inevitably it implied its antinomy, moral voluntarism, since the very existence of a feminist movement meant that some women had in some sense transcended their conditioning.

All the disparate versions of radical feminist analysis shared two basic weaknesses that contributed to the movement's demise. First, commitment to the sex-class paradigm pinned women's hopes for radical change on a millennial unity of women across barriers of class, race, cultural values and sexual orientation. The gap between what radical feminism promised and what it could deliver without a more complex, multivalent theory and strategy was immense. That gap was all too soon filled by attempts at individual liberation through "overcoming female conditioning," fantasies of benevolent matriarchies, the equation of woman-bonding, an alternative women's community and/or a "politically correct lifestyle" with feminism, and moralizing about the iniquity of men and "male values." Underlying these individualist and countercultural revisions of radical feminism was an unadmitted despair of real change. That despair is expressed more overtly in the work of cultural feminist theorists like Andrea Dworkin, who has reified the sex-class paradigm, defining it as a closed system in which the power imbalance between men and women is absolute and all-pervasive. Since the system has no discontinuities or contradictions, there is no possibility of successful struggle against it—at best there can be moral resistance.

The movement's second major weakness was its failure to develop a coherent analysis of either male or female psychology—a failure so total that to me it indicates a willed ignorance rooted in terror. While there was a dissenting minority, radical feminists as a group were dogmatically hostile to Freud and psychoanalysis, and psychoanalytic thought—especially its concept of the unconscious and its emphasis on the role of sexual desire in human motivation—had almost no impact on radical feminist theory. Since I agree with Juliet Mitchell that psychoanalysis is not a defense of patriarchal culture but an analysis of it—though I don't subscribe to her Lacanian interpretation of Freud—I think radical feminists' closed-mindedness on the subject was an intellectual and political disaster.

As I've discussed elsewhere, I basically agree with Freud's model of how children develop a masculine or feminine psychology in response to parental suppression and channeling of infantile sexuality.[4] Of course, as a radical I also believe that the social context in which this takes place is subject to change: male superiority is not a biological fact, and the patriarchal family and sexual repression are not prerequisites of civilization. But Freud's sexism and pessimism are not sufficient to explain why most radical feminists were so blind to his subversive insights, while they had no comparable qualms about selectively criticizing and appropriating other male theorists, Marx, for instance. I believe—and I know this is the kind of circular argument that drives anti-Freudians crazy—that the movement's violent rejection of psychoanalysis was in part a response to its hitting too close to home. At a time when feminism itself was tearing off layers of protective skin and focusing our attention on feelings we'd spent our lives suppressing, it was not surprising that women should resist any further attack on their defenses. To analyze women's behavior psychoanalytically was to risk unmasking all our secret strategies for coping with the traumatic linking of our sexual organs to our class inferiority, and with the resulting unconscious feelings of irrevocable violation, shame, global terror and dangerous rage. And those cherished strategies would not necessarily pass political muster, since — if you accept Freud's basic assumptions—it's precisely through women's attempt to manage their unconscious conflicts that femininity is reproduced. For instance, one typical feminine strategy is to compensate for the humiliation of sexual "inferiority" with self-righteous moralism and asceticism. Whether this is rationalized as religious virtue or feminist militance, the result is to reinforce patriarchal values. As I see it, a psychoanalytic perspective is crucial to understanding and challenging such self-defeating tendencies in feminist politics, and for that reason it is anathema to feminists who confuse the interests of women with their own unconscious agenda.

Redstockings did not succeed in defining psychology as a nonissue. Most radical feminists recognized that there were aspects of male and female feelings and behavior that eluded pragmatic, common-sense explanation. But their attempts to acknowledge the psychological dimension have been fragmented and muddled. In general, the inheritors of the radical feminist movement have followed the path of New York Radical Feminists and endorsed some version of behaviorism, biological determinism, or an ad hoc, contradictory mêlange of both. Given the history of biologism as the enemy's weapon, most feminists who draw on it prefer to pretend it's something else, and behaviorist terminology can be useful for this purpose. The present "radical feminist" antipornography movement provides a good example. It claims that pornography conditions men to sexual sadism, which is the foundation and primary expression of their power over women, and conditions women to accept their victimization. But if you examine the argument closely, it doesn't hang together. If men have the power, create the pornography, and define the values it embodies, conditioning might perhaps explain how some men transmit a sadistic mentality to others, but not how or why that mentality arose in the first place. And in fact it is clear from the rest of their rhetoric that antiporn theorists equate male sexuality, per se, with sadism. As for women, the antipornography movement explicitly defines authentic female sexuality as tender, romantic, and nongenitally oriented, despite the suspicious resemblance of this description to the patriarchal stereotype of the good woman. It is only women who disagree with this view of their sexuality who are proclaimed to be victims of male-supremacist conditioning. (How antiporn activists have managed to avoid being conditioned is not explained.) In this case, the language of behaviorism serves not only to deflect charges of biologism, but to inflate the importance of pornography as a target and dismiss political opponents.

The disintegration of radical feminism took several forms. First of all radical feminist ideas caught the attention of large numbers of women, especially educated, upper-middle-class women, who had no radical perspective on other matters and often were uninterested in, if not actively hostile to, left politics as such. These women experienced sexual inequality in their own lives, and radical feminism raised their consciousness. But their awareness of their oppression as women did not make them radicals in the sense of being committed to overall social transformation, as the early radical feminists had naively assumed it would. Instead they seized on the idea of women's oppression as the primary oppression and took it to mean not that feminism was or should be inclusive of other struggles, but that left politics were "male" and could be safely ignored.

This idea became a prominent theme of cultural feminism. It also led to the development of a new kind of liberal feminism. Many women reacted to radical feminism with an intense desire to change their lives, or the social arrangements that immediately affected them, but had no intention of supporting changes that would threaten their (or their husbands') economic and social class status. Many of the same women were reluctant to explicitly attack male power—not only because of the personal consequences of militance, but because the whole subject of power is uncomfortable for people who are basically committed to the existing socioeconomic order. The result was a brand of politics best exemplified by *Ms.* magazine, which began publishing in 1972. The traditional reformism of organizations like NOW was economistic and hostile to the "personal" sexual and emotional issues radical feminists were raising. *Ms.* and the new liberals embraced those issues, but basically ignored the existence of power relations. Though they supported feminist reforms, their main strategy for changing women's lives was individual and collective self-improvement. They were partial to the argument that men and women are fellow victims of sex-role conditioning. But where the "politicos" in the early movement had blamed this conditioning on capitalism, the liberals blamed it vaguely on "society," or the media, or the schools, ignoring the question of who runs these institutions and on whose behalf. In terms of their political ethos and constituency, the difference between the *Ms.*-ites and NOW was roughly analogous to the difference between the McGovern and Humphrey wings of the Democratic Party, and *Ms.* was to radical feminism what the "new politics" Democrats were to the new left.

On one level *Ms.*-ism and cultural feminist anti-leftism were the inevitable and predictable distortions of a radical movement that reaches far beyond its founders. They were testimony to people's desire to have it both ways—to fight their oppression while holding on to their privileges—as well as their tendency to take refuge in simple if illusory solutions. But the specific forms the distortions took were inspired by the idea of sex as the primary division and reflected the inadequacy of the sex-class paradigm as the basis for a radical movement. Although the early radical feminists were appalled by these uses of our ideas, we can't avoid some responsibility for them.

Within the radical feminist movement itself, the original momentum almost immediately began giving way to a bitter, immobilizing factionalism. The first issue to create permanent rifts was equality in the movement. Partly out of rebellion against hierarchical structures (especially in the new left), partly because consciousness-raising required informality, radical feminists, like the w.l.m. as a whole, had chosen the putatively structureless small group as their main form of organization. Yet every group had developed an informal leadership, a core of women—I was part of that core in Redstockings—who had the most to do with setting and articulating the direction of the group. Women who felt excluded from equal participation challenged not only the existing leaders but the concept of leadership as a holdover from male-dominated organizations. Debates about group process, the oppressive behavior of some members toward others, and leaders' alleged exploitation of the movement for personal ends began to dominate meetings, to the exclusion of any engagement with sexism in the outside world.

The problems of elitism, class bias, differences in power within the movement, and opportunism were certainly real—they were much the same kinds of problems that had surfaced elsewhere on the left—but by and large the attempts to confront them were ineffective and in the long run disastrous. Obviously, there are inherent difficulties in trying to build a democratic movement. You can't create a perfect society in microcosm while the larger society remains the same, and you can't change the larger society if you spend all your time and energy trying to create a utopian microcosm. The goal should be to strike a balance—work on finding ways to extend skills, experience and confidence to everyone, but at the same time encourage people who already have these assets to use them for the movement's benefit, provided they are accountable for *how* they use them in the movement's name. What makes this so difficult is not only the leaders' desire for personal power or their resistance to being held accountable and sharing their skills, but the rage of those who find themselves at the bottom of yet another hierarchy. They tend to want instant redress, and since there's no way to instantly create a situation where everyone has equal power—because the differences come from years of differential opportunities—some people resort to the pseudo-solution of demanding that those who have the skills or other forms of social power not use them, either for the movement or for themselves. Which is a dead end in terms of creating an effective movement, as well as an unreasonable demand on individuals trying to live their lives within the present social system.

These issues come up in all egalitarian movements, but the premises of radical feminism made them especially intense. The assumption that women's oppression is primary, and that the differences among women can be worked out entirely within an antisexist context, shaped the movement's predominant view of women and class: that a woman's position in the class hierarchy derived solely from the men she was attached to, that women could oppress other women by virtue of their class status but not men, that class conflict among women was a product of false consciousness, and that any form of class striving or power-mongering was therefore "male-identified" behavior. For some women this category extended to any form of individual achievement, intellectual activity, articulateness or self-assertion, the assumption being that these could only derive from some unholy connection with male power. The implicit corollary was that traditionally feminine behavior was the only truly sisterly behavior. These ideas too became staples of cultural feminism. Of course, many radical feminists disagreed and pointed out that charges of pushiness and overachieving were always used by dominant groups to keep oppressed groups in their place. But since the dissenters were operating out of the same basic framework as their adversaries, they tended to adopt some version of the mirror-image position that since women's common interest transcended class differences, this democracy in the movement business must be a sexist plot to cut down feminist leadership and keep the movement weak.

Though this idea was literally absurd, there was a grain of emotional truth in it. Much of the opposition to elitism took the form of unworkable, mechanistic demands for an absolutely random division of labor, taking no account of differences in skill, experience or even inclination. (As usual, The Feminists carried this tendency the furthest, instituting a strict lot system for the distribution of all tasks. When the group decided that no member could talk to the media unless chosen by lot, Ti-Grace Atkinson quit.) These demands were often coupled with personal attacks on individuals that were little more than outbursts of fury and *ressentiment* against any woman who seemed to have achieved some measure of autonomy, recognition or influence. Some feminist leaders reacted with defiance, some quit the movement, and others—myself included—tried to respond to the criticism by echoing it and withdrawing from our leadership roles, in classic guilty liberal fashion. With all the accusations and breast-beating, there was relatively little honest effort to deal with the concrete problems involved in creating a movement that was both egalitarian and effective. The result was not democracy but paralysis. And part of the reason, I'm convinced, was unconscious fear that feminists' demands for freedom and power would provoke devastating retribution. The movement was stripping away our protective mask of feminine compliance, and its leaders were the most visible symbol of that.

During the same period, working-class women in the movement began talking to each other about their experience with class oppression and confronting middle-class feminists. This new application of the consciousness-raising process educated feminists about the workings of the class system on the level of personal relations, but it did not significantly change class relations in the movement or help to unify women across class lines. As I've noted, there was no way within the parameters of radical feminism to connect the struggle for internal democracy with active opposition to the class system per se. This split between internal and externally oriented politics was exacerbated by a total emphasis on class as a set of oppressive personal relations. It was assumed that the strategy of challenging men's sexist behavior could be applied with equal success to challenging women's class-biased behavior. But this assumption overlooked fundamental differences in the dynamics of class and sexual politics. While the basic institutions of sexist oppression are located in personal life, a realm in which men have a great deal of personal power, the basic institutions of class oppression are located in the public world of the political economy, where middle-class people (women, especially) have little power. That does not mean there is no personal aspect to class oppression, but it does suggest that personal politics are not the cutting edge of class struggle.

For some radical feminists, however, consciousness-raising about class led to a political identity crisis. I was one of those who became convinced that women *were* implicated in the class system and had real class interests, that women could oppress men on the basis of class, and that class differences among women could not be resolved within a feminist context alone. Which meant that a feminist movement purporting to represent all women had to connect in some organic way to a workers' movement, and by extension to a black liberation movement and other movements of oppressed groups—in short, to a left. Some women reacted to this realization by going back to the existing left to promote feminism from within; some moved off in search of a socialist-feminist synthesis. My own experience left me with a lot of new questions and no answers. In the fall of 1969 I had moved to Colorado Springs to work in a G.I. organizing project, intending at the same time to start a radical feminist movement in the area. Obviously, I was already interested in somehow combining feminist and leftist organizing, less out of any abstract commitment to the idea than from the impulse to integrate different sides of my life and politics. Two radical feminists from New York, including Joyce Betries, who was working-class and had raised the class issue in Redstockings, came out to work with me, and we started a women's liberation group. Betries also began confronting the oppressive class relations between middle-class and working-class members of the project and between civilians and G.I.s. After going through this confrontation in a sexually mixed group, in which the women were also raising feminist issues, I had no doubt that the standard radical feminist line on class was wrong.

Unlike Betries, who became active in Youth Against War and Fascism, I continued to regard myself as a radical feminist. I still believed that male supremacy was a structure of domination at least as basic as class or race, and so far as I could tell neither the "male" left nor the socialist-feminists—who struck me as updated versions of 60s politicos—agreed. But I rejected the idea of the primacy of women's oppression and began reluctantly to reject the global sisterhood model of feminist revolution. I saw that the fate of feminism at any given time and place was bound up with the fate of the larger left, though I had no idea how to translate this perception into a political strategy. At this point—1971—our G.I. project had fallen apart along with the rest of the new left, radical feminism was doing the same, and the prospects for any kind of radical politics looked grim. If I felt confused and stymied, I was not alone.

The final blow to the radical feminist movement as a vital political force was the gay-straight split, which took place in the early 70s. Lesbian separatists added a crucial ingredient to existing female separatist ideology —a positive vision of community. While early separatism offered only the moral reward of revolutionary purity, lesbian feminism offered in addition the more concrete social and sexual benefits of a women's counterculture. It then defined that culture not simply as a strategy for achieving women's liberation or as a form of sustenance for its troops but as the meaning and purpose of feminism.

At a time when the enormous obstacles facing the movement were becoming apparent, this vision had an understandable appeal. And while it had particular advantages for women already committed to lesbianism (and oppressed as lesbians), it could not have been a transforming influence on the movement if it had not exerted a strong pull on the feelings of radical feminists generally. Not only did many women break with heterosexuality to join the lesbian feminist counterculture, and even more experiment with it; many feminists who remained practicing heterosexuals identified with that culture and its ideology and considered themselves failed or incomplete feminists. Others argued that sexual orientation was irrelevant; what mattered was whether a woman accepted the *values* of female culture. By this route, cultural feminism evolved into a politics that anyone could embrace, that had little to do with sexual separatism or lesbianism as a sexual practice. The "female values" cultural feminists proclaimed—either with openly biologistic arguments, as in Jane Alpert's influential article, "Mother Right," or with behaviorist window dressing—were none other than the traditional feminine virtues. Once again we were alleged to be loving, nurturing, in tune with nature, intuitive and spiritual rather than genital in our eroticism, while men were violent, predatory, alienated from nature, committed to a sterile rationalism and obsessed with genital sex. (There was some disagreement on whether men were hopeless cases or whether women could teach them female values and thereby "humanize" them.) Thus "radical feminism" came full circle, from challenging the polarization of the sexes to affirming it and embracing a reverse sexism.

Insofar as cultural feminists translated their ideas into political activism, their chief focus was male violence against women. Radical feminists had defined rape and other forms of male aggression as weapons for enforcing male dominance—for punishing "uppity" female behavior or simply reminding women who was boss. But their lack of attention to psychology had left a gap in their analysis: in discussing sexual violence as a more or less deliberate, instrumental choice, they ignored it as a sexual and emotional experience. The movement was inconsistent in its view of the relation between rape and sexuality. On the one hand it noted the continuity between rape and "normal" male sexual aggressiveness, and the resulting social tendency to rationalize rape as fun and games. Yet in reaction to this confusion, and to the related myth that men rape out of uncontrollable sexual need, the radical feminist mainstream asserted that "rape is violence, not sex"—a tidy slogan that avoided disturbing "unmaterialist" questions about the nature of male desire, the relationship of pleasure to power. And the iconoclastic Feminists, who implicitly equated heterosexuality with rape, declined to recognize sexual pleasure as a motive in either.

Cultural feminists leaped into this psychological breach, rightly (and therefore effectively) insisting on the reality of sexual violence as an erotic experience, an end in itself. Unfortunately, they proceeded to incorporate this insight into their neo-Victorian caricature of men's sexual nature and to generalize it to all patriarchal relations. New York Radical Feminists had broken with earlier radical feminist thought to argue that men wanted power for its intrinsic satisfactions, not its concomitant rewards; cultural feminists spelled out the implication of this position—that all sexist behavior is an extension of the paradigmatic act of rape. From this standpoint sexual violence was the essence and purpose of male dominance, the paradigmatic "male value," and therefore feminism's central concern.

In the late 70s, cultural feminists' emphasis shifted from actual violence against women to representation of sexual violence in the media and then to pornography. Groups like Women Against Pornography and Women Against Violence in Pornography and Media adopted pornography as the quintessential symbol of a male sexuality assumed to be inherently violent and oppressive, then made that symbol the focus of a moral crusade reminiscent of the 19th-century social purity and temperance movements. Predictably, they have aimed their attack not only at male producers and consumers of porn, but at women who refuse to define lust as male or pornography as rape and insist without apology on their own sexual desires. While continuing to call itself radical feminist—indeed, claiming that it represents the only truly feminist position—the antiporn movement has in effect collaborated with the right in pressuring women to conform to conventionally feminine attitudes.

Though there was surprisingly little resistance to the collapse of radical feminism, some movement activists did fight back. In 1973 Kathie Sarachild, Carol Hanisch, and several other women revived Redstockings, which had disbanded three years before, and in 1975 they published a journal, *Feminist Revolution. FR* was an ambitious attempt to analyze the deradicalization of the movement and contained the first major critiques of cultural feminism and *Ms.* liberalism. Its publication was an important political act, especially for those of us who felt alienated from what was passing for the radical feminist movement—or, as it was coming to be called, the "feminist community"—and were trying to make sense of what had gone wrong without the help of any ongoing group. But the journal also revealed the limitations of Redstockings politics when carried to their logical conclusions. *FR*'s critique did not contain any second thoughts about the premises of radical feminist materialism, including its rejection of psychology. On the contrary, the editors blamed the devolution of radical feminism entirely on deviations from these premises. From this unreconstructed viewpoint they could explain the deviations only as deliberate sabotage by "Agents, Opportunists, and Fools" (a section heading). One article, which provoked brief but intense controversy in the "feminist community" and eventually led Gloria Steinem to threaten a libel suit, contained a detailed account of *Ms.*'s corporate connections and Steinem's past work with the Independent

Research Service, an outfit that had received CIA funds, with Steinem's knowledge, to send students to European youth festivals. While the information provided useful commentary on *Ms.*'s and Steinem's political perspective, many of the implications drawn from it were tortuous at best, including the overall implication that Steinem's ascendancy as a feminist leader, and *Ms.* itself, were a government and/or corporate plot to supplant radical feminism with liberalism.[5]

The implicit heterosexual chauvinism of the original Redstockings became overt homophobia in *FR*. Like the dominant tendency in lesbian feminism, Redstockings talked about sexual orientation in terms of political choice rather than sexual desire. But where orthodox lesbian feminists defined heterosexuality as entirely political, a patriarchal imposition on women, Redstockings took heterosexuality for granted and argued that homosexuality, both male and female, was a product of male supremacy. For the *FR* editors, lesbianism was at best one of the many compromises women made with a sexist system, a substitute for the equal heterosexual relationships we all really wanted. At worst it was a copout, a futile attempt to escape from men and male supremacy instead of struggling. By the same logic, *FR* condemned male homosexuality as a form of male supremacy: it was misogynist in that it did not simply subordinate women as lovers and sexual partners but rejected them altogether; and it was a resistance to feminism in that it allowed men to evade women's demands for equality by turning to each other. In a sense, *FR* implied, men who did not need women were the greatest threat of all. Like their cultural feminist opponents the *FR* editors filled the gap in their understanding of sexual psychology with political reductionism on the one hand and biological determinism on the other. But their uncritical acceptance of the concept of a natural, normative heterosexuality was especially ironic for self-proclaimed materialists.

Feminist Revolution crystallized my opposition to cultural feminism and stimulated a long-dormant desire to think seriously about the state of the movement and its future. But it also reinforced my suspicion that simply reviving the old-time radical feminist religion was not the answer, that while we needed to affirm and learn from what we had accomplished, we also needed to move on—to what was still unclear. I had similar reactions to *Meeting Ground*, a radical feminist and socialist journal that Carol Hanisch began publishing in 1977. Though *MG* was intended as a forum for debate and hopefully an impetus to renewed organizing—Hanisch and her coeditors solicited readers' articles and comments—for the most part its content reflected Redstockings' orthodoxy and embattled isolation. And though it was concerned with exploring the connections between feminism and antiracist, anticapitalist politics—a concern I shared—its conception of socialist revolution was based on Marxist-Leninist-Maoist assumptions with which I had little sympathy.

During the last few years — dating roughly (and not coincidentally) from the start of the Reagan era—there has been a more promising resurgence of dissident feminist voices, coming from several different directions. Yet another attempt to reconstitute a radical feminist movement began in 1980, when Brooke, a radical feminist, a lesbian, and one of the earliest critics of cultural feminism (her essay, "The Retreat to Cultural Feminism," appeared in *Feminist Revolution*), published an article in a feminist newspaper calling for a new radical offensive. Response to the piece led its author and several other women to form the Radical Feminist Organizing Committee, which set out to create a network of radical feminists by circulating a newsletter, *Feminism Lives!*, and inviting readers' responses. RFOC now has about 70 members and is starting a national organization. Its basic stance is materialist; besides opposing cultural feminism and lesbian vanguardism it has taken an explicit stand against heterosexual chauvinism (Brooke broke with Redstockings over its line on homosexuality). Otherwise the group does not have developed positions; it is at the stage where virtually everything but opposition to male supremacy is open for discussion. As a result, *Feminism Lives!* has been largely free of the sectarian, defensive tone that *Feminist Revolution* and *Meeting Ground* tended to fall into. The terms of the discussion—its vocabulary and underlying assumptions—are still those of 60s radical feminism. But if RFOC makes a serious effort to revive militant feminist activism in a political climate and social situation that have changed dramatically since the 60s, it may well end up questioning some of those terms and breaking new ground.

Another, more publicly visible challenge to cultural feminism, and to the antisexual strain in radical feminist thought that dates back to Ti-Grace Atkinson, has come from feminist opposition to the antipornography movement. The antiporn groups, which emerged as an organized political force in 1979, quickly captured the attention of the media and dominated public discussion of feminism and sexuality. Because their ideas resonated with the conservative social climate and appealed to women's fears at a time when real freedom and equality seemed increasingly remote, they exerted a strong influence on the liberal mainstream of the women's movement and on the public perception of feminism. I found these developments alarming, as did many other women who felt that feminists should be fighting the right's assault on women's sexual freedom, not reinforcing it. Our opposition has generated a fierce intramovement debate on the significance of sexuality for feminist politics.

The sex debate has recapitulated the old division between those radical feminists who emphasized women's right to equal sexual pleasure and those who viewed sex primarily in negative terms, as an instrument of sexist exploitation and abuse. But contemporary "pro-sex" feminists (as the dissidents have been labeled) are also doing something new—placing a specifically feminist commitment to women's sexual autonomy in the context of a more general sexual radicalism. Bound by its theoretical framework, the radical feminist movement analyzed sexuality as a function of sex class; it did not concern itself with sexual repression versus liberation as a problematic distinct from that of male power over women. Accordingly, most radical feminists in all factions equated women's sexual oppression with male domination and rejected the idea of sexual liberation for men as at best redundant, at worst a euphemism for license to exploit women with impunity. Within this framework there was no way to discuss the common elements in women's and men's (particularly gay men's) subjection to sexual repression; or to explore the extent to which men's sexual guilt, fear and frustration contribute to their sexism (and specifically to sexual violence); or to understand the complexities of lesbian sexuality; or to examine other variables besides sexism that influence sexual formation—such as the parent-child relationship, race, class and anxieties shared by both sexes about the body, pleasure, emotional vulnerability and loss of control.

The pro-sex feminists are raising all these questions and others, provoking an explosion of intellectual activity and reintroducing the spirit of critical inquiry to a movement all but ossified by cultural feminist dogma. The emphasis has been on questions rather than answers. There is a good deal of ideological diversity within the pro-sex camp, a loose, informal network that consists mostly of lesbian dissenters from the lesbian feminist consensus, women with political roots in early radical feminism, and feminist academics influenced by Marxism, structuralism, and psychoanalysis. We also maintain friendly relations and an ongoing exchange of ideas with parallel tendencies in the gay movement and the neo-Marxist left.

At the same time, black women and other women of color have begun to create the context for a feminist radicalism based on efforts to analyze the web of race, class and sex/gender relations. Like pro-sex theorizing, these explorations break with prevailing assumptions—in this case the competing orthodoxies of radical and cultural feminism, black nationalism and Marxist socialism. Each of these movements has insisted on hierarchies of oppression and primary causes, forcing women who suffer from racial and class oppression to subordinate some aspects of their identity to others or be political schizophrenics. While socialist feminists have purported to address this dilemma, in practice their economistic bias has tended not only to vitiate their feminist analysis but to reduce racism to its economic component. Many women of color have shared this perspective and its limitations. What is novel and exciting about the current discussions is their concern with the totality of a culture and their recognition that sexism, heterosexism, racism, capitalism and imperialism intersect in complex, often contradictory ways. When this multidimensional analysis is applied to bedrock issues of sexual politics—marriage and motherhood, sexual repression and violence, reproductive freedom, homophobia—it does not simply correct for white middle-class feminists' neglect of other women's experience; it shows that whatever a woman's particular social vantage point, her experience of femaleness is charged with class and racial meanings.

Though the emergence of this tendency and the burgeoning of the predominantly white pro-sex coalition happened independently (a small number of black and Hispanic women have been involved in both) they end up raising many of the same questions from different angles. They also reflect a common impulse toward a decentered radicalism sensitive to difference, ambiguity and contradiction, and critical of all forms of hierarchical thinking. The same impulse informs contemporary cultural radical revisions of Marxist and Marxist-feminist theory. It seems to me that these convergences represent a first fragile step toward the creation of a multiracial left that will include feminism as a basic assumption. At the moment, helping this process along is my own political priority; I think a "new new left" is the prerequisite for a third feminist wave.

Still, the paradox posed by early radical feminism remains unresolved and may be unresolvable in any definitive way. An antisexist politics abstracted from a critique of familialism, a commitment to sexual liberation, and race and class struggle cannot sustain itself as a radical force; a movement that attempts such an abstraction is bound to fragment into bitterly opposed factions and/or turn conservative. Yet so long as sexist power relations exist there will be a need for an autonomous, specifically feminist women's movement. It is the legacy of radical feminism that makes it possible to talk even tentatively of a feminist left. And it would be naive to imagine that a left intellectually committed to feminism would automatically be free of sexism either in theory or in practice. In the foreseeable future, any feminist movement that aims to be radical will somehow have to negotiate this tension between the need to preserve its political boundaries and the need to extend them. It will help to remember that radical feminism named the boundaries in the first place.

NOTES

1. In this essay, as in common usage on the left, the term "socialist feminism" refers primarily to an activist tendency and "Marxist feminism" to a body of theory. There is of course some overlap between the two, but by no means a one-to-one correspondence. As a movement, socialist feminism has generally been more socialist than feminist, assuming that economic relations are fundamental, while sexual political questions are "cultural" or "ideological," i.e., epiphenomenal. Often socialist-feminists have adopted a cultural feminist view of these "ideological" questions and thereby reduced feminism to a matter of lifestyle.

Marxist feminism has displayed a similar weakness for economic reductionism, but it has also used Marxist methodology to expand feminist theory; in recent years, especially, Marxist feminists have both influenced and been influenced by the cultural radical critiques that have generated the "crisis in Marxism" debate. On the other hand, since Marxist-feminist theorizing has been carried on mostly in the academy, it has suffered badly from lack of contact with any organized feminist movement.

2. In any case, postrevolutionary China is hardly a model for those of us whose definition of liberation includes individual freedom. This does not invalidate the process of self-assertion by peasants against landlords, women against men and autocratic matriarchs that Hinton describes. But it does raise the question of whether the Maoist model of struggle can have more than limited success only in a revolution in which individual autonomy and cultural diversity are not important values.
3. Alice Echols, "The New Feminism of Yin and Yang," in *Powers of Desire: The Politics of Sexuality,* ed. Christine Stansell, Ann Snitow and Sharon Thompson (Monthly Review Press, 1983).
4. Ellen Willis, "Toward a Feminist Sexual Revolution," *Social Text,* 6, Fall 1982.
5. Before publishing *Feminist Revolution*, Redstockings held a press conference on the Steinem-CIA connection and distributed copies of the *FR* article. At the time I was working part-time at *Ms.*, editing book reviews, and had just concluded that I ought to quit, having come to the limits of my tolerance for the constant (and usually losing) battles involved in being the token radical on a magazine with mushy corporate liberal politics. The Redstockings flap pushed me over the edge. I had mixed feelings about the article and was upset about the press conference, which by villainizing Steinem and implying a conspiracy could only undercut the credibility of Redstockings' valid critique of *Ms.*'s politics and impact on the movement. But I was incensed by Steinem's response, a disdainful who-are-these-people dismissal of Sarachild, Hanisch et al. as crazies and not real Redstockings. I resigned from *Ms.* and wrote an open letter to the movement press detailing my own criticisms of the magazine and its editor. Redstockings included it in *FR.*

In 1979, Random House published an "abridged edition with additional writings" of *Feminist Revolution.* The chief abridgement was "Gloria Steinem and the CIA," which Random House deleted in response to Steinem's threat to sue, although the facts of her involvement with IRS had long been public information and the article had already survived a libel reading. Though Redstockings organized a protest, this act of censorship provoked little interest outside of radical and cultural feminist circles, and cultural feminists mostly supported Steinem. In the end, the entire episode was a depressing defeat for radical feminism, albeit largely self-inflicted. Not only did Redstockings fail to provoke significant debate about *Ms.*-ism; most people who heard about the controversy at all were left with the impression that Steinem had been attacked by a lunatic fringe.

THE ETHNIC QUESTION

COLIN GREER

The mid-60s and early 70s saw a so-called ethnic revival sweep the United States, celebrating the idea of a multi-ethnic nation. While this revival was a component in the general upsurge of the decade, it was not a component with a clear and simple message. It marked the recognition that the promise of mobility and inclusion was yet to be fulfilled for large numbers of Americans, a promise usually expressed in terms of what was taken to be the "up-from-poverty story" of the model white ethnic. At the same time, while recalling the legendary strength of the immigrant's rugged, do-it-yourself scramble up the ladder of socio-economic opportunity, ethnic revivalists and activists also sought government intervention to secure repetition of that story. More recently, another current in ethnic convention has become popular, namely the notion that government intervention to aid the unsuccessful and excluded has been inimical to their progress—and to those who are ready to help themselves.[1]

These contradictory emphases draw on ever-present elements in ethnic consciousness, but we have yet to understand this from a perspective which sees the revival both as a proponent and opponent of the progressive agenda of the 60s. Clearly, this is not simply a scholastic problem. What we as people believe the nation to be has great effect on what people take to be their just claims on, and expectations of, political and economic life. So far, ethnic revival and ethnicity stand so poorly informed or misinformed by attempts at historical perspective that the current conservative prejudices of the newly dubbed moral majoritarians seem even to drop ethnic identification out of most popular and scholarly recollections of the social movements of the 60s. The clouding of the contradictions between immigrant and native-American values and goals is central to the powerful, but conservative meanings given to "Americanness" via immigrant imagery.

However, an initial clarification is necessary. Since the turn of the century "immigrant" and "ethnic" have been used more or less interchangeably to designate what is in fact the former. The historical roots of the creation of ethnic characterization of Americans thus tend to become the demographic reality of their immigrant origins: immigrant history serves as ethnic history. The actual conditions of today's ethnically identified American are obfuscated by this emphatic immigrant identity, an image of the self-reliant and community-supported newcomers on their way up, of hyphenated Horatio Algers. In truth, we have no real ethnic history. What we have are studies of ethnic patterns of voting, housing and language, all seeming to confirm the trajectory from immigrant to mainstream. Yet the issues where ethnic votes *can* be perceived today are instructive because they show groups of Americans seeking to advance their position via government (e.g., school busing, controls of undocumented Mexican workers, support for Israel). This resort to government is basic to contemporary ethnicity.

Conventional wisdom has it that traditional immigration came to an end with the quota system instituted in the 1920s; but except for the lull during the Depression, both legal and illegal entry has remained high and are today equal to the floodtide years before World War I. In the ten years before 1974, about 4 million immigrants entered legally and at least as many came via exceptions (refugees, for example) or illegal means. These immigrants have, for the most part, remained a national supply of cheap labor, in which capacity they have been met with hostility and suspicion by the settled children of previous immigrants. Simultaneously, the latter will often celebrate the immigrant of the past as the *real* immigrant, while the immigrant of the present, by inference, is a *false* one. The new immigrants are thus seen to threaten and undermine the Americanness of the established groups in whom the "true" immigrant inheritance lives on. This hostility can also be expressed against business interests which use cheap labor. The threads of antagonism to new immigrants and business, and resort to government protection have, as in the cases of all 20th-century immigration restriction efforts, been the little noted basis for an ethnic history distinct from, and in direct relation to, immigration history.[2]

THE RISE OF TODAY'S ETHNIC

Americans are linked to immigration by an ideology which seems to present them to themselves as an aristocracy of labor over newcomers: contemporary ethnics, in other words, embody immigrant achievement, and as ethnics they are also working people who profit from the harshness of the struggles of their ancestors. This is reflected in scholarly analyses which depict ethnicity entirely through the lens of historic immigration. Present immigrants hence tend to be excluded from what we may call the public ethnicity, which in turn is the ethnicity of the ethnic revivalism in popular culture. This conception came of age in the 1950s and 60s with the growth of state intervention in the economic struggles between classes, when ethnicity came to characterize various interest groups, competing "beyond ideology," as the parlance of the time framed it, in the arena of American political pluralism.

Immigration has not always been a major perspective from which to look at American history. It only became one through the successive struggle by blacks, white ethnics, and blacks again, for legal protection against discriminatory exclusion, a struggle spanning the half century between 1920 and 1970. The scholarly reflection of this is interesting to follow.

Immigration scholarship arose in the 1920s, in fact, with the advent of restriction when the whole process of immigration seemed to have come to an end. This was a time when native Americans were writing immigrant history and southern whites were writing black history. Indeed, blacks produced more indigenous scholars of their own experience than did the "new" immigrants and their offspring. What little there was came in the form of reminiscences of the struggle for livelihood in the new land and plaudits for the success achieved. Even the most politically active immigrants tended to represent the United States as a land of opportunity, albeit a land of great and unequal struggle.

It was the idea of the room for struggle, both political and economic, which dominated the testimonies of the personal and group-devoted order. This idea was a powerful one. Scholars took it over after World War II and reinvented the frontier image of American life in the process: the immigrant was now the archetypal hero escaping poverty and repression for opportunity and freedom. After a war against tyranny and racial persecution, a major shift against the fortress of American racial hostility was undertaken. Now "new" immigrant offspring set about writing immigrant history too. The national consciousness was ready for non-Anglo-Saxon Americans to occupy a more comfortable home in American folklore, memory and convention—they were after all an enormous part of the nation and could now, after two wars and restrictionism had cut them off from Europe, be seen as Americans.

Harvard University Press's recent *We the Peoples: An Encyclopedia of American Ethnic Groups* is illustrative in this regard. The result of years of scholarly and popular attention to American ethnic character, *We the Peoples* sets out to carefully survey a scene set rhetorically by such as Michael Novak (*The Rise of the Unmeltable Ethnics*) and to underscore its fulfillment in definitions of the U.S. population. The book's title is, of course, a pun on its Bill of Rights precursor, "we the people," and as such indicates the shift to the gradual inclusion of a diversity of groups in the American community; indeed in the very definition of community by the presence and inclusion of these groups. Here on an equal basis are those groups who were for so long despised and discriminated against fully instated as the very backbone of the nation. Whereas in the past there was a people, defined largely by WASP identity, to which the offspring of immigrants must assimilate, now that WASP "people" is but a number of groups occupying the mainstream of national identity. Postwar prosperity obviously also provided room for this shift, allowing a new social contract with labor from which, however, most of the continuing stream of newcomers to the labor force were excluded through loopholes in immigration and labor protection legislation, by mutual labor and capital agreement.

Indeed, the unceasing flow of immigrants to the U.S., despite restrictive legislation passed in the 1920s and 30s, remains a rarely told story. There are the proverbial highs in the decades around the turn of the century but it is worth noting that the nation's character as a nation of immigrants precedes these highs—although it was, of course, intensified by them. If that characterization was reasonable before 1890, it certainly remains reasonable after 1920. This is especially so when one recognizes the hard-to-specify numbers of unrecorded immigrants entering since the quota restrictions of the 1920s. In addition to illegal immigrants, there are the various sources of legal entrants not recorded as quota immigrants: Mexicans who have entered the U.S. in large and encouraged numbers since at least 1880, and for whom there was no quota until 1965; contract workers during and since the 1940s and 1950s from Mexico and the West Indies; and refugees from Europe, Asia, the Caribbean and Latin America.[3]

It is fascinating that the historical assumption of "completed" immigration has been an axial point of view sustained, respectively, by those who seek to push their analyses toward conservative, liberal, and left advantage. For conservatives, the past success of immigrants is to be the basis for present national policy. For liberals, that achievement argues for the continuing involvement of the institutional cushion, derived from the 19th-century charity system. For left observers, the early 20th-century immigrant locale serves as the basis of people's self-support, sometimes in their own advancement and sometimes in resistance to the technical rationality of capitalism. Those traditional communities, they argue, contain oppositional elements to the atomism of modern society through long-time personal bonds and social networks. Despite significant divergencies, all three confirm the key role of pre-restrictionist immigration as the basis for understanding America's current native born.

Yet the newcomer continued to be a signpost of somebody else's status. Just as immigrants perennially experienced upgrading and movement from neighborhood to neighborhood as more immigrants came in from different sources, so ethnics identified with the upgrading of their forebears by defining and defending their position in opposition to other groups. Seen from this angle, ethnic is part of a history of group identity which in fact originated with WASP identity and the aggressive defensiveness of WASPs against newcomers of diverse origin. It was the first and most thorough-going definition of ethnicity, the conflation of ethnicity and the operative notion of what it was to be American.

ETHNICS, IMMIGRANTS AND GOVERNMENT

The 1965 immigration laws ended country-by-country quotas in favor of hemispheric quotas. Preference was still European. The ending of preferences *between* European countries meant the equalization of the hitherto disfavored southern and eastern Europeans with the highly prized northern and western Europeans. The nation of nations was confirmed and celebrated as white ethnic offspring of a largely completed immigration were included in the newly politicized economy. Meanwhile, third-world newcomers, without the force of congressional pressure, faced continuing limits on entry far below the level produced by the pressures on them to seek work in the U.S. Hence, the construction of the undocumented alien as a major labor source largely outside the old American integrative promise made to immigrants which ethnicity was, by the 60s, seen to represent.[4]

The interventionist state was in many ways anticipated in the restrictionist solution to native-born conflict with new immigrants. Two things should be remembered in this context. First, the flow of immigration has continued despite periodic legislation to restrict it; neither antipathy to immigrants nor restrictive legislation has changed the basic immigrant character of the American labor force. Second, from the earliest, acts of immigration restriction have all in great measure served as response both to popular distress in depressed economic circumstances and to the failure of settled Americans to feel secure in such times in the existing tradeoffs between immigrant and native labor opportunities.

Restriction legislation and the campaign for it may thus be seen as part of an "assimilation curtain" raised periodically and made out of the cloth of government protections for citizens and corollary redefinitions of who is to be included in that status. Such government assurance has never been easily won—but each time it has been advanced to include new elements, it has also been accompanied by caveats protecting some inflow of foreign labor to satisfy powerful business interests. With each restrictionist advance, a framework of "backdoor" immigration was developed—illegal in many instances and invisible in the case of the Mexican. Indeed, each act was in some ways a new definition of who was now an acceptable American and who might still provide much needed cheap labor without the benefit of social and political inclusion. Hence, since the earliest restrictions, there has been a category of immigrants not invited to join the mainstream of society. With this perennial backdrop came a constant flow of the worse racist ideology directed at various Asian, Catholic, Jewish, and European entrants, who came to the United States between 1840 and 1940. Popular and scholarly literature alike reeked with it, giving questions of immigration and assimilation a strongly genetic and sociological hue.[5]

This framework of overt control and covert flexibility has been operating through periodic health and desirability regulations, as well as in restriction and legalization legislation. Two important conditions follow from this. First, the ethnic basis for American self-definition was established and confirmed. Restrictive legislation has broadened the meaning of "American" and helped produce a consciousness of Americans as ethnics. Second, those who for long periods have inhabited the social space created by limitation and exclusion are those we currently recognize as "minorities." Those groups, for instance, currently forging the Hispanic identity are so known, as are blacks, although they are only reluctantly recognized as immigrant in origin—those who have not yet reached their "majority" in ethnic America.

The significance both of the emerging "ethnic" landscape of identity and of the strength of non-American origins in the articulation of such identity was not lost on contemporaries of the early explicitly restrictive legislation up to 1920. This is especially clear in the relation of immigrants to black Americans. To black leaders of the time, it was clear that future security and prosperity were being created by newcomers who were displacing blacks in urban employment and housing. They also saw that blacks had limited capacity to struggle for similar opportunities because slavery had reduced them to a marginal role in the political economy, one which, as easy displacement by immigrants demonstrated, remained fundamental in black life.

The struggle to gain access to majority status, to the protections and opportunities associated with citizenship, has been a clear objective among blacks for a long time. Indeed, that struggle has been an important contributing force to the construction of ethnicity itself. Already at the end of the 19th century, black leaders like B.T. Washington and W.E.B. Dubois favored one brand or another of immigration restriction: Chinese immigrants were the first to be seen as inimical to the interests of American workers (including blacks), and later European immigrants were taken to be a threat. But immigrants were also set as an example for black workers, North and South, to advance the task of what Washington called "constructing" a society in which blacks could work on equal terms with other Americans once having completed—through Emancipation—the task of "destroying" the legality of inequality along racial lines. The threat came, as both Washington and Dubois saw it, as immigrants displaced black workers from previously secure employment opportunities in the North, and undermined access to opportunities in the newly industrialized South. The example came in the form of native-origin solidarity, in these black leaders' view. The identification with non-American origins formed the basis on which group tradition transcended U.S.-determined value and status norms; the power of the *padrone* and political ward systems in northern cities seemed to allow foreign newcomers to make particular industries and neighborhoods their province.

Along with support for immigration restriction, black leaders favored the concentration of blacks in the South where there was both a history and current numerical predominance of black labor to build on, where there was recognition of African origins as the authentic root and alternative to slavery at the core of black American identity, and where there was a base for pressure on government and political processes to help reverse the discriminatory centuries of the "color line." Limitations on black opportunity were created by government; they were, it seemed easily to follow, to be undone by government too.[6]

In this turn-of-the-century focus we see the beginning of the framework of ethnic identification as a baseline of activist identity in American political life. After slavery, blacks sought to defend against, and to learn from, the pattern of development which embodied the operations of the American promise among the newcomers who perpetually arrived to realize it. In the formation of this black articulation, however, the world post-slavery blacks confronted was different; conditions which, as Dubois noted, made them "slaves to industry," and a political social context in which their status had long been determined through functions of legislative and administrative government.

These elements (self-definition by national origins, looking to government for support and protection, and competitiveness with newcomers) are basic ingredients of what today represents ethnic identity. The use of the term ethnic in this manner is distinct from the simultaneous turn of the century use of it to refer to foreign-born residents of the U.S. What is usually not recognized is that it is the former usage which defines the current meaning of the term and obscures its effective social content.

The conditions in which this contemporary version of ethnicity are identifiable in the political sphere in relation to blacks are also worth tracing. The initial context of the late 19th century was the particular vulnerability of blacks in newly flourishing U.S. cities to job displacement and large-scale discrimination in law, education, and housing. On one hand, they were U.S. citizens who, along with others, found themselves threatened by immigrant workers. On another, they were ex-slaves over whom employers and landlords preferred immigrants—forcing them into the same kind of marginal relation with immigrants (e.g., as strikebreakers) as immigrants occupied with respect to the white native-born. Progessives of the period called on government policy to address the living and working conditions of both these experiences of marginality.

The character of the ethnic claims on government which were carved out originated in the urban poverty conditions of whites and blacks. At the turn of the century, ethnic was used to describe poor white immigrants. But as blacks contested the discriminatory fabric in their lives in succeeding decades, the word "ethnic" shifted in popular usage to describe black Americans. Used at first to describe immigrants at the margins of socioeconomic life, the term was appropriated briefly for blacks uniquely condemned to such conditions. Their perpetual marginality meant that, as the decades wore on, the lack of progress could be framed against claims and assumptions of wide-scale immigrant success. The continuity of urban black life was forgotten and they were cast as new immigrants—yet to be included in the mainstream. The term "ethnic" then became reasonable nomenclature.[7]

During the 40s and 50s the children and grandchildren of immigrants fought their way out of discriminatory codes and overwhelming material deficiencies to the point where educational opportunities for expanding technological and professional employment were possible. In a highly technological industrial life blacks made similar demands; education seemed essential to the first steps out of poverty. Both sets of efforts required a newly expanded role for government in defending against discriminatory practices, in building educational institutions and goals, and in supporting the massive growth of highways, urbs and suburbs which made the mainstream potentially wide enough for unprecedented numbers to enter. The new emergent American "majority" (later to be called "silent" and "moral") and the newly mobilized "minority" turned to government. That majority, less persuaded of the security of their middle-class all-Americanness than their ideology would have it, bristled at black demands and government responses, and in both the 1950s and 1970s a "revival" of consciousness of the disparate native origins of most Americans competed with and challenged black (and/or Afro-American) demands for government support in fulfilling B.T. Washington's "construction" imperative. Not usually noticed at the time, "ethnic" came to represent demands on government on the one hand, and the assertion, on the other, that numerous Americans felt themselves very distant from the fulfillment of American promises. Federal "ethnic" heritage and "ethnic neighborhood" funds sounded the reclamation of "ethnic" for the offspring of turn-of-the-century, primarily European immigrants. (The creation of the term "minority" was developed at the same time to include in the ethnic motif the fact of other hyphenated Americans for whom life and work remained marginal in the socioeconomic reality which had for a long time made particular and separate definition appropriate.)

As the civil rights and Great Society era unfolded, "ethnic" was used to describe those who were supposed to have made it. Set apart from the black experience with which it was perennially contrasted, the ethnic label lost its newcomer emphasis and was regarded instead as a record of an alternative, a more truly American style. However, blacks were following an old style—a style, in fact, very close both to the ethnocentric style of native Americans who sought legislative and educational resources to protect them and to the ethnically centered style of earlier newcomers and their offspring who frequently called on government to provide better schools, social services, and employment conditions.[8]

The competitiveness which characterized bitter struggles and diatribes between white ethnic groups (e.g., Irish, Jewish and Italian) and blacks in the late 1960s and 1970s over school desegregation and school ownership struggles was testament at once to the new significance of educational preparation in the society and to the significance of government in the security of life and work of citizens which had been confirmed by the New Deal and in which public education was a basic component.[9]

Ironically, the ideal of free enterprise and do-it-yourself marketplace opportunities, a long-standing sacred truth among those who have long sought government intervention against competitors (i.e., immigrants), has served to hide the extent to which the call on government has also been a means of protection against employers who so readily sought to import and hire foreign labor as an alternative to meeting demands for adequate working pay and conditions. Indeed, where resistance to blacks' successive claims for representation in and control of the government institution aimed to serve them (i.e., public schools) occurred, it usually revealed the limited security and tenuous hold the quite recently empowered felt outside the domain of such government-supported institutions as the public school.

By 1965, amid the flourish of government social welfare programs, legislative action changed the basic immigration law. This time hemisphere rather than national origins was the major factor in permitting entry into the United States. The Immigration Act, issued in 1965 as amendments to the McCarran-Walter Act, abolished the national origins system. Numerical restrictions were still imposed on the eastern hemisphere, subject to an overall limitation with each European country given an equal limit. For the first time, in a kind of civil-rights declaration for southern and eastern Europeans, all European nations were given equal status in American pluralism. The 1965 amendments removed, under pressure from ethnics, the national-origins preference system established and followed after World War I. At the same time the western hemisphere was for the first time given a numerical ceiling, reducing legal immigration from that part of the world where in fact it now mostly originated.

But the 1965 legislation actually changed very little. While it reformed the nation-over-nation preference system, it in effect erected a quasi-racial preference system, making the European normative dominance in the United States as explicit as ever. Even McCarran-Walter, with its strong antipathy to any immigration, was clear about its European preference, maintaining country-by-country quotas, McCarran-Walter also allotted almost 90 percent of all annual quotas to Europe. The shift from national to hemispheric determination was of a piece with this tradition. In effect, it updated U.S. pluralism at the very time Congress sought to confirm an end to black inequity in the Civil Rights Act of that year. After 1965 the tacit recognition of legitimate hyphenated American identity, always the hidden agenda of restriction quotas, was expanded beyond national grouping so that the hierarchy of desirability among national origins was redefined in the broader hemispheric categorization. This did not, of course, have the effect that Italian and Greek Americans, for example, now identified themselves as European-American. Quite the contrary. The inclusion of diverse groups in a category which reformed the international quasi-racial preferences implied in previous quotas meant that all European groups were accorded a freshly dignified place in definitions of American identity. European origin was the preferred category, and so all in it were free to identify with their particular version of it now that the particular was an aspect of preference, not a measurement of distance from it.

Quotas among western hemisphere countries punctuated the different status of this continuing heavy stream of immigrants, most of them illegal. The restrictionist force in this situation is subtle but clear since the question of differential demand is paramount. Emigrants from western hemisphere countries far outnumber quota allowances, as is confirmed by deportation and undocumented residence as well as by applications for entry and consequent waiting lists. The rough quota equivalence given western and eastern hemispheres actually draws two critical lines of exclusion. One line was predicated on an even balance between hemispheres in the makeup of total legal immigrant numbers, as if, regardless of demand, certain sources would be undesirable in greater numbers. A second line determined a preference system for entry which amounts to a class discrimination system, tacked onto the national origins discrimination system; it allowed worldwide privileged entry to professional and skilled emigrants, while restricting the entry of the poorest and least skilled and making illegal entry their most likely prospect.[10]

Finally, following a series of amendments during the succeeding decade, the 1965 Immigration Act has been said to equalize restriction entirely. western hemisphere countries as well as eastern are now relieved from country-by-country preferences. An intriguing byproduct of the hemispheric quota system, coming as it does at the point of large-scale entry of western hemisphere (widely Spanish-speaking) immigrants, is the programming of an Hispanic identity on people from quite diverse Spanish-speaking cultures. This occurs as newcomers struggle to achieve political strength in a government-emphatic framework which Daniel Bell has referred to as the political delivery of economic and social rewards.

The broadening of national image via ethnic characterization of the populace coincided with the relocation of economic and industrial tension in the political arena, a thrust which meant a shift away from the explicit class focus of the Depression years to an increasingly origins-based focus which identified individuals in groups, regardless of class—thereby attaching them to achievement in this society.

It is in relation to these processes, and the intrinsically related emergence of the state, that ethnicity must be understood. Both restrictionists and progressives in the 19th and 20th centuries have turned to the state to work out the terms of acceptable Americanness. At the same time, business turned to the state to work out the terms of a revised free enterprise in the face of labor shortage and recalcitrance, and international competition. Generally favorable to immigration, American business has been able to protect its access to immigrant labor despite successive restriction legislation through its influence on legislative and administrative government processes. Each restriction victory or progressive compromise meant that the state was central to the economic and demographic life of the nation. Basic economic and demographic forces were politicized, and the political arena became, by the end of the New Deal, a framework within which the hitherto private sector conflicts were to be managed and resolved.

At the heart of restrictionist mobilization among native-born and long-settled workers has run a double-edged paradox with predictably counterproductive outcomes. Opposition to new immigrants, however, framed in racist and inhuman rhetoric, was always at root a defense against business interests. To the great extent that immigration has withstood all legislative attack, it is because immigrants are wanted by employers. To the extent that native (ethnic) Americans express fear for their jobs via restrictionism, hostility for newcomers is antagonistic to the nation's powerful business interests. The miscalculation in the focus is clear when we recognize that the most restrictive measures have never been accompanied by employer sanctions of any weight. But it has been difficult to disentangle symptom and cause in all this since ethnics have looked to establish their integration in American society most often by joining their identity in it with its myth of laissez-faire individualism and enterprise. While both capital and labor have looked increasingly to government and corporate styles of organization, the basic imagery of settled Americans derives from their immigrant ancestors lionized as rugged and successful individualists.[11]

When Nathan Glazer in the early 60s questioned black demands for integration via government intervention as a challenge to the pluralism by which other groups had, on their own, entered American community life, he underscored the ruling convention about pluralism and ethnic experience. But in making that case he failed to notice that the groups he regarded as having made their own way had been strenuously involved in efforts to remove the discrimination which operated in their lives and invoked the state on behalf of their efforts to advance in American society, both in terms of economic opportunity and social status.[12]

That black civil rights leaders developed an early focus on schools in the fight for social justice was not a unique development. They drew directly on the recognition that schools were major instruments of government in a context of government's increasing role as the balance wheel in post-New Deal capital-labor relations. By World War II, following federal government involvement in social problems, the role of public education became more and more central to the post-New Deal political economy. New Deal and post-New Deal state management of the political economy, actually initiated at the local and state level before and after World War I, was the product of both private and public interests. Employers and employees alike, after decades of virtual warfare, settled on a social wage to resolve their historic deadlock and the exhaustion of old-style competitive capitalism. Like the 1965 Immigration Act and Civil Rights Act, the G.I. Bill of Rights was central to this emergent framework. The bill established the need for the state to facilitate the reentry of demobilized manpower following the war, a labor force which before the war had been the victim of an unprecedented unemployment. These were the children of immigrants not by any means making it by virtue of a free-enterprise economy.[13]

Daniel Bell has gone farther in clarifying the nature of the society in which ethnic identity is intrinsic to national identity. For Bell, such a society is one which has been increasingly politically determined. Drawing on the view of a technology-determined society that he shares with other observers from quite varied shades of political opinion, Bell writes in "Ethnicity and Social Class" (in *Ethnicity*, Nathan Glazer and D.P. Moynihan, eds., Harvard University Press) that a fusion of the status order of society with the political order has occurred:

> . . .generally, we find a subtle but pervasive change, namely, that the revolution of rising expectations. . .has become a sustained demand for entitlements.

As skill and education have grown in importance, so credentials and certification have become central for individuals striving to get ahead:

> . . .for our purposes the essential point is that as the mechanisms for occupational advancement become increasingly specialized and formalized, the political route becomes almost the only major means available for individuals and groups without specific technical skills to "upgrade" themselves in society.

The resulting demand is for "social rights" (jobs, insurance against unemployment, adequate health care, and a minimum, decent standard of living) to be delivered via political rather than economic processes. Bell sees the upsurge of ethnicity to be directly related to national political life:

> In the competition for the values of the society to be realized politically, ethnicity can become a means of claiming place of advantage. And it is a means for disadvantaged groups to claim a set of rights and privileges which the existing power structures have denied them.

Intrinsic to the fusion of status order with political order which Bell describes is the growth of the modern state. As the state has become a central arbiter of economic well-being between classes in society, so the issues of economic well-being have become increasingly political. Ethnicity is a critical variable in this complex of ideology and power intrinsic to the political nature of society.

This view is not meant to diminish the significance of class and race in the operations of society. In fact, as Milton Gordon argues, ethnicity is a dependent variable of these elements; further examination in this perspective is warranted.[14]

Key in this framework is the continuing stream of immigration which has remained a basic ingredient in society. It is at once an aspect of active ethnic self-definition and a focus of the struggle between capital and labor in the context of which ethnic ideology derives. Ethnicity, then, can be seen as a central characteristic of American identity which is most clearly observed in relationship with, not by any means simply as a successor to, immigration.

It would be a mistake to take this line of reasoning to suggest that ethnic is synonymous with group mobilization for government support. It is entirely accurate, however, to argue that ethnicity summarizes the extensive framework of government support which has developed since the New Deal. The state has been perceived by the last two generations of American workers to be their basic defense against the ability of corporate interests to exploit and mobilize government resources. As government was targeted as an agent of progressive social change, as the nature of civic value and priority was fought out through its offices and through corollary definition of the "public good," the power of the state increased. The women's group leader and the union leader, for example, have justified their emphases in political and legislative activities as a crucial extension of their responsibility to defend those they represent. At the same time, however, this bargaining context for struggle between workers and employers has also served to empower certain combinations of workers against other workers.

Ethnic identity has expressed this context. But its importance must also be sought in its mediating role between two distinct functions in U.S. life. In effect, two basic, semi-autonomous realms are merged in the ethnic idiom: on the one hand, the belief in the do-it-yourself marketplace of immigrant achievement continues to justify an immigrant stream; on the other, the reality of government involvement in the lives of most Americans and their reliance on government is both hidden and justified through the identification with immigrant forebears.

Basic to the structure of this ethnicity is the ongoing presence of newcomers against whom native identity is constantly recreated. Without this context other means of labelling contemporary Americans would work as well. As is, ethnicity remains an active consciousness which captures powerful societal forces on several levels. It captures a geneological and sociological reality for broad sectors of the American public. It embraces confused historical memories and myths which lead numerous Americans to national ideals directly counterproductive to their class interests. And it embodies the core issue in the American labor market, the perpetuation and disenfranchisement of an immigrant labor pool. The ethnic group, like the corporation, faces the state in an "as if" relationship. Each adopts the legendary status accorded individuals and their rights to property and its protection—as if the ethnic group and the corporation were, respectively, an actual immigrant and an actual business entrepreneur. With state relations legitimated via this nostalgic mythology, actual immigrants become to ethnics what workers are to employers-competitors.[15]

TOWARD A PERSPECTIVE

In a strong sense the concept of public ethnicity, advancing a view of national identity which confirms, at once, the efficacy of political pluralism, immigrant success, and government support of valued citizens, provides the American counter-argument to Marx's prediction of "increasing misery" as one of the variables which could contribute to social upheaval. The ethnic, by an intricate web of implicit historical and current comparisons, presents an image of decreasing misery which seems to suggest that social upheaval is not necessary.

Immigrants still enter to improve their condition and realize their dream. The confidence at the bottom expands the sense of historical improvement—even if threatened and in need of defense—experienced in the relatively higher circles. And it is with this image that we hear periodically, despite all the strong evidence to the contrary, that American blacks have yet to stake their claim to the rewards of the society—delayed, supposedly, by slavery and allegedly late arrival in the cities.

What emerges is an obvious, logical conclusion, perhaps even a political-economic law: the process of inclusion is simultaneously a process of exclusion, and vice-versa. In this society the perpetual pattern of misery at the bottom is justified by the expectation of its serial demise for successive waves of newcomers. Thus, even if it were true that ethnic Americans, the children of immigrants, are secure in the improvements their parents and grandparents made, it would be equally true that the presence of misery in the society is inevitable and justifiable.

With that principle at the gut of our social-economic-political processes, it's no wonder that misery has a way, at periodic intervals, of leaping up and grabbing some few millions who thought themselves safe from it. The hungry wolf will be fed.

National community, Ortega y Gasset wrote, requires both a vision of the past and an historical project. As we examine the confused packaging of past and project in public ethnicity, two key myths can be seen to make it distinct from immigration and the particular studies of immigrant groups on the basis of which ethnic history has been written by conservative, liberal, and left scholars:

1) in the failure to include ongoing immigration in the historiography of immigration and the general persuasion that current ethnics are the nation's cherished immigrant record to be understood by reference to their immigrant past, and

2) in the denial of ethnic reality (most especially, of struggle for government protection and support and of ongoing relations with new immigrants), simultaneously with the identification of the ethnic with the historic, self-reliant immigrant.

In this way, the past becomes the historical project and so the character of pluralist ideology is defined. In this backwards conviction not only of a better past but of a past worthy of restoration, we recognize a backlash against the character of reality in American history, a backlash now enhanced regressively but with its own seeds of rebellion, given the actual enfranchisement scenario in U.S. history.

Unfortunately, when buoyed by the confounding ideology of an heroic and completed "immigrant" past, progressive potential in U.S. life is self-defeated. While the struggle for enfranchisement has been unequivocally important for those who benefit from it, the security it offers is greatly distorted, as the current national economic and political retrogression demonstrates.

Those limits have expressly to do with the exclusionary principle implicitly at work in the operations of the inclusionary one. Just as with the ancient Greeks, freedom in America depends on a disenfranchised baseline. But unlike the Greek project, of course, the American Dream offers the promise of movement up from the bottom—indeed the very symbolic strength of ethnicity serves as a record of the efficacy of that promise. Meanwhile, the baseline remains absolutely necessary.

And yet continuing distress at the bottom means an enormous insecurity in the middle, among ethnics, because their position in the social and economic scheme of things depends on the ground of achievement indicated and shored up by certain work being done by others lower down—more often than not, by immigrants. But in order for the ethnic to represent immigrant success and self-reliance (i.e., to achieve inclusion in American cultural biases), the force of government through which insecurity in the middle has been cushioned is seriously denied or downplayed. Indeed, part of the significance of recognizing the restrictionist and progressive reliance on government is precisely to underscore both the state-emphatic character of what has been erected and the demise of the promise represented in ethnicity in the predominance of illegals in the ranks of immigrants.

A few years ago when ethnics were roundly celebrated in America, immigrants went largely unnoticed—except as the ancestors of ethnics. Actual immigrants were virtually invisible. While ethnics recorded the nation's success with immigrants in the past, current immigrants were popularly regarded as "illegal," and so occupied a fringe in American society not at all akin to the massive immigration phenomenon of years gone by. The "real" historic immigrant was known as the heroic base from which contemporary Americans took their identity—a kind of birthright. And both whites and blacks, headlined in those days as central to social progress and social problems respectively, competed for inclusion in it.

Nowadays, white and black ethnics are not central. Indeed, their attachment to government for opportunity and security is under severe attack. Trade unions, the political base of the most prosperous ethnic workers, are equally battered down as the boundaries between primary and secondary labor are under assault. Leaders in government and business are fast persuading public opinion that the force which workers mobilize through ethnic pressures on government and through unions has been detrimental to the nation and must be reversed. The Reagan administration strongly favors a more open resort to cheap immigrant labor, preferring guest-worker options over the current reliance on illegal aliens. Meanwhile, the salience of ethnic identity is much less strong now that alliances between citizens of similar market position seem to be the target of supply-side recovery.

Enter the immigrant, exit the ethnic. Re-enter laissez-faire, exit the welfare state. A new order of recognition is emerging for the actual immigrant, arriving today to do as well as possible in whatever conditions are available. The absence of regulation on behalf of workers' health, security, etc., is the clarion proclaimed for national economic recovery. The immigrant of the past, who struggled amid similar conditions, is the predecessor now of today's immigrants more than of today's ethnics, those further up the ladder who were so valued just a few years ago. It's the continuation of the immigrant struggle which will supply-side us back to broadscale economic health. The myth is reinforced and the reality is obfuscated.

Meanwhile, ethnic workers are led to ethnicity as an expression of class which stops short of class consciousness. Generally, they express the two most conventional appraisals of ethnicity. Their own immigrant origins are regarded as ethnic, the American creation of ethnicity is not understood, and their own fragmented and politically imposed ethnic identification is only rarely noticed. For some, ethnic identification is seen as a diversion from class; for others, ethnic identification reflects the effective workings of American pluralism offering wide access to prosperity.

Defined as the continuous thread which links contemporary America with its heroic, independent immigrant past, ethnics are cut off from their own history as co-creators of the state as ground for economic and social struggle. In the course of two waves of ethnic revival, native-born Americans have denied themselves even as they sought to claim themselves. Ethnicity remains a powerful summary of the political emphasis in a state-centered socio-economy and as such has won left and liberal as well as conservative scholars to the recognition of contemporary Americans in it. Before the next "ethnic revival" we need to look beyond the obvious foreign antecedents of ethnicity to its American roots.

Throughout, a public ethnicity emerged as distinct from particular ethnic affiliation. Even very low particular identification was compatible with high public ethnic identification. It is in this perspective that ethnicity may be seen at the crossroads of celebration and lament: to settled Americans immigrants built America and immigrants threaten Americans because employers profit from their labor. And while the state has increasingly become the source for an operational social contract between workers and employers, it has done so by bowing especially deeply to employers—in this case allowing their continuing access to a cheaper, less protected labor supply. So new immigrants are a lively ground of struggle with employers, and the state is berated for its failure to support and protect workers. American ethnics share a recognition of themselves as immigrant-originated and an awareness of the limits on security that national reliance on immigration represents for the capitalist economy.

Furthermore, the inclusionary power of ethnic identification as a national self-characterization keeps these same Americans shackled to public ethnicity. Through restriction, workers persistently looked to government to resolve their conflict with employers in search of cheaper labor. The New Deal and its aftermath in government expansion on behalf of citizens institutionalized and broadened that scenario. Ethnics, American workers, caught between their ideological tie to immigrant heroes (on which they have so strongly pinned their identity) and government intervention (on which their very security in America has depended), turn more easily to and on government for its failure to protect them from upstart competition than they resist the effective use of government by the corporate interests which perpetually demand immigration.

NOTES

1. The general revival is illustrated by Michael Novak's *The Rise of the Unmeltable Ethnics* (N.Y.: Simon and Schuster, 1973) and Peter Schrag's *The Decline of the WASP* (N.Y.: Simon and Schuster, 1972). The revival as social action is summarized in the record of Harry Boyte's *Backyard Revolution* (Philadelphia: Temple University Press, 1981). The currently popular anti-government perspective is exemplified in Thomas Sowell's *Ethnic History* (N.Y.: Basic Books, 1982).
2. Robert A. Devine, *American Immigration Policy: 1924–52* (New Haven: Yale University Press, 1957); John Higham, *Strangers in the Land* (New Brunswick, N.J.: Rutgers University Press, 1955); Marc Riesler, *By the Sweat of Their Brow* (Westport, Conn.: Greenwood Press, 1976); *Select Commission on Immigration and Refugee Policy* (Washington, D.C.: Government Printing Office, 1980).
3. A.M. Schlesinger, *New Viewpoints in American History* (New York: Macmillan, 1922); Edward Saveth, *American Historians and European Immigrants: 1875–1924* (New York: Columbia University Press, 1948); O.F. Ander, *In the Trek of the Immigrant* (Rock Island, Ill.: Augustana College Library, 1964).
4. Paul Erlich et al, *The Golden Door* (New York: Ballantine Books, 1979); Also see Devine, *American Immigration Policy, op. cit.*,; Higham, *Strangers in the Land, op. cit.*,; Riesler, *By the Sweat of Their Brow, op. cit.*
5. Riesler, *By the Sweat of Their Brow, op. cit.* Unconventional views of this kind of entry are available in both Cecil Woodham Smith's *The Great Hunger* (New York: Harper and

Row, 1962) and Marion T. Bennet's *American Immigration Policies* (Washington, D.C.: Public Affairs Press, 1963).

6. Eric Foner, *America's Black Past* (New York: Harper and Row, 1970); W.E.B. Dubois, "Crisis Editorials Circa World War I" W.E.B. Dubois Memorial Issue, *Freedomways* (1965); Louis R. Harlan, *Booker T. Washington,* New York: Oxford University Press, 1972); Rayford Logan, *The Betrayal of the Negro* (New York: Macmillan, 1965).

7. Thomas Lee Philpot, *The Slum and the Ghetto* (New York: Oxford University Press, 1978); John D. Buenker, *Urban Liberalism and Progressive Reform* (New York: W.W. Norton, 1978). These works illustrate the progressive politics and urban reform which paralleled immigration restriction efforts. Indeed progressives who worked hard at the local and national levels to win protections for immigrant workers and their families must be included with restrictionists among those who put government at the center of relations between employers and employees.

8. Nathan Glazer, "Negroes and Jews: The New Challenge to Pluralism," *Commentary* 38: 1964. For a recent general review of this context, see Alan Wolfe, *The American Impasse* (New York: Pantheon, 1981).

9. Colin Greer, *The Divided Society: The Ethnic Experience in America* (N.Y.: Basic Books, 1974); Colin Greer, *The Solution as Part of the Problem: Educational Reform in the 1960's* (N.Y.: Harper and Row, 1974). The economic struggle at the core of much of the inter-ethnic conflict around schools is being well developed in the work in progress of Jennifer L. Hochschild at the Woodrow Wilson School at Princeton University.

10. Charles Keely, *American Immigration Policy* (New York: Population Council, 1982).

11. Novak, *The Rise of the Unmeltable Ethnics;* Sowell, *Ethnic History*; Wolfe, *American Impasse.*

12. Glazer, "Negroes and Jews," *op. cit.*

13. Stanley Aronowitz, *Working Class Hero* (N.Y.: Pilgrim Press).

14. Both Daniel Bell and Milton Gordon make these arguments in their respective essays in Nathan Glazer and Daniel Patrick Moynihan (eds.), *Ethnicity* (Cambridge: Harvard University Press, 1982).

15. Joshua Cohen and Joel Rogers, on *Democracy: Toward A Transformation of American Society* (N.Y.: Penguin, 1983); Colin Greer and Josh DeWind, "A Labor Perspective on Immigration Policy" in Colin Greer, et al. (eds.) *After Reagan* (N.Y.: Harper and Row, 1984).

VIETNAM: THE THOUSAND PLATEAUS*

HERMAN RAPAPORT

In *Mille Plateaux*, Gilles Deleuze and Felix Guattari ask how one can make a body without parts or organs; that is, how can one make oneself into a schizo? In French this reads, "comment se faire un corps sans organes," which strategically can be reinterpreted as, how is one to produce a corps without organs, a military corps like an "I Corps"[1]? How does the "unit" disarticulate, dematerialize, frag? It is a military question, but also geographical, for I am thinking of the corps as corpse of Vietnam, of the thousand plateaus which Deleuze and Guattari pass over: the body of a country, object of dismemberment, extermination, defilement, supporting so many heterogeneous groups, cultures, languages—a third world overcoded with countless layers of political ideologies, many imports, essentially, while Buddhist monks self-destruct and children walk up to strangers with explosive charges in Coke cans. The thousand plateaus . . . Vietnam.

"In the mountains, there you feel free," a voice says in *The Wasteland*, but not in the plateaus, not in the Nam, that rhizomic landscape webbed with paddies, bomb craters, villages, jungle, camps, roads, and rivers, what amounted to an evasion of any concrete sense of territory. The bridge made by day was blown up every night, and the next day it had to be erected again by our troops. The Bailey Bridge. To us it was a "sign" of peace, a certainty that we could learn to live with. For what we coded by day, they de-coded by night. And we thought, maybe they're trying to let us know they are like us, or, better a bridge than a rocket attack, better this game of mastery. We learned that to "code" the Orient as if it were a blank map, with our hill numbers, nicknames, strategies, zones, mines, camp sites, that to "code" the Orient with concertina wire, was to enter into a dialogue with an "other" who would allow us our "code" if we really wanted it, but only for half the day. As if western territories could be reduplicated over a rhizomic landscape that had seen decades of deterritorialization.

"A plateau is always in the midst, neither the beginning nor the end. A

for Rick Berg

rhizome is made up of plateaus."[2] This notion of the plateau is borrowed from Gregory Bateson's *Steps to an Ecology of Mind* and signifies a level without climax, a development of intensities which never break or crest. At night with the starscope nothing can be seen on the treeline, no climax can be reached, nothing comes to a head. The stifling heat, the crushing permanence of tropical conditions, and the probability that nothing will happen (it is already late in the war) simply draws out whatever one feels to points of boredom beyond conscious definition, to a meditation on death whose double is the uncertainty of knowing whether one hears anymore or not, whether the eyes can see, whether the mind processes, or the self is still reacting. And then at once another level or plateau manifests itself, totally unmotivated, unattached, disconnected, and this is hyper-sensitivity, paranoia, the knowledge that something has arrived, the moment has come. And then again nothing. Vietnam: "a region of unceasing intensities, vibrating upon themselves, which develop by avoiding every orientation towards a culminating point or towards an exterior end."[3] Nguyen Van Ba of the National Liberation Front puts it less poetically when he writes that the "Elite U.S. units were rushed about from one front to another, [illustrating] better than anything else the strategic passivity to which the U.S. command had been driven."[4]

In Balinese society, Bateson writes, there is a lack of climax. "In general the lack of climax is characteristic for Balinese music, drama, and other art forms."[5] Could the same be said about the Viet Cong, that for them the art of war is anticlimactic, just a movement, "derived from the logic of its formal structure, and modifications of intensity determined by the duration and progress of the working out of these formal relations"[6]? And what might we say about the violence as interpreted in this framework? Balinese culture "avoids" quarrels; the Viet Cong avoid direct, head-on contact. But at ambush, at the trap, they are devastating. A rifleman from the 1st Cavalry Division relates how his unit is moving into a valley and suddenly hears the V.C. talking through bullhorns: "kill G.I., kill G.I." An invisible speaking, and then suddenly mortar fire into the center of the unit, widening out so that the men cannot hold a perimeter, and the wounded G.I.s crying out, "Kill me! Kill me!" followed by misdirected ammo drops which the enemy recovers and uses, followed by more wounded, and terrified bystanders with empty clips. And still the steady rain of mortar fire. "I always had a bad habit of being afraid of wounded guys. A wounded guy crying, I didn't know what to do." Paralysis, fragmentation, and then just blur. "When [the N.V.A.] made the rush there was a lot of shooting. They shot all our wounded, killed them. During the course of the fighting all the horror of people being wounded, parts of their body being blown off, became a blur."[7] Typical of the Army, one was always without ammo at such points—alone, terrified, impotent before the screaming of the enemy which had caught one "off guard," in a position which was not a "position" from which to encounter the enemy, a trap or deadly rhizome without sides, bearings, directions, but only a disembodied violence, like being shot point blank. As the North Vietnamese rightly described their perception of the war during the first years of America's commitment to the struggle, it was the U.S. elite troops which took a brutal mauling at the hands of the communist guerrillas and regulars.

And yet this "mauling" never occurred in the form of "decisive battles." Truong Son of the N.L.F. reports that the North Vietnamese took very much into account the American expectation that one ought to win "decisive battles" in Vietnam. "Though somewhat disheartened, the Americans, obdurate by nature and possessed of substantial forces, still clung to the hope for a military solution, for decisive victories on the battlefield." Truong Son's comments are based on the perception that an American view of an all-or-nothing victory can easily be converted to a tactic by which the "superior forces," anxious for quick victory, are by way of a certain fracturing, reduced to something less than victory. That is, the North Vietnamese immediately realized that a molecularization of its forces among those of the Southern resisters would force the United States to spread its resources thin. Son's assessment of the American strategy is that "it did not specifically center on anything" and that "the Americans and their puppets had no definite way of utilizing their mobile and occupation forces . . ."[8] For this reason, even when conflict was "head on," that conflict would be articulated in terms of a certain passivity, since action did not necessarily lead to anything more than action itself. Moreover, the communists saw to it that the "corps" would be disarticulated along various mobile "fronts" all at the same time. In doing so they insured that "action" would be reduced to random or marginalized events which even if successfully won by the Americans would not mean victory. As so many soldiers said to themselves over and over again, "what a waste . . ."

For us the violence and terror which occurred appeared illegitimate and ethically perverse, that sudden blitz out of nowhere, and the mysterious dissolution of the enemy. It was a violence which we could not experience as violence, for nothing really felt like it "engaged" anything else. There is just catastrophe and then Medivac. These various levels of experience, each more or less detached and disarticulated from the other: this constituted the thousand plateaus. It is the recognition that violence or combat is not part of a teleological experience, part of a personally coherent state of affairs in which events can be linked, explained, discussed, argued. For the word "combat" itself was made somewhat obsolete, since it suggests a relation, an active fighting with or against someone. In Vietnam, however, we either launched attacks or sustained them, at least in some regions. But there were no battles, necessarily. Perhaps the tendency to mutilate corpses after a fight was merely an attempt by some of our people to recapture a sense of combat, but here again there was only a certain passive frustration. The enemy was already dead, occupied another plateau, was cut off from the living.

All of our military forces were split up into separate units and separate operations, again, as a general rule. One group may have been extraordinarily well supplied, another stricken by internal dissension which no officer could reconcile, another refusing to go out on missions beyond a certain point. Moreover, certain zones of Vietnam may even have been dumping groups for recalcitrant units, territories of the damned, internal penal colonies within a deterritorializing machinery of war, like the Russian front in World War II where the Nazis sent undesirables. Within the corps, the penal colony within a penal colony. . . Nam as Gulag for the lower classes in America, as re-education center for bad boys who did not make it to college or for former inmates. At the draft board in Santa Ana, California, a man in a red plaid shirt looks across a long table. "Jew boy: you goin'." There were ex-cons too and former mental patients, people with violent tendencies. Within the individual unit, a fracturing of contacts, for there were many noncommunicators, and those plugged-in people who were upward bound ended up in swamps with bullets in their backs. Some called it "friendly fire." And for the dead no climax, and for the living no relief: there were always eager replacements. The plateau is always in flux or motion. Even fragging did not put an end to sergeants, lieutenants, captains, majors, and so on. It is not as if we didn't try.

To talk about the American Army as a *corps sans organes* goes somewhat against the thesis of Deleuze and Guattari about nomad versus the State, because in Vietnam it was the culture of capitalism which played the nomadic role of crazy and the communists who were curiously well directed and unified, much more than we care to believe. As Michael Herr writes in *Dispatches*, "going crazy was built into the tour."[9] Or, as a SEAL scout puts it, ". . . the off times are just as insane as the on-duty times. We'd get in fights, and blow things up . . . . We didn't make much distinction about who the enemy was . . . . All you were supposed to do over there was be crazy."[10] The American intervention: a play of territorialization—deterritorialization—reterritorialization, a movement in which zones would be captured, cleaned out, and then let go again to "other" forces, in which people would be "pacified," killed or relocated, their property annihilated, their bodies often tortured for "information," then left to rot in camps. They were eventually let go, dead or alive, only to face relocation again as refugees, perhaps even after the fall of Saigon, an activity that mimicked the soldiers who were suddenly "dropped" in various "strategic" zones, pulled out, living, wounded, or dead, rested for a time, and "dropped" somewhere else, some place detached from every other place, shuttled back to base or left in the field (who knew where?) in that land without places, that body devoid of any real parts. In Vietnam, the American soldier was the nomad, and not so much because he wanted to be, but because that is what the technology demanded of him. Herr writes, "Airmobility, dig it, you weren't going anywhere. It made you feel safe, it made you feel Omni, but it was only a stunt, technology. Mobility was just mobility. . . ."[11] Here too a plateau is being described in which even the most apparently libidinal movement cannot climax. It is this nomadic movement, this production of the plateau disarticulated from all others that capitalist industry made possible in the skies of Vietnam when it created the Chinook which rode a boundless cushion experienced as if without limits and which produced the sense of a landscape at every point accessible, penetrable, and nonrestricted; a panopticon, in theory, overlooking the rhizome, but from within, and not realizing that. The Chinook, Dust-off, Cobra. . . . Back in the States so many Vets still hear the choppers overhead, the sound of the blades, pitched just right, and the thought, "I'm going to get airlifted. They're going to get me out of here, now, any moment. They're going to land, pick me up, take me away."

Not only air power but tape power accompanies the men in the hovercraft, which is to say, the Vietnam conflict was the first "rock and roll" war. Introjected into the technology, the libidinal impulses of rock became the lure by which some men killed with pleasure, the lure of "heavy metal." Certainly, we don't want to give the impression soldiers walked through the jungles with blaring radios or that all chopper pilots fought to "Light My Fire." Nevertheless, rock had its influence, too. Certainly, if the Frankfurt School could argue that "rationality" legitimized technology and its applications in capitalist society, it must acknowledge too the legitimation of technology not only by means of the Military System's *Herrschaft*, but also by incorporation of libidinal pulsations which strictly speaking reproduce that *Herrschaft* (rock groups as Star, Master, Leader, Hero, Christ Figure) via the so-called "free market,": pulsations whch are not so much "rational" but "desiring," in the sense of Deleuze and Guattari's "desiring machines." Such a machine couples continuous flows and partial objects but itself in turn breaks or punctuates the flows, not unlike a machine gun. And it is this breaking which produces the sense of plateau, the wearing down of that feeling of being omnipotent.

Inevitably, shooting takes on a musical equivalent, and putting the weapon on "automatic fire" was called putting it on "rock and roll." Such locutions make it clear that man's relationship with equipment becomes very complex, that the difference between man and machine, interiority and exteriority, depends largely upon how man interprets his relation to equipment, and that this relation is subject to interpretations in which the equipment a soldier or workers uses is easily introjected into his libidinal or desiring economies. In *Saint Genêt*, Jean-Paul Sartre points out this awareness of a relation between worker, machine, and pop music, a relation which promotes a rich sexual fantasy life. Genêt himself lists the words or thoughts which the factory worker utters while running the machines, and these words are all taken from popular songs. "...Dear stranger, gilded room...lovely lady...my heart adores you...color of the evening ..." Genêt writes: "those fiercely luxurious words, words which must slash their flesh like a ruby-crested dagger."[12] Genêt cannot consider these words without shame, these words whose edge is the violence of the ornamental dagger. Worker, machine, and song, these are but ingredients of crime, of violence, and they breed in the workhouse, in the fantasy-land of the factory, what for Genêt amounts to a penal colony. Indeed, the distance between this and Vietnam is just another matter of time and geography.

The relation between man and technology is of course not simply fantastic, but also hermeneutic, and this has significant bearings on the "meaning" of our means to win the war: aircraft, recoilless rifles, chemicals, rockets, automatic weapons, and all the rest. Heidegger developed the idea of "concern" to characterize our relation to equipment.[13] Technology cannot be defined merely by way of objective cultural representations or ideologies, whose purpose is to master or dominate persons within rational modes of technological production; for technology is itself an order or structure which penetrates and is penetrated by human consciousness. The interface is a hermeneutic enframing, *Gestell*. This covers the Frankfurt School notion of instrumental reasoning, but goes beyond it, complementing Deleuze and Guattari by suggesting that such an enframing is subject to a peculiar deterritorialization. From a third world perspective, the *Gestell* might be seen as an open structure composed of plateaus which do not necessarily connect. In Vietnam, the *Gestell* was in a sense reinterpreted by the enemy as what Deleuze and Guattari call the *machine de guerre*: a nomadic, schizoid, and rhizomic technology that is always inscribed into western technology. Vietnam is exemplary because there the *Gestell* immediately reveals itself as a thousand plateaus, as a disarticulating structure which evades any logical or predictable economy of relations.

If Heidegger's point is that the *Gestell* can be experienced as a "destining or revealing," that man must learn how to conduct his *Daseinanalyse*, his interpretation of Being, in terms of his "concern" with that very *Gestell* in which his "concern" is already produced, revealed, destined, who is he to say that such an interpretation must conform to Western historical and cultural expectations? Indeed, capitalism "invests" its war material with its own *Daseinanalyse* which is peculiarly sensitive to the horizon of death which any piece of weaponry is specifically designed or coded to define. To make the M-16 is already to articulate a consensus of meaning, to arrive, via the Pentagon, at an interpretation of what a given piece of equipment signifies in terms of death, but also in terms of what the West considers compassion, of what the private sector (i.e. Remington, Colt, Mattel, etc.) thinks about such "concerns." The rifle must produce terror, enormous fire power, but must delimit the "amount" of pain and suffering involved. The bullet of the M-16 is designed to kill, mainly, but also to wound in a very specific manner, for its bullet tumbles when hitting the body, shearing off portions of flesh and bone. To be wounded by this bullet is to sustain extensive physical damage, but not so much that the body will never recover, not so much as to be "inhuman." The bullet's purpose: to render man inactive, to make him historically impotent, as far as the *West* is concerned. The bullet must take a man out of political action, must prevent him from affecting us. It is such attitudes which, among much else, inhere in a particular social *Gestell* with respect to the technology of weaponry. Yet, it is myth that any Vietnamese child with a hand-grenade was able to dispel. The release is off, the child walks towards a group of American soldiers, asks for something, and suddenly three people are seriously wounded or killed beside the fragments of what once was a five-year-old talking to G.I.s.

For the Americans the weapon carried much symbolic potential, most notably speed, a sense of power or omnipotence. The weapon must carry not only its horizon of morally acceptable death (a kind of clean or merciful death) but of desire and *Herrschaft*. It belongs to what is still in the Western imagination a Holy Knight or "Red Crosse" Knight of sorts. And it produces the burst, climax, flow, explosion of "busting of caps," effects interpreted as the climax of an on-going process in which violence is the logical consequence (legitimation by means of reason) of one's activities or works in the field (humping). As if one were performing in a kind of theater in which the romance or tragedy mounts until the violence erupts in the last act. Reason, but also desire: for to put the weapon on "rock and roll" or to "bust caps" was to experience the discharge of bullets libidinally, phallically, anally. To fire: to make love to the victim, show him compassion (the wound will not hurt too much, says Red Cross; we are humane), show him the peace sign, that code for "rock and roll" in the 60s. Peace as undecidability, as love/hate without the bar in between. To make peace with the rifle was to make piece, to "fuck" the enemy. To make peace: to rest or dwell in peace, as in death, to pacify the people, as in terror, to let them have "it. . .": the Id or the *es*? To shoot is to decode everything and to produce the rhizome with so many interconnecting plateaus which cannot be coherently accounted for. Like the fragged major in the swamp.

But if we considered the enemy from within such a *Gestell*, this humane export from the United States, so did the Viet Cong in their remarkable third world way. Like the Balinese mother who, Bateson reports, sexually stimulates her child only in order to reject him, to give him a firm slap of disapproval, the Viet Cong similarly stimulated the schizo from America, and not only with whores, but with the lure of its own body, its own corps: the lure of military "engagement." But just as the schizo expects gratification, he finds mommy absent. The trail is cold, the "other" has disappeared without sound. For the Viet Cong knew that what Westerners want is a shoot-out at the "Okay" corral, that they see history in terms of a fascistic sacrificial machine where excess or surplus is ignited, the buildup of the Heideggerian "standing reserve" of the *Gestell* expended in some sort of libidinal climax or *Herrschaft*. To sacrifice, to reconcile groups, to overcome conflict, to make peace, this the Viet Cong and the N.V.A. frustrated at every point. "Let the Americans keep their reserves . . . it will destroy them!" Unlike Heidegger who calls for an exposure of the reserve, its "consumption" in the interpretive process—what amounts to nothing more than a lifting of the veil—the Viet Cong allow that reserve to remain, to let capitalism choke on its surplus values. For surplus has to be expended, if not on the other, then on the self. Already this could be seen in Saigon where G.I.s had more money than they could spend and had to spend it no matter what. The consequences were often disastrous, a fact revealed in the vernacular expression, "he bought it" (got killed). The anxiety coupled with spending wages probably appeared to the Viet Cong as equivalent with the anxiety coupled with the need to fight or engage, to produce body counts by means of the expenditure of the "standing reserve" of that *Gestell* called the arsenal or dump. The Viet Cong, for its part, was content to evade the desire for combat, for peace, the erotics of fighting which the sacrificial machinery, called Western warfare, represented. Indeed this sacrificial technology was thus prevented from producing the kinds of difference the fascistic mimetic model requires, the kinds of separability Westerners depend upon for social coherence, unity, hierarchy, i.e. civilization. And what was particularly astute of the Viet Cong was that it saw within the weaponry itself the deterritorializing power which would prevent it from ever achieving its sacrificial purposes, those libidinal flows which I have called "rock and roll."

Like an analyst, the guerrilla must punctuate the discourse of the psychotic, the schizo, the West, must penetrate its libido with the right response. Like the Lacanian analyst, the Viet Cong remains silent, plays the role of being the "Other" in the forest, behind the treeline. Perhaps the Cong listens, perhaps not. But this does not matter, for the psychotic hears "Charlie" (as American double who is othered) at all times and has lost touch with the real, since he can no longer perceive any boundary between inside and outside. He has become bound by the moebius strip, as a Lacanian might put it, his body cast into different plateaus which do not manage to distinguish themselves unambiguously from one another, yet also do not collapse. In terms of René Girard's theory of sacrifice, this means the psychotic is trapped in a zone of violence which has no borders; thus, the *Gestell* of this sacrificial machine "intends" to at once open and close such a zone, to structure it into acceptable, capitalist social behavior for means of control. But in Vietnam it is as if this machine, once entering the zone of violence (Girard), undecidability (Derrida), the *tourbillon* (Serres), the catastrophe (Thom), the event (Morin), cannot find its way out of the rhizome again, out of the thousand plateaus. Indeed, it is at this point the sacrificial machine has entered, has arrived, and has become Vietnam. Suddenly the country itself turns into a moebius strip, for that blank map, Vietnam, which is written on by Western politics and its technology, has fallen back on itself, and has over-coded, written itself, on the West.

Such reterritorialization extends even to *Daseinanalyse*, for the Viet Cong immediately perceived that using the West's standing reserve of weapons against the West itself, it would be most effective if one did not interpret or use these weapons as the Americans did. Indeed, the Viet Cong did not enter into the capitalist "mirror of production and consumption," but interpreted into the *Gestell* all those "repressed" layers of terror and suffering, coded over by the "civilized" Americans with their notions of domination, drama, and desire. Whereas the Americans could only see war in the macro-terms of all or nothing, everybody lives or everybody dies, the Viet Cong settled for the interstices of liquidation, for the fragmentary victory. Merely to inflict pain by means of taking what was at hand and subjecting it to a bricolage, itself an interpretive field, like the home-made grenade, for example, immediately revealed a strange contradiction in the capitalist invader, one that says everything about his relationship with technology. And with this point we will close.

For all his deterritorialization, the American had still one unshakable faith in a defined zone: his own body. To lose a leg or a hand or foot in American society is a most terrible consequence in a society that believes everyone must be "whole." To be missing the capacity to move, as in paraplegia, or to be missing an arm or a leg contradicts the ideology that insists libido is only attracted to unities. When "Charlie" castrated the corpses of its enemy, it wasn't anything else but a sign pointing to the fact that dismemberment means a loss of sexuality, a ruining of Western man's acceptability as man in the eyes of his peers. To come back without all one's parts, all one's organs, this thought destroyed the effectiveness of Americans in the field. The Westerner always wants to interpret the *Gestell* of war within an all-or-nothing ideology. The body is totally wiped out or must remain totally intact. There is no in-between. But the guerrilla was there to threaten that one last bit of coherence, to reduce not only the corps but the body to *corps sans organes*, to expose the myth of total annihilation by means of a Coke can, a bullet, and a nail. Step on it and you lose your foot.

For the West, power was a matter of presence and absence, of wholes and nothings. Refusing to give up any part, the West insists upon total extermination, which in larger geographical terms amounts to nuclear holocaust, or peace at any price. But communism sees through this myth of totalization. The difference between all or nothing is absolute. It is still two separate entities we are considering, two fragments. Thus one is already talking within the rhizome with its fractures, its plateaus, about the *corps sans organes* which desires to be omnipotent. In this sense the political threat of the West is but an economy of dis-articulating parts, an ideology inherently cloven or dis-membered. Put another way, we are saying that the "whole" body, that sexual and libidinized corps, is perceived by the third world as inherently castrated, and that for this reason it was so easy to terrify troops in the field by simply bringing up again a forgotten trauma, the lack of a phallus, the body as partial object. Enter the guerrilla as schizo-analyst. Indeed, the "unity" which the Military Corps maintained was only another register of the rhizome, split down the middle by an all-or-nothing ideology, de-totalized and fragmented. The Vietnamese's ability to see this contradiction was to sight Vietnam, the Thousand Plateaus, within the metaphysical geo-psychography of the West, to have entered our paradigms only to overcode them with theirs, to liberate from within our *machine de guerre,* in true antipsychiatric fashion, the *corps sans organes.*

Not so much a conflict as a cure . . .

NOTES

1. *Mille Plateaux* (*A Thousand Plateaus*) [Paris: Minuit, 1980], by Gilles Deleuze and Felix Guattari, is the second volume of their work *Capitalism and Schizophrenia*, whose first volume, *Anti-Oedipus*, has been translated into English (Viking, 1977). By way of an attack on orthodox Freudianism, the first volume stages social life as a confrontation between the ideal schizophrenic (revolutionary and "molecular") and the ideal paranoiac (fascist and "molar")—two figures of individual consciousness who will in the untranslated second volume become the nomadic war machine and the State respectively. The rhetoric of the first volume valorizes the mechanical over the organic, individuals being described as "desiring machines," or, in a related formulation, as "bodies without organs" on which certain libidinal "codes" are inscribed. (The same formulations are extrapolated to the outer world of those individuals, to their social and geographical "bodies" which are coded, over-coded, decoded and recoded in a play of what Deleuze and Guattari call "territorialization" and "deterritorialization.") The language of machinery is then replaced in *Mille Plateaux* by a different type of figuration which the authors derive from Christopher Alexander's famous essay, "A City is not a Tree," where the architectonics of the tree is seen as hierarchical: instead, the supreme symbol of the *rhizome* is proposed, which, like schizophrenic consciousness, or like a cancer or a potato, grows out in all directions indifferently and without centralizing or repressive order.
2. *Mille Plateaux*, p. 32.
3. *Ibid*., p. 32.
4. *Vietnamese Studies*, Vol. 20 ("American Failure"), ed. Nguyen Khac Vien, North Vietnamese Government Publication, Hanoi (Dec. 1968). *Vietnamese Studies* is a series of pamphlets written during the 1960s and 1970s which cover various aspects of Vietnam, from medicine, farming, history, to chemical warfare (Agent Orange). These pamphlets have been distributed through Foreign Languages Publishing House in Hanoi and are no longer permitted to be imported into the United States, by order of the United States Government. Still, these studies can be found in various bookstalls. A separate monograph, not part of *Vietnamese Studies*, entitled *National Liberation War in Viet Nam* by General Vo Nguyen Giap is also of great interest.
5. *Steps to an Ecology of Mind* (New York: Ballentine, 1972), p. 113.
6. *Ibid*., p. 113.
7. Al Santoni, *Everything We Had* (New York: Ballentine, 1981), p. 39. The account is by Thomas Bird, a rifleman in the 1st Cavalry Division, August, 1965, to August, 1966.

8. *Vietnamese Studies*, Vol. 20, pp. 13, 16. Truong Son's account is extremely important from our perspective, since he outlines the Vietnamese struggle in terms of varying levels of combative intensification whose purpose is to erode the difference between the sense of an inside and an outside, a front and a rear, a regular army and merely civilians, etc. Some quotations are in order.

> Our combat methods are flexible, diverse and highly effective as they prevail over our adversary's not only in situations of a single type, for a definite time and in a definite theatre, but also in situations of various types, for different durations and in theatres of different sorts. While attaching importance to knocking out enemy forces on the move, just after their landing from the air or in their provisional encampments, etc., by means of ambushes, surprise attacks, mobile warfare or artillery shelling and so on, the PLAF and people of South Vietnam have taken advantage of every opportunity to strike at them in their fortifications (strong points or rear bases) in skillful and bold attacks. Using sometimes only few troops, they succeeded in limiting the effect of the enemy's firepower, scoring major successes and reducing their own losses. (47)

And yet, as Son insists, the Vietnamese who fought for communist ideals did not simply act on small scales.

> Our combat methods derived their superiority from the fact that they made it possible for every fighter and every unit either to independently search out the enemy to knock him out or to closely co-operate with other fighters and units according to a common plan in a whole series of actions or a whole campaign. That is why we fight the enemy in every theatre ... [Our combatants] carry out independent activities simultaneously with small and large-scale operations and coordinated actions lasting for many days. (51)

Again,

> With our combat methods everything in our people's hands can be turned into a weapon against the enemy, even a stick, a carrying pole or a heap of stones. With rudimentary weapons used very skillfully, cleverly and widely, we have caused heavy losses to the GI's. And it is only natural that these American "playboys" dread the spiked pits and booby traps laid by our guerrillas and people, into which they fall everyday. (52)

The point in all of these comments is that the third world redefines the divisions or categories of the westerner. There is a fluidity of combinative intensities which allows at once for the most primitive and most advanced methods of warfare. The American enemy is on all sides at once, working in all kinds of heterogeneous modes and combining or recombining them at will. Here, too, there is a *corps sans organes*. The aim is not quick victory, of course, but what the North Vietnamese call "nibbling tactics," a "sapping" which produces a kind of "quagmire" or sea of disarticulated and hostile activities whose climaxes are never really peaks, but merely plateaus of various intensities which take their toll and then subside. In this we notice a very Batesonian example of a form of social activity which defies the western sense of climax and purpose.

9. *Dispatches* (New York: Knopf, 1978), p. 61.

10. *Everything We Had*, p. 212. Related by Mike Beamon, U.S. Navy SEALS, August, 1968 –February, 1969.

11. *Dispatches*, p. 12.

12. (New York: Signet, 1971), p. 252.

13. *The Question Concerning Technology* (New York: Harper and Row, 1977).

INTRODUCTION

An intriguing aspect of the radicalization in the 60s was the appearance in the West of Maoism, a Maoism which assumed very different forms in the various national contexts.[1] This essay is about a type of French Maoism—referred to here as "antihierarchical Maoism"—which was rooted both in Mao's thought itself and in specifically French political phenomena. Though it never had any equivalent in the United States, there are good reasons to expose American readers to it. First, we all learn from experience, our own as well as that of others. National singularity should not be taken to mean that the relevance of a struggle is necessarily limited: some of its aspects will be and some will not, but to see which is which presupposes knowledge. Parochialism, in other words, can only be debilitating. Second, antihierarchical Maoism raised basic questions about the nature of oppressive power, about the problematic of the personal/cultural/political, and about the criteria of emancipatory struggle. One does not have to accept the positions or actions of this political movement to recognize the transnational importance of these issues. Finally, to give an account of this particular Maoist experience is also to add "life" to some of the outstanding theoretical work coming out of France during and since the 60s. Sartre, Lefebvre, Althusser, and Foucault all had a relation of one kind or another with antihierarchical Maoism. Sartre was a particularly important figure for he directly and consistently participated in the work of the largest and most enduring of the antihierarchical Maoist groups.

Despite the historical strength of the left, France still has one of the most inegalitarian economic structures in the western world. The class distinctions are sharp and everywhere in evidence. But the victims of French capitalism are not only internal. For France, like the United States, has been very active militarily in order to keep third world peoples within the orbits of western capitalism. It was France which tried, with American financial support, until the defeat in 1954 at Dien Bien Phu to maintain its Indochinese colonies by military force; France which fought a war between 1956 and 1962 to preserve Algeria as an administrative part of the country; and

France which has kept a military presence throughout its former West African colonies to this day.

However, the war in Algeria differed from the earlier war in Indochina in terms of who did the fighting and the impact upon the political system at home. A deliberate decision was made not to use conscripts in Indochina. In Algeria, they were used. The war in Indochina posed no real threat to the political system in the metropole. The war in Algeria resulted in the fall of the Fourth Republic and the institution of the more authoritarian Fifth Republic under de Gaulle. It also stimulated a considerable antiwar movement in which students played a major role.

The conflict between the authoritarian regime and the students survived the termination of the war in 1962. The Algerian War proved to be a crucial stimulus for a much more general radicalization of youth in the 60s. It played a key role in the delegitimization of a variety of adult-dominated structures. The educational system, for instance, came to be viewed as a conduit funneling young people into military bureaucracies to fight imperialist wars, or into capitalist bureaucracies, whether public or private, to earn a living as a supporting cog in a system of repressive privilege. Such lack of control over one's own destiny, and the oppressive archaism of the educational system itself, generated among radicalized youth more than an empathetic relation to other victims of the overall system.

This alienation extended to the traditional political parties on the left as well as to the ruling Gaullists. For it was under a "socialist," Guy Mollet, that the Algerian War began in earnest. Premier Mollet also intervened in 1956, together with the British and the Israelis, to seize the Suez Canal. Mollet's party, the SFIO, predecessor of today's Socialist Party, thus appeared to many young people not only to be playing along with the inegalitarian bourgeois system but to be one of the most aggressively colonialist forces in the country. Even the traditionally anticolonialist Communist Party was tarnished because its parliamentary deputies had voted to give the military emergency powers in Algeria and had voted for the military budget during the war. Moreover, the party's leaders denounced the more militant antiwar movement for what was regarded as adventuristic tactics.

Radicalized youths thus alienated from these two parties gravitated toward other structures, such as the national student union (UNEF), which had become the leading power in the antiwar movement; the *Parti Socialiste Unifié*, a new party created by antiwar socialists and dissidents from the Communist Party, the Catholic MRP, and the Radical Socialists; and the *Union des Etudiants Communistes* (UEC). Despite its affiliation with the Communist Party, the UEC was actually controlled between 1963 and 1965 by a melange of young Marxist dissidents: infiltrating Trotskyists, "Togliattists" influenced by the more independent-minded Italian Communists, and Maoists.

Initially in dealing with antiwar demonstrations, and after 1962, with regard to demonstrations around educational issues as well, the Gaullist regime introduced more blatantly repressive measures. For the first time, massive police violence was used not only against workers and the poor but also against the sons and daughters of the upper middle and middle classes who took to the streets to demonstrate their opposition. In constricting the range of what would be accepted as legitimate oppositional activity, the Gaullist regime forced people into much more basic and deliberate transgression. Antihierarchical Maoism was one expression of this transgression, the refusal to work within the confines of "legitimacy" established by those holding power.

In all of this—the imperialist war, the delegitimization, the repression and the radicalization — France bore striking similarities with the United States. But France had a vastly larger old left and movements like the Maoists found themselves fighting against both capitalism and against what was considered the conservative hold of the established leftist parties over the working class. Another difference with the United States was the strong and largely indigenous tradition of anarchism/syndicalism/utopianism within the French working class, powerfully expressed in the general strikes of 1936 and 1968, and in the demand for *autogestion*, workers' control over the work place.

This tradition meshed in a very interesting way with one aspect of Maoism, the suspicion that no matter how dedicated an agent might be to the general welfare, there will always be an unfortunate tendency to confuse the agent's welfare with the general welfare. The resemblance to Rousseau, an important source for the French tradition in question, is strong: for he had argued that, though necessary, the executive structure would have to be forced to take direction from the masses and to be held accountable to them. In Mao, this becomes the "mass-line."[2] Lenin's model, in which the masses learn from the party,[3] is transformed by Mao into one in which the party learns from, and is accountable to, the masses, in this instance the Chinese peasantry. The chief example of this was of course the Cultural Revolution, where the General Will (represented by the Red Guards) forced the functionaries, professors and officers back out into the fields and work places so as to reconnect government and masses.[4] This fit the indigenous French radical tradition well and provided the originating source of inspiration for antihierarchical Maoism.

The United States has neither an enduring antihierarchical radical heritage nor large hierarchical parties on the left. Rather than emerging against the backdrop of such parties, U.S. Maoism appeared in the context of the loosely organized and largely countercultural Students for a Democratic Society. Reacting negatively to these characteristics of SDS and the countercultural milieu in general, Maoist groups in the United States were uniformly hierarchical in structure and "proletarian" rather than "countercultural" in morality. The U.S. group which most resembled the French antihierarchical Maoists was Weatherman but it had a general anti-imperialist rather than a specifically Maoist orientation. With this in mind we may now turn to the specifics of the development of anti-hierarchical Maoism in France.

FRENCH MAOISM UP TO 1968

The Delegitimization of the French Communist Party

Maoism in France had two distinct points of origin, reflective of the generational cleavages of the 1960s. One was the "adult" Communist Party itself. The early 60s was difficult for that party. The leadership, under the chairmanship of Maurice Thorez, was rigidly Stalinist and had become a subject of ridicule, particularly when compared with the less doctrinaire and more "realistic" positions of the Italian party led by Palmiro Togliatti. The Italian model gave many western Marxists a basis for viewing the French party as ossified without learning capacity.

"Doctrinaire," however, was not the opposite of "pragmatic." Internally, the party was being severely judged for its "pragmatism," especially during the Algerian War. While the party had always maintained a formal opposition to colonialism, its parliamentary representatives did vote for the granting of special powers to the military in Algeria and for the military budget. The party took the position that the war should be ended by a negotiated settlement and it severely denounced those elements of the left which gave aid to or took to the streets in support of the Algerian National Liberation Front. In fact, it looked disfavorably on any demonstrations that it did not sponsor. Its pragmatic and nationalist political position on Algeria (which, unlike the formal colonies, was juridically an integral part of France) was of course enforced within the party and was to carry a considerable price in terms of the image of the party among youth.

What the party did not need at that point was Khrushchev's de-Stalinization campaign and the Sino-Soviet split. The split came in 1962, precisely the year when the Algerian War ended, and the youthful antiwar movement was at its height. The Chinese viewed de-Stalinization as a cover for a right-wing revisionist position adopted by the Soviets under Khrushchev. In their eyes, Stalin had indeed been guilty of excesses and of establishing a personality cult, but the general thrust of Stalin's substantive policies had been positive. They saw de-Stalinization as a foil to justify the self-serving revisionism of his successors.

The French party was caught in a dilemma. It was caught between the commitment which it had made to Stalin and his policies, and its commitment to the line of the Soviet party as the leading communist party in the world.

It should be understood that the commitment to Stalin within the French Communist Party was not simply a phenomenon imposed from the top down. For many in the rank and file, especially those who had been active in the underground during World War II, Stalin was the leader who had initially been abandoned by the West to deal with Hitler alone and, after that, the one who provided the leadership by which the Russian people resisted defeat by the Nazis at such high cost in human life and suffering. There was a kinship between the resistance of the French Communists (after so many other supposed antifascists had caved in to Vichy) and the resistance of the Russians in the East. Many thus accorded Stalin the same kind of esteem and respect that they accorded to the leaders of the French Resistance. This basis of support for Stalin is often overlooked. It was also more difficult for the younger generation of the 60s to understand, as well as for Americans who did not experience the fighting of World War II on their soil and who did not have to hope with the same desperation that the Russians would be able to contain the Nazis on the Eastern Front.

Ultimately, the French party leadership demanded more explanations from the Kremlin and took a longer period of time to adapt than most of the other parties, but eventually it came around to accepting de-Stalinization and to defending the Soviet Union in its theoretical and ideological conflict with the Chinese party.

An Autonomous Maoist Movement Begins

Prior to the Sino-Soviet rupture, however, there were members of the French Communist Party who had taken a special interest in China and who had affiliated with the Franco-Chinese Friendship Association: something which, of course, presented no problems as long as the Soviet and Chinese parties were still "fraternal." As the pressures to accept de-Stalinization and to side with the Soviet party against the Chinese intensified, pro-Chinese party members began to form "Marxist-Leninist Circles." These "circles" provided the pro-Chinese party members with a means of resistance to de-Stalinization and an anti-Chinese position—both of which were covers for a severe distortion of Marxism-Leninism in their eyes.

By 1964, it became impossible for these people to maintain their foothold within the party. After passing through two less centralized pre-party stages from 1964 to 1967, they constituted the *Parti Communiste Marxiste-Lêniniste de France* (PCMLF) in the latter year. This party was immediately accorded recognition by the Chinese and Albanian parties.

The young Maoists in the *Union des Etudiants Communists* (UEC) were able to remain in the UEC longer than their Maoist elders were able to remain in the parent party and even longer than the Trotskyists and Togliattists were able to remain in the UEC. Stalinism was not the emotional issue for them that it was for their elders. While they were influenced by the critiques that party member Louis Althusser was beginning to make of the party leadership and while they were strongly opposed to the party's backing of Mitterrand's 1965 presidential candidacy, they muted their criticisms.

Like Althusser, who remained in the party, the young Maoists in the UEC apparently still hoped that they could be an effective voice in preventing the party from irreparably divorcing itself from the "science" of Marxism-Leninism.[5]

In late 1965, the purge of the UEC Maoists began. In February 1966, a group called the *Union des Jeunesses Communistes (Marxiste-Lêniniste)*, or UJCML, was created by purged and to-be-purged UEC Maoists. Initially it was cautious and did not wave the Little Red Book or pictures of Mao before the party leadership. But at the UEC's April Congress, held the month after Althusser's positions had been officially denounced by the party's Central Committee, the UJCML distributed a tract which contained a broadside attack on the positions of the Central Committee. The party immediately completed the purge of the Maoists from the UEC.

The PCMLF, whose members were older and predominantly workers, felt that the young and almost exclusively student members of the UJCML needed an affiliation with their party, but the younger students refused. Against arguments that youth and intellectual status cannot serve as a sufficient basis for organizing mass struggle, the UJCML responded that what it did not know about the direct experience of workers—and such "secondary categories" as small and tenant farmers and even elements of the bourgeoisie — it could find out by going out to the people and learning from them. This was a technique which the Maoists referred to as the *enquête*. The party structure of the PCMLF was viewed as too closed to maintain this kind of openness to input from the masses. The PCMLF and the UJCML thus wound up exchanging charges of elitism.

The UJCML did not reject the PCMLF's party conception in principle; it only rejected its appropriateness at that particular stage in the struggle. And the Chinese were going through a stage of their own revolution which proved very helpful to the UJCML's arguments against the PCMLF's overtures in France: this was the Cultural Revolution, embarked upon in 1966, in which Mao elevated the young Red Guards to the position of defenders of the revolution against middle-aged cadres of the party as well as against those of the bureaucracy, army, and universities who were accused of insulating "their" positions from the people. The rejection of the PCMLF's party conception and the emphasis upon the *enquête* ultimately rested upon the same legitimizing principle as the Chinese Cultural Revolution, Mao's theory of the "mass line."

But it did not take long for both the PCMLF and the UJCML to split internally over the party issue. Some of the intellectuals within the PCMLF argued for a loosely knit "grand alliance" of Maoists with more fluid organizational patterns. Some in the UJCML became concerned that the people conducting the Cultural Revolution in China were supporting the PCMLF, and grew convinced that they themselves were indeed manifesting petit-bourgeois elitism by remaining apart from it. A "liquidationist" current thus developed within the UJCML, and it was during this period of self-questioning and self-criticism that the 1968 student revolt exploded.

The UJCML was caught completely off balance. Its militants went into the streets not to mount the barricades but to argue for their dismantling. They argued that only the workers could make a true revolution and that without them the confrontations would be meaningless. Ironically, the PCMLF was more supportive of the students, and some of its members or sympathizers were on the barricades. Once labor unions began to demonstrate support for the students and workers began to conduct strikes and plant occupations, the UJCML attempted to join forces with the broader movement by organizing "long marches" out to the factories in support of the workers.

But this did not save the organization. The liquidationists argued that the regime had survived the 1968 uprising because there was no disciplined party willing and able to give direction to the energy unleashed by the revolt, and they gained the majority. UJCML people who had taken jobs in factories were called out. Some withdrew from the world of practice into the world of texts in order to seek guidance. Others went directly into the PCMLF. Still others cut new paths, one of which was "antihierarchical Maoism."

ANTIHIERARCHICAL MAOISM

In the late 60s and in the 70s, the French used different words to signify a hierarchical Maoist organization such as the PCMLF and the kind of antihierarchical groupings that we are about to examine. The former was referred to as *Marxist-Léninist* (needless to say the Communist Party did not accept this as accurate) while the latter were referred to as *les Maoistes* or simply *les Maos*. This was more than a linguistic device to differentiate. It was a ranking. The antihierarchical Maoists managed to steal Mao's name away from the hierarchical PCMLF and subsequent hierarchical groups. They did this by their daring actions and high visibility at a time when the PCMLF (which had been banned after the 1968 revolt) was trying to survive clandestinely.

The antihierarchical Maoists were characterized by fluid organizational patterns, a refusal to be bound by the orthodoxy of any texts, and a highly confrontational posture. Two of these movements were of particular importance. One had a much shorter life-span than the other but managed to make its mark in that brief period.

Vive la Révolution

Vive la Révolution (VLR) was a small movement of no more than a few hundred people which did not last beyond July of 1971.[6] VLR, like most Maoist movements, sent its members into factories to organize. Although

VLR militants worked in approximately twenty factories in the Parisian area, its special target was the Citroën plant in Paris' 15th Arrondissement. This was a brave choice because Citroën was known for its company unionism and its very tight discipline.

VLR centered its criticism of bourgeois society around the concept of "everyday life" developed by the philosopher Henri Lefebvre.[7] As this concept was elaborated by the VLR in its paper *Tout*, greater and greater emphasis was devoted to the libidinal aspects of life stressed by Wilheim Reich. *Tout*, of which sixteen issues were produced, was the first widely circulated publication on the French left to analyze problems of sex, women's liberation, and homosexuality. The inclusion of this dimension proved to be the undoing of the VLR. One particularly salty issue, Number 12, had wide-ranging repercussions. VLR's factory organizers protested that the editorial staff had produced something which was totally useless for their task; the Norman Bethune Maoist Bookstore refused to sell it; the government banned and seized it. The government also brought an obscenity charge against Jean-Paul Sartre who had agreed to serve as its nominal editor.[8]

The remaining four issues were devoted to an analysis of the puritanical attitudes of the French far left and of its unwillingness or inability to see that any truly emancipatory revolution would have to combat sexual as well as economic and political repression. It should be recalled that there was no "counterculture" in France equivalent to the American phenomenon up to this point. French leftists tended to be very conventional people socially and culturally. While the VLR put itself out of existence by taking such a position, it was in fact helping to set the stage for the appearance of the countercultural phenomena which did manifest themselves in France by the mid-70s. And, according to Remi Hess, both the women's liberation movement (the *Mouvement de Libération des Femmes*, MFL) and the gay movement in France (the *Front Homosexuel d'Action Révolutionnaire*, FHAR) grew out of the VLR experience and were initially led by former VLR militants.[9]

LA GAUCHE PROLÉTARIENNE

The Nature of the "Movement"

In September 1968, a current of the non-liquidationists called "Mao-spontex" ("spontex" referring to spontaneity) created a movement called the *Gauche Prolétarienne* (the Proletarian Left or GP). Simultaneously, a newspaper called *La Cause du Peuple* (the People's Cause or CDP) was started. The GP became the most aggressive and durable action arm of the antihierarchical Maoist movement, and the CDP its public and information arm.

A fragment of the former UJCML, the GP did not involve many people at the very beginning. But it did receive a shot in the arm in terms of numbers and energy when some of the militants from the Nanterre

Mouvement du 22 mars came into the GP in February and March of 1969. The *22 mars* played a catalytic role in the 1968 revolt on the Nanterre campus of the University of Paris. Although it was actually a coalition which included people inclined toward Maoism as well as Frankist Trotskyists and their sympathizers, the dominant tone and public image of the *22 mars* was set by Daniel Cohn-Bendit (the famous "Danny the Red") and his anarchist comrades. Also, some of the fence-straddlers in the dispute between the "liquidationists" and the Mao-spontex current decided to enter the GP about this time.

During the last year and a half of the 60s the GP and the CDP caused sufficient grief to the French establishment that the movement was outlawed and the editors of the newspaper prosecuted and imprisoned. This time, however, the charges had nothing to do with obscenity. They were strictly political in the conventional sense of the term.

In the first two years of existence, the GP attempted to close the gap between what it called the "antiauthoritarian youth revolt" and the proletarian revolution. It sent its members into the Renault automobile plant at Flins, a plant which had erupted in 1968. The government, the management of the nationalized plant, and the CGT local were extremely sensitive about political work in the plant. The confrontations turned into violent conflict and the plant which had been stormed by the police during the 1968 uprising was once again the scene of police action.

Priority was also placed upon organization in and around the high schools, much the way Weatherman was doing in the United States. Atypically drawing upon a World War II image, the high school students were encouraged to join the GP in its "nonarmed but violent battle of the partisans"[10]—not only in Flins and other plants but in the ghettos and working-class suburbs.

These first two years of the life of GP Maoism represented the high point of organizational structure for the movement. During this stage there was a committee structure at the national, regional and local level. The committees called and coordinated periodic "general assemblies of workers" at which the real decisions were supposed to be made. The people within the movement were convinced that they were fighting against the distinction between leaders and nonleaders in the making of decisions, and the general assemblies were supposed to maximize political equality. Although this was the conscious goal, some people did emerge as more influential than others and these "leaders" were disproportionately male. The men in the GP did not display the same sensitivities as the men in the VLR.

The government was increasingly fed up with the trouble the Maoists were causing in the plants. But firing and/or arresting militant workers did not work because more always seemed to take their place. And even though the movement was more highly structured at this early point than later, it was still too amorphous for the government to attack directly.

In March 1970, therefore, the government decided to strike at the only visible and accessible organ of the GP movement—its newspaper. The two editors of *La Cause du Peuple*, Le Bris and Le Dantec, were arrested and arraigned for trial. The police also began to seize the paper and to attack and arrest the vendors. Simply selling the paper could result in a year in prison and perpetual loss of civil rights.

After the arrests of Le Bris and Le Dantec, Alain Geismar, a former university teacher and leader of one of the professors' unions who was also one of the three most prominent personalities involved in the 1968 revolt (along with Cohn-Bendit and student union leader Jacques Sauvageot), stepped in to fill the gap as editor of the CDP. Geismar, who had been fired from his teaching position because of his activities in '68, moved closer to the *22 mars* people and came into the GP with some of them in early 1969.

Geismar, however, was also arrested, under the so-called "Anti-Wrecker Law" (*Loi Anti-Casseur*) which the Gaullists had passed after the 1968 revolt. Under its terms, anyone who participated in a demonstration or in a process leading to a demonstration could be held culpable for the actions committed by any demonstrator. Two days before the trial of Le Dantec, a number of groups sponsored a rally. Geismar spoke. There was to be a demonstration on the day of the trial itself. The police banned the demonstration—which was their usual practice. The demonstration took place anyway; the police broke it up; there were approximately 490 arrests; and Geismar was charged with incitement even though he was not there. Although no one was killed or charged for murder during this affair, the process employed by the government to get Geismar was similar to that used to hunt down and punish the anarchists who were not at the Haymarket Massacre in Chicago.

Unlike some of those people, however, Geismar was not hanged. Liberal democracy showed its more humane face. He was sentenced to, and served, eighteen months in prison, five of them in solitary confinement. Le Bris had already drawn an eight month term and Le Dantec was sentenced to a year. These two were charged only with editing the CDP. In addition to the prison sentences given to the CDP's editors, the government banned the *Gauche Prolétarienne* by a ministerial decree during Geismar's trial.

But the GP did not cease to exist. It changed its name to the "ex-GP." Nor did *La Cause du Peuple* cease publication. On the contrary, after Geismar's arrest, Jean-Paul Sartre once again assumed the nominal directorship of a publication, this time the CDP. Publisher François Maspéro also went out on the streets to sell the paper. This was a clear challenge to the government to arrest personalities with world-wide reputations and to try them for the same acts for which lesser known younger militants had been imprisoned. Maspéro was arrested but slapped only with the minor charge of vending without a license but the government took no action at all against Sartre.

The GP militants were convinced that there was an inner dialectic at work so that the movement "naturally" arrived at certain stages at certain points in time, a dialectic which neither they nor the government could completely control. Thus, while committed to a highly voluntaristic conception of the "politics of the act," the movement also had a strong element of nonvoluntarism. For example, the reaction to the government's banning of the GP was to see the underground stage as the next "natural" one anyway. Even if the government had not banned the GP, this stage would have been dictated by other factors in the environment and the internal, ineluctable dynamics of the movement.

The theme for 1970–71 became "Widen the Resistance" and emphasis was placed upon action through local, decentralized groups. Some of these groups were already in existence; a number had to be created from scratch. The base committees in the factories (*comités de base*) were in the former category. But in the spring of 1971 new militant strike forces were created in the plants to deal physically with the attempts to suppress the work of the base committees and to punish individual bosses or management personnel who abused workers. Committees were organized in the secondary schools. Support groups for the Vietnamese and the Palestinians were set up, and, finally, a wide network of GP support groups was established. The most important of these was *Secours Rouge* which was directed by Maspéro and which enjoyed the participation or active support of a good number of prominent intellectuals, including Sartre. There were also *Les Amis de la Cause du Peuple*. People in this sold papers and extended other support to the CDP. The *Comités Vêrité et Justice* were a little different. They did not engage in illegal activity as the other two did. Rather, they investigated, determined, and publicized specific cases in which bourgeois legality was unjustly twisted to the detriment of the deprived and to the benefit of the wealthy and powerful. They judged the dominant powers in ways that the latter did not and could not be expected to judge themselves.

GP Maoism was now conforming more to Kenneth Keniston's definition of a "movement" than to a formal organization.[11] Both in terms of their internal transformations and in terms of their actions directed at the external environment, the GP and ex-GP Maoists were the most *dynamic* people on the French far left. Their actions were almost always dramatic. They were sometimes even the stuff that movies were made of, particularly in the hands of Maoist or Maoist sympathizing directors such as Jean-Luc Godard, who directed *La Chinoise* and (with his collaborator Jean Pierre Gorin) the even more widely known *Tout Va Bien*.[12] Add to this the support of Sartre, Maspéro, and other literary and artistic figures, the charisma of Geismar, and the aura of 1968 and one can begin to understand the drama—even the glamour—which surrounded GP Maoism.

Let us now take a closer look at the concrete practice of the GP Maoists, both prior to and after the banning, in four different areas.

THE GP AND EX-GP IN ACTION
(1) The Assault on Renault

The most daring and dangerous of the movement's activities was its factory work. The GP and then the ex-GP operated in a number of plants and work settings throughout France including Brandt and Berliet in Lyon, Batignolles in Nantes, the shipyards in Dunkerque, and the coal mines in the North. However, the Renault automobile plant at Billancourt, on the perimeter of Paris, became a special target.

First, the GP Maoists wanted to pick up on and generalize the sabotage which was already going on inside the plant and which was part of an overall increase in worker militancy at that time.[13] Secondly, they wanted to pass from clandestine instances of sabotage to a more open campaign against what they called "the terrorism of the administration."[14] This brought the Maoists into open and direct conflict with the CGT—dominated by the Communist Party—which was trying to keep the focus of the workers on bread and butter issues.

After encouraging the organization of approximately a dozen *comités de lutte* (committees of struggle, patterned after the 1968 "action committees") in various sections of the plant, the Maoists engaged in their first major battle which incurred the wrath of the CGT. In response to an increase in the metro fares, the Maoists organized workers into large groups which jumped over the turnstiles and refused to pay any fares. When eight metro police officers attempted to intervene, they were roughed up and chased away. The CGT attacked the Maoists for beating up public employees. The Maoists refused to recognize police of any nature as normal employees with whom they had a proletarian bond. They were seen simply as the enforcers of the legal norms of the established order. In response to the action of the Maoists, massive deployments of regular police were sent to the station near the plant and the police sought their own violent revenge.

The Maoists also ran afoul of the CGT in a campaign against an increase in meal prices in the plant restaurant, an increase in which the CGT was directly complicit because it dominated the *Comité d'Etablissement* which administered the restaurant. The Maoists distributed tracts against the increase and called for action. Some workers took food without paying in a tactic similar to that applied in the metro. Fights broke out in the canteen between Maoists and CGT militants. The Maoists claimed to enjoy the support of a good number of immigrant workers and accused the CGT of bringing in members of the Communist youth movement to help them battle the Maoists. While the Maoists won on neither the metro nor the lunchroom issue, they felt that they had unmasked the CGT as a bureaucratic structure which was not looking after the interests of the workers.

After these initial campaigns, the Maoists turned their attention to the work process itself. They adopted a task rotation strategy to challenge pay differentials based upon the hierarchical division of labor. Each worker in a particular unit would teach every other worker how to perform his or her task. When every worker could perform every task, all of the workers demanded the pay of the highest paid among them on the grounds that all were equally qualified.

They also encouraged the direct confrontation of supervisory personnel. Workers began timing themselves rather than accepting the word of the supervisors. Supervisors who complained about the quality of the work were forced into the pits to do the work themselves. And what was regarded as grossly arbitrary behavior toward any worker or demonstrations of racism toward immigrant workers was punished by the *Groupes Ouvriers Anti-Flics* (the GOAF or Anti-Cop Workers Groups). Some supervisory personnel were beaten up and at least one foreman in the painting section had a bucket of paint poured over his head.

As violent resistance against the management increased, so did conflict with the CGT. But even one hierarchical Maoist group with no love for the CGT attacked the GP Maoists for being so indiscriminate in their tactics that on two occasions they attacked anyone who came into range wearing the white smock characteristic of lower management and supervisory personnel in the plant.

More and more plant police were added to the Billancourt factory. Firings for political activity, violent or nonviolent, accelerated. Some of the fired workers were handed over to the regular police stationed at the factory gates and were charged with crimes. Others, who were just fired and ejected from the plant, went on a hunger strike. Two important sources of moral support were Sartre, whom the GP Maoists managed to smuggle into the plant for an inspection trip but who was quickly ejected by plant police, and actress Simone Signoret who paid supportive visits to the hunger strikers. While Signoret was supporting this concrete action of the GP Maoists, her husband Yves Montand was making *Tout Va Bien* with Jane Fonda, a film which provided a supportive dramatization of the tactics of GP Maoists.[15]

The confrontations reached a peak in February and March 1972. Pierre Overney, a twenty-three year old ex-GP Maoist Renault worker who had been fired along with a number of his politically active comrades, returned to the factory gates on Friday, February 25. He and the others were distributing tracts to the workers as they entered and left the gates. He got into a verbal dispute with one of the heads of the security section at the plant, a M. Tramoni. Standing a good distance from Overney, Tramoni pulled a gun and fatally shot him.

The next day, Renault workers found the plant completely surrounded by the paramilitary police, the CRS, who checked the papers of all of the workers. Seven workers who had known of the killing on Friday and who had participated in a demonstration against it were fired. On Tuesday police circled the plant in convoys and four more workers were fired. On

Thursday, eleven workers who had been dismissed before or after the killing managed to get into the plant and issued a public call to resistance. They were attacked by Tramoni's security personnel and turned over to the police. Five were charged under the Anti-Wrecker Law.

But the Maoists did not rest content with a protest over the killing of one of their own and the firings of their militants and supporters. An ex-GP commando group, the *Groupe Pierre Overney de la Nouvelle Résistance Populaire*, seized and held in an undisclosed location the chief personnel officer at Billancourt, Robert Nogrette. The Maoists had previously engaged in holding bosses prisoner in plants until they granted concessions (or were freed by the police) and in a plant of a subsidiary of Renault they had "fired" a boss by kicking him out of the plant and obliging him to remain out for several days. But the Nogrette action was one which was perceived as being of a more serious order, serious enough to attract the personal attention and denunciation of President Pompidou.

The commando group demanded, in return for Nogrette's release, that criminal charges be dropped against the workers who had been turned over to the police and that all workers fired after Overney's death be reinstated. There was never a threat to kill Nogrette. And, despite the fact that the police were not able to find him and that the concessions were not made, he was released unharmed after approximately forty-eight hours. The Maoists had expected the labor unions to denounce the action and they did so. But it is not so clear that they had expected pressure from another source, the negative reaction of most of the other far left groups which had declared their solidarity with the ex-GP in the massive street processions and demonstrations which had followed Overney's killing.[16] Even the *Ligue Communiste Révolutionnaire*, the most confrontational of the Trotskyist organizations and one which had good relations with the GP Maoists, joined with most of the other far left organizations in publicly criticizing the operation. The *Ligue*, which at the time was a major supporter of guerrilla warfare tactics in Latin America, felt that the act made no sense in the French political context, particularly when the Maoists clearly had no intention of killing Nogrette if their demands were not met. Indeed, those demands were not met, Nogrette was released unharmed, and it became virtually impossible to do political work at the Renault plant after this affair.

(2) Work with the Immigrants

The second major thrust of the work of the GP and ex-GP Maoists was directed at the large immigrant worker population. These workers are disproportionately clustered at the lowest job classifications and hence at the lowest wage rates—sometimes at variance with their actual skills or with the tasks which they actually perform. They are thus also the least able to absorb increases in such costs at metro fares, food prices, and rents. The Maoists hoped that by protesting the price increases, adopting the task rotation tactic, and physically punishing supervisory personnel who exhibited racist behavior against Arab or black African workers, they would gain the support of the immigrant workers and trigger off greater militancy on their part.

An additional tactic designed to appeal to Arab workers from Algeria, Morocco, and Tunisia was the creation of Palestine Support Committees in the plants. Initially, the GP Maoists gave considerable attention to the war in Indochina. Their own *Comités Vietnam de Base* extended uncritical support to the efforts of both the Provisional Revolutionary Government in the South and the government of North Vietnam. The Maoists' tactics brought them into a number of violent clashes with the police, once after they had taken over the South Vietnamese embassy in Paris and run the flag of the National Liberation Front up over it. However, in the ex-GP stage, they shifted the emphasis of their work away from Vietnam towards the Palestinian issue, which had more appeal to the immigrant worker population that they were trying to reach. Indeed, support for the return of the Palestinian Arabs to their homeland was virtually the only non-French issue to which the ex-GP devoted substantial attention.[17]

However, the Maoists did not limit their attempt to reach the immigrant worker population to agitation within the plants. From its formation in 1968, GP Maoism directed its attention to the plight of immigrant workers who were forced to live in the shantytowns (*bidonvilles*) spread across France but more numerous in the Parisian region. The word *bidon* means a drum (such as an oil drum) and the huts were made of any such materials which could be stuck together to form a roof and walls. Heating, sanitation, or running water were luxuries not to be found in these make-shift structures. These certainly contributed to the high rates of disease, particularly tuberculosis, among the immigrant workers and their families.

The Maoists were active on several fronts in the *bidonvilles*. While denouncing their existence, they insisted that acceptable alternate housing be provided before the *bidonvilles* were destroyed. They thus attempted to avoid urban renewal, American style. The GP Maoists fought this battle particularly strenuously in Argenteuil, a Parisian suburb in which the Communist Party controlled city hall. *Secours Rouge*, the GP support group, attempted to supply services which were supplied inadequately or not at all by public authorities. In one of the more highly publicized actions of a Maoist commando group, Fauchon, the fashionable food shop, was raided and delicacies were distributed in the *bidonvilles*. While a hierarchical Maoist group created in 1970 also began to work in the *bidonvilles*, the GP Maoists were there first. Together, they called national and international attention to the existence of these abysmal conditions and this activity undoubtedly played a major role in the French government's determination to dismantle them in a remarkably short period of time. By 1975, almost all of the *bidonvilles* were gone.

The GP and the ex-GP Maoists also worked within the regular immigrant ghettos in the larger cities as well as within the residences constructed specifically to house immigrant workers. In the former, they attempted to organize around the issues of police harassment, violent racist attacks by whites, and the irresponsibility of landlords. Particularly favored tactics were rent strikes, resistance to eviction, and squatting in vacant housing. In 1972, the ex-GP Maoists aided French families in working-class suburbs who were engaging in the same tactics. In the residences constructed for single immigrant workers or those who came to France to spend eleven months out of the year without their families, the GP Maoists encouraged and supported the immigrants' attempts to fight against the racism of some of the residence managers (many of whom were former military people from the colonial service), to gain control over the governance of the houses, to insist upon proper physical maintenance, and to resist the rent increases which had been levied against the residents at fairly regular intervals. This early work on the part of the GP Maoists, as well as the continuing work of some of its former Arab members and of the hierarchical Maoist UCFML, was an important encouraging and supportive element in a process of conflict which led to a national rent strike within the residences. Over a period of four years, the largest corporation running such residences was unable to collect the full rents.

(3) Work Outside of the Urban Context

All of the above actions took place within the urban areas. However, the GP and ex-GP Maoists broke out of the urban context to a much greater extent than did the hierarchical Maoists. They did so in three ways. First, a year after their creation, the GP Maoists mounted the barricades set up by rural and small town merchants to protest what they felt to be unfavorable legislation in 1969. Some on the left, including Sartre, criticized the Maoists for fighting the police alongside petit-bourgeois merchants. The GP was accused of aiding not a progressive movement but a more likely resurgence of right-wing Poujadism.

Secondly, the GP and ex-GP Maoists supported nationalistic movements in two areas of France, Brittany in the West and Occitanie in the South. In the late 1970s, Corsican nationalism attained very violent levels, but the strongest expressions of a desire for cultural and political separatism in the early and mid-70s came from the populations of Brittany and Occitanie. While the GP and ex-GP Maoists supported the struggle of these movements against the status quo, the complexities of such questions were not any easier for them to handle than the question of racial separatism has been for American Maoists. On the one hand they knew that nationalistic movements can often be quite reactionary and they did not want the movements in Brittany and Occitanie to evolve in that direction. On the other hand they were loath to impose upon them any specific structure. They chose to see them as struggles for decolonization which would develop their own specific configurations in struggle.[18] In fact, this is the same flexible attitude that Mao adopted towards revolutionary movements in countries other than China—i.e., each will cut its own path.

The most active attempts made by the GP and ex-GP Maoists to reach out beyond the urban environment, however, were two summer campaigns conducted in 1971 and 1972 in the Loire-Atlantique, the southeastern portion of Brittany. This was an area in which militant farmers had driven their crops into the cities and dumped them in the streets, erected barricades on the roads, occupied processing facilities, and, in 1969, even held the visiting Minister of Agriculture captive until he was freed by the police. A number of the above activities entailed physical combat with the police.

While the GP Maoists had made *ad hoc* attempts to establish contacts with the rural population prior to this, in 1970 and 1971 they organized an actual program in which students and other young people from the cities were recruited to go out and live with farming families. There were two precise political motives. One was to counteract the propaganda campaign that the government had been conducting against the far left since 1968. The young revolutionaries wanted to show the farmers that, despite what they saw and heard on the government controlled television regarding the 1968 uprising and the government's enactment of the "Anti-Wrecker Law" in 1970, they were not simply people intent upon delivering France over to havoc. This was a public relations task.

On the other hand, most of these young people were urban and knew as little about rural life and the rural population as the farmers knew about them. They wanted to come to know that life and the feelings of the farmers first-hand by living and working with them. The summer programs were thus also designed to serve as *enquêtes*. On the basis of this experience they came to the conclusion that small and tenant farmers had been subjected to tremendous pressures by inflation and the European Common Market. The justification of technological efficiency and the pressures exerted by the international European capitalist market were seen quite simply as an attempt to get the small farmer off of the land and the latter into the hands of those who had the wealth to work it more "efficiently." The dominant capitalist economic organization of Western Europe was condemned as totally insensitive to the farmer's relationship with the land and the Maoists strove to demonstrate a respect for that relationship:

> Among the poorest farmers, there are many who possess a patch of earth on which they survive miserably. And they cling to that earth. There is no question of telling them that *'property is theft'* and tearing it away from them. Certain problems require time before their resolution. We are told that in China, in order to prove the merits of land collectivization, those who want to work individually are permitted to do so until they see for themselves that they are wrong. There is no other way of persuasion.

And then, what endears the earth to the farmer is not primarily money but what the earth represents, the investment of soul. In the cities, in the factories, work is not humane. One works for someone else, a boss, in the heat and according to the speed of the assembly line. One makes a piece of a car, of a machine. One does not see the result. One does not have a feeling of control over one's work. The farmer's love of the earth is also the love for a labor by which one creates something that one has control over, something living.

The present battles for survival of the small farmers are not like the *'selfish demands of the petite bourgeoisie'* that can be managed by capitalism's offering of higher prices and representatives in Parliament. They are becoming more and more struggles of a new type, turned toward a progressive future, conforming to the development of humanity. Aiming more and more at the same enemies as the mass of the people, the farmers, in this epoch of a general wave of worker contestation, are discovering that they are not alone.[19]

The feeling for the relationship between the farmer and the land and the generally high value placed upon agricultural life are much more characteristic of the writing of Rousseau and Proudhon than of Marx and Engels. The GP Maoists did not make the distinction between usufruct and ownership, a distinction which Proudhon took from Rousseau in the hope of permitting that special relationship with the land to be preserved under conditions of greater equality. In contradistinction to Proudhon's attempt to preserve rural individualism through a national credit system available to small scale farmers, the GP Maoists saw collectivization, on the model of the Chinese agricultural communes, as the optimal answer. But they felt that it was a viable answer only if the landless and small farmers came to it themselves. They shared the anarchist Proudhon's revulsion at the thought of bureaucratic compulsion in the form of forced collectivization and rejected Trotsky's pessimism over the capability of the peasantry to determine their own destiny.

(4) Prisoners' Rights

Many of the above actions of GP Maoism involved illegal activity. Thus, it is not surprising that of the 1,035 far leftists claimed to have been sentenced to prison between June 1, 1968 and March 20, 1972 by Minister of Interior Marcellin as well as of additional people who were held in pretrial detention but not convicted, the GP and ex-GP Maoists more than filled their quota.[20] However, even inside the prisons, these Maoists found another arena for agitation.

The tactic of the Maoists was to claim the status of "political prisoners." Such a status would entitle the Maoists to certain rights under French law. Once their claim was recognized, the Maoists intended to claim that all prisoners should be extended this more humane treatment simply by virtue of being human beings. The government responded by denying that there were any political prisoners in France and calling the demands a publicity stunt.

The prisoners' claims were supported outside the prison walls by demonstrations organized by *Secours Rouge* and families of the imprisoned militants. In some cases, these demonstrations brought further arrests and confinement. Trials were taken advantage of as forums where parents of people presently detained or former detainees could talk about prison conditions. On September 1, 1970, thirty Maoist prisoners began a hunger

● GLOSSARY OF ORGANIZATIONS AN

Les Amis de la Cause du Peuple	a support group which sold *La Cause du Peuple* and extended other support to the Maoist paper.
La Cause du Peuple (CDP)	the newspaper of the anti-hierarchical *Gauche Prolétarienne.*
Les Comités de Lutte	committees of struggle patterned after the 1968 "action committees." They were created by the GP Maoists in the factories where they did political work.
Les Comités Vérité et Justice	committees created by the GP Maoists to investigate, determine, and publicize cases of bourgeois legal injustice.
L'ex-Gauche Prolétarienne (ex-GP)	the name adopted by the GP after it had been banned by the government.
Front Homosexuel d'Action Révolutionnaire (FHAR)	a revolutionary homosexual group which former members of *Vive la Révolution* took part in creating.
La Gauche Prolétarienne (GP)	the largest and longest-lasting of the anti-hierarchical Maoist movements in France.
Groupes Ouvriers Anti-Flics (GOAF)	groups created by the GP in factories which sometimes violently punished bosses or plant security personnel for abusing workers.
Groupe Pierre Overney de la Nouvelle Résistance	the ex-GP commando group which arrested and held the chief personnel officer at the Renault plant after Pierre Overney had been killed and militants fired from the plant.

strike to demand recognition of their status as political prisoners, an end to the common practice of putting the Maoists in solitary confinement from the very beginning of their stays, a common location where all of the political prisoners could meet, a more liberal visitation system, and a general improvement in the conditions of detention including an end to harassment on the part of the prison guards.[21]

UBLICATIONS REFERRED TO IN THIS ARTICLE

La Ligue Communiste Révolutionnaire (LCR)	the "Frankist" Trotskyist group in France which was not usually hostile to the GP but which did criticize the Nogrette "arrest" (see above).
Mouvement de Libération des Femmes (MLF)	here used in its generic sense as the multitude of groups struggling against patriarchy. Legally, the name has been taken by one group, the former *Politique et Psychanalyse*. This group claims to be inspired by Freud and Lacan as well as by Marx, Lenin, and Mao. Its putting a legal claim on the name and initials MLF has caused considerable bitterness on the part of other groups within the movement.
Mouvement des Travailleurs Arabes (MTA)	a militant organization of Arab immigrant workers.
Mouvement du 22 mars	a coalition of radical students at the University of Paris' Nanterre campus which played a crucial catalytic role in the 1968 student uprising. Daniel Cohn-Bendit and his anarchist comrades set the dominant tone.
Parti Communiste Marxiste-Léniniste de France (PCMLF)	a party created in 1967 by supporters of China who were forced out of the French Communist Party. It is recognized as a fraternal party by the Chinese party.
Section Française de l'Internationale Ouvrière (SFIO)	the name of the French affiliate of the Second International before it was reconstituted and renamed simply the Socialist Party in the early 70s.

As the hunger strike and the supportive demonstrations continued, the government gave in on some of the points in regard to pretrial detainees. By September 22, all of the strikers in pretrial detention except Geismar were transferred to prison hospitals. And, on September 28, a court accorded the status of political offense to the writing of a slogan on the wall which had earned its author three months of solitary confinement up to that point. The changes in the treatment of the prisoners, however, seemed to have been limited to pretrial detainees as Geismar himself served more time in solitary after his October conviction.[22]

The two most important sources of public information on the conditions of prisoners and on their revolt were the Maspéro publishing house and *La Cause du Peuple*. Maspéro published the pamphlet entitled *The Political Prisoners Speak* which publicized the hunger strike. Maspéro also published extracts from Geismar's testimony at his trial during the following month. These materials received wider distribution than they would have if the Maoists had published and distributed them through their own little press, *Editions Liberté-Presse*. An additional source of publicity for the struggle of the imprisoned Maoist militants was obtained during the September 24 concert of the Rolling Stones in the Palais des Sports in Paris. Before the huge audience, the lights were dimmed and the group turned the microphone over to a Maoist militant to explain why the Maoists were in prison and what they were doing there. The Rolling Stones then sang "Street Fighting Man."[23]

Approximately a year after the hunger strike, in the winter of 1971–72, France experienced a surge of general prison revolts. While it is impossible to establish a tight causal relationship between Maoist agitation and those revolts, the fact is that the GP Maoists were still circulating through the prisons and that the movement and its newspaper were supportive of the revolt against the general conditions prevailing in the French prisons which they had come to know so well.[24] But then the GP Maoists never claimed to "start" anything. The limit of their claims was that they lent their energy, skill, and dedication to struggles that had already been commenced by the masses.

THEORY OR JUST PRACTICE?

To orthodox Marxists or Marxist-Leninists, GP Maoism appeared to be blatantly antitheoretical. The movement was nonspecific in terms of a programmatic commitment (e.g., it had nothing comparable to the Common Program of the Communists and Socialists or to the Transitional Program of the Trotskyists); it held no core of Marxist or Marxist-Leninist theory to be sacrosanct; and it was convinced that there were more lessons to be learned from practical action in support of the masses than in any theoretical texts.

Aside from this priority of practice over textual theory, a priority assigned by Mao himself in his essay *On Practice*,[25] there were three commitments which comprised the theoretical axis around which the GP movement revolved.

(1) The Rejection of Hierarchy

The rejection of hierarchy had a dual thrust for the GP Maoists. In terms of the revolutionary movement itself, the GP Maoists were convinced that the hierarchical democratic-centralist form of party advocated by Lenin was an elitist formulation which would structurally cut the self-designated vanguard off from the masses. Such a party, in their eyes, would be bound to approach the masses in a highly directive manner. It would come armed with superior theoretical weaponry which would be used to establish entitlement to such a directive role. While Mao attempted to synthesize the democratic-centralist party with his conception of the mass line, the GP Maoists felt that a choice was necessitated. At least during one period of Chinese history, that of the Cultural Revolution, Mao came close to the same conclusion in practice. The rejection of a hierarchical party was linked to the GP Maoists' commitment to a very limited time span for their movement. Hierarchy implies permanence, at least intended permanence. This is the root difficulty which confronts "stage" theories of socialism which posit a controlled and time-limited continuation of hierarchical structures.[26] The GP Maoist *movement* was thought of as being one of temporary assistance to the masses. These Maoists shared Rousseau's conviction that hierarchy breeds permanence and that permanent structures inevitably develop a corporate will of their own at odds with the general will of the masses.

Hierarchy was also seen as the way in which capitalism maintained control over the masses. Within the industrial plant itself, hierarchy was a form of discipline over the workers. Hierarchical job classification systems were designed to convince some workers that they were more capable than others, brighter than others, and deserving of greater remuneration and status than others. It was used not only to divide the indigenous French working class, but also to foster racism. Arab and black African immigrant workers were designated as inherently inferior by virtue of being clustered at the bottom of the classification ladders.[27]

The GP Maoists shared Marx's and Engels' contention in the *German Ideology* that the root of human alienation lies in the division of labor. However, the GP Maoists displayed a blind spot regarding the implications of the sexual division of labor to which Engels was particularly sensitive. Secondly, the GP Maoist analyses came very close to collapsing the concepts of hierarchy, division of labor, and technology. For example, GP Maoist Philippe Olivier wrote: "To fight against 'authority' in the workshop is to fight against the capitalist hierarchical system and, in particular, against one of its ruses, 'technology.' "[28]

Whereas Marx saw technology as the phenomenon which would make possible the release of humanity from the detrimental effects of the division of labor, the GP Maoists at least implied that technology, division of labor, and hierarchy were necessary correlates — if not the same thing viewed from different perspectives — which served as the basis of both inequality and alienation. This analysis comes closer to that of some earlier utopian writers such as Fourier or to contemporary antitechnological writers such as Jacques Ellul and Theodore Roszak than that of any other Marxist group known to this writer.

(2) The Configuration of the Struggle

The GP Maoists unabashedly rejected a clear class-versus-class analysis. When they talked about the masses they talked about all people who were exploited by capitalism. When they went into action, they did so at the side of anyone who struggled against exploitation by the capitalist system.

The earliest break with the class-versus-class, dichotomous analysis came as a self-criticism of the position taken by the UJCML against the erection of the barricades in 1968. It will be recalled that the UJCML's position was that nothing could be done until the workers were on the barricades. The founders of GP Maoism, who came out of the UJCML, had to live down the fact that they had opted out of the most intense battle on the streets of Paris since the Liberation. Indeed, the workers had followed the lead of students and young people in 1968.

The lesson was that anyone who rose up should be supported. They completely shed Marx's distrust of the lumpenproletariat and recruited and organized particularly among immigrants and rebellious young people who did not seem to have much of a future in the present system. The terrain of the latter was the streets rather than the industrial plants. But revolutionary activity could not be confined to any one terrain. The GP Maoists supported the farmers who were barricading roads and dumping products in the city streets in protest against the squeeze of the capitalist Common Market's policies. They fought alongside shopkeepers when the latter mounted the barricades—despite their supporter Sartre's criticism that the substance of the battle was not at all progressive. They supported the nationalistic struggles of separatists in Brittany and Occitanie. For the GP Maoists, the question was not what class or occupation one was attached to. The question was: "is the group in struggle?" They were convinced that struggle was where consciousness was attained. The fact that a group or category of people was not "progressive" before struggle did not mean to them that they wouldn't learn more about capitalism by struggling against its agents.

Conversely, even those who were wage earners and poorly paid were enemies if they supported the capitalist structure. The GP Maoists were totally unsympathetic with the criticisms of the Communist Party and CGT that in beating up plant security people, the metro police, or even the regular police, they were in fact turning on workers. They were just as unsympathetic to the charge of one of the hierarchical Maoist organizations that they were indiscriminate in turning on even lower supervisory personnel. To the GP Maoists, anyone who put on the white smock symbolic of supervisory status was complicit in the system of hierarchical control and a legitimate target of struggle. No one was obliged to become a cop or a boss.

Class-versus-class analysis based upon roles in the productive process thus gave way to an analysis revolving around complicity in or struggle against the system of dominance.

(3) The Qualitative Attributes of Struggle

While the GP Maoists would support virtually all struggles of people who felt that they were being exploited under the system of dominance regardless of actual class position, there were two qualitative criteria by which certain struggles were seen as more advanced than others.

One of the criteria was illegality. Respect for the bounds of legality represented capitulation to the bourgeois capitalist state without extracting any cost from that state. Strategies such as those of the Communist and Socialist parties and the labor confederations were seen as legitimizing the system of dominance. They accepted and abided by the rules of bourgeois capitalism and their complicity provided it with a facade.

The only way to break out of this trap for the GP Maoists was to refuse to play by the established rules, constantly to transcend the limits of legality. Illegal action broke through the facade of competition centered around agreed-upon norms and forced the state to demonstrate its repressiveness in a blatant way. The confrontations which centered around illegal activity were thus to be a lesson for those who really could not see the repressive nature of the capitalist system when it was permitted to dominate without being fundamentally challenged.

A second criterion was creativity. The GP Maoists looked back to some of the occupations of the university facilities, particularly that of the *Ecole des Beaux Arts* in Paris, as models for liberating and creative work. Passive occupations were rejected as contributing little to the spread of revolutionary consciousness. Under such conditions — and this was demonstrated in the undercutting of the plant occupations in 1968—time is on the side of the regime and such perceived counter-revolutionary forces as the Communist Party and the CGT. But active and creative occupations like that at the *Beaux Arts*, where autonomous self-governing committees were created and revolutionary graphics produced, were looked upon as prototypes for occupations of plants and other work sites in which the very structure of productive relationships had to be changed.

It will be recalled that the *Comitês Vêritê et Justice* was the one organization created by the GP Maoists which did not transcend the boundaries of bourgeois legality. Rather, the function of these committees was to reveal the hypocrisy and inconsistency of the bourgeois legal system itself. It is interesting that this was singled out by Michel Foucault for criticism on the grounds that, far from being creative, the form of the committees (judges seated around a table) was a replica of the bourgeois court. And it is also interesting that the defense of such a process by the GP Maoists was made in quite traditional Leninist terms—i.e., that in the battle for socialism some of the forms of the bourgeois state are going to have to be used against it. Although the movement was largely of non-Leninist inspiration, it was not completely anarchist and it could still draw upon a more Leninist logic when challenged from a clearly non-Marxist perspective.[29]

THE DEMISE OF THE GP

Those who created the GP Maoist movement in 1968, and those who entered the movement from the *22 mars* in 1969, never envisioned that the movement would be permanent. It would serve as a facilitator and a stimulus but as soon as the masses themselves engaged upon the path of creative illegality, there would be no reason for the GP Maoist movement to exist.

The 1973 Lip strike, in which the workers of the Besançon watch factory took over the plant and assumed the governance and productive functions themselves, convinced most of the older GP Maoists that they were no longer needed within the industrial setting. On the other hand, the Chilean coup of that year convinced the same people that unless an important segment of the middle class—and not just lumpens, farmers, and small-town shopkeepers—were included in work for social change, they would and could destroy any such attempts. The combined impact of Lip and Chile in 1973 was an attempt by the older militants in the ex-GP and the *Cause du Peuple* to disband the final semblance of organizational coherence and to cease publishing the paper. They advocated emphasis upon "cultural work" spread widely across social issues and milieux.[30]

Some of the younger militants failed to see the logical relationship between Lip, Chile, and the liquidationist movement. They saw the older liquidationists as simply burned out by the intensity of the activity and the repression. They managed to maintain sufficient coherence to continue publishing and distributing the CDP on an irregular basis for at least four years after its founders left the paper. But the vitality of the earlier years was never regained by those who tried to keep the GP going after 1973.

WHAT HAS ENDURED? WHAT WAS THIS MOVEMENT IN RETROSPECT?

GP Maoism was a child of the 60s. It was rooted, if in a curious and contradictory way, in the spontaneous uprising of 1968. Its theoretical complexity was completed when the *22 mars* activists who had been on the barricades joined with the former Maoists of the UJCML who engaged in a self-criticism because they had not been on those barricades, indeed had argued for their dismantling.

From 1969 to 1973, these former members of the UJCML more than made up for their inactivity on the Night of the Barricades. Whether one accepts the relevance of events like Lip and the downfall of the Allende government to the GP's liquidation, whether one accepts the concept of structural mortality as the only sure guarantee against substitutionism, or whether one agrees with the young bucks that hyperactivity and repression simply burned out the older leaders who tended to identify themselves with the movement and who could not overcome their own possessiveness sufficiently to permit others to guide the movement—however one interprets the situation—the fact is that the older militants are now spread a bit all over in a multitude of national, decentralized, and individual contexts.

Geismar and some of the comrades with whom he was closest started a commune. They took to heart the message of the old VLR and began experimenting with changes in family structure and living and work arrangements. This involved revising Marx back in the direction of utopian socialism, particularly of the Fourierist variety.

Further, approximately half of the staff of the left countercultural daily *Libération*, which was begun at the end of 1972 under the omnipresent formal editorship of Sartre (who had also been called upon to declare himself editor of *Tout* and the *Cause du Peuple* during periods of severe repression), is composed of former GP militants. Here too, as Remi Hess points out, these people are involved in an endeavor which has a striking similarity to what *Vive la Révolution* attempted in its paper *Tout.*[31] By a different and much more arduous route, these people are now part of a much larger counterculture which the VLR attempted to introduce into France from 1969 to 1971 but which destroyed that group in the process.

Still other former GP Maoists are in the arts, the women's movement, the gay movement, the environmental movement, or more nationally or ethnically specific movements. Some of the former Arab members have transferred their efforts to completely Arab groups, such as the *Mouvement des Travailleurs Arabes*, which operate almost exclusively within the immigrant milieu. Former CDP editor Le Dantec is attempting to find a new political orientation in the historical thought and folkculture of his native Brittany which he believes to contain an appropriate blend of concern for the collectivity and respect for the individual.

But the former GP Maoists who have received the most international publicity are those who belong to a group referred to as the *Nouveaux Philosophes* or the New Philosophers. André Glucksmann and Michel Le Bris (also a former CDP editor along with Le Dantec and Geismar) have gone from their modifications of traditional Marxism-Leninism as GP activists to a more systematic criticism of Marxism itself as intellectuals detached from and reflecting upon their past practice.[32] Many leftists see this recantation as the ultimate proof that this ultra-leftist movement was petit-bourgeois all along. This is certainly one of the few things that Trotskyists, hierarchical Maoists, and the French Communist Party would all agree upon.

But whatever evaluation one might make of the whole phenomenon of GP Maoism, it is striking how distinctly *French* it was. In its refusal to fetter the workers with a hierarchical political organization and its emphasis upon action and clear cleavages within the industrial plant itself, it resembled the thought of the anarcho-syndicalist theorist Georges Sorel. In the value which it placed upon rural life and the relationship between land and the people who work it, it shared the sentiments of the Genevan Rousseau and the French anarchist Proudhon. It shared both Proudhon's distaste for hierarchical authoritarianism and the negative view of the division of labor held by the utopian thinker Fourier.

Thus the GP movement represented a melange of early Marxism and Maoism with French utopianism and anarchism as well as with the French experience. Even the older generation of contemporary Western theorists who had an impact upon its origins, development, and termination (Althusser, Sartre, and Foucault) were all French. And with the exception of the Chilean coup, all of the events which served as theoretical points of reference as the movement progressed were French. While GP Maoism probably served as a suggestive model to some extent for the "autonomist," "autoreductionist," and even the urban guerrilla movements in Italy, the GP movement itself had virtually no ties with the outside world.[33] Even the symbolic tie represented by the little picture of Mao on the masthead of the *Cause du Peuple* was removed for a time because it was too foreign.

GP Maoism was the most distinctively French movement within the far left. Perhaps that is why it was able to strike the imagination of French people who were not even sure of what it was. It was largely a synthesis of their own radical heritage, but one presented by the generation of the 60s and early 70s which had been inspired by a third world theorist and practitioner.

NOTES

1. This introduction draws on A. Belden Fields, *Student Politics in France: A Study of l'Union Nationale des Etudiants de France* (New York: Basic Books, 1970), and "The Effects of Student Activism in Industrialized Countries" in R. Perrucci and M. Pilisuk (eds.), *The Triple Revolution Emerging* (Boston: Little, Brown, 1971), pp. 585–606.
2. On Mao's theory of the "mass line" see his *On Practice* and Extracts from a Directive of the Central Committee of the Chinese Communist Party dated 1 June 1943 and attributed to Mao himself in the *Selected Works*. Reprinted in Stuart R. Schram, *The Political Thought of Mao Tse-tung* (New York: Praeger, 1963), pp. 316–317.

3. V.I. Lenin, *What Is To Be Done?*, Chapter IV.
4. Jerome Ch'ên stresses the impact of Russian anarchism on the young Mao, particularly the work of Kropotkin, Bakhunin, and Tolstoy. But we know from Mao's conversations with Edgar Snow that he had also been attracted to utopian socialism and that he had read Rousseau's work. We know further that he had a keen interest in France and its intellectual life. See Ch'ên, *Mao and the Chinese Revolution* (London: Oxford University Press, 1965), pp. 52–54 and Edgar Snow, *Red Star Over China* (New York: Random House, 1938), pp. 134–164. For a study which also stresses the Leninist and non-Leninist tensions within Maoism see Maurice Meisner, "Leninism and Maoism: Some Populist Perspectives on Maoism," *The China Quarterly*, 45, January–March 1971, pp. 40–93.
5. For intellectuals Althusser's theories, particularly his work on ideology, are of great importance. But for the party's leadership, the thrust of Althusser's work was subversive in a Platonic sense. In their eyes, Althusser was using his position in the *Ecole Normale Supêrieure* to train a new cadre of philosopher kings who would be able to understand the difference between theory (science) and ideology (images), who would be able to read *Capital* in ways that the present party leadership did not and could not. This "subversive" effect was not appreciated and it aggravated the tension that had already developed between the party and its young intellectual adherents. Once the young Maoists whom he had influenced were clearly separated from the party and attacking it from the outside, Althusser offered no support. His overt criticisms of the party leadership subsided until the rupture of relations between the Socialists and the Communists prior to the 1978 elections. Althusser then delivered an extremely severe criticism of the party leadership for placing all the blame on the Socialists rather than offering or even permitting a theoretical self-criticism within the party. He charged them with a Stalinist use of "theory" as an instrument to manipulate the militants. There is a curious irony in the argument since Maurice Thorez, perhaps the epitome of Stalinism in the 40s and 50s, is held up by Althusser as one who knew how to use theory correctly. Despite these attacks by Althusser, and despite the fact that the latter attack was delivered in the public pages of *Le Monde*, Althusser was not given hemlock by the party leadership. He was not even purged before the tragic turn of events which resulted in his being committed to a mental health facility. He was a great if sometimes very inconsistent theorist who enlivened intellectual discourse and debate among Marxists and between Marxists and non-Marxists. His purging would have had negative national and international repercussions for the party.
6. Bernard Kouchner and Michel-Antoine Burnier, *La France sauvage* (Paris: Editions Publications Premières, 1970), p. 187. The estimate of "several hundred" involved in the VLR in 1970 compares with "about fifteen hundred" for the *Gauche Prolêtarienne* (p. 159). The limited validity of such an estimate for the GP must be kept in mind given the fluid nature of the movement and the fact that in the following year a number of support groups were created.
7. Remi Hess, *Les Maoistes Français* (Paris: Anthropos, 1974), p. 151. Also see Henri Lefebvre, *Everyday Life in the Modern World,* trans. Sacha Rabinovitch (New York: Harper and Row, 1971).
8. Hess, pp. 163–167.
9. *Ibid.*
10. Michèle Manceaux, *Les Maos en France* (Paris: Gallimard, 1972), p. 203.
11. Kenneth Keniston, *Young Radicals* (New York: Harcourt, Brace, and World, 1968). "The term 'movement' suggests a spontaneous, natural, and non-institutional group; it again points to their feelings that they are in motion, changing, and developing. . ." (p. 217).
12. The attraction which this brand of Maoism held for people involved with the cinema is also attested to by the fact that two French journals of film criticism, *Cahiers du Cinêma* and *Cinêthique*, adopted Maoist orientations with *Cahiers* turning itself into a Maoist

writing collective. See Julia Lesage, "*Tout Va Bien* and *Coup pour Coup:* Radical French Cinema in Context," *Cinéaste*, V, 3, Summer 1972, p. 45.

13. The number of disputes in industrial settings increased from 2,949 in 1970 to 4,318 in 1971 and the number of working days lost due to industrial conflict increased from 1,742,175 to 4,387,781. *Yearbook of Labor Statistics* (Geneva: International Labor Organization, 1976), p. 831.

14. *Pour l'Union des comités de lutte d'atelier, Renault-Billancourt* (Paris: Editions Liberté-Presse, supplement à *La Cause du Peuple*, No. 11, 1971), p. 31.

15. Signoret apparently did bring other prominent people along with her on some of her supportive visits. On her role see Jean-Pierre Le Dantec (the former CDP editor who made contact with Signoret), *Les Dangers du soleil* (Paris: Les Presses d'Aujourd'hui, 1978), pp. 239–240.

16. The first demonstration in response to the killing was held on February 28. *Le Monde* estimated the number of participants at 30,000. The same paper estimated that approximately 120,000 people participated in Overney's funeral procession on March 4. *Le Monde*, le 7 mars 1972, p. 8. *La Cause du Peuple* estimated that 250,000 people marched in the funeral procession. Having witnessed all of the major demonstrations in Paris between July 1963 and January 1965 and the second wave of demonstrations from June 10 to July 10 in 1968, I can say that the funeral procession was the largest demonstration that I have ever seen in Paris.

17. On this issue, Sarte disagreed with the GP Maoists. He did not see Israel simply as an outpost of capitalist imperialism and he saw the problem as one of the reconciliation of the rights of two peoples.

18. "Occitanie: 'Des luttes paysannes á la révolte d'un peuple,'' *Les Temps Modernes*, 310 Bis, 1972, pp. 141–170.

19. Centre d'Action Paysanne, *Où En Sont Les Paysans?* (Paris: Editions Liberté-Presse, 1971), pp. 6–7.

20. The figures are from *Le Monde*, le 21 mars 1972, p. 32.

21. *Les Prisonniers politiques parlent* (Paris: Maspéro, 1970), pp. 28–29.

22. Information on Geismar's treatment is based upon conversations with him.

23. *Les Prisonniers politiques parlent*, pp. 12–13.

24. The December 9, 1971 and January 15, 1972 issues of *La Cause du Peuple* carried information and supportive articles on revolts in seven French prisons.

25. Mao Tse-tung, *On Practice* in *Four Essays on Philosophy* (Peking: Foreign Languages Press, 1968), pp. 1–22.

26. For an interesting discussion of how hierarchical structures justified by "stage" theories of socialism have ultimately resulted in male dominance in countries claiming to be socialist, see Batya Weinbaum, *The Curious Courtship of Women's Liberation and Socialism* (Boston: South End Press, 1978), Chapter VII.

27. The French have some interesting slang in their language as it relates to work which perpetuates images of racial inferiority. "*Travail Arabe*" means a job poorly done regardless of who does it; "*nègre*" is used to designate the low person on the totem pole in a professional office despite the fact that the position is usually occupied by a white French person with the least seniority.

28. Philippe Olivier, "Après la Bataille de Renault," *Les Temps Modernes*, 310 Bis, 1972, p. 29.

29. Michel Foucault, "Sur la Justice Populaire: Débat avec les Maos," *Les Temps Modernes*, 310 Bis, 1972, pp. 335–336. This has recently been translated into English by Colin Gordon in Foucault, *Power/Knowledge* (New York: Pantheon Books, 1980), pp. 1–36.

30. For insight into the thinking of those involved with the GP movement at this late stage, see P. Gavi, J-P Sartre, and P. Victor, *On a Raison de se révolter* (Paris: Gallimard,

1974). It is interesting to compare this statement at the end with the very early statement of the analysis and intentions of the movement in A. Geismar, S. July, and E. Morane, *Vers La Guerre civile* (Paris: Editions et Publications Premières, 1969).

31. Hess, pp. 177–181.

32. See André Glucksmann, *Les Maitres Penseurs* (Paris: Grasset, 1977) and *La Cuisinière et le mangeur d'hommes* (Paris: Seuil, 1975) and Michel Le Bris, *L'Homme aux semelles de vent* (Paris: Grasset, 1977). Both writers have been heavily influenced by Michel Foucault.

33. While the GP movement used violence, it recognized limits in a way that the Italian urban guerrillas have not. The one case in which there was the killing of an adversary was that of M. Tramoni, the Renault security officer who had killed Pierre Overney. In 1977, after his release from a two year prison sentence for the Overney killing, he was assassinated by a commando group and the deed was applauded by those who continued to publish *La Cause du Peuple* (mai-juin 1977, No. 15, p. 3). Former CDP editor Le Dantec denounced the act and the CDP's support of it and reflected that the movement in which he had played so important a role probably had had an unfortunate effect upon the later German and Italian armed urban guerrillas. Le Dantec, op. cit., pp. 246–248. For a discussion of "autonomia" and the "autoreductionist" movements in Italy, which must not be confused with armed guerrilla groups like the Red Brigades, see *Semiotext(e)*, III, 3, 1980, pp. 36–78.

PERIODIZING THE 60s

FREDRIC JAMESON

Nostalgic commemoration of the glories of the 60s or abject public confession of the decade's many failures and missed opportunities are two errors which cannot be avoided by some middle path that threads its way in between. The following sketch starts from the position that History is necessity, that the 60s had to happen the way it did, and that its opportunities and failures were inextricably intertwined, marked by the objective constraints and openings of a determinate historical situation, of which I thus wish to offer a tentative and provisional model.

To speak of the "situation" of the 60s, however, is necessarily to think in terms of historical periods and to work with models of historical periodization which are at the present moment theoretically unfashionable, to say the least. Leave aside the existential fact that the veterans of the decade, who have seen so many things change dramatically from year to year, think more historically than their predecessors; the classification by generations has become as meaningful for us as it was for the Russians of the late 19th century, who sorted character types out with reference to specific decades. And intellectuals of a certain age now find it normal to justify their current positions by way of an historical narrative ("then the limits of Althusserianism began to be evident," etc.). Now, this is not the place for a theoretical justification of periodization in the writing of history, but to those who think that cultural periodization implies some massive kinship and homogeneity or identity within a given period, it may quickly be replied that it is surely only against a certain conception of what is historically dominant or hegemonic that the full value of the exceptional—what Raymond Williams calls the "residual" or "emergent"—can be assessed. Here, in any case, the "period" in question is understood not as some omnipresent and uniform shared style or way of thinking and acting, but rather as the sharing of a common objective situation, to which a whole range of varied responses and creative innovations is then possible, but always within that situation's structural limits.

Yet a whole range of rather different theoretical objections will also bear on the selectiveness of such a historical narrative: if the critique of periodization questions the possibilities of diachrony, these involve the problems of synchrony and in particular of the relationship to be established between the various "levels" of historical change singled out for attention. Indeed, the present narrative will claim to say something meaningful about the 60s by way of brief sketches of but four of those levels: the history of philosophy, revolutionary political theory and practice, cultural production, and economic cycles (and this in a context limited essentially to the United States, France and the third world.) Such selectiveness seems not merely to give equal historical weight to base and superstructure indifferently, but also to raise the specter of a practice of homologies—the kind of analogical parallelism in which the poetic production of Wallace Stevens is somehow "the same" as the political practice of Che Guevara — which have been thought abusive at least as far back as Spengler.

There is of course no reason why specialized and elite phenomena, such as the writing of poetry, cannot reveal historical trends and tendencies as vividly as "real life"—or perhaps even more visibly, in their isolation and semiautonomy which approximates a laboratory situation. In any case, there is a fundamental difference between the present narrative and those of an older organic history which sought "expressive" unification through analogies and homologies between widely distinct levels of social life. Where the latter proposed identities between the forms on such various levels, what will be argued here is a series of significant homologies between the *breaks* in those forms and their development. What is at stake then is not some proposition about the organic unity of the 60s on all its levels, but rather a hypothesis about the rhythm and dynamics of the fundamental situation in which those very different levels develop according to their own internal laws.

At that point, what looked like a weakness in this historical or narrative procedure turns out to be an unexpected strength, particularly in allowing for some sort of "verification" of the separate strands of the narrative. One sometimes feels—especially in the area of culture and cultural histories and critiques—that an infinite number of narrative interpretations of history are possible, limited only by the ingenuity of the practitioners whose claim to originality depends on the novelty of the new theory of history they bring to market. It is more reassuring, then, to find the regularities hypothetically proposed for one field of activity (e.g., the cognitive, or the aesthetic, or the revolutionary) dramatically and surprisingly "confirmed" by the reappearance of just such regularities in a widely different and seemingly unrelated field, as will be the case with the economic in the present context.

At any rate, it will already have become clear that nothing like a history of the 60s in the traditional, narrative sense will be offered here. But historical representation is just as surely in crisis as its distant cousin, the linear novel, and for much the same reasons. The most intelligent "solution" to such a crisis does not consist in abandoning historiography altogether, as an impossible aim and an ideological category all at once, but rather—as in the modernist aesthetic itself—in reorganizing its traditional procedures on a different level. Althusser's proposal seems the wisest in this situation: as old-fashioned narrative or "realistic" historiography became problematic, the historian should reformulate her vocation—not any longer to produce some vivid representation of History "as it really happened," but rather to produce the *concept* of history. Such will at least be the gamble of the following pages.

1. THIRD WORLD BEGINNINGS

It does not seem particularly controversial to mark the beginnings of what will come to be called the 60s in the third world with the great movement of decolonization in British and French Africa. It can be argued that the most characteristic expressions of a properly first world 60s are all later than this, whether they are understood in countercultural terms—drugs and rock—or in the political terms of a student new left and a mass antiwar movement. Indeed, politically, a first world 60s owed much to third-worldism in terms of politicocultural models, as in a symbolic Maoism, and, moreover, found its mission in resistance to wars aimed precisely at stemming the new revolutionary forces in the third world. (Elsewhere in this work, Belden Fields suggests that the two first world nations in which the most powerful student mass movements emerged—the United States and France—became privileged political spaces precisely *because* these were the two countries involved in colonial wars, although the French new left appears after the resolution of the Algerian conflict.) The one significant exception to all this is in many ways the most important first world political movement of all—the new black politics and the civil rights movement, which must be dated, not from the Supreme Court decision of 1954, but rather from the first sit-ins in Greensboro, North Carolina, in February of 1960. Yet it might be argued that this was also a movement of decolonization, and in any case the constant exchange and mutual influences between the American black movements and the various African and Caribbean ones are continuous and incalculable throughout this period.

The independence of Ghana (1957), the agony of the Congo (Lumumba was murdered in January 1961), the independence of France's sub-Saharan colonies following the Gaullist referendum of 1959, finally the Algerian Revolution (which might plausibly mark our schema here with its internal high point, the Battle of Algiers, in January–March 1957, as with its diplomatic resolution in 1962)—all of these signal the convulsive birth of what will come in time to be known as the 60s:

> Not so very long ago, the earth numbered two thousand million inhabitants: five hundred million *men* and one thousand five hundred million *natives*. The former had the Word; the others merely had use of it. . . .
>
> Sartre, "Preface" to *The Wretched of the Earth*

The 60s was, then, the period in which all these "natives" became human beings, and this internally as well as externally: those inner colonized of the first world — "minorities," marginals, and women — fully as much as its external subjects and official "natives." The process can and has been described in a number of ways, each one of which implies a certain "vision of History" and a certain uniquely thematized reading of the 60s proper: it can be seen as a decisive and global chapter in Croce's conception of history as the history of human freedom; as a more classically Hegelian process of the coming to self-consciousness of subject peoples; as some post-Lukácsean or more Marcusean, new left conception of the emergence of new "subjects of history" of a nonclass type (blacks, students, third world peoples); or as some poststructuralist, Foucaultean notion (significantly anticipated by Sartre in the passage just quoted) of the conquest of the right to speak in a new collective voice, never before heard on the world stage—and of the concomitant dismissal of the intermediaries (liberals, first world intellectuals) who hitherto claimed to talk in your name; not forgetting the more properly political rhetoric of self-determination or independence, or the more psychological and cultural rhetoric of new collective "identities."

It is, however, important to situate the emergence of these new collective "identities" or "subjects of history" in the historical situation which made that emergence possible, and in particular to relate the emergence of these new social and political categories (the colonized, race, marginality, gender and the like) to something like a crisis in the more universal category that had hitherto seemed to subsume all the varieties of social resistance, namely the classical conception of social class. This is to be understood, however, not in some intellectual but rather in an institutional sense: it would be idealistic to suppose that deficiencies in the abstract idea of social class, and in particular in the Marxian conception of class struggle, can have been responsible for the emergence of what seem to be new nonclass forces. What can be noted, rather, is a crisis in the institutions through which a real class politics had however imperfectly been able to express itself. In this respect, the merger of the AFL and the CIO in 1955 can be seen as a fundamental "condition of possibility" for the unleashing of the new social and political dynamics of the 60s: that merger, a triumph of McCarthyism, secured the expulsion of the Communists from the American labor movement, consolidated the new antipolitical "social contract" between American business and the American labor unions, and created a situation in which the privileges of a white male labor force take precedence over the demands of black and women workers and other minorities. These last have therefore no place in the classical institutions of an older working-class politics. They will thus be "liberated" from social class, in the charged and ambivalent sense which Marxism gives to that word (in the context of enclosure, for instance): they are separated from the older institutions and thus "released" to find new modes of social and political expression.

The virtual disappearance of the American Communist Party as a small but significant political force in American society in 1956 suggests another dimension to this general situation: the crisis of the American party is "overdetermined" by its repression under McCarthyism and by the "revolution" in the Soviet bloc unleashed by Khrushchev's deStalinization campaign, which will have analogous but distinct and specific equivalents for the European Communist Parties. In France, in particular, after the brief moment of a Communist "humanism," developed essentially by philosophers in the eastern countries, and with the fall of Khrushchev himself and the definitive failure of his various experiments in 1964, an unparalleled situation emerges in which, virtually for the first time since the Congress of Tours in 1919, it becomes possible for radical intellectuals to conceive of revolutionary work outside and independent of the French Communist Party. (The older attitudes—"we know all about it, we don't like it much, but nothing is to be done politically without the CP" — are classically expressed in Sartre's own political journalism, in particular in *Les Communistes et la paix*.) Now Trotskyism gets a new lease on life, and the new Maoist forms, followed by a whole explosion of extraparliamentary formations of all ideological complexions, the so-called "groupuscules," offer the promise of a new kind of politics equally "liberated" from the traditional class categories.

Two further key events need to be noted here before we go on. For many of us, indeed, the crucial detonator — a new Year I, the palpable demonstration that revolution was not merely a historical concept and a museum piece but real and achievable—was furnished by a people whose imperialist subjugation had developed among North Americans a sympathy and a sense of fraternity we could never have for other third world peoples in their struggle, except in an abstract and intellectual way. Yet by January 1, 1959, the Cuban Revolution remained symbolically ambiguous. It could be read as a third world revolution of a different type from either the classical Leninist one or the Maoist experience, for it had a revolutionary strategy entirely its own, the *foco* theory, more about which later. This great event also announces the impending 60s as a period of unexpected political innovation rather than as the confirmation of older social and conceptual schemes.

Meanwhile, personal testimony seems to make it clear that for many white American students—in particular for many of those later active in the new left—the assassination of President Kennedy played a significant role in delegitimizing the state itself and in discrediting the parliamentary process, seeming to mark the decisive end of the well-known passing of the torch to a younger generation of leadership, as well as the dramatic defeat of some new spirit of public or civic idealism. As for the reality of the appearance, it does not much matter that, in hindsight, such a view of the Kennedy presidency may be wholly erroneous, considering his conservatism and anticommunism, the gruesome gamble of the "missile crisis," and his responsibility for the American engagement in Vietnam itself. More significantly, the legacy of the Kennedy regime to the development of a 60s politics may well have been the rhetoric of youth and of the "generation gap" which he exploited, but which outlived him and dialectically offered itself as an expressive form through which the political discontent of American students and young people could articulate itself.

Such were some of the preconditions or "conditions of possibility"—both in traditional working class political institutions and in the arena of the legitimation of state power — for the "new" social forces of the 60s to develop as they did. Returning to these new forces, there is a way in which their ultimate fate marks the close of the 60s as well: the end of "third-worldism" in the U.S. and Europe largely predates the Chinese Thermidor, and coincides with the awareness of increasing institutional corruption in many of the newly independent states of Africa and the almost complete militarization of the Latin American regimes after the Chilean coup of 1973 (the later revolutionary triumphs in the former Portuguese colonies are henceforth felt to be "Marxist" rather than "third-worldist," while Vietnam vanishes from American consciousness as completely after the ultimate American withdrawal as did Algeria from French consciousness after the Evian accords of 1963). In the first world of the late 60s, there is certainly a return to a more internal politics, as the antiwar movement in the United States and May 68 in France testify. Yet the American movement remains organically linked to its third world "occasion" in the Vietnam War itself, as well as to the Maoist inspiration of the Progressive Labor-type groups which emerge from SDS, such that the movement as a whole will lose its momentum as the war winds down and the draft ceases. In France, the "common program" of the left (1972) — in which the current Socialist government finds its origins—marks a new turn towards Gramscian models and a new kind of "Eurocommunist" spirit which owes very little to third world antecedents of any kind. Finally, the black movement in the U.S. enters into a crisis at much the same time, as its dominant ideology—cultural nationalism, an ideology profoundly linked to third world models—is exhausted. The women's movement also owed something to this kind of third world inspiration, but it too, in the period 1972–1974, will know an increasing articulation into relatively distinct ideological positions ("bourgeois" feminism, lesbian separatism, socialist feminism).

For reasons enumerated above, and others, it seems plausible to mark the end of the 60s around 1972–74; the problem of this general "break" will be returned to at the end of this sketch. For the moment we must complete our characterization of the overall dynamic of third world history during this period, particularly if it is granted that this dynamic or "narrative line" entertains some privileged relationship of influence on the unfolding of a first world 60s (either through direct intervention—wars of national liberation—or through the prestige of exotic political models—most obviously, the Maoist one—or finally, owing to some global dynamic which both worlds share and respond to in relatively distinct ways).

This is of course the moment to observe that the "liberation" of new forces in the third world is as ambiguous as this term frequently tends to be (freedom as separation from older. systems); to put it more sharply, it is the moment to recall the obvious, that decolonization historically went hand in hand with neo-colonialism, and that the graceful, grudging or violent end of an old-fashioned imperialism certainly meant the end of one kind of domination but evidently also the invention and construction of a new kind—symbolically, something like the replacement of the British Empire by the International Monetary Fund. This is, incidentally, why the currently fashionable rhetoric of power and domination (Foucault is the most influential of these rhetoricians, but the basic displacement from the economic to the political is already made in Max Weber) is ultimately unsatisfactory: it is of course politically important to "contest" the various forms of power and domination, but the latter cannot be understood unless their functional relationships to economic exploitation are articulated—that is, until the political is once again subsumed beneath the economic. (On the other hand—particularly in the historicizing perspective of the present essay — it will obviously be a significant historical and social *symptom* that, in the mid-60s, people felt it necessary to express their sense of the situation and their projected praxis in a reified political language of power, domination, authority and antiauthoritarianism, and so forth: here, second and third world developments — with their conceptions of a "primacy of the political" under socialism—offer an interesting and curious cross-lighting.) Meanwhile, something similar can be said of the conceptions of collective identity and in particular of the poststructuralist slogan of the conquest of speech, of the right to speak in your own voice, for yourself: but to articulate new demands, in your own voice, is not necessarily to satisfy them, and to speak is not necessarily to achieve a Hegelian recognition from the Other (or at least then only in the more somber and baleful sense that the Other now has to take you into consideration in a new way and to invent new methods for dealing with that new presence you have achieved). In hindsight, the "materialist kernel" of this characteristic rhetoric or ideological vision of the 60s may be found in a more fundamental reflection on the nature of cultural revolution itself (now independent of its local and now historical Chinese manifestation).

The paradoxical, or dialectical, combination of decolonization and neocolonialism can perhaps best be grasped in economic terms by a reflection on the nature of another process whose beginning coincides with the general beginnings we have suggested for this period as a whole. This is a process generally described in the neutral but obviously ideological language of a technological "revolution" in agriculture: the so-called Green Revolution, with its new applications of chemical procedures to fertilization, its intensified strategies of mechanization, and its predictable celebration of progress and wonder-working technology, supposedly destined to free the world from hunger (the Green Revolution, incidentally, finds its second world equivalent in Khrushchev's disastrous "virgin lands" experiment). But these are far from neutral achievements, and nor is their export — essentially pioneered by the Kennedys — a benevolent and altruistic activity. In the 19th and early 20th century, capitalist penetration of the third world did not necessarily mean a capitalist transformation of the latter's traditional modes of production. Rather, they were for most part left intact, 'merely' exploited by a more political and military structure. The very enclave nature of these older agricultural modes—in combination with the violence of the occupier and that other violence, the introduction of money—established a sort of tributary relation that was beneficial to the imperialist metropolis for a considerable period of time. The Green Revolution carries this penetration and expansion of the "logic of capital" into a new stage.

The older village structures and precapitalist forms of agriculture are now systematically destroyed, to be replaced by an industrial agriculture whose effects are fully as disastrous as, and analogous to, the moment of enclosure in the emergence of capital in what was to become the first world. The "organic" social relations of village societies are now shattered, an enormous landless preproletariat "produced," which migrates to the urban areas (as the tremendous growth of Mexico City can testify), while new, more proletarian, wage-working forms of agricultural labor replace the older collective or traditional kinds. Such ambiguous "liberation" needs to be described with all the dialectical ambivalence with which Marx and Engels celebrate the dynamism of capital itself in the *Manifesto* or the historical progress achieved by the British occupation of India.

The conception of the third world 60s as a moment in which all over the world chains and shackles of a classical imperialist kind were thrown off in a stirring wave of "wars of national liberation," is an altogether mythical simplification. Such resistance is generated as much by the new penetration of the Green Revolution as it is by the ultimate impatience with the older imperialist structures, the latter itself overdetermined by the historical spectacle of the supremacy of another former third world entity, namely Japan, in its sweeping initial victories over the old imperial powers in World War II. Eric Wolf's indispensable *Peasant Wars of the Twentieth Century* underscores the relationship between possibilities of resistance, the development of a revolutionary ethos, and a certain constitutive distance from the more absolutely demoralizing social and economic logic of capital.

The final ambiguity with which we leave this topic is the following: the 60s, often imagined as a period in which capital and first world power are in retreat all over the globe, can just as easily be conceptualized as a period in which capital is in full dynamic and innovative expansion, equipped with a whole armature of fresh production techniques and new "means of production." It now remains to be seen whether this ambiguity, and the far greater specificity of the agricultural developments in the third world, have any equivalent in the dynamics with which the 60s unfold in the advanced countries themselves.

2. THE POLITICS OF OTHERNESS

If the history of philosophy is understood not as some sequence of timeless yet somehow finite positions in the eternal, but rather as the history of attempts to conceptualize a historical and social substance itself in constant dialectical transformation, whose aporias and contradictions mark all of those successive philosophies as determinate failures, yet failures from which we can read off something of the nature of the object on which they themselves came to grief—then it does not seem quite so far-fetched to scan the more limited trajectory of that now highly specialized discipline for symptoms of the deeper rhythms of the "real" or "concrete" 60s itself.

As far as the history of philosophy during that period is concerned, one of the more influential versions of its story is told as follows: the gradual supercession of a hegemonic Sartrean existentialism (with its essentially phenomenological perspectives) by what is often loosely called "structuralism,' namely, by a variety of new theoretical attempts which share in common at least a single fundamental "experience"—the discovery of the primacy of Language or the Symbolic (an area in which phenomenology and Sartrean existentialism remain relatively conventional or traditional). The moment of high structuralism—whose most influential monuments are seemingly not philosophical at all, but can be characterized, alongside the new linguistics itself, as linguistic transformations of anthropology and psychoanalysis by Claude Levi-Strauss and Jacques Lacan respectively — is however an inherently unstable one which has the vocation of becoming a new type of universal mathesis, under pain of vanishing as one more intellectual fad. The breakdown products of that moment of high structuralism can then be seen on the one hand as the recution to a kind of scientism, to sheer method and analytical technique (in *semiotics*); and on the other, as the transformation of structuralist approaches into active ideologies in which ethical, political and historical consequences are drawn from the hitherto more epistemological "structuralist" positions; this last is of course the moment of what is now generally known as *post-structuralism*, associated with familiar names like those of Foucault, Deleuze, Derrida and so forth. That the paradigm, although obviously French in its references, is not merely local can be judged from an analogous mutation of the classical Frankfurt School via problems of communication, in the work of Habermas; or by the current revival of pragmatism in the work of Richard Rorty, which has a home-grown American "post-structuralist" feeling to it (Peirce after all having largely preceded and outclassed Saussure).

The crisis of the philosophical institution and the gradual extinction of the philosopher's classic political vocation, of which Sartre was for our time the supreme embodiment, can in some ways be said to be about the so-called death of the subject: the individual ego or personality, but also the supreme philosophical Subject, the cogito but also the *auteur* of the great philosophical *system*. It is certainly possible to see Sartre as one of the last great systembuilders of traditional philosophy (but then at least one dimension of classical existentialism must also be seen as an ideology or a metaphysic: that of the heroic pathos of existential choice and freedom in the void, and that of the "absurd," more particularly in Camus). Some of us also came to *Marxism* through dialectical elements in the early Sartre (he himself then turning to follow up this avenue in his own later, more Marxian work, such as the *Critique of Dialectical Reason* [1960]). But on balance that component of his work which underwent the richest practical elaboration at other people's hands as well as his own was his theory of interpersonal relations, his stunning rewrite of Hegel's Master/Slave chapter, his conception of the Look as the most concrete mode in which I relate to other subjects and struggle with them, the dimension of my alienation in my "being-for-other-people," in which each of us vainly attempts, by looking at the other, to turn the tables and transform the baleful alienating gaze of the Other into an object for my equally alienating gaze. Sartre will go on, in the *Critique*, to try to erect a more positive and political theory of group dynamics on this seemingly sterile territory: the struggle between two people now becoming dialectically transformed into the struggle between groups themselves. The *Critique* was however an anticipatory work, whose import and significance would not finally be recognized until May 68 and beyond, whose rich consequences indeed have not even fully been drawn to this day. Suffice it to say, in the present context, that the *Critique* fails to reach its appointed terminus, and to complete the projected highway that was to have led from the individual subject of existential experience all the way to fully constituted social classes. It breaks down at the point of the constitution of small groups, and is ultimately usable principally for ideologies of small guerrilla bands (in a later moment of the 60s) and of microgroups (at the period's end): the significance of this trajectory will soon be clear.

However, at the dawn of the 60s, the Sartrean paradigm of the Look and the struggle for recognition between individual subjects will also be appropriated dramatically for a very different model of political struggle, in Frantz Fanon's enormously influential vision (*The Wretched of the Earth,* 1961) of the struggle between Colonizer and Colonized, where the objectifying reversal of the Look is apocalyptically rewritten as the act of redemptive violence of Slave against Master, the moment in which, in fear and the anxiety of death, the hierarchical positions of Self and Other, Center and Margin, are forcibly reversed, and in which the subservient consciousness of the Colonized achieves collective identity and self-affirmation in the face of colonizers in abject flight.

What is at once significant is the way in which what had been a technical philosophical subject (the "problem" of solipsism, the nature of relationships between individual subjects or "cogitos") has fallen into the world and become an explosive and scandalous political ideology: a piece of the old-fashioned technical philosophical system of high existentialism breaking off and migrating outside philosophy departments altogether, into a more frightening landscape of praxis and terror. Fanon's great myth could be read at the time, by those it appalled equally well as by those it energized, as an irresponsible call to mindless violence: in retrospect, and in the light of Fanon's other, clinical work (he was a psychiatrist working with victims of colonization and of the torture and terror of the Algerian war), it can more appropriately be read as a significant contribution to a whole theory of cultural revolution as the collective reeducation (or even collective psychoanalysis) of oppressed peoples or unrevolutionary working classes. Cultural revolution as a strategy for breaking the immemorial habits of subalternity and obedience which have become internalized as a kind of second nature in all the laborious and exploited classes in human history—such is the vaster problematic to which, today, Gramsci and Wilhelm Reich, Fanon and Rudolf Bahro, can be seen as contributing as richly as the more official practices of Maoism.

3. DIGRESSION ON MAOISM

But with this new and fateful reference, an awkward but unavoidable parenthetical digression is in order: Maoism, richest of all the great new ideologies of the 60s, will be a shadowy but central presence throughout this essay, yet owing to its very polyvalence it cannot be neatly inserted at any point nor exhaustively confronted on its own. One understands, of course, why left militants here and abroad, fatigued by Maoist dogmatisms, must have heaved a collective sigh of relief when the Chinese turn consigned "Maoism" itself to the ashcan of history. Theories, however, are often liberated on their own terms when they are thus radically disjoined from the practical interests of state power. Meanwhile, as I have suggested above, the symbolic terrain of the present debate is fully as much chosen and dictated by the right as by left survivors: and the current propaganda campaign, everywhere in the world, to Stalinize and discredit Maoism and the experience of the Chinese cultural revolution — now rewritten as yet another Gulag to the East—all of this, make no mistake about it, is part and parcel of the larger attempt to trash the 60s generally: it would not be prudent to abandon rapidly and without thoughtful reconsideration any of this terrain to the "other side."

As for the more ludicrous features of Western third-worldism generally—a kind of modern exotic or orientalist version of Marx's revolutionaries of 1848, who "anxiously conjure up the spirits of (the Great Revolution of 1789) to their service and borrow from them names, battle cries and costumes" — these are now widely understood in a more cynical light, as in Régis Debray's remark: "In France, the Columbuses of political modernity thought that following Godard's *La Chinoise* they were discovering China in Paris, when in fact they were landing in California."

Most paradoxical and fascinating of all, however, is the unexpected and unpredictable sequel to the Sino-Soviet split itself: the new Chinese rhetoric, intent on castigating the Soviet bureaucracy as revisionistic and "bourgeois," will have the curious effect of evacuating the class content of these slogans. There is then an inevitable terminological slippage and displacement: the new binary opposite to the term "bourgeois" will no longer be "proletarian" but rather "revolutionary," and the new qualifications for political judgements of this kind are no longer made in terms of class or party affiliation but rather in terms of personal life — your relationship to special privileges, to middle-class luxuries and dachas and managerial incomes and other perks — Mao Tse-tung's own monthly "salary," we are told, was something in the neighborhood of a hundred American dollars. As with all forms of anticommunism, this rhetoric can of course be appropriated by the anti-Marxist thematics of "bureaucracy," of the end of ideology and social class, etc. But it is important to understand how for western militants what began to emerge from this at first merely tactical and rhetorical shift was a whole new political space, a space which will come to be articulated by the slogan, "the personal is the political," and into which —in one of the most stunning and unforeseeable of historical turns—the women's movement will triumphantly move at the end of the decade, building a Yenan of a new and unpredictable kind which is still impregnable at the present moment.

4. THE WITHERING AWAY OF PHILOSOPHY

The limit as well as the strength of the stark Fanonian model of struggle was set by the relative simplicity of the colonial situation; this can be shown in two ways, first of all in the sequel to the "war of national independence." For with the Slave's symbolic and literal victory over the (now former) Master, the "politics of otherness" touches its limit as well; the rhetoric of a conquest of collective identity has then nowhere else to go but into a kind of secessionary logic of which black cultural nationalism and (later on) lesbian separatism are the most dramatic examples (the dialectic of cultural and linguistic independence in Quebec province would be yet another instructive one). But this result is also contradictory, insofar as the newly constituted group (we here pick up Sartre's account in the *Critique*) *needs* outside enemies to survive as a group, to produce and perpetuate a sense of collective cohesion and identity. Ultimately, in the absence of the clear-cut Manichaean situation of the older imperialist period, this hard-won collective self-definition of a first moment of resistance will break up into the smaller and more comfortable unities of face-to-face microgroups (of which the official political sects are only one example).

The gradual waning of the Fanonian model can also be described from the perspective of what will shortly become its "structuralist" critique. On this view, it is still a model based on a conception of individual subjects, albeit mythical and collective ones. It is thereby both anthropomorphic and transparent, in the sense in which nothing intervenes between the great collective adversaries, between the Master and the Slave, between the Colonizer and the Colonized. Yet even in Hegel, there was always a third term, namely matter itself, the raw materials on which the slave is made to labor and to work out a long and anonymous salvation through the rest of history. The "third term" of the 60s is however rather different from this. It was as though the protracted experiences of the earlier part of the decade gradually burned into the minds of the participants a specific lesson. In the United States, it was the experience of the interminable Vietnam War itself; in France, it was the astonishing and apparently invincible technocratic dynamism, and the seemingly unshakeable inertia and resistance to deStalinization of the French Communist Party; and everywhere, it was the tremendous expansion of the media apparatus and the culture of consumerism. This lesson might well be described as the discovery, within a hitherto antagonistic and "transparent" political praxis, of the opacity of the Institution itself as the radically transindividual, with its own inner dynamic and laws, which are not those of individual human action or intention, something which Sartre theorized in the *Critique* as the "practico-inert," and which will take the definitive form, in competing "structuralism," of "structure" or "synchronic system," a realm of impersonal logic in terms of which human consciousness is itself little more than an "effect of structure."

On this reading, then, the new philosophical turn will be interpreted less in the idealistic perspective of some discovery of a new scientific truth (the Symbolic) than as the symptom of an essentially protopolitical and social experience, the shock of some new, hard, unconceptualized, resistant object which the older conceptuality cannot process and which thus gradually generates a whole new problematic. The conceptualization of this new problematic in the coding of linguistics or information theory may then be attributed to the unexpected explosion of information and messages of all kinds in the media revolution, about which more in the following section. Suffice it to remark at this point that there is some historical irony in the way in which this moment, essentially the Third Technological Revolution in the West (electronics, nuclear energy)—in other words, a whole new step in the conquest of nature by human praxis—is philosophically greeted and conceptually expressed in a kind of thought officially designated as "antihumanist" and concerned to think what transcends or escapes human consciousness and intention. Similarly, the Second Technological Revolution of the late 19th century—an unparalleled quantum leap in human power over nature—was the moment of expression of a whole range of nihilisms associated with "modernity" or with high modernism in culture.

In the present context, the Althusserian experiment of the mid- to late 60s is the most revealing and suggestive of the various "structuralisms," since it was the only one to be explicitly political and indeed to have very wide-ranging political effects in Europe and Latin America. The story of Althusserianism can be told only schematically here: its initial thrust is two-fold, against the unliquidated Stalinist tradition (strategically designated by the code words "Hegel" and "expressive causality" in Althusser's own texts), and against the "transparency" of the eastern attempts to reinvent a Marxist humanism on the basis of the theory of alienation in Marx's early manuscripts. That Althusserianism is essentially a meditation on the "institutional" and on the opacity of the "practico-inert" may be judged by the three successive formulations of this object by Althusser himself in the course of the 60s: that of a "structure in dominance" or *structure à dominante* (in *For Marx*), that of "structural causality" (in *Reading Capital*), and that of "ideological state apparatuses" (in the essay of that name). What is less often remembered, but what should be perfectly obvious from any re-reading of *For Marx*, is the origin of this new problematic in Maoism itself, and particularly in Mao Tse-tung's essay "On Contradiction," in which the notion of a complex, already-given *overdetermined* conjuncture of various kinds of antagonistic and non-antagonistic contradictions is mapped out.

The modification which will emerge from Althusser's "process of theoretical production" as it works over its Maoist "raw materials" can be conveyed by the problem and slogan of the "semi-autonomy" of the levels of social life (a problem already invoked in our opening pages). This formula will involve a struggle on two fronts: on the one hand against the monism or "expressive causality" of Stalinism, in which the "levels" are identified, conflated, and brutally collapsed into one another (changes in economic production will be "the same" as political and cultural changes), and, on the other, against bourgeois avant-garde philosophy, which finds just such a denunciation of organic concepts of totality most congenial, but draws from it the consequence of a post- or anti-Marxist celebration of Nietzschean heterogeneity. The notion of a semi-autonomy of the various levels or instances, most notably of the political instance and of the dynamics of state power, will have enormous resonance (outstandingly in the work of Nicos Poulantzas), since it seems to reflect, and to offer a way of theorizing, the enormous growth of the state bureaucracy since the war, the "relative autonomy" of the state apparatus from any classical and reductive functionality in the service of big business, as well as the very active new terrain of political struggle presented by government or public sector workers. The theory could also be appealed to to justify a semi-autonomy in the cultural sphere, as well, and especially a semi-autonomous cultural politics, of a variety which ranges from Godard's films and *situationnisme* to the "festival" of May 68 and the Yippie movement here (not excluding, perhaps, even those forms of so-called "terrorism" which aimed, not at any classical seizure of state power, but rather at essentially pedagogical or informational demonstrations, e.g., "forcing the state to reveal its fundamentally fascist nature").

Nonetheless, the attempt to open up a semi-autonomy of the levels with one hand, while holding them all together in the ultimate unity of some "structural totality" (with its still classical Marxian ultimately determining instance of the economic), tends under its own momentum, in the centrifugal force of the critique of totality it had itself elaborated, to self-destruct (most dramatically so in the trajectory of Hindess and Hirst). What will emerge is not merely a heterogeneity of *levels* — henceforth, semi-autonomy will relax into autonomy *tout court*, and it will be conceivable that in the decentered and "schizophrenic" world of late capitalism the various instances may really have no organic relationship to one another at all—but, more importantly, the idea will emerge that the struggles appropriate to each of these levels (purely political struggles, purely economic struggles, purely cultural struggles, purely "theoretical" struggles) may have no necessary relationship to one another either. With this ultimate "meltdown" of the Althusserian apparatus, we are in the (still contemporary) world of microgroups and micropolitics—variously theorized as local or molecular politics, but clearly characterized, however different the various conceptions are, as a repudiation of old-fashioned class and party politics of a "totalizing" kind, and most obviously epitomized by the challenge of the women's movement whose unique new strategies and concerns cut across (or in some cases undermine and discredit altogether) many classical inherited forms of "public" or "official" political action, including the electoral kind. The repudiation of "theory" itself as an essentially masculine enterprise of "power through knowledge" in French feminism (see in particular the work of Luce Irigaray) may be taken as the final moment in this particular "withering away of philosophy."

Yet there is another way to read the destiny of Althusserianism, a way which will form the transition to our subsequent discussion of the transformation of the cultural sphere in the 60s; and this involves the significance of the slogan of "theory" itself as it comes to replace the older term "philosophy" throughout this period. The "discovery" of the Symbolic, the development of its linguistic-related thematics (as, e.g., in the notion of understanding as an essentially synchronic process, which influences the construction of relatively ahistorical "structures," such as the Althusserian one described above), is now to be correlated with a modification of the practice of the symbolic, of language itself in the "structuralist" texts, henceforth characterized as "theory," rather than work in a particular traditional discipline. Two features of this evolution, or mutation, must be stressed. The first is a consequence of the crisis in, or the disappearance of, the classical *canon* of philosophical writings which necessarily results from the contestation of philosophy as a discipline and an institution. Henceforth, the new "philosophical" text will no longer draw its significance from an insertion into the issues and debates of the philosophical tradition, which means that its basic "intertextual" references become random, an *ad hoc* constellation which forms and dissolves on the occasion of each new text. The new text must necessarily be a commentary on other texts (indeed, that dependence on a body of texts to be glossed, rewritten, interconnected in fresh ways, will now intensify if anything), yet those texts, drawn from the most wildly distant disciplines (anthropology, psychiatry, literature, history of science), will be selected in a seemingly arbitrary fashion: Mumford side by side with Antonin Artaud, Kant with Sade, pre-Socratic philosophy, President Schreber, a novel of Maurice Blanchot, Owen Lattimore on Mongolia, and a host of obscure Latin medical treatises from the 18th century. The vocation of what was formerly "philosophy" is thereby restructured and displaced: since there is no longer a tradition of philosophical problems in terms of which new positions and new statements can meaningfully be proposed, such works now tend towards what can be called metaphilosophy—the very different work of coordinating a series of pregiven, already constituted codes or systems of signifiers, of producing a discourse fashioned out of the already fashioned discourse of the constellation of *ad hoc* reference works. "Philosophy" thereby becomes radically occasional; one would want to call it disposable theory, the production of a *metabook*, to be replaced by a different one next season, rather than the ambition to express a proposition, a position or a system with greater "truth" value. (The obvious analogy with the evolution of literary and cultural studies today, with the crisis and disappearance of the latter's own canon of great books—the last one having been augmented to include the once recalcitrant "masterpieces" of high modernism—will be taken for granted in our next section.)

All of this can perhaps be grasped in a different way by tracing the effects of another significant feature of contemporary theory, namely its privileged theme in the so-called critique of representation. Traditional philosophy will now be grasped in those terms, as a practice of representation in which the philosophical text or system (misguidedly) attempts to express something other than itself, namely truth or meaning (which now stand as the "signified" to the "signifier" of the system). If, however, the whole aesthetic of representation is metaphysical and ideological, then philosophical discourse can no longer entertain this vocation, and it must stand as the mere addition of another text to what is now conceived as an infinite chain of texts (not necessarily all verbal—daily life is a text, clothing is a text, state power is a text, that whole external world, about which "meaning" or "truth" were once asserted and which is now contemptuously characterized as the illusion of reference or the "referent," is an indeterminate superposition of texts of all kinds). Whence the significance of the currently fashionable slogan of "materialism," when sounded in the area of philosophy and theory: materialism here means the dissolution of any belief in "meaning" or in the "signified" conceived as ideas or concepts which are distinct from their linguistic expressions. However paradoxical a "materialist" philosophy may be in this respect, a "materialist theory of language" will clearly transform the very function and operation of "theory," since it opens up a dynamic in which it is no longer ideas, but rather texts, material texts, which struggle with one another. Theory so defined, (and it will have become clear that the term now greatly transcends what used to be called philosophy and its specialized content) conceives of its vocation, not as the discovery of truth and the repudiation of error, but rather as a struggle about purely linguistic formulations, as the attempt to formulate verbal propositions (material language) in such a way that they are unable to imply unwanted or ideological consequences. Since this aim is evidently an impossible one to achieve, what emerges from the practice of theory—and this was most dramatic and visible during the high point of Althusserianism itself in 1967–68—is a violent and obsessive return to ideological critique in the new form of a perpetual guerrilla war among the material signifiers of textual formulations. With the transformation of philosophy into a material practice, however, we touch on a development that cannot fully be appreciated until it is replaced in the context of a general mutation of culture throughout this period, a context in which "theory" will come to be grasped as a specific (or semi-autonomous) form of what must be called postmodernism generally.

5. THE ADVENTURES OF THE SIGN

Postmodernism is one significant framework in which to describe what happened to culture in the 60s, but a full discussion of this hotly contested concept is not possible here. Such a discussion would want to cover, among other things, the following features: that well-known poststructuralist theme, the "death" of the subject (including the creative subject, the *auteur* or the "genius"); the nature and function of a *culture of the simulacrum* (an idea developed out of Plato by Deleuze and Baudrillard to convey some specificity of a reproducible object world, not of copies or reproductions marked as such, but of a proliferation of trompe-l'oeil copies *without originals*); the relation of this last to media culture or the "society of the spectacle" (Debord), under two heads: 1/ the peculiar new status of the image, the "material" or what might better be called the "literal," signifier: a materiality or literality from which the older sensory richness of the medium has been abstracted (just as on the other side of the dialectical relationship, the old individuality of the subject and his/her "brushstrokes' have equally been effaced); and 2/ the emergence, in the work's temporality, of an aesthetic of *textuality* or what is often described as schizophrenic time; the eclipse, finally, of all depth, especially *historicity* itself, with the subsequent appearance of pastiche and nostalgia art (what the French call *la mode rêtro*), and including the supercession of the accompanying models of depth-interpretation in philosophy (the various forms of hermeneutics, as well as the Freudian conception of "repression," of manifest and latent levels).

What is generally objected to in characterizations of this kind is the empirical observation that all of these features can be abundantly located in this or that variety of high modernism; indeed, one of the difficulties in specifying postmodernism lies in its symbiotic or parasitical relationship to the latter. In effect, with the canonization of a hitherto scandalous, ugly, dissonant, amoral, anti-social, bohemian high modernism offensive to the middle classes, its promotion to the very figure of high culture generally, and perhaps most important, its enshrinement in the academic institution, postmodernism emerges as a way of making creative space for artists now oppressed by those henceforth hegemonic modernist categories of irony, complexity, ambiguity, dense temporality, and particularly, aesthetic and utopian monumentality. In some analogous way, it will be said, high modernism itself won its autonomy from the preceding hegemonic realism (the symbolic language or mode of representation of classical or market capitalism). But there is a difference in that realism itself underwent a significant mutation: it became *naturalism* and at once generated the representational forms of mass culture (the narrative apparatus of the contemporary bestseller is an invention of naturalism and one of the most stunningly successful of French cultural exports). High modernism and mass culture then develop in dialectical opposition and interrelationship with one another. It is precisely the waning of their opposition, and some new conflation of the forms of high and mass culture, which characterizes postmodernism itself.

The historical specificity of postmodernism must therefore finally be argued in terms of the social functionality of culture itself. As stated above, high modernism, whatever its overt political content, was oppositional and marginal within a middle-class Victorian or philistine or gilded age culture. Although postmodernism is equally offensive in all the respects enumerated (think of punk rock or pornography), it is no longer at all "oppositional" in that sense; indeed, it constitutes the very dominant or hegemonic aesthetic of consumer society itself and significantly serves the latter's commodity production as a virtual laboratory of new forms and fashions. The argument for a conception of postmodernism as a periodizing category is thus based on the presupposition that, even if *all* the formal features enumerated above were already present in the older high modernism, the very significance of those features changes when they become a cultural *dominant*, with a precise socioeconomic functionality.

At this point it may be well to shift the terms (or the "code") of our description to the seemingly more traditional one of a cultural "sphere," a conception developed by Herbert Marcuse in what is to my mind his single most important text, the great essay on "The Affirmative Character of Culture." (It should be added that the conception of a "public sphere" generally is a very contemporary one in Germany in the works of Habermas and of Negt and Kluge, where such a system of categories stands in interesting contrast to the code of "levels" or "instances" in French poststructuralism.) Marcuse there rehearses the paradoxical dialectic of the classical (German) aesthetic, which projects as play and "purposefulness without purpose" a utopian realm of beauty and culture beyond the fallen empirical world of money and business activity, thereby winning a powerful critical and negative value through its capacity to condemn, by its own very existence, the totality of *what is*, while at the same time forfeiting all ability to social or political intervention in what is, by virtue of its constitutive disjunction or autonomy from society and history.

The account therefore begins to coincide in a suggestive way with the problematic of autonomous or semi-autonomous levels developed in the preceding section. To historicize Marcuse's dialectic, however, would demand that we take into account the possibility that in our time this very autonomy of the cultural sphere (or level or instance) may be in the process of modification; and also, that we develop the means to furnish a description of the process whereby such modification might take place, as well as of the prior process whereby culture became "autonomous" or "semi-autonomous" in the first place.

This requires recourse to yet another (unrelated) analytic code, one more generally familiar to us today, since it involves the now classical structural concept of the *sign*, with its two components, the signifier (the material vehicle or image—sound or printed word) and the signified (the mental image, meaning or "conceptual" content), and a third component—the external object of the sign, its reference or "referent"—henceforth expelled from the unity and yet haunting it as a ghostly residual aftereffect (illusion or ideology). The scientific value of this conception of the sign will be bracketed here since we are concerned, on the one hand, to historicize it, to interpret it as a conceptual symptom of developments in the period, and on the other, to "set it in motion," to see whether changes in its inner structure can offer some adequate small-scale emblem or electrocardiogram of changes and permutations in the cultural sphere generally throughout this period.

Such changes are already suggested by the fate of the "referent" in the "conditions of possibility" of the new structural concept of the sign (a significant ambiguity must however be noted: theorists of the sign notoriously glide from a conception of reference as designating a "real" object outside the unity of Signifier and Signified to a position in which the Signified itself—or meaning, or the idea or the concept of a thing—becomes somehow identified with the referent and stigmatized along with it; we will return to this below). Saussure, at the dawn of the semiotic revolution, liked to describe the relationship of Signifier to Signified as that of the two sides, the recto and verso, of a sheet of paper. In what is then a logical sequel, and a text which naturally enough becomes equally canonical, Borges will push "representation" to the point of imagining a map so rigorous and referential that it becomes coterminous with its object. The stage is then set for the structuralist emblem par excellence, the Moebius Strip, which succeeds in peeling itself off its referent altogether and thus achieves a free-floating closure in the void, a kind of absolute self-referentiality and autocircularity from which all remaining traces of reference, or of any externality, have triumphantly been effaced.

To be even more eclectic about it, I will suggest that this process, seemingly internal to the Sign itself, requires a supplementary explanatory code, that of the more universal process of reification and fragmentation at one with the logic of capital itself. Nonetheless, taken on its own terms, the inner convulsions of the Sign is a useful initial figure of the process of transformation of culture generally, which must in some first moment (that described by Marcuse) separate itself from the "referent" the existing social and historical world itself, only in a subsequent stage of the 60s, in what is here termed "postmodernism," to develop further into some new and heightened, free-floating, self-referential "autonomy."

The problem now turns around this very term, "autonomy," with its paradoxical Althusserian modification, the concept of "semi-autonomy." The paradox is that the Sign, as an "autonomous" unity in its own right, as a realm divorced from the referent, can preserve that initial autonomy, and the unity and coherence demanded by it, only at the price of keeping a phantom of reference alive, as the ghostly reminder of its own outside or exterior, since this allows it closure, self-definition and an essential boundary line. Marcuse's own tormented dialectic expresses this dramatically in the curious oscillation whereby his autonomous realm of beauty and culture both returns upon some "real world" to judge and negate it, at the same time that it separates itself so radically from that real world as to become a place of mere illusion and impotent "ideals," the "infinite," etc.

The first moment in the adventures of the Sign is perplexing enough as to demand more concrete, if schematic, illustration in the most characteristic cultural productions themselves. It might well be demonstrated in the classical French *nouveau roman* (in particular, the novels of Robbe-Grillet himself), which established its new language in the early 1960s, using systematic variations of narrative segments to "undermine" representation, yet in some sense confirming this last by teasing and stimulating an appetite for it.

As an American illustration seems more appropriate, however, something similar may be seen in connection with the final and canonical form of high modernism in American poetry, namely the work of Wallace Stevens, which becomes, in the years following the poet's death in 1956, institutionalized in the university as a purer and more quintessential fulfillment of poetic language than the still impure (read: ideological and political) works of an Eliot or a Pound, and can therefore be numbered among the literary "events" of the early 60s. As Frank Lentricchia has shown, in *Beyond the New Criticism*, the serviceability of Stevens' poetic production for this normative and hegemonic role depends in large measure on the increasing conflation, in that work, of poetic practice and poetic theory:

> This endlessly elaborating poem
> Displays the theory of poetry
> As the life of poetry . . .

"Stevens" is therefore a locus and fulfillment of aesthetics and aesthetic theory fully as much as the latter's exemplar and privileged exegetical object; the theory or aesthetic ideology in question being very much an affirmation of the "autonomy" of the cultural sphere in the sense developed above, a valorization of the supreme power of the poetic imagination over the "reality" it produces. Stevens' work, therefore, offers an extraordinary laboratory situation in which to observe the autonomization of culture as a process: a detailed examination of his development (something for which we have no space here) would show how some initial "set towards" or "attention to" a kind of poetic *pensée sauvage*, the operation of great preconscious *stereotypes*, opens up a vast inner world in which little by little the images of things and their "ideas" begin to be substituted for the things themselves. Yet what distinguishes this experience in Stevens is the sense of a vast systematicity in all this, the operation of a whole set of cosmic oppositions far too complex to be reduced to the schemata of "structuralist" binary oppositions, yet akin to those in spirit, and somehow pregiven in the Symbolic Order of the mind, discoverable to the passive exploration of the "poetic imagination," that is, of some heightened and impersonal power of free association in the realm of "objective spirit" or "objective culture." The examination would further show the strategic limitation of this process to landscape, the reduction of the ideas and images of things to the names for things, and finally to those irreducibles which are place names, among which the exotic has a privileged function (Key West, Oklahoma, Yucatan, Java). Here the poetic "totality" begins to trace a ghostly mimesis or *analogon* of the totality of the imperialist world system itself, with third world materials in a similarly strategic, marginal yet essential place (much as Adorno showed how Schoenberg's twelve-tone system unconsciously produced a formal imitation of the "total system" of capital). This very unconscious replication of the "real" totality of the world system in the mind is then what allows culture to separate itself as a closed and self-sufficient "system" in its own right: reduplication, and at the same time, floating above the real. It is because of this essential lack of content in Stevens' verse that his poetry ultimately comes to be auto-referential with a vengeance, taking as its primal subject matter the very operation of poetic production itself. This is an impulse shared by most of the great high modernisms, as has been shown most dramatically in the recent critiques of architectural modernism, in particular of the International style, whose great monumental objects constitute themselves, by projecting a protopolitical and utopian spirit of transformation, *against* a fallen city fabric all around them and, as Venturi has demonstrated, end up necessarily displaying and speaking of themselves alone. Now, this also accounts for what must puzzle any serious reader of Stevens' verse, namely the extraordinary combination of verbal richness and experimental hollowness or impoverishment in it (the latter being attributable as well to the impersonality of the poetic imagination in Stevens, and to the essentially contemplative and epistemological stance of the subject in it, over and against the static object world of his landscapes).

The essential point here, however, is that this characteristic movement of the high modernist impulse needs to justify itself by way of an ideology, an ideological supplement which can generally be described as that of "existentialism" (the supreme fiction, the meaninglessness of a contingent object-world unredeemed by the imagination, etc.). This is the most uninteresting and banal dimension of Stevens' work, yet it betrays along with other existentialisms (e.g., Sartre's tree root in *Nausea*) that fatal seam or link which must be retained in order for the contingent, the "outside world," the meaningless referent, to be just present enough dramatically to be overcome within the language: nowhere is this ultimate point so clearly deduced, over and over again, as in Stevens, in the eye of the blackbird, the angels or the Sun itself—that last residual vanishing point of reference as distant as a dwarf star upon the horizon, yet which cannot disappear altogether without the whole vocation of poetry and the poetic imagination being called back into question. Stevens thus exemplifies for us the fundamental paradox of the "autonomy" of the cultural sphere: the sign can only become autonomous by remaining semi-autonomous and the realm of culture can absolutize itself over against the real world only at the price of retaining a final tenuous sense of that exterior or external world of which it is the replication and the imaginary double.

All of which can also be demonstrated by showing what happens when, in a second moment, the perfectly logical conclusion is drawn that the referent is itself a myth and does not exist, a second moment hitherto described as postmodernism. Its trajectory can be seen as a movement from the older *nouveau roman* to that of Sollers or of properly "schizophrenic" writing, or from the primacy of Stevens to that of John Ashbery. This new moment is a radical break (which can be localized around 1967 for reasons to be given later on), but it is important to grasp it as dialectical, that is, as a passage from quantity to quality in which the *same* force, reaching a certain threshold of excess, in its prolongation now produces qualitatively distinct effects and seems to generate a whole new system.

That force has been described as reification, but we can now also begin to make some connections with another figural language used earlier: in a first moment, reification "liberated" the Sign from its referent, but this is not a force to be released with impunity. Now, in a second moment, it continues its work of dissolution, penetrating the interior of the Sign itself and liberating the Signifier from the Signified, or from meaning proper. This play, no longer of a realm of signs, but of pure or literal signifiers freed from the ballast of their signifieds, their former meanings, now generates a new kind of textuality in all the arts (and in philosophy as well, as we have seen above), and begins to project the mirage of some ultimate language of pure signifiers which is also frequently associated with schizophrenic discourse. (Indeed, the Lacanian theory of schizophrenia — a language disorder in which syntactical time breaks down, and leaves a succession of empty Signifiers, absolute moments of a perpetual present, behind itself—has offered one of the more influential explanations and ideological justifications for postmodernist textual practice.)

All of which would have to be demonstrated in some detail by way of a concrete analysis of the postmodernist experience in all the arts today: but the present argument can be concluded by drawing the consequences of this second moment—the culture of the Signifier or of the Simulacrum—for the whole problematic of some "autonomy" of the cultural sphere which has concerned us here. For that autonomous realm is not itself spared by the intensified process by which the classical Sign is dissolved: if its autonomy depended paradoxically on its possibility of remaining "semi-autonomous" (in an Althusserian sense) and of preserving the last tenuous link with some ultimate referent (or, in Althusserian language, of preserving the ultimate unity of a properly "structural totality"), then evidently in the new cultural moment culture will have ceased to be autonomous, and the realm of an autonomous play of signs becomes impossible, when that ultimate final referent to which the balloon of the mind was moored is now definitively cut. The break-up of the Sign in mid-air determines a fall back into a now absolutely fragmented and anarchic social reality; the broken pieces of language (the pure Signifiers) now falling again into the world, as so many more pieces of material junk among all the other rusting and superannuated apparatuses and buildings that litter the commodity landscape and that strew the "collage city," the "delirious New York" of a postmodernist late capitalism in full crisis.

But, returning to a Marcusean terminology, all of this can also be said in a different way: with the eclipse of culture as an autonomous space or sphere, culture itself falls into the world, and the result is not its disappearance but its prodigious expansion, to the point where culture becomes coterminous with social life in general: now all the levels become "acculturated," and in the society of the spectacle, the image, or the simulacrum, everything has at length become cultural, from the superstructures down into the mechanisms of the infrastructure itself. If this development then places acutely on the agenda the neoGramscian problem of a new cultural politics today—in a social system in which the very status of both culture and politics have been profoundly, functionally and structurally modified—it also renders problematic any further discussion of what used to be called "culture" proper, whose artifacts have become the random experiences of daily life itself.

6. IN THE SIERRA MAESTRA

All of which will have been little more than a lengthy excursion into a very specialized (or "elite") area, unless it can be shown that the dynamic therein visible, with something of the artificial simplification of the laboratory situation, finds striking analogies or homologies in very different and distant areas of social practice. It is precisely this replication of a common diachronic rhythm or "genetic code" which we will now observe in the very different realities of revolutionary practice and theory in the course of the 60s in the third world.

From the beginning, the Cuban experience affirmed itself as an original one, as a new revolutionary model, to be radically distinguished from more traditional forms of revolutionary practice. *Foco* theory, indeed, as it was associated with Che Guevara and theorized in Regis Debray's influential handbook, *Revolution in the Revolution?*, asserted itself (as the title of the book suggests) both against a more traditional Leninist conception of party practice and against the experience of the Chinese revolution in its first essential stage of the conquest of power (what will later come to be designated as "Maoism," China's own very different "revolution in the revolution" or Great Proletarian Cultural Revolution, will not become visible to the outside world until the moment in which the fate of the Cuban strategy has been sealed).

A reading of Debray's text shows that *foco* strategy, the strategy of the mobile guerrilla base or revolutionary *foyer*, is conceived as yet a third term, as something distinct from *either* the traditional model of class struggle (an essentially *urban* proletariat rising against a bourgeoisie or ruling class) *or* the Chinese experience of a mass peasant movement in the countryside (and has little in common either with a Fanonian struggle for recognition between Colonizer and Colonized). The *foco*, or guerrilla operation, is conceptualized as being neither "in" nor "of" either country or city: geographically, of course, it is positioned in the countryside, yet that location is not the permanently "liberated territory" of the Yenan region, well beyond the reach of the enemy forces of Chiang Kai-shek or of the Japanese occupier. It is not indeed located in the cultivated area of the peasant fields at all, but rather in that third or non-place which is the wilderness of the Sierra Maestra, neither country nor city, but rather a whole new element in which the guerrilla band moves in perpetual displacement.

This peculiarity of the way in which the spatial coordinates of the Cuban strategy is conceived has then immediate consequences for the way in which the class elements of the revolutionary movement are theorized. Neither city nor country: by the same token, paradoxically, the guerrillas themselves are grasped as being neither workers nor peasants (still less, intellectuals), but rather something entirely new, for which the prerevolutionary class society has no categories: new revolutionary subjects, forged in the guerrilla struggle indifferently out of the social material of peasants, city workers or intellectuals, yet now largely transcending those class categories (just as this moment of Cuban theory will claim largely to transcend the older revolutionary ideologies predicated on class categories, whether those of Trotskyist workerism, Maoist populism and peasant consciousness, or of Leninist vanguard intellectualism).

What becomes clear in a text like Debray's is that the guerrilla *foco*—so mobile as to be beyond geography in the static sense—is in and of itself a *figure* for the transformed, revolutionary society to come. Its revolutionary militants are not simply "soldiers" to whose specialized role and function one would then have to "add" supplementary roles in the revolutionary division of labor, such as political commissars and the political vanguard party itself, both explicitly rejected here. Rather, in them is abolished all such prerevolutionary divisions and categories. This conception of a newly emergent revolutionary "space" — situated outside the "real" political, social and geographical world of country and city, and of the historical social classes, yet at one and the same time a figure or small-scale image and prefiguration of the revolutionary transformation of that real world—may be designated as a properly utopian space, a Hegelian "inverted world," an autonomous revolutionary sphere, in which the fallen real world over against it is itself set right and transformed into a new socialist society.

For all practical purposes, this powerful model is exhausted, even before Che's own tragic death in Bolivia in 1967, with the failure of the guerrilla movements in Peru and Venezuela in 1966; not uncoincidentally, that failure will be accompanied by something like a disinvestment of revolutionary libido and fascination on the part of a first world left, its return (with some leavening of the newer Maoism) to their own "current situation," in the American antiwar movement and May 68. In Latin America, however, the radical strategy which effectively replaces *foco* theory is that of the so-called urban guerrilla movement, pioneered in Uruguay by the Tupamaros: it will have become clear that this break-up of the utopian space of the older guerrilla *foco*, the fall of politics back into the world in the form of a very different style of political practice indeed—one that seeks to dramatize features of state power, rather than, as in traditional revolutionary movements, to build towards some ultimate encounter with it—will be interpreted here as something of a structural equivalent to the final stage of the sign as characterized above.

Several qualifications must be made, however. For one thing, it is clear that this new form of political activity will be endowed, by association, with something of the tragic prestige of the Palestinian liberation movement, which comes into being in its contemporary form as a result of the Israeli seizure of the West Bank and the Gaza Strip in 1967, and which will thereafter become one of the dominant worldwide symbols of revolutionary praxis in the late 60s. Equally clearly, however, the struggle of this desperate and victimized people cannot be made to bear responsibility for the excesses of this kind of strategy elsewhere in the world, whose universal results (whether in Latin America, or with Cointelpro in the United States, or, belatedly, in West Germany and Italy) have been to legitimize an intensification of the repressive apparatus of state power.

This objective coincidence between a misguided assessment of the social and political situation on the part of left militants (for the most part students and intellectuals eager to force a revolutionary conjuncture by voluntaristic acts) and a willing exploitation by the state of precisely those provocations suggests that what is often loosely called "terrorism" must be the object of complex and properly dialectical analysis. However rightly a responsible left chooses to dissociate itself from such strategy (and the Marxian opposition to terrorism is an old and established tradition that goes back to the 19th century), it is important to remember that "terrorism," as a "concept," is also an ideologeme of the right and must therefore be refused in that form. Along with the disaster films of the late 60s and early 70s, mass culture itself makes clear that "terrorism"—the image of the "terrorist"—is one of the privileged forms in which an ahistorical society imagines radical social change; meanwhile, an inspection of the content of the modern thriller or adventure story also makes it clear that the "otherness" of so-called terrorism has begun to replace older images of criminal "insanity" as an unexamined and seemingly "natural" motivation in the construction of plots—yet another sign of the ideological nature of this particular pseudo-concept. Understood in this way, "terrorism" is a collective obsession, a symptomatic fantasy of the American political unconscious, which demands decoding and analysis in its own right.

As for the thing itself, for all practical purposes it comes to an end with the Chilean coup in 1973 and the fall of virtually all the Latin American countries to various forms of military dictatorship. The belated reemergence of this kind of political activity in West Germany and in Italy must surely at least in part be attributed to the fascist past of these two countries, to their failure to liquidate that past after the war, and to a violent moral revulsion against it on the part of a segment of the youth and intellectuals who grew up in the 60s.

7. RETURN OF THE "ULTIMATELY DETERMINING INSTANCE"

The two "breaks" which have emerged in the preceding section—one in the general area around 1967, the other in the immediate neighborhood of 1973 — will now serve as the framework for a more general hypothesis about the periodization of the 60s in general. Beginning with the second of these, a whole series of other, seemingly unrelated events in the general area of 1972–1974 suggests that this moment is not merely a decisive one on the relatively specialized level of thirdworld or Latin American radical politics, but signals the definitive end of what is called the 60s in a far more global way. In the first world, for example, the end of the draft and the withdrawal of American forces from Vietnam (in 1973) spell the end of the mass politics of the antiwar movement (the crisis of the new left itself—which can be largely dated from the break-up of SDS in 1969—would seem related to the other break mentioned, to which we will return below), while the signing of the Common Program between the Communist Party and the new Socialist Party in France (as well as the wider currency of slogans associated with "Eurocommunism" at this time) would seem to mark a strategic turn away from the kinds of political activities associated with May 68 and its sequels. This is also the moment at which, as a result of the Yom Kippur war, the oil weapon emerges and administers a different kind of shock to the economies, the political strategies, and the daily life habits of the advanced countries. Concomitantly, on the more general cultural and ideological level, the intellectuals associated with the establishment itself (particularly in the United States) begin to recover from the fright and defensive posture which was theirs during the decade now ending, and again find their voices in a series of attacks on 60s culture and 60s politics which, as was noted at the beginning, are not even yet at an end. One of the more influential documents was Lionel Trilling's *Sincerity and Authenticity* (1972), an Arnoldian call to reverse the tide of 60s countercultural "barbarism." (This will, of course, be followed by the equally influential diagnosis of some 60s concept of "authenticity" in terms of a "culture of narcissism".) Meanwhile, in July 1973, some rather different "intellectuals," representing various concrete forms of political and economic power, will begin to rethink the failure in Vietnam in terms of a new global strategy for American and first world interests; their establishment of the Trilateral Commission will at least symbolically be a significant marker in the recovery of momentum by what must be called "the ruling classes." The emergence of a widely accepted new popular concept and term at this same time, the notion of the "multinational corporation," is also another symptom, signifying, as the authors of *Global Reach* have suggested, the moment in which private business finds itself obliged to emerge in public as a visible "subject of history" and a visible actor on the world stage—think of the role of ITT in Chile—when the American government, having been badly burned by the failure of the Vietnam intervention, is generally reluctant to undertake further ventures of this kind.

For all these reasons it seems appropriate to mark the definitive end of the "60s" in the general area of 1972–1974. But we have omitted until now the decisive element in any argument for a periodization or "punctuation" of this kind, and this new kind of material will direct our attention to a "level" or "instance" which has hitherto significantly been absent from the present discussion, namely the economic itself. For 1973–1974 is the moment of the onset of a worldwide economic crisis, whose dynamic is still with us today, and which put a decisive full stop to the economic expansion and prosperity characteristic of the postwar period generally and of the 60s in particular. When we add to this another key economic marker—the recession in West Germany in 1966 and that in the other advanced countries, in particular in the United States a year or so later—we may well thereby find ourselves in a better position more formally to conceptualize that sense of a secondary break around 1967–68 which has begun to surface on the philosophical, cultural, and political levels as they were analyzed or "narrated" above.

Such confirmation by the economic "level" itself of periodizing reading derived from other, sample levels or instances of social life during the 60s will now perhaps put us in a better position to answer the two theoretical issues raised at the beginning of this essay. The first had to do with the validity of Marxist analysis for a period whose active political categories no longer seemed to be those of social class, and in which in a more general way traditional forms of Marxist theory and practice seemed to have entered a "crisis." The second involved the problem of some "unified field theory" in terms of which such seemingly distant realities as third-world peasant movements and first-world mass culture (or indeed, more abstractly, intellectual or superstructural levels like philosophy and culture generally, and those of mass resistance and political practice) might conceptually be related in some coherent way.

A pathbreaking synthesis by Ernest Mandel, in his book *Late Capitalism*, will suggest a hypothetical answer to both these questions at once. The book presents, among other things, an elaborate system of business cycles under capitalism, whose most familiar unit, the 7-to-10 year alternation of boom, overproduction, recession and economic recovery, adequately enough accounts for the mid-point break in the 60s suggested above.

Mandel's account of the worldwide crisis of 1974, however, draws on a far more controversial conception of vaster cycles of some thirty to fifty year periods each—cycles which are then obviously much more difficult to perceive experientially or "phenomenologically" insofar as they transcend the rhythms and limits of the biological life of individuals. These "Kondratiev waves" (named after the Soviet economist who hypothesized them) have according to Mandel been renewed four times since the 18th century, and are characterized by quantum leaps in the technology of production, which enable decisive increases in the rate of profit generally, until at length the advantages of the new production processes have been explored and exhausted and the cycle therewith comes to an end. The latest of these Kondratiev cycles is that marked by computer technology, nuclear energy and the mechanization of agriculture (particularly in foodstuffs and also primary materials), which Mandel dates from 1940 in North America and the postwar period in the other imperialist countries: what is decisive in the present context is his notion that, with the worldwide recession of 1973–74, the dynamics of this latest "long wave" are spent.

The hypothesis is attractive, however, not only because of its abstract usefulness in confirming our periodization schemes, but also because of the actual analysis of this latest wave of capitalist expansion, and of the properly Marxian version he gives of a whole range of developments which have generally been thought to demonstrate the end of the "classical" capitalism theorized by Marx and to require this or that postMarxist theory of social mutation (as in theories of consumer society, postindustrial society, and the like).

We have already described the way in which neocolonialism is characterized by the radically new technology (the so-called Green Revolution in agriculture: new machinery, new farming methods, and new types of chemical fertilizer and genetic experiments with hybrid plants and the like), with which capitalism transforms its relationship to its colonies from an old-fashioned imperialist control to market penetration, destroying the older village communities and creating a whole new wage-labor pool and lumpenproletariat. The militancy of the new social forces is at one and the same time a result of the "liberation" of peasants from their older self-sustaining village communities, and a movement of self-defense, generally originating in the stabler yet more isolated areas of a given third world country, against what is rightly perceived as a far more thoroughgoing form of penetration and colonization than the older colonial armies.

It is now in terms of this process of "mechanization" that Mandel will make the link between the neocolonialist transformation of the third world during the 60s and the emergence of that seemingly very different thing in the first world, variously termed consumer society, postindustrial society, media society, and the like:

> Far from representing a postindustrial society, late capitalism . . . constitutes *generalized universal industrialization* for the first time in history. Mechanization, standardization, overspecialization and parcellization of labor, which in the past determined only the realm of commodity production in actual industry, now penetrate into all sectors of social life. It is characteristic of late capitalism that agriculture is step by step becoming just as industrialized as industry, the sphere of circulation [e.g., credit cards and the like] just as much as the sphere of production, and recreation just as much as the organization of work.

With this last, Mandel touches on what he elsewhere calls the mechanization of the superstructure, or in other words the penetration of culture itself by what the Frankfurt School called the culture industry, and of which the growth of the media is only a part. We may thus generalize his description as follows: late capitalism in general (and the 60s in particular) constitute a process in which the last surviving internal and external zones of precapitalism—the last vestiges of noncommodified or traditional space within and outside the advanced world—are now ultimately penetrated and colonized in their turn. Late capitalism can therefore be described as the moment in which the last vestiges of Nature which survived on into classical capitalism are at length eliminated: namely the third world and the unconscious. The 60s will then have been the momentous transformational period in which this systemic restructuring takes place on a global scale.

With such an account, our "unified field theory" of the 60s is given—the discovery of a single process at work in first and third worlds, in global economy and in consciousness and culture, a properly *dialectical* process, in which "liberation" and domination are inextricably combined. We may now therefore proceed to a final characterization of the period as a whole.

The simplest yet most universal formulation surely remains the widely shared feeling that in the 60s, for a time, everything was possible: that this period, in other words, was a moment of a universal liberation, a global unbinding of energies. Mao Tse-tung's figure for this process is in this respect most revealing: "Our nation," he cried, "is like an atom . . . . When this atom's nucleus is smashed, the thermal energy released will have really tremendous power!" The image evokes the emergence of a genuine mass democracy from the breakup of the older feudal and village structures, and from the therapeutic dissolution of the habits of those structures in cultural revolutions: yet the effects of fission, the release of molecular energies, the unbinding of "material signifiers," can be a properly terrifying spectacle; and we now know that Mao Tse-tung himself drew back from the ultimate consequences of the process he had set in motion, when, at the supreme moment of the Cultural Revolution, that of the founding of the Shanghai Commune, he called a halt to the dissolution of the party apparatus and effectively reversed the direction of this collective experiment as a whole (with consequences only too obvious at the present time). In the west also, the great explosions of the 60s have led, in the worldwide economic crisis, to powerful restorations of the social order and a renewal of the repressive power of the various state apparatuses.

Yet the forces these must now confront, contain and control are new ones, on which the older methods do not necessarily work. We have described the 60s as a moment in which the enlargement of capitalism on a global scale simultaneously produced an immense freeing or unbinding of social energies, a prodigious release of untheorized new forces: the ethnic forces of black and "minority" or third world movements everywhere, regionalisms, the development of new and militant bearers of "surplus consciousness" in the student and women's movements, as well as in a host of struggles of other kinds. Such newly released forces do not only not seem to compute in the dichotomous class model of traditional Marxism; they also seem to offer a realm of freedom and voluntarist possibility beyond the classical constraints of the economic infrastructure. Yet this sense of freedom and possibility—which is for the course of the 60s a momentarily objective reality, as well as (from the hindsight of the 80s) a historical illusion—may perhaps best be explained in terms of the superstructural movement and play enabled by the transition from one infrastructural or systemic stage of capitalism to another. The 60s were in that sense an immense and inflationary issuing of superstructural credit; a universal abandonment of the referential gold standard; an extraordinary printing up of ever more devalued signifiers. With the end of the 60s, with the world economic crisis, all the old infrastructural bills then slowly come due once more; and the 80s will be characterized by an effort, on a world scale, to proletarianize all those unbound social forces which gave the 60s their energy, by an extension of class struggle, in other words, into the farthest reaches of the globe as well as the most minute configurations of local institutions (such as the university system). The unifying force here is the new vocation of a henceforth global capitalism, which may also be expected to unify the unequal, fragmented, or local resistances to the process. And this is finally also the solution to the so-called "crisis" of Marxism and to the widely noted inapplicability of its forms of class analysis to the new social realities with which the 60s confronted us: "traditional" Marxism, if "untrue" during this period of a proliferation of new subjects of history, must necessarily become true again when the dreary realities of exploitation, extraction of surplus value, proletarianization and the resistance to it in the form of class struggle, all slowly reassert themselves on a new and expanded world scale, as they seem currently in the process of doing.

A VERY PARTIAL

The million-year period to which the burned junk from the museums and archives related would be summed up in the history books in one sentence, according to Koradubian: Following the death of Jesus Christ there was a period of readjustment that lasted for approximately one million years.

Kurt Vonnegut, The Sirens of Titan

1957 Battle of Algiers
Independence of Ghana
The Sputnik

1958 Return of de Gaulle; the Fifth Republic
EEC

1959 The Cuban Revolution
Urban renewal in New Haven

1960 Sino-Soviet split
First sit-ins, Greensboro, N.C.
A student sit-in conference at Shaw College, N.C., becomes the start of the Student Nonviolent Coordinating Committee (SNCC)

1961 John F. Kennedy is inaugurated as President of the United States
Lumumba, the radical Congolese leader, is murdered
Invasion of Cuba at Bay of Pigs, a dismal failure
Generals' putsch in Algiers (OAS)
Gagarin becomes the first man in space

Compiled by Fredric Jameson, Anders Stephanson, and Cornel West.

CHRONOLOGY

The first Freedom Ride buses (organized by CORE) are burned in Alabama
Interstate Commerce Commission desegregates bus and train stations
The Berlin Wall
Joseph Heller's *Catch 22*

1962 Students for a Democratic Society (SDS): the *Port Huron Statement*
Algerian independence
Pope John XXIII opens Vatican Council II
The Beatles hit England with *Love Me Do*
The Cuban Missile Crisis
John Glenn, first American to orbit Earth in space

1963 King's *Letter From a Birmingham Jail*
Assassination of Medger Evers, NAACP, Miss.
Massive civil rights March on Washington: *"I have a Dream"*
Black rebellion in Birmingham, Ala., after church bombing
Fall of Ngo Dinh Diem in Saigon
Assassination of John F. Kennedy
Lacan is excluded from the French Psychoanalytic Society

1964 Malcolm X leaves the Nation of Islam after a schism
Free Speech Movement begins at Berkeley
Herbert Marcuse, *One-Dimensional Man*
Stanley Kubrick, *Dr. Strangelove*

Freedom Summer in Mississippi
Gulf of Tonkin "incident"
Khrushchev falls, enter Kosygin and Brezhnev
Congress passes the Civil Rights Act
King receives the Nobel Peace Prize
Betty Friedan, *The Feminine Mystique*

1965 First regular US combat troops in Vietnam
US intervenes with 20,000 troops in the Dominican Republic
The first teach-ins at the University of Michigan
Large-scale bombings of North Vietnam
Anti-war March on Washington
Riots in the Watts ghetto in Los Angeles
The Voting Rights Act is signed
The Great Society Program
Malcolm X is assassinated
Bob Dylan goes electric with *Bringing it all back home*
Cultural Revolution begins in China
Sukarno is overthrown in Indonesia; hundreds of thousands of Communists are murdered in the aftermath

1966 King comes out against the war in Vietnam
Mao, *Quotations of Chairman Mao*
Jefferson Airplane has its first record success
The National Organization for Women (NOW)
The Black Panther Party is founded in Oakland, Cal.
Louis Althusser's *For Marx* appears in France
The Great Coalition (CDU-SPD) in West Germany

1967 The Shanghai Commune
Military takes over in Greece
Black uprisings in the United States, e.g., Detroit
Six-Day War; Israel occupies the West Bank, Sinai and the Gaza Strip
de Gaulle visits Quebec
Psychedelic summer of love in San Francisco
Beatles' *Sgt. Pepper's Lonely Hearts Club Band*
Che Guevara is killed in Bolivia
Siege of Pentagon
NOW adopts the Bill of Rights for Women

1968

The Tet Offensive in Vietnam
The Prague Spring
Student uprisings in Warsaw and Mexico City
Student uprising at Columbia University, New York
Founding of the *March 22 Movement* in Paris
May '68 in France
King is assassinated
Eldridge Cleaver, *Soul On Ice*
Robert F. Kennedy is assassinated
Democratic Convention in Chicago
Soviet invasion of Czechoslovakia
Nicos Poulantzas' *Political Power and Social Classes* is published in France
Tommie Smith and John Carlos make a Black Power salute while receiving their medals at the Mexico City Olympics

1969

End of Cultural Revolution
Armed clashes along the border of the Soviet Union and China
Breakup of the SDS
Woodstock and Altamont music festivals
League of Black Revolutionary Workers founded in Detroit
The *Red Stocking Manifesto*, and the *Bitch Manifesto*
Repression against the Black Panthers; murder of Fred Hampton *et al.*
US puts man on the moon
Rudi Dutschke is shot in Berlin
Days of Rage in Chicago
Dennis Hopper, *Easy Rider*
Willy Brandt and the SPD come to power in West Germany
Beginning of civil rights movement in Northern Ireland
Trial of the Chicago Eight
Richard Nixon

1970

Kate Millett, *Sexual Politics*
Hawaii, Alaska and New York, first states to liberalize abortion laws
Cambodian invasion; Kent State murders
Black September in Jordan

Women march on the Republican Convention hall, Miami Beach, 1968. Photo by Jean Raisler, courtesy of Liberation News Service.

Black students take over building at Cornell University, Spring 1969. Courtesy of the *Guardian*.

The October Crisis, Quebec
Strike in Gdansk
Senate holds ERA-hearings, the first since 1956

1971 Attica Prison rebellion
New York Radical Feminists stage *Speakout Against Rape*
Fourth World Manifesto by Detroit feminists and Indochinese women

1972 *Common Program*, Socialist and Communist Parties in France
National Conference of Puerto Rican Women founded
McGovern becomes the Democratic nominee and is defeated by Nixon
Women make up 40% of Democratic Convention (13% in 1968)
Judy Chicago, Miriam Shapiro and others open *Womanhouse* exhibition at the California Institute of the Arts

1973 Wounded Knee
Benjamin Spock denounces his early childcare books as sexist
Last US troops leave Vietnam
Allende is overthrown and killed in Chile
Yom Kippur War; the oil crisis
National Black Feminist Organization is formed

1974 Revolution in Portugal
The Three Marias are freed in Portugal after international feminist campaign
Symbionese Liberation Army kidnaps Patricia Hearst

1975 Liberation of Saigon
Independence of Angola and Mozambique

1976 Soweto rebellion
Victory of Partie Quebecois
Mao dies, and so does Zhao, in Peking

PART 2 READING FOR WHAT? (Thanks, Robert Lynd)

Grace Paley on the beach in North Vietnam, 1969

She begins, in one poem about the villages behind her:

THREE VILLAGES

Last week
seven Americans swam in the Gulf of Tonkin
guarded by the sampans of the Nhan Tracn
Fishing Cooperative
This village was attacked 846 times
For each inhabitant, 260 bombs were dropped
There isn't a home left or a household that's intact

•

The North Vietnamese had offered to release three POWs to the peace movement; Paley, Linda Evens (SDS), Jimmy Johnson (of the Fort Hood Three) and four filmmakers went to receive them. Courtesy of Grace Paley.

INTRODUCTION

SOHNYA SAYRES

"Reading for What?" gathers the responses of over forty writers to the question of what issues in the 60s, what books, what people drove home their commitments. These authors open themselves here and make assessments that sound long overdue. In some cases they write of their own development and transformations or of debates time has made more vivid; in other cases, they argue for a way to think about the period as a whole. Sometimes they share present experiences to account for what is needed to be remembered: sometimes, as in Finvola Drury's work, "Children Have No Freedom. They Are Property Just Like a Book," they recall the desperate acts which exposed the depths of the confrontation. Together they begin to explain how to read and how to write when events make large claims.

This collection grew out of a difficulty I had in deciding how to read Goodman's, Mailer's, and Sontag's work from those years. I started out writing in the summer of '82 what I thought would be not a discussion of ideology, which it has trailed off into, but a grudging appreciation. I felt they deserved to be remembered for being more than infuriating, that theirs was a special case of American novelists and critics who wrote as political intellectuals—the kind of Camus-Sartre-de Beauvoir an American left may not have needed, but would have welcomed to hold down the fort, a fort in which the troops were jumping around inside to Fanon, Malcolm X, and bitch manifestoes of all kinds and who, when stepping out, were getting framed and arrested before they had a chance to finish *Capital*. Many were young, and these writers had longevity, scope. They wrote a lot, they stood up, they had gotten through the 50s with some of their integrity, they knew about liberal America. (And Goodman, especially, had borne some abuse for it.) They were drawn to what was happening and they tried to explain it: Mailer, in Miami and Chicago and on the marches; Sontag, in essays as game as "What's Happening in America," in Cuba and Vietnam; Goodman to his audiences when he told about schooling and alienation and anarchist sympathies. When I looked at their mistakes, their caution, their worrying over the roles of intellectuals, it seemed, well, what I might do to someone else's movement: single out utopian excesses and historical blindnesses because I really couldn't believe and couldn't trust what this new movement overleapt.

In other words, I found I could forgive more. Mailer's *Miami and the Siege of Chicago* was better than I remembered, at least where he describes coming into the cities. His hightailing back to the hotel in Chicago still galls, as Sontag's constant dichotomizing in Vietnam does, as Goodman's avuncular handholding of middle America does, but few had their record for being near enough to the fray to risk being wrong.

Risk they did, and they lost a little. They backed away from America more astir than it had been in their memories to hold out for style, for modernist selfhood, from a communalism so vague it talked piety and little else. Then, too, they missed the revolution of this time—they misjudged the new subjectivity. Mailer's gropings about sex and women put him outside the pale. Goodman had the fashionable, but objectionable habit of tossing off sexism and racism as a recent invention that would disappear under the rule of nature in politics. Sontag got stuck on what I would call the objective correlative of negation. Her energies got siphoned off into self-confrontation and the parodic idea that "disburdenment" was the most honest way to be modern.

Their writings seemed just one realization or two behind what they could have said had they recognized the intellectual's new responsibility: to step to the side. They were needed to criticize, warn, embrace, to be sure, but they needed to stop using themselves as the measurement of the validity or authenticity of a project. They needed to decenter themselves, but not apocalyptically—not in a version that repeats the kinds of contradictions already the ratchet and socket of their lives.

I came to believe, for example, that it wasn't the challenge of feminism to Mailer's sexology of the rusty barb and the ethical payload that showed him so lacking, nor his fixation on violence. These were the man, the positions from which he could see better the meanness of American life, which gave him the uncanny bad luck of being almost right about Gary Gilmore and Jack Abbott, which made his Henry Miller closer to present feminist arguments for desire, for the fantasies of dread and power we swell our sexuality with, than Kate Millett's. The underside to Mailer, or to keep my metaphor, the bite of his gears, was his indebtedness to these views. He saw the world in terms of fight and readiness, existentially, then kept wondering why the fight wasn't in him, why literary quarrels and cocktail party attacks constituted his ring and his criminality. America politicizing caught him off balance. He had been leading with his style and his sense of personal heroics, and he got caught shadow boxing. Women writers, blacks, gays, third world authors presumed to speak for themselves about struggles he was barely privy to. They were making a tradition, in Amiri Baraka's fine phrase, and what is more they were in the streets. Even the young could not be relied upon to be beat or hip. There were plenty who were impulsive and ignorant, grasping for an identity and an aesthetic to follow, but plenty more were piecing together arguments for a new world order. Some did both. I remember nights when you couldn't hold your own in a Buffalo bar without a willingness to strip, a taste for quaaludes, and a good line on Althusser.

Yet, despite these objections, I wanted to confess that I could now more appreciate Mailer's turn to journalism (he was able to subordinate himself to events that much), that I wanted to thank Goodman for his energy. They were there, if not for us, then as self-appointed ambassadors to the outside, and when our morale was low their interest, their documents counted. Goodman's neolithic conservatism is still a puzzle, I should add, but fortunately, we have here in this collection Arnold Sachar's and Arnold Krupat's clarifications.

Sontag's contribution came harder to me. She took culture more seriously than the other two; she was less touched by the pleasure of writing and less enthralled by the beat of America's heart. She brought the history of European intellectual crises to whatever she wrote about. Yet the new politics wanted to believe, anyway, that these crises could be circumvented. It was making discoveries about those previously invisible and marginalized, about people and perspectives conspicuously missing, in other words, from her sample of European intellectual thought. When Sontag did write about these missing people too often her insights depended on oppositions she found within herself as a western, complicating, hyper-self-conscious writer, glutted on ideas and empty of certainty. Her critique of styles of radical will stayed put, square in the midst of her dilemma. What else can she do now, in good conscience, but write her series of disavowals—of her naiveté, her politics, even the vehicle of prose itself?

I am reminded of Flo Kennedy's remark, in the interview at the end of this collection, that "all struggles pay off," but not of course equally. The struggle to purify the self earns so little compared to the struggle to find out how to act and how to be willing to be surprised by addition to thought, not just contradiction. Consider how we are learning to add the operatic sexuality of the gay movement to our politics, how we are trying to repossess the spectacle in the society of spectacle, how we are chancing to sublimate the paranoia of a mass society in nuclear stalemate into world peace. Consider the meaning that accumulated as we listened to the identity-cheated as they shifted into being subjects with power.

It was their knowledge from their struggle that exposed my difficulty. I know of few books canonized before the end of the 60s a woman, black, indigenous, or third world person can read without feeling like a heretic under the rule of misrule; one waits for the alarm that would send one to the stake, or for the tolerance absent-mindedly patting one's head. I put my essay aside.

But when thinking about a bibliography for this book, I was thrown back onto the same question: what do we learn from writers when in a moment of danger (as Benjamin said) we remember history, when what they write seems at once stunning and insufficient? Can we forgive them their writerly reserve when the events before them cost them little? In retrospect, do we too much admire their caution and common sense? And what about the other issue to reading in such moments? Danger turned relevance into an obligation; danger made Plato practically leer and Nietzsche whisper in the back of the head. It made Hegel and Freud unshakable ghosts. Marx stayed a good man—as good as one could expect from a man—to have around. What was certain was that whomever one read, one read with an ear for the rending of fabric.

For over a year, then, I asked those who had been active in the 60s to reflect on the books they still thought about, the figures they had looked at or listened to. The very first pieces to come in—Jay Boyer's description of waiting for the right Vietnam War novel, Paula Gunn Allen's telling of the books that helped make her an Indian, Paul Buhle's advice on doubting one's own recollections—reinforced the old lesson: no theory can predict the number of parts that exceed the whole nor reveal their meaning as voices can, interpreting themselves. Each piece after struck new chords, and I began to hear a liberating celebration of rare memories and rare assessments and paths shaped unexpectedly by events which, in turn, illuminated the texts.

I want to thank each contributor to "Reading for What?" for turning a bibliography into an occasion, and I want to thank members of the *Social Text Collective*, like Nancy Anderson, who offered their time and encouragement. I want to thank Robert Roth for (a) scouting around and (b) hour upon hour prodding me away from editorial temptations with exchanges like the one printed below.

> "So you want to know what I think about *Social Text*? I like it about as much as I can any publication that was designed from the beginning not to publish anything I wrote.
>
> "Furthermore the trouble with most left wing publications is that they sound like one highly intelligent person wrote all the articles. Sohnya, you're writing about Paul Goodman. Well, Paul Goodman couldn't appear in *Social Test*—unless, of course, he was already Paul Goodman. And then only maybe.
>
> "I think one real problem is that writers now are so nervous about being edited and revised or rejected, etc., that before anything can ever come out of them, they have already done a good deal of editing and revising and rejecting—which is one reason that so much work has become constricted—all objections are sure to be met—and even that doesn't matter because the work will be revised and edited again because that is what editors and editorial collectives do.

> "People now almost compulsively talk about the need for standards — as if somehow talking that way relieves whatever doubts they or anyone else might have about their own abilities. I think most of this talk about standards, this new toughness reflects a need to keep things under control, a need not to stumble and sprawl in the pursuit of new things, a need to constrict imagination. It is I suspect some type of violent reaction to the explosion of possibility that was the most beautiful aspect of the 60s."

Thanks again, Robert. As usual you made me reach for my politics. What follows collects those loosened spirits as they remember what was important (in "Memories"), acknowledge their influences (in "Acknowledgments"), and take up issues that changed their lives (in "[Re]takes"). After a graphic break with Richard Metz and Alex Jeavins, and Tuli Kupferberg, the section concludes with interviews with feminists Silvia Federici and Flo Kennedy. Federici argues how to "put feminism back on its feet," and Flo Kennedy remarks on how, "since it's damn slick out there," we should pardon our errors and get on with it. Finally, with relish, Donald Foss and Ralph Larkin offer quips about some old rhetoric.

◀ 1. ▲ 2.

▲ 3. 4. ▶

1. Paul Goodman and draft resister at the Greenwich Village Peace Center, 1967. Photo by Karl Bissinger. 2. Allen Ginsberg, resting, NYC, 1968. Photo by Diana Davies, courtesy of the War Resisters League. 3. Poet David Henderson at the largest of the antiwar demonstrations, Washington, DC, November 15, 1969. Photo by Karl Bissinger. 4. A.J. Muste and Judith Malina, Hiroshima Day Sit-Down, NYC, 1963. Photo by Neil Haworth, courtesy of the War Resisters League.

MEMORIES

New wine in old bottles

IRVING WEXLER

It's the early 60s; I'm alone, jobless, a dispirited post-Stalinist on the loose. Years after the Khrushchev confessions, I'm still mired in its aftermath. . ., still paralyzed politically, with a lifetime of radical consciousness and practice stored in mothballs during the long sedation of the conformist fifties. From afar I hear dim echoes of an incipient social, political and cultural convolution. Some of its manifestations—sit-ins, freedom rides, campus confrontations, militancy—I greet with enthusiasm. Other aspects—the drug scene, youth cult, nirvana-seeking, extravagantly sexual, occult, antirational, blissed-out—I dismiss out of hand. How characteristic of the petit-bourgeois young, I observe self-righteously, to try to liberate society out of a narcissistic pleasure principle rather than from truly objective (that is to say Marxist) social concerns.

It is in this ambiguous mindset that I am literally catapulted into the ambience of the 60s when a young friend takes me to the Fillmore East to hear the Jefferson Airplane. After milling around for hours in the midst of a stoned crowd, I find myself seated at the Fillmore's midnight concert, deliriously dissolving in the acid meanderings of Grace Slick. And I realize through the grass clouds—with a mixture of panic and ecstasy, acceptance and rejection, attraction and repulsion—that what I am experiencing is in the nature of a personal conversion. . . a revelation. . . a leap into a whole new state of consciousness.

Now everybody knows that hard-edged older leftists don't undergo born-again transformations at rock concerts. There is no place for this kind of mystical shtick in historical materialism. Yet here I am, at a sleazy rock palace, with an audience half my age, so moved by the shared ritual of spontaneous self-expression that the music is melting away decades of psychic armoring. Later, shaken and dislocated, I know that I am on the edge of a profound and deep spiritual opening.

This is an exciting and at the same time disoriented stage in my life. "In me," as C. Day Lewis writes, "two worlds at war trample the willing flesh." Dogmas of the past bind me like chains; contradictions follow me like shadows. On the one hand, I am responding with warmth and gratitude to the utopian vision of the sixties at their best: the insistence that personal liberation and social change go hand in hand; the idea that spontaneity, openness and subjective participation must be part of the process of achieving socialism. On the other hand, coming as I do from an orthodox Marxist-Leninist perspective, I am hooked on the presumptions of dialectical materialism, bottom-line economic determinism, and a set pattern of revolutionary strategy and tactics. Can the ascetic old left find love with the sexy new left? Can a Leninist sit at the same table with millennianism? Will Freedom set sail into the sunset with Necessity? Transcendentalism and iron-bound historicism—it isn't what you'd call a marriage made in heaven.

Reacting to the ferment around me with conflicting sets of values is inducing a kind of dialectical schizophrenia. For example, I read the *Port Huron Statement* with two totally different minds. One applauds the passionate appeal for social change, the attack on consumer capitalism, the commitment to struggle for personal and political metamorphosis. My other mind is appalled at the SDS contention that middle-class students are to replace the working class as the major agency for revolutionary transformation. The malaise of the young rather than the exploitation of the basic worker as the cutting edge of revolution? The Marxist in me bristles at this revisionist tripe.

Since I reject the cliches of the old left, and am bewildered by the romantic, personalized or theatrical concepts of the new left, where does that leave me politically? Too old for SDS, alienated from the radical sectarian groups, dumped by my black friends as part of their separatist strategies, I go through the turmoil of the middle 60s—the civil rights demonstrations, the marches to Washington, the anti-Vietnam War actions—as a political party of one. Later, for a brief time, I relive my old coalition days when I join the Peace and Freedom Party and go upstate to gather petitions for Cleaver as President. God, it reminds me of my young CP days, when the Irish workers in Chelsea would bang the door shut in my face. Only this time, I'm a middle-aged bearded man calmly discussing ecological and political issues with incredulous farmers who sometimes—out of sheer Yankee cantankerousness—actually sign my petitions. When this effort falls apart, I join a radical ecology group out of a basic need for political community, even though I am quite at odds with their politics. For the same reasons, I become a supporter and warm personal friend of the War Resisters' League, despite my theoretical objections to nonviolence. Still later, I join the collective staff of a nonauthoritarian radical underground paper, *Against the Grain*. Here, as the house Marxist in a group of assorted anarcho-syndicalists, I remain for two years and six issues—managing quite nicely to learn from, tolerate and respect my comrades until the paper falls apart when it prints an issue attacking Marxism as the opposite side of the coin of dictatorship.

As with so many so-called radical men, ambiguity marks my first response to the feminist rumblings in the early 60s. Typically, I take it for granted that class rather than gender is the primary oppression of all societies—including of course capitalism. Accordingly, it is not good politics to raise the issue of sexism—as pervasive as it may be—since it will become a divisive factor in the movement. Simone de Beauvoir's *The Second Sex* profoundly shakes my views, on a theoretical level at least, but leaves my basic attitudes untouched. Doris Lessing's *Golden Notebook*, with its powerful evocation of the psychological subjugation of Anna in her relationship with men, is a turning point in my perception. But again, the author's muted and compassionate tone towards the male characters allows me to rationalize: "Well, Anna is a completely exceptional woman, and besides, I'm not the kind of shit her men are."

My first real awareness of the fury of movement women at male chauvinism comes, as I recall, from a reading of the 1967 *Manifesto of the Women's Caucus in SDS.* On its heels, like shock waves, come a series of more violent attacks on sexism, from within the SDS, from lesbians, radical feminists, writers like Jill Johnston, Ti-Grace Atkinson—all of whom I read with great apprehension. For me, the height of women's anger at men is Robin Morgan's demand in RAT for men to "surrender their cock privilege or else join the power establishment." Confused, guilty, indignant, vulnerable, I sense however that the women have irrevocably changed the course of radical politics in America. How grateful, I remember being, to read socialist feminist literature as confirmation from women themselves that men, however flawed, are still necessary in achieving basic social changes. Who wants to be read out of the human race on biological, sociological or existential grounds?

Aside from feminist and later, gay literature, the books during this decade that affected me most were the ones that challenged and upset long-crystallized patterns of thinking. As a poet I was most strongly influenced by Allen Ginsberg's prophetic and openly homosexual work. I also remember myself being shaken by the Afro-American poetry of young writers like (then) Leroi Jones, Don Lee, Ethridge Knight, Nikki Giovanni—with their biting portrayal of the new black consciousness, the mixture and street and high diction, their tensions, vitality, and above all, white-hot anger at white oppression.

The three authors whom I particularly battled with and returned to throughout this era were Paul Goodman, Norman Brown and Herbert Marcuse. At one and the same time I was moved tremendously by Goodman's (*Growing Up Absurd*) compassion for the alienated young in a meaningless world and irritated by his almost Victorian conservative prescription for change. With Brown's apocalyptic *Life Against Death* I carried on one of those incompatible yet fervent love affairs, simultaneously seduced by its shimmering promises of a new consciousness, body mysticism, transcendent sexuality and ecstatic vision of a new world acoming beyond our comprehension—and coldly critical of its mystical excesses entirely outside the realms of Marxist scientism. And of course Marcuse, despite his dense often impenetrable style, exposing the illusions of bourgeois freedom, contrasting autonomy with one-dimensionality, urging us to look into the internal as external terrain for the libertarian impulse. Ah, Herbert, our Freudo-Marxian Papa, the oldest and therefore for me the dearest new leftist of them all.

As far as I was concerned, the 1960s officially came to an end not with a bang, or even a whimper, but on twanging guitar note, when a group of us in Movement for a Democratic Society voted to close our People's Coffee House in the west eighties one bitter-cold winter night. We couldn't pay the rent, our constituency had dwindled to near zero, and the new left was virtually defunct. So, sitting in the heatless dreary storefront, we packed up some books, shook hands, sat around smoking a joint and singing a medley of songs—from Guthrie to Dylan—accompanied by the offkey playing of my friend Joel. Before shutting the lights, we promised to keep in touch until we could find a way of reconstituting our group. Alas, we never did.

In *Gates of Eden*, Morris Dickstein notes that the books of the 60s come across today as quaint, distant, nostalgic and out of touch with today's realities. Not so for me. Preparing this brief paper, I noticed that the only organized section of my otherwise chaotic bookshelves contained a reasonably good selection of 60s materials—from Alinsky and Bookchin, through Fanon and Ferlinghetti, through Mills and Morrison, to Rich and Vonnegut. I read this orderliness as a subconscious metaphor on my part that the turbulent 60s were the most cohesive and liberating times in my life. Rereading this literature reminds me poignantly how much the corporate 80s need the utopian ethos, hopes, and visions of the 60s.

All the good indians

PAULA GUNN ALLEN

Yesterday, a student said something that forced me to contemplate a world without Indians. He said that the elder people knew that we were disappearing, and when something is ending, it gets smaller. He said it's like a shutter on a camera, the opening grows smaller as it closes. That is why, he said, so many of us have begun to write: to write everything down so that there will be a record.

The student is the second chief of his tribe, the Narragansett; he has been an active and involved Indian, working for his tribe and his people for well over a decade. He is at Berkeley studying Native American studies and anthropology, readying himself to research and record everything he can about his own tribe and others accurately in terms of both perspectives.

The class let out after five o'clock. I left the U.C. Berkeley campus walking down Telegraph toward the parking lot. As I walked I saw people going past me. I saw the shops, the goods on display in the windows. I went by restaurants and coffee houses. Nowhere did I see an Indian, an item produced by or even reminiscent of Indians, a food or beverage for sale that was identified in my mind or in the mind of those others around me, as Indian. Coffee is Indian, but not really. Corn, turkey, tomatoes. Pumpkin, chili, tortillas. So many things. But no Indian visible anywhere, not even me.

Less than 24 hours later, I still haven't begun to deal with his remark.

But walking along Telegraph I remembered a time when I had lived in an Indianless world; I was in Oregon, attending the University in Eugene. For the first year or so I never saw or heard of an Indian. I was the only Indian I knew. That was around 1967. Sometime in 1968, a package arrived in the mail from my parents. It was a signed copy of N. Scott Momaday's *House Made of Dawn*. I believe that book saved my life.

How do you touch extinction?

How do you comprehend that the entire world is about to vanish?

Sitting Bull did that. He comprehended the totality of death. He went with Buffalo Bill's Indian circus, like the last exotic striped quagga goes with the zoo. He told the people to see to it that the children got educated in the white man's schools, and he worked to get schools opened so they could. They left the wondrous way of the Sioux. He left it. They became ranchers and farmers; Christians and bureaucrats, soldiers in the conqueror's armies, welfare recipients. Their life-expectancy was as much as 44 years in the 60s. It hasn't increased.

Crazy Horse chose to fight and to die instead. They bayoneted him when he came to the fort to talk. They bayoneted him because they couldn't shoot him. His medicine was such that he was invulnerable to bullets.

They used to dance the ghost dance. They wept. They knew what they had lost, what was gone. They tried to dance it back.

In Oregon, I didn't know the name of the disease I was suffering from. I was seeing a shrink. I didn't know that I was only grieving and lost. I thought I was mentally ill.

In Oregon I was involved. In the civil rights movement; in the peace movement. I taught and spoke and wrote. I struggled. One night at the local campus bar I was in a conversation with some people—two radical black men, a white man (my husband) and a couple of SDS-types. We were talking about why the movement was important. One black man said I couldn't know how significant it was. That I had no reason to care. He said I was a "groupie," a "voyeur." The other one said that wasn't so; I had at least the same difficulties black people had. I faced the same oppression, repression, depression. "She's a woman," he said. "For her it's even worse." Nobody said, "She's an Indian." Not my husband. Not even me.

It is 1982. I live in California. I teach at Berkeley. In Native American Studies. The Indians I see are in my classes (2 Indians out of 40 students) or in the department's offices. Out of some 30,000 students enrolled at "Cal," something like 160 are American Indian.

Out of 200.6 million people (more or less) in the United States, slightly over 1 million are American Indian.

When I think of the figures, I wonder how I could have lived 43 years thinking the world was *not* bereft of Indians.

But, I think, there are millions of us south of here. In Mexico and Central America, in South America. But just a day or so ago I read that the Guatemalan regime recently massacred 2,500 Indians. A few months ago I read that the Sadinistas massacred several hundred or a thousand Indians. A few years ago I read that they hunt Indians in Brazil with airplanes; when they spot them they bomb them, napalm them, throw nets over them and haul them away to camps where they are raped, beaten to death, starved. Or in the time honored fashion of the invader, they just throw down some bundles that contain poisoned food, pestilence-infected clothing and blankets. Scratch scores, hundreds, thousands, millions of Indians.

Some say that upwards of 45 million Indians lived in what is now the United States on the eve of contact. Government records put our numbers at 450,000 in the 1970 census. The population of Indians in the United States hasn't doubled in ten years; the count was just more accurate.

Some health workers say that over 25 percent of Indian women and 10 percent of Indian men in the United States have been sterilized without their knowledge or consent. Scratch several hundred thousand future Indians. Many Indians "marry out." Go to the cities and get lost. Over two-thirds of all American Indians live in cities now. Maybe more. They walk down Telegraph, or Central, or Market, or Fifth Avenue. They see themselves nowhere they look. Scratch several hundred thousand more. They say, the only good Indian is a dead Indian. There are millions of good Indians somewhere.

Do you remember the child's song, "One Little, Two Little, Three Little Indians?" The first part counts one, two, three, up to ten. The second part counts backwards: ten, nine, eight little Indians, seven, six, five little

Indians, four, three, two, little Indians, one little Indian. It's on my mind right now. I learned it in the 40s. I forgot it later. It comes up today.

Lens closing. So light doesn't get through. But the camera leaves a picture for posterity.

I remember the 60s. A time when American hippies discovered Indians, rediscovered Indians. A decade-long Columbus day. In the early 70s a story about that was published in Rosen's *The Man To Send Rain Clouds* anthology. It was written by Simon J. Ortiz. You should read it. It's about an old Pueblo man who goes to San Francisco looking for his granddaughter who has disappeared. He goes to the Indian Center on Valencia Street to see if anyone there has seen her. But there are no Indians there. The building is locked. He is befriended by some hippies. They are practicing to be Indians. They take him back to their pad, hoping he can turn them on to the proper Indian uses of peyote. He doesn't find his granddaughter—they don't know her. A picture, a record, left by an Indian, a Pueblo writer named Ortiz.

And *House Made of Dawn*, another picture. From which the hero, a longhair Pueblo Indian who can't speak, disappears. The only Indian book I read in the 60s was *House Made of Dawn*. At the time, I didn't realize what the end of it meant. I thought Abel ran into life, into tradition, into strength. It was not until the late 70s, when I saw a film rendition of the book made by a group of Indian filmmakers, that I realized that in the end Abel ran into another world; that he reclaimed himself as a longhair Pueblo Indian man by running out of this particular world-frame, this particular universe, this reality. In other words, he died. Abel was a good Indian.

When my student spoke, I thought of *House Made of Dawn*, about what it meant. I understood the record Momaday had made. The one about how the Indian vanishes, with a fine, soundless song; the one that got him the Pulitzer Prize.

And I have known for a long time that what an Indian is supposed to be is dead. But I didn't until just that instant, as my student spoke, understand that what Sitting Bull said was not a statement wrung from him by defeat in a years-long war; it was a statement about who and what Indians are in America. More than forgotten, more than oppressed, more than terminated, relocated, removed; the word for it is extinguished. Dead.

The only book by an Indian I read in the 60s was about the reality of Indianness. Just as the book I began writing in 1970 and finished last spring is. Which I didn't realize until today.

I can imagine a world without Indians. It is a world that has surrounded me most of my life. I only just now recognized it—a world that will have records—pictures, foods, artifacts, heritages of Indians, all transformed into something unrecognizable to an Indian. But it won't matter, I guess. All of us who cannot live in such a world won't, and all of us will be good.

Notes from the 60s

MARTIN DUBERMAN

George Kennan's "Rebels Without a Program" [*The New York Times*, Sunday magazine, Jan. 21, 1968] is appalling. There is barely a sentence in the article free of false accusation, self-enclosed argument, misplaced indignation. It is a gross misrepresentation of the radical left on the campus —just the sort of patronizing and distorted account which confirms 20 year olds in their view that "liberals" are incapable of understanding either the new generation or the new problems which confront our society. It is, moreover, a dangerous article, for it lends the weight of Kennan's name to a perspective and rhetoric usually associated with a Ronald Reagan. . . .

I cannot believe that Kennan has read extensively in the position papers frequently issued by Students for a Democratic Society (SDS), the national organization which represents radical left opinion on the campus. If he had, he could not possibly refer to their "massive certainties," their "screaming tantrums," their consuming interest in "violence for violence's sake". . . . Because they believe there can and should be less suffering in the world hardly makes them "utopians."

True, they have no "blueprints" for creating a better world. If they had, the charge of naiveté *would* apply, for only a simpleton would pretend to have a detailed set of answers for the multiple problems which beset us . . . . But let there be no pretense that today's youthful radicals have no line of argument. If Kennan will read the literature written by members of SDS, he will find any number of proposals for "constitutional amendment or political reform," as well as that very wealth of "reasoned argument and discussion" he claims does not exist. . . . It's the old story: when radicals do produce plans for a better society, they're denounced for attempting to straightjacket fluid reality. When they fail to produce plans, they're denounced as visionaries. Those who oppose substantive change can always find some reason for doing so. . . .

—To the Editor, *Times*, 1968

In our racist culture, bigotry is ingested with our pablum. We would be foolish to expect it can be readily exorcised, to hold out the unrealistic hope that this generation can achieve *feelings* of brotherhood. We will do well if we can bring it to *act* in accordance with those principles. Perhaps some future generation, brought up in a more truthful and humane spirit, will move from outward conformity to inner conviction. But for now, to achieve even the limited goal of equality before the law, we must rely on additional federal legislation, demand it be forcefully executed (unlike the acts of 1964 and 1965), and be prepared for a fair amount of social upheaval. . . .

It would be better if change came voluntarily; enforced legislation is not the ideal way. But given the lateness of the hour and the intransigence of the opposition, it is apparently the only way. It will be argued that imposed change cannot produce lasting results; one cannot legislate against prejudice; stateways cannot change folkways. But this argument mistakes the primary intention of egalitarian legislation, which aims not at eradicating prejudice but at curtailing its outward expression. And this much, legislation *can* accomplish. *If* enforced, if people are made to obey the law regardless of how they feel about the law. It can even be argued—as Gordon Allport has in his book, *The Nature of Prejudice*—that in the long run forcing changes in outward behavior ultimately affects inner convictions, bringing the two into greater conformity. . . .

History is not the story of inevitable, continuing progress, however fondly Americans cherish that view. The reform impulse often spends itself before reaching its goals, a reverse trend sets in which erases previous gains. In 1967, as in 1877 (the "first Reconstruction"), there are again clear signs that such a trend has in fact begun. If it is not resisted, it may well accelerate. We can hardly afford to rest on our laurels—pitiful as they are. If further gains toward racial equality are to come, they will result from hard work—*not* from reliance on the presumed benevolence of Time, or the Deity.

—Preface to *A Civil Rights Reader*
(Leon Friedman, ed.), 1967

John Bunzel is angry at patsies and bleeding hearts. He particularly dislikes those who treat the "tough, pragmatic" (i.e. "real") world of politics with contempt, trying to convert it into something it is not—ethics, say, or theology—and then lambasting it for failing to measure up. In so doing, Bunzel claims (in his new book *Anti-Politics in America*), they refuse to recognize that politics—its give and take, its compromises and accommodations—are the very lifeblood of a democratic society seeking to contain, with a minimum of coercion, inevitable conflicts of individual and group interests. Politics has one and only one valid function: to prevent inherently divisive social and economic issues from disrupting the "consensual basis" of society.

Bunzel declares he *is* for principled politics, but proceeds to define all examples of it from our history in such a way as to make them seem ridiculous, misguided, unpalatable. In the process, he distorts a good part of that history. The most egregious example is his treatment of the Populists. Bunzel portrays their leaders as entranced by a "conspiracy theory," as anti-Semitic, Anglo-phobic and nativistic, and as wedded to schemes of reform that were abstract or inappropriate or both. . . . In this portrait nothing is lost save truth. Bunzel has based his version of Populism on a stereotype briefly fashionable 10 to 20 years ago, but effectively shattered since. . . . Bunzel is either unaware of recent scholarship or unwilling to acknowledge the challenge it offers to his simplistic perspective on the history of the American left. . . .

The counterpart of devaluing all structural criticism of our policies and institutions is to magnify the accomplishments of "politics as usual," to imply that our political system does its work of reconciliation between class and interest groups so well, as to make sharp contrast protest unnecessary: "The left-wing critiques of American society . . . have been unable to see that the created development of our democratic institutions has largely been responsible for making concentrated economic power in the United States more and more the servant of society."

What can Bunzel be referring to? Surely not to the fact that 2 percent of American families own between two-thirds to three-quarters of all corporate stock (an increasing concentration since the 1920s). Nor to the fact that two hundred–three hundred families own controlling blocks of stock in the one hundred and fifty "super-corporations." And certainly not to the fact that in 1959 five of the nineteen American families with incomes over 5 million dollars paid no income tax at all, and of the remaining fourteen not one paid a tax in the top brackets.

Bunzel enjoys contrasting our political system with totalitarian ones. Ours, he claims, puts the accent on innovation, provides for "the free interplay of antagonistic forces competing freely with each other for popular support," ensures that "differences in society are sympathetically understood, intelligently discussed, and peacefully resolved."

Since Bunzel and I live in the same United States, we must at least live in different territories of the mind. To me—one of those deplorable leftists—Bunzel's definition of a totalitarian system stands not in direct contrast to our own but in uncomfortable proximity to it: a "static and disciplined world of the closed society, where the accent is on stability. Harmony, unity, order—these are the themes."

***—Village Voice,* 1967**

We are not short these days of critiques of American power. Unlike many radical critics Noam Chomsky [in *American Power and the New Mandarins*] does not build his case against our country's foreign policy by magnifying the innocence or goodness of those who oppose us internationally. While arguing brilliantly against the official American view that our interventionist policies are merely a defensive reaction to Russian or Chinese aggression, that we intervene only to defend the people of Asia (or Africa, or Latin-America) from the horrors of communist totalitarianism, Chomsky can also . . . "react with dismay, perhaps even outrage, to the authoritarian and repressive character of the Chinese state," can refer to the Soviet Union "consolidating its eastern European empire with brutality and deceit." He knows that the case against our imperialist ventures is so strong it does not require the varnishing of our "antagonists" for its force. . . .

He emphasizes, moreover, that . . . we have finally reached the peace table at Paris, not because the peace movement has produced a fundamental change of heart about our country's right to intervene in the internal affairs of other nations, but simply because the public has come to feel that our involvement in Vietnam is costing too much. . . . One could argue that Chomsky mistakenly equates the peace movement's failure to produce fundamental results with its unwillingness to try for them . . . but the basic facts remain as Chomsky states them: most opponents of the war think Johnson was a usurper and Vietnam an aberration; *ordinarily*, they argue, we do not interfere with the affairs of other nations—or when we do, it is only because *someone* must dictate "acceptable" patterns of social and political organization . . . liberal intellectuals have done much to encourage the view now so common in our country (especially among the "well-educated") that the masses are "objects, incapable of political expression or allegiance, to be 'controlled' by one side or the other." The repercussions of such a view need not be spelled out. . . .

***—The New Republic*, 1969**

James Meredith set off on his march from Memphis to Mississippi to demonstrate, he said, that Negroes had nothing to fear. Could he have believed this? Only a few years ago, when trying to integrate Ole Miss, Meredith personally experienced the Anglo-Saxon wrath awaiting those who boldly challenge established patterns. . . .

Had Meredith not been shot, had he completed his march without being harmed, the common reaction, I suspect, would have been that he was lucky, protected by fame and publicity. The average Negro tenant-farmer would never have been foolish enough to imagine that his own anonymity and helplessness would prove safeguards of equal weight. Few men have the resources (whatever their complex origin) to face up to the probability of physical injury, perhaps death, with equanimity. And one would be as sanctimonious in telling men that they should, as one would be naive in expecting that they will. Much of the shock at hearing that Meredith has been shot is based on the assumption that in his case "they wouldn't dare!" But they did dare. . . . The likely, and human, reaction in the Negro community—there is something supra-human about Meredith—will be a redoubling, not an easing of fear. And of anger. And of disillusion with the benefits likely to derive from continuing to rely on the tactics of nonviolence.

The civil rights movement, under the weight of accumulating frustrations, had begun to shift ground before Meredith's march, the shift dramatically symbolized by the recent emergence of Stokely Carmichael and the Black Panthers. Rejecting "politics," emphasizing "blackness," they reject hitherto sanctified tactics for assaulting segregation. And who is to say that their "alienation" is other than an appropriate response to the seemingly endless evasions of white America? . . .

The shooting of James Meredith is bound to swell the ranks of the disaffected. He set out on his march to demonstrate "progress" and encourage hope. Encouraged at the prospect of a bullet? Hopeful when even a Meredith is gunned down? Hardly. James Meredith, congenital optimist, has unwittingly given fuel to growing pessimism within civil rights ranks.

—***The Village Voice,* 1966**

From the novel Burning Questions: "the happiness question"

ALIX KATES SHULMAN

Right here, before I go one more page, I have a ticklish confession to make. At this very moment, when it looks as though we blew our revolution, I find myself happier than I ever dreamed I could be. I am full of energy, confidence, little pleasures, big plans . . . .

Of course, being a veteran, one who has watched the decades come and go, I know my happy state is probably temporary. I know, too, that I ought to keep my satisfaction to myself; for to those who don't share it I'm afraid it must look like callous or mindless complacency. No matter that even such an unassailable rebel as the martyr Rosa Luxemburg could write from her prison cell, "the more the infamy and monstrosity of daily happenings surpasses all bounds, the more tranquil and more confident becomes my personal outlook . . . . I lie here alone in silence, enveloped in the manifold black wrappings of darkness, tedium, unfreedom, and winter — and yet my heart beats with an immeasurable and incomprehensible inner joy." She is above suspicion. No matter that the large-souled Angelica Balabanoff should not hesitate to write (though her revolution too was betrayed): "I knew that I was a very fortunate person. [My] suffering and struggle . . . had meaning and dignity because they were linked to those of humanity. *Life lived in behalf of a great cause is robbed of its personal futility.*" (My italics) No matter that the free-spirited Emma Goldman should insist: "I do not believe that the cause which stood for a beautiful ideal, for anarchism. . . should demand the denial of life and joy. . . . If it meant that I did not want it." These precedents can't vindicate me. Not only am I, unlike them, no martyr, but I suddenly find myself in the compromised position of having for the first time in my life almost everything I've ever desired, short of a different world. Having had the incredible luck to be on hand at almost the exact moment when the Third Street Circle was forming, I am now a veteran of the passion of my time—never again can my life be discounted. . . .

●

I'm not the only one to feel uneasy about the ironies of the present moment. Some time earlier, a former sister of the Third Street Circle back in town on a visit from California where she'd moved like so many around '72, called me to catch up on the East Coast News. (I'll call her Phyllis.) From the way a certain name kept thudding awkwardly into the conversation I could tell something was up.

"Are you in love with him?" I asked. ("We must destroy love," the Feminists, now disbanded, had boldly proclaimed in their earliest manifesto. "Love promotes vulnerability, dependence, possessiveness, susceptibility to pain, and prevents the full development of woman by directing all her energies outward in the interests of others.")

Phyllis hesitated.

"You can tell me, Phyllis," I reassured her. I might have felt ashamed myself to be "in love" with a man that year, but I tried to be tolerant with my friends. Though I was half sorry to watch our old certainties slip away, I already knew you can't force certainty. So much we had rashly renounced in the 60s had been gradually resumed in the 70s that all the old pieties had to be rethought. For example: though I had once seriously contemplated living outside the world of men, now that Sammy's voice had changed it was obviously out of the question.

Phyllis hesitated, then finally confessed. "Well, yes—actually I am in love. But please, Zane, for god's sake don't tell anyone. I'm afraid it doesn't look good."

"To whom?"

"You know. The movement."

The movement, the movement! Shades of the past when we cared only if the movement loved us. When inside the movement we found comfort and protection and outside a jungle of preying men. But things were no longer so simple as they'd once seemed. *The personal is political* had a larger meaning now.

I tried to reassure Phyllis. "Listen," I said, "Golda's in law school—should she feel guilty about it? We need lawyers, too." And then, summoning all my courage, I confessed with that honesty our Circle had once unleashed as our secret weapon: "And look at me."

"Are you in love too?" she asked eagerly.

"No, not in love; worse! I'm happy."

Into the silence I dropped my shameful secret. "I mean—here I am, teaching at the New School, . . . writing articles, debating—must I feel guilty?" Blurting out my list of sins, my satisfactions, the question sounded more like a plea for indulgence than the reassurance I'd intended . . . . "The 60s are over, Phyllis," I reminded her. . . . It was foolish, even arrogant, of us to have presumed the revolution would be won at precisely the moment when we arrived on the scene. You're born when you're born, you fight as well as you can—that's all. "Listen, Phyllis," I said, "it's not your fault we didn't bring it off. Even Mao predicts the revolution will take five hundred years."

"Mao is a man."

"People have to live."

"Well, still," said Phyllis. "I'll feel a lot better if no one knows about John."

●

Those days it was hard to fathom who had really changed. On the surface at least, everyone had: rulers, liberals, and misogynists alike all claimed to have come around. Those who denied us our rights in the old days by saying we didn't need them could now deny us our rights by pretending we already had them. Every morning over coffee one could read in the *Times* about the "new equality" and "women's takeover of key positions." The whole world had gotten into the act. Some of the most fashionable new movies were about women's condition. And Leo Stern himself, who had once been so quick to denounce the movement, had launched a new series of books called Women and Society for which his company had made him a vice president. Now he sat across the table, trying to reassert his power.

". . . You may as well know why I've invited you to lunch. If you can write without such barbarisms as 'oppressed,' how would you like to do a book for me?" asked Leo.

A book? I was stunned. But something warned me to refuse. "What's the matter with 'oppressed'?" I asked.

Leo shrugged and wrinkled up his nose. "It's one of those dated propaganda words."

Propaganda? Dated? It seemed to me descriptive. If one thing had always been with us, it had been oppression.

"You know— " he went on, "it smacks of the 60s which are over, thank god . . . ."

The 60s—how different they had been for women and men, anyway men like Leo. Of course, *they* hated the 60s; of course *they* were glad to see them over. Naturally they called them "barbaric" and "chaotic"—I could see why. By the time the 60s were going strong *they'd* already wrapped up their degrees, their positions, their futures. But for us, who could so easily have spent the rest of our lives letting the men speak for us, the 60s were anything but chaotic. Not that we lived serenely in those years, but we took our first steps on our own. We learned organization, discipline, caring . . ., how to be civilized. We stood up for each other, made community, tried to provide sympathy and support and something lasting for all of us and our children—what could be more civilized than that? . . .

"The book I have in mind," said Leo, "would be something of a popular history of women, maybe title it *The Book of Firsts* . . . . A book of positive images. What do you think?"

To hear Leo Stern ask me like that with real concern, *What do you think*? I would have once rented out my soul; and for the chance to do a book (a book!), I wouldn't have hesitated to throw my body in as well. But —surprise—even as I savored my fancy lunch, I knew I couldn't consider the offer now. Not because of the movement's one-time condemnation of individual authorship as elitist, opportunist individualism. That hard line that had once frightened some of us into silence and conformity, telling us where to work, how to dress, whom to love, how many children to bear, whether to breastfeed or bottlefeed, marry or not, till droves of converts fled for air, didn't work on me. Nor was it because Leo Stern was a man, one in the pay of an establishment publishing house owned by a multinational corporation that was the sworn enemy of our revolution. The list of works by true heroes of the revolution that were published and even commissioned by "the enemy" could stock a small library. No, if I rejected this latest inducement to sell out it was less to "combat self" (Mao) than because I now, miraculously, had integrity to defend and a community of sisters to answer to. What student or comrade of mine wouldn't see instantly that Leo's *Book of Firsts* could as well be called a *Book of Lasts* or a *Book of Lies*? Those "positive images" he was so eager to peddle implied that women's liberation was in the bag, that oppression and struggle were passé, that there was little to get upset about any more . . . .

. . . The 60s were over, yes, but some of us were still fighting our holding actions, keeping in precious touch.

●

As the bus pulled up to the New School stop I leaped over the melting slush to the dry curb. In two minutes my favorite class would begin—the one on Revolutionary Women: the text was Luxembourg's prison letters, on the question of Happiness.

Personally, I would never claim to feel, like Rosa Luxembourg, "as if I were the possessor of a charm which would enable me to transform all that is evil and tragical into serenity and happiness." To me happiness was a mysterious, delicate thing which might vanish like a snowflake if you tried to catch it. It wasn't solid like comfort, which you could sit on or wear or chew or grow used to or do without. It was like a delicate flower that unexpectedly blooms on a plant you've nurtured for its leaves: at once offshoot and seed. As with luck, you'd be foolish to pluck it: better simply to rejoice in it. It was a charm, as Luxemburg said, but only if you didn't count on it.

Still, at that moment, basking in the pride of having won one more draw from my old adversary Leo Stern, I knew that if ever a teacher could be inspired, it would be I, that day.

Those beats!

MARILYN COFFEY

Imagine me in 1959: I was 22 years old, living in Nebraska where I'd lived virtually all of my life, renting my first apartment, starting to earn my living by writing headlines for society-page stories on the Lincoln (Neb.) *Evening Journal*, nursing wounds received from discovering that I was not going to get married and live happily ever after, like my mother and Cinderella. I was a member of the so-called Silent Generation, and silent many of us were, back in the fifties, in the aftermath of Joe McCarthy and the Korean War. Speechless. A strange condition for a woman who aspired to be a writer. I had trained in journalism and creative writing at the University of Nebraska, worked as a political reporter on the school newspaper, and followed, as a discipline, Joseph Conrad's adage that a writer, above all else, must make a reader see. I practiced the fine art of observation, posting myself on the edge of events and mentally translating images into words: that, and eating and fucking, were my extra-curricular preoccupations. I was terribly distraught that I was still living in Nebraska. The state, at that time, seemed to me to be the epitome of hypocrisy and sterile living. Behind the habitual midwestern smile lurked, I believed, a judgment as harsh as that of the Bible-belt Jehovah on which it was based. Living seemed largely a question of minding your P's and Q's, something I was not particularly adept at. Something I resented.

Then chance, or fate, or serendipity dropped Jack Kerouac's *On the Road* into my hands. I read the book avidly, its words pouring directly into my veins as fast as they must have flowed out of Kerouac's fingers: nonstop onto an unbroken roll of United Press teletype paper. I read so rapidly I didn't half understand what I was reading, but something of the life being described was comprehensible to me, foreign as it was to the young woman who'd been born and bred in the conservative Midwest. Yeow! The words shot through me like a fusillade of bullets. I was undone, a changed person. I immediately went out, bought myself a straw-covered bottle of Chianti, a candle, and a pad of paper. Then I went home and, slightly inebriated, began to write by candlelight, scribbling words onto paper as fast as my hand could compose, following instinctively Kerouac's model of Spontaneous Prose. My classes at the University were forgotten. The novel liberated me as it did many others of my generation. There was that instantaneous recognition of self. For the first time since I began writing in 1948, I felt free to say anything I wanted to. Kerouac obviously felt free to; why shouldn't I? For I, in those blissfully naive pre-feminist days, felt the equal of any man.

Kerouac's impact was lasting. Delightfully troubling as dark rich chocolate in a cavity, I worked him over and over, finally writing one journal entry: "You have made one error in your interpretation of Kerouac's *On the Road*. His characters are not fleeing from life nor running away from something. They are on a search more deeply spiritual than the quest for the Holy Grail." Kerouac sees, as William Carlos Williams put it, "with the eyes of the angels." Quite a contrast to Conrad.

By September, I had a good idea of Kerouac's weaknesses as seen by his critics. I wrote, "Even if Kerouac propounds no more than a single idea —I like people who are enthusiastic—I have a feeling I shall become one of his devoted disciples. Although I must agree that as a writer Kerouac is loose-jointed; his material, ill-constructed; yet I feel he has something to say that should be said to this generation. Should have indeed been said long before now.

"Listen: 'Man, wow, there's so many things to do, so many things to write! How to even *begin* to get it all down and without modified restraints and all hung-up on like literary inhibitions and grammatical fears. . . .' "

Still, the contrast between my life and that of Kerouac's characters was almost too much for me to bear. "I must admit I was in an excellent mood to absorb the man [Kerouac] tonight," I wrote on Sept. 14. "For this afternoon, to my utter horror, Gil, my boss, told me that I was to work permanently on society copy. Man, wow, I mean like nausea! The thought quelled me, even though I knew it was coming. But so soon, so soon. I hadn't even had a chance to learn the market page, namely because I'm a girl, blast it. What a crime to be born with a few brains and a bosom in this country! I was depressed like nothing before. I couldn't even work. I spent all afternoon writing 1–14–1's for society filler and dreaming about my exit from the dull, dull, dull routine of the place. I went to Bourbon Street, via a bicycle, with my blue jeans, my heavy shoes, my baggy shirt, my red sweatshirt and a pair of leather gloves. I mean I traveled. From Louisiana on to Florida and beachcombed to my heart's delight."

For Kerouac certainly romanticized the journey as adventure. As soon as I could, I followed in his footsteps. From Nebraska, I went to Denver where, in the Greyhound Bus Depot, I twirled a girlfriend, eyes closed, arm extended, in front of a gigantic map of the United States. She pointed, and we set off—to New Orleans, and eventually across Texas, etc., to the West Coast, up the Coast to Portland, Oregon, and from there, to New York. Like Ed Sanders, who abandoned Kansas for New York, I came with a copy of *On the Road* in my hand.

But not even Kerouac prepared me for Allen Ginsberg. The opening lines of Ginsberg's "Howl" exploded in my brain like a fireball. Again, the material was completely foreign: I'd never heard of a fix. But on another level, the words struck home: hadn't I seen the best minds of my generation destroyed by conformity? Hadn't I howled myself through black streets at dawn? Certainly I knew the dark night of the soul he seemed to be describing.

Then I encountered Moloch; I had to look him up to discover that he was a deity to whom parents sacrificed children. The ensuing lines begat a kind of terror in me, as I fell further under the spell of Ginsberg's chanting, his rhythmic repetitions. This reading was like listening to music, utterly satisfying on some sensual level. By the last refrain, I was mesmerized. I didn't know who Carl Solomon was to him, but on some other, deeper level, I knew! I knew! The electricity flowed to me; I was dazzled.

"It's the Holy Ghost comes through you" when you write, wrote Kerouac. And now more than ever I knew what he meant. I released myself to my own Holy Spirit, which seemed to exist in me although I was no longer a Christian. And the impulse to write, which had been with me since I was eleven, seemed to take on a more tangible form, become more heated, move in me and through me in ways that I could never have foreseen. I decided to trust it completely.

But Ginsberg worked on me not only as a writer; he appealed to me on a human level as well. Much as I had been influenced by Kerouac, I couldn't imagine ever wanting to meet him. I knew his kind: either we'd go to bed or I'd be ignored, perhaps even put down. But Ginsberg was another case. For one thing, he was homosexual, so that allowed the possibility of sexual interaction to be set aside. For another, he seemed to be accessible, as I found indeed he was.

As a member of the Silent Generation, I had fallen in love with the Beats, that bearded bunch of Falstaffs. Not only was there Ginsberg and Kerouac, there was Michael McClure whose "The Beard" I saw produced in New York, whose recreation of Jean Harlow and Billy the Kid left me with a legacy of "Stars! Stars! Stars!" And Gregory Corso, whose outrageous antics on the stage never failed to amuse me. And The Fugs, that putrid outgrowth on the edges of the movement. I loved them all. "Honest" was how they seemed to me; "anti-intellectual" was the critic's charge. But this crew seemed less against the intellect than proposing a new one, an intellect that would encompass passion and humor. "Ideas gripped with intensity become powerful," I wrote in 1959, and certainly the Beatniks' ideas seemed gripped.

As I've aged, I've watched the Beatniks spawn the Hippies, as the Bohemians once spawned the Beats, and I wait, impatiently, for the next manifestation of this urge in American literature, this transcendental thrust, which dates back to Whitman, Emerson, and Thoreau, which interconnects with the Romantic movement in Europe. Ah! fascinating. How life goes on! How it refuses to be put down.

Outside readings

FRED PFEIL

Three kinds of texts and/or ways of reading ran without resolution through virtually all my 60s experience. One kind came out of the small factory town I am from, born into a working-class family on my mother's side, petit-bourgeois on my father's. For my present purposes, though, these class specificities are less important than the overall white working-class character of the entire town, defining both itself and the world as a place where you worked hard for little, took it gratefully and kept your mouth shut; where you voted Republican because they were right, and expected nothing for it; where in fact you expected nothing for anything, especially nothing in the end. That was the way the clenched world read in that poor drab region of silent Swedes, and still reads, for as far as most of the people there are concerned nothing has changed. Nor does this view or reading have anything to do with the papers or TV, except insofar as certain news stories bear out its hopeless truths, e.g. the crucifixion of hard-working, graceless Nixon at the hands of the Democrats and smart boys of the Press, or the loss of the Vietnam War. It is a viewpoint which in fact does not require reading at all in the narrow sense of the word, and since it does not know how to respond to any music either it is silent, no jukeboxes in bars, no hit stations on in cars on the way in to work at the plant. Yet it does produce its own texts now and then nonetheless, stories and jokes which can only be read in its own way of reading, and this joke, which I heard the last summer I worked down at the plant, is one of its kind! It seems there are these two guys, Pete and Charlie, and they've both been working at the plant fifteen, twenty years, eating lunch every day in the lunchroom, and one day they knock off and sit down in the lunchroom and Pete opens up his bucket and lets out a yell. *Peanut butter!* he says. *Goddamn peanut butter every goddamn day, I can't stand it any more!* and he throws the sandwich up against the wall.

So his best friend Charlie, when Pete stops kicking the shit out of the sandwich, steps in. *Hey calm down old buddy*, says Charlie, *no reason to fly off the handle like that. If you don't want peanut butter no more, tell your wife to fix you something else.*

You keep my wife out of this goddammit! says Pete. *I make my own goddamn lunch!*

The second kind of reading I learned in the 60s sprang from this same fear and fury in a new context, Amherst College, Class of 1971. The night before my freshman year began, while my mother and sister lay sleeping in our Howard Johnson's motel room I sat up in the john to finish my book of Sophocles plays. A few months later and I was up all night standing on a chair to get *Dr. Faustus* under my belt. Stand on a chair to read and if you fall asleep you get hurt. Go to sleep instead and leave that much more chance of getting cut down tomorrow, recognized as the dumbo cultural ape from a hick town that you really are. "Only for the sake of the hopeless," wrote Benjamin, "are we given hope," and though of course he was not hot or classical enough at the time to make my list of assigned readings, my motivation was much the same: I had four years to catch up and beat every one of those rich bastards my classmates, lift and wrestle down every scrap of goddamn culture they'd always had. Otherwise, I had no right to be there at all.

No one paid more explicit allegiance than I to Western Civ in the years 67 to 71; no one had more contempt for student activists and their politics alike. When Amherst's student radicals dragged their weary asses down to the dining hall after a long night of running mimeos, there to continue their tumultuous discussion of the Cultural Revolution or the next week's anti-war march, I was the one who scraped their Marlboro butts, their uneaten eggs and toast into my buscart; while they went off to study the aftermath of May 68 in Paris the following summer, I would be back busting my ass in the plant, packing in their Nietzsche and Shakespeare and Joyce whenever I could between punching out and falling asleep. That was why when they shut down the campus in spring 1970, I hunted up my English prof and demanded he and I discuss the last book on the syllabus—*Swann's Way* by Marcel Proust; why in that whole four years at the 60s' dazzled heights I did exactly one piece of active political work, canvassing working-class neighborhoods in nearby Northampton on the war only so that none of my rich bastard classmates would do it instead. I was that sure their idea of canvassing meant telling people what to think. So while on the surface what this reading looked like, and was, was the most reactionary grade-grinding shit-eating obeisance conceivable, it was also a private perverse class war wholly sanctioned by the folks back home, who not only seemed to understand but practically expected it of me, up to and including my increasing detachment from them, the very signal of our triumph and success.

On the other hand, no matter how "organically" this second kind of reading developed from the first, it still led to a class double-bind whereby to succeed was to fail, to behave according to the town inside me was to find myself alone. There had to be a third set of texts, another reading which neither blotted out the outside world in impacted rage nor appropriated highbrow culture as weapon in an undeclared and doomed guerrilla war. Already, even before leaving home, I had taken the unprecedented step of buying two records, *Surrealistic Pillow* by the Airplane and the Beatles' *Sergeant Pepper*, to my knowledge the only extant copies in my town, which I played and studied again and again. Likewise, at Amherst I bought a hardbound anthology of articles culled from various underground papers, *Notes from the New Underground*, ed., Jessie Kornbluth, and read it behind closed doors in my spare time, replaying certain pieces as if they were cuts on any one of the Doors or Hendrix or Cream albums I took in with the same hagiographic devotion; and when I read Allen Ginsberg's "everybody who hears my voice, directly or indirectly, [should] try the chemical LSD at least once, every man woman and child American in good health over the age of 14" (Kornbluth, p. 54) I took some right away, it was that simple and important a means of escape. So in all its antinomian delirium, its white consumerist surrealism on the cheap, that counterculture became my official scripture, its precepts and prophecies serving to cover my redneck American Legion anger without ever quite replacing it. That way, thanks to all my gospel reading from Zap Comix to Grateful Dead, everything from Chicago '68 to Attica '71 was about the same revolt of young against old, hip vs. square, stoned vs. straight, madness vs. reason, life vs. death, etc.: so when the going got rough all you had to do was hang tight, stay cool until the old farts died off and we took over, after which everything would be all right.

Thus defined as the space of time during which all three of these readings vied with and fed off each other, my 60s started late and ended early, running roughly from September '67 and my night with Sophocles to an afternoon seven years later in Berkeley, 1974, when a woman I was dating took me to the alumni pool for a swim and I looked at all those golden skins, spendy trunks and halters fresh out of the water, stretched out on their towels reading *The Gulag Archipelago*. There must have been a hundred people there my age, our age, around that pool, all of whom must have gone through college in those same late 60s, out there on the cutting edge; and a good twenty-five of them were reading Solzhenitsyn, the book's silver cover kept flashing in my eyes; and at last I knew Charles Reich was wrong, the New Age was not on the way. More and other epiphanies would soon follow—not least from a trip on a U.S. Navy destroyer to Southeast Asia at the real end of the war, a voyage which pushed me into an explicitly radical politics at last. Yet even today I have to admit that radicalism exists as a kind of alternating current generated in the arc between an ongoing affiliation with the "hip-wazee" and all its goofball fears and dreams on the one hand, on the other that same relentless suffering anger of all those still left unrepresented, both back home and around the world, all those whose only freedom lies still all too often in their own refusal to read. Such a circuit, whose positive and negative poles are constantly reversed, is my chief inheritance from the 60s' reading of me.

New left: old america

JAMES GILBERT

When I began to write about the 1960s as a historical period, I realized I had to face up to an unpleasantness; not just of sensing the tragedy and violence that hung over the decade like a wisp of tear gas, but of recognizing that I had seen it somewhere before. I do not mean that I had lived it before—it is, after all,inevitable that we believe in the uniqueness of our own share of history—but as a historian I recognized some surprising shapes. From the perspective of the late 1970s and early 1980s, the 60s had a familiar silhouette, much like the 1830s and 1840s when a similar social and political malaise gripped the United States. Such a thought was about as welcome to me as the election of Richard Nixon; something I knew couldn't happen until it did, at which time I realized why it happened, why it had to happen. I have been troubled by *déjà vu* ever since.

I suppose that what distressed me most was the impossibility of believing as I once had in international solidarity in quite the terms that made this an exhilarating concept. Before the excesses of the Cultural Revolution in China, during the days of 1968 in France when friends of mine spoke for hours (collect) to the students camped inside the Sorbonne in Paris, the uprising of youth had appeared to be a revolution of interchangeable parts. Proponents as well as opponents agreed to that. Sometimes I had been jarred by incongruity, as when an international student convention at Columbia I was attending marched off to gather up the New York working class to picket the Mexican Embassy in support of a strike in that nation. Still, I rarely suspected that the faces of new international heroes that went up and down on the walls of student housing and apartments might really represent very different forces than I hoped they did. My assumption was grounded in the belief that finally we had stepped outside history and beyond the clutches of American culture. It is easy to see now that these faces of international radicals did have at least one common element: they had been transformed and homogenized by our own faith in them. Just as the rebellion of youth in the 1960s was truly international in one sense, in part, it was an American export. Some of the glimmer of revolutionary fervor was, thus, reflected light.

When I tried to look seriously and dispassionately through the bifocal lens of history, with a close and a distant perspective, I realized that my own vision, while living through the decade, required correction. Two conclusions now seem certain. The period had important echoes in American history—imagine, if you will, the present echoing back into the past. Specifically these echoes were associated with the great age of "Perfectionism," in the 1830s and 1840s, when communal experiments, sexual utopianism, political radicalism, feminism, conservative evangelical religion, and abolitionism swayed American history onto a course that led straight to the Civil War. This period had its "burned-over" districts of rapid-fire religious revivals just as our age has had its "burned-out" followers of one political or moral cause after another. The point is that the seeming particular, peculiar, unique blend of 1960s radical politics and liberated life styles turns out not to be peculiar and unique at all, for its antecedents lie well established in a similar uprising of young Americans in the early Victorian Age. The second point is that whatever the international ties of our age, however much we might try to abandon the notion of a cultural "city on the hill," we cannot do so. New left, perhaps; but old America.

Looking back, what intrigues me now about the 1960s is my effort, and that of many friends, to steer clear of other movements that might have compromised our own aims. This meant either denying that contemporary music, drug culture, revival religion or sexual liberation had much to do with the tasks of radical politics. Or it meant that everything called the "youth movement" would eventually cast off its frivolous apparel and don a political uniform. I was often angriest when I heard the opposite advice (for I half believed it) that the new left was associated, cross-ways, with American culture, with generational politics, a new religious spiritualism, drug culture, and a hundred other manifestations I disliked.

Like anyone engaged in politics, I saw America in political terms, and struggled to prevent the impulse of dissent from chasing into the blind alleys of cultural change. That is why I so much disliked Charles Reich's

Greening of America. Not because it was right (it wasn't, in fact his major premise was almost 180 degrees wrong); but because his book symbolized a terrible failure of politics. By 1969, when the book appeared, the political phase of the new left had turned to descent and destruction. For better or worse — and it turned out worse — the emphasis had to be on cultural change and a new consciousness. Reich, despite his squishy optimism, was right in predicting that radical cultural ideas were about to be incorporated into the mainstream of American culture, like so many eggs being folded into a batter.

Looking back from the perspective of today, we must try to understand the political perfectionism and activist moralism that characterized all of the dissenting movements of the 1960s, both left and right. This peculiarly American uprising had happened before, in the face of the profound moral crisis of slavery. It happened again in the late 1950s and 1960s with the crisis of segregation, overlaid, compounded and complicated by the war in Vietnam and pushed by the Cold War and the threat of the bomb. Under the circumstances, and given our heritage to flee into some sort of desperate communitarianism, it is amazing that drop-outs remained a minority, not a majority.

That common element, which allowed the free interchange of members between a wide variety of political and cultural movements with scarcely a scuff of conscience, was a common element of moral perfectionism that they all shared. This has as much to do with the traditions of a Protestant culture as it does with the particular events of the day. The impulse to expect and demand perfection in politics and society, to live by absolutes alone, is an old tradition that wends it way in American history, through Puritanism, Perfectionism, Teetotalism, Prohibition, and a thousand other reforms and schemes. What we did not recognize at the time was the hidden Americanism of our demands: the spiritual slogans about equality; the abhorrence of privilege and elitism; the burning intensity of our rejection of the old—meaning compromised—left. In fact, nothing could have been more traditional or more in character.

I suppose the low point of my spirits when it came to this question, occurred about 1963, during a Vietnam vigil (a term that always made me uncomfortable). It was a very cold February night and a small group of us gathered in the middle of the University of Wisconsin campus. Staughton Lynd addressed the small band, beginning: "Tonight, we are like the Abolitionists of old. . . ." I don't remember anything else he said, but my anger etched these words in my memory. Of course, he was right, although not exactly in his intended sense of paying homage to a respected tradition. In a curious and direct way he had raised a central dilemma of the day, acknowledging our existence inside a culture that could only equate change with moral revolution. We supposed in demanding a pure politics, that we were safely out of the path of moral storms and harbored away from the intellectual compromises of American religion. But purity—not politics—was the true badge of our protest—and we protested too much.

Looking back to the 1960s now, I think it is important to see with all the good and bad of that decade, the fundamental ambiguity of our moralistic culture when it is put to the task of political change. There were some very positive elements to this. For one, Martin Luther King recognized and exploited the power and contradictions of American secular religiosity with great skill. The new left and the student movement showed a blinding light on the war in Vietnam and destroyed the political power of one President and the mental stability of another. But the new left could never master its own intensity and spiritualism, could never keep on a political track. Anymore, I believe, than the new right today will be able to withstand the temptations of moralism.

Thinking back on the 1960s, I see this period as one of enormous energy and change, of a movement in civil rights that altered American history as much as anything ever has done. But I also see it as a profoundly antipolitical decade, nothing, in its premises or effects like the 1930s during the heyday of the old left. And, I am forced to wonder what might have happened—what still might happen—if the moral energy of the 1960s were ever joined to the political shrewdness of the 1930s.

Between the 30s and the 60s

MURRAY BOOKCHIN

I strongly doubt if we will ever understand—and fully evaluate—the 60s without placing it against the background of another radical decade, the 30s. Having lived out both periods up to the hilt, I find that my older contemporaries as well as the younger people with whom I worked twenty years ago have seldom been able to distance themselves sufficiently from their time to draw these crucial comparisons adequately. Recent biographies by old New York socialists and communists who lived with such nostalgic exhilaration in the era climaxed by the Spanish Civil War and CIO organizing drives seem utterly estranged and uncomprehending in their attitudes toward the "new left" and counterculture. By the same token, the younger people of '68 and of New York's Lower Eastside and San Francisco's Haight-Ashbury have either romanticized the era of their elders or disdained it as completely irrelevant.

None of these viewpoints and attitudes does justice to the issues that relate these two decades in a strangely symbiotic interaction. We get much closer to the truth, I think, if we recognize that the 60s are particularly significant because they tried to deal with problems that 30s' radicalism left completely unresolved. And both decades lacked a clear consciousness of how these problems were rooted in the need to create a radical movement *for* the United States. Let me emphasize my remarks on the need for an American movement—a movement that could deal with uniquely American problems and function within a distinctively American context. The failure of 30s' radicalism to meet this need played a major, if negative, role in the emergence of the "new left" and the counterculture of the 60s—this, to be sure, and the special social conditions that marked the postwar era. Ironically, neither generation fully understood the dynamics of its own development in these terms. In both decades, "the movement" collapsed in large part for lack of this understanding, each generation maliciously back-biting the other, drifting in large numbers into the "system" or splintering into a variety of dogmatic sects and exotic academic conclaves that live a largely campus-bound existence.

Let me start this comparison by emphasizing two features about the "red 30s." 30s' radicalism was neither an American movement nor a movement whose "revolution had failed." The word "betrayal" springs much too easily into radical accounts of a movement whose fate was already predestined by the nature of the workers' movement as a whole. For the moment, it suffices to point out that the sizeable communist and smaller socialist parties that gave their imprint to the 30s were rooted in European immigrants who had brought thoroughly exogenous ideas of socialism and anarchism to the United States. The radical periodicals of the 1930s with the largest circulations were published in foreign languages and reflected experiences, often preindustrial and artisan in nature, that were nourished by central, eastern, and southern European problems — problems discussed with considerable insight in Stanley Aronowitz's *False Promises*. A curious mix of issues that had been formed by highly stratified, quasi-feudal societies and a highly incestuous community life was simply transferred to Anglo-Saxon America with its more fluid, libertarian, and individualistic traditions. These two traditions never fused. In fact, to a great extent, they were deeply hostile to each other. Nor did the American-born offspring of the European radicals succeed in melding the two. They simply preserved the dualities within themselves without coming to terms with the fairly consolidated outlook of their parents on the one hand and the strangely "primitive" American tradition on the other. Drifting into the academy or into labor unions, they became a self-enclosed clique after the Second War—basically social-democratic, indulgently "pluralistic" (which concealed a deep-seated social schizophrenia) or cold warriors, following in the tow of the

Jay Lovestones, Max Schachtmans, and perhaps the most perceptive of the lot, Bertram D. Wolfe—all, larger or smaller lights in the founding years of the American Communist Party.

What helped to conceal this cultural failure of 30s' radicalism from itself were the last great upsurges of the classical workers' movement. Europe, which always had formed the focal point of this 30s' radicalism, was playing out the last stage of an era that began with the French Revolution, unfurled itself with the Parisian workers' barricades of June, 1848, reached its highpoint in the Bolshevik and central European revolutions of 1917–21, and perished in the terrifying bloodbath of the Spanish Revolution of 1936–39. In the years directly following World War II—a war which did not end in a European revolution as the 30s' radicals had so devoutly hoped—"the movement" waited patiently, to no avail, for the 30s to recur. The staggering armamentorium and the restored vitality of capitalism, particularly as revealed by its ability to dissolve the workers' movement of its mythic "historic role" as a revolutionary class, soon made it evident that an entire historical era had passed. The dwindling of the old radical immigrant population merely removed the body politic of that era and left its children stranded—indeed, bitterly resentful of a loss of ideals, organizations, constituencies, and a sense of self-importance that was to surface in the form of incredible arrogance when the 60s movements emerged. This sense of "betrayal" by history, even more than the "betrayals" of Stalin, explains in great part the distempers of the "old left" and its innumerable defections to liberalism and reaction that preceded the emergence of the "new left."

Almost unknowingly, the young people who entered SNCC, SDS, the counterculture, and many less conspicuous and long-forgotten groups were dealing with the barely visible problem which 30s' radicals had faced but never confronted. Twice removed from the old leftist immigrants—and composed numerically of many young Americans of old ethnic backgrounds—they began to weave a uniquely American populist "agenda" of their own—an "agenda" that could influence Americans as a whole in the "affluent" era of the sixties. This "agenda" stressed the *utopian* aspects of the "American Dream" as distinguished from its *economic* aspects: the eschatological ideal of a "New World," of frontier mutualism, of decentralized power and "participatory democracy," of republican virtue and moral idealism. The American landscape was to be planted with flowers, not paved with gold. Intuitively, these young people knew that a different social configuration, largely populist in character and promising in its abundance of the material as well as spiritual means of life, had replaced the hard, labor-oriented, self-denying vision of proletarian socialism. Perhaps no era in American history seemed more rich with the promise of freedom than the early and mid-60s. Its glow of optimism, more moral than economic and more cultural than political, found its most remarkable expression in the founding documents of the civil rights movement and SDS, particularly *The Port Huron Statement*, which I frankly regard as the most authentically American expression of a new radicalism.

One can adduce many reasons, now conventional features of the retrospective sociology on the 60s' "phenomenon," to explain why this movement declined: the end of the Vietnam War, the desertion by the black leadership of the black "masses," the theoretical and intellectual naivete of the "flower children," the inevitable degradation of the drug culture from an ideology of "mind expansion" into "mind numbness," the commercialization of every facet of the counterculture, and the "Leninization" of the "new left." Yet, ironically, it may have been the Vietnam war itself, so often regarded as its most important stimulus, that more significantly than any other factor prevented the 60s' movements from developing *slowly*, *organically*, and *indigenously* into *lasting*, *deeply rooted* American phenomena, charged by a deeper sense of consciousness and a more historic sense of mission than it was to achieve. Set against the background of the 30s, the 60s had confronted problems and, in certain respects, begun to resolve issues that a dying era with its dying constituencies could never deal with. Until the Vietnam war had created a 30s-like image of violent insurgency, polarization, and shopworn ideological dogmatism, the 60s was fully indigenous in character. Given time and a deepening of consciousness, it might have spoken to the American people in comprehensible terms and greatly altered the American social climate. That was not to be. Guilt-ridden, literally anti-American rather than anti-imperialist, "third-world" oriented without any sense of the redeeming features of the libertarian elements in the American tradition, the "new left" was literally strait-jacketed by its ideologues into a sleazy Leninism. If this seems like a simplification of an account of the decline of the 60s, we would do well to place it against the background of the 30s. It then becomes evident that what subverted the 60s decade was precisely the percolation of traditional radical myths, political styles, a sense of urgency, and above all, a heightened metabolism so destructive in its effects that it loosened the very roots of "the movement" even as it fostered its rank growth. Having already sounded its death-knell with '68 and after, the American culture which the 60s opposed to the European movements of the 30s could now become faddist, ephemeral, and co-optable, much to the delight, I suspect, of my own dear 30s comrades.

If there are lessons to be learned, aside from those that may be raised by the vast social changes that lie before us, they are the need for organicity of growth, patience in commitment, localism in scale, consciousness in practice—and the development of an American radicalism, largely woven from indigenous traditions rather than European, Asian, African, and Latin importations. We do the "third world" no service by ignoring the "first," and we do Europe, restless with anxiety, no service by ignoring America and its utopian traditions.

Surviving contradictions

GRETA NEMIROFF

The 60s penetrated the membrane of my most private vision only in 1969. I had taught at all levels from elementary through university where I was then teaching a standard English curriculum with great conviction. At thirty, I had spent twenty-five years in schools and disliked all but one of them. I had not, however, formulated an analysis of them because I couldn't grasp how something as impersonal as their structure militated against good education. Perilously naive, I thought that at best, most teachers were boring and wrong-headed; and at worst, they were as sadistic as the social class of their students permitted.

The university where I taught had a fairly large black population for a Canadian university of the time. We in Canada like to pretend that racism begins south of the border. Nonetheless, in 1969, as a result of a very provocative and complex situation, a group primarily composed of black students occupied and then set fire to the university's computer center. Many faculty members, who had never discussed race before, felt licensed to make gross racist public statements. I felt alienated from my colleagues; the shock of their behavior changed the direction of my life. I began to devour the "sacred texts" of the times: Fanon, Malcolm X, Cleaver, Jackson, histories of the slave trade, the underground railway, the black community in Canada, and individual autobiographical accounts like those of Frederick Douglass. When I resumed lecturing, the literary exegesis of Alexander Pope seemed of dubious validity as I looked out at the forgetful faces of my students. Clearly, they wanted to forget and "get on with it." I wished for the tools to give them a more radical vision, but I was just beginning to learn myself.

Almost simultaneously, I became caught up in the women's movement where I have remained. In 1970 I co-taught one of the first university women's studies courses in Canada, and eventually co-founded a women's studies program. At the beginning there were few books in print: de Beauvoir, Friedan, Engels-Marx-Lenin, on the "woman question," Virginia Woolf and later Kate Millett. Our courses were huge and there was a pioneering excitement in them. It was exhilarating to see women becoming empowered through knowledge about themselves and their history, discussion with one another, and above all through a feminist analysis of their own lives. The best stories, though, are always individual ones and we have yet to see great waves of social change resulting solely from individual raised consciousness. While there is a burgeoning body of research on all facets of women's lives, we are in dire need of a coherent praxis which can move women towards consolidated radical action.

In 1967, as a result of the "quiet revolution," Québec instituted changes in its educational system. In an effort to democratize education through increasing access to post-secondary students, a system of free community colleges called C.E.G.E.P.'s [Collèges de l'enseignement général et professionel] was inaugurated. To avoid the separation of an educated élite from those in "trades," the colleges would have compulsory programs for pre-university students as well as for those going directly into "career" programs. Students from all sectors would mix socially in the compulsory language, humanities/philosophy and physical education courses, thus eliminating the alienation of the past when students were streamed in high school. The *Rapport Parent*, the text on which the C.E.G.E.P.'s are based, optimistically ignores the many systemic barriers to the completion of high school faced by many oppressed people in Québec.

The C.E.G.E.P.'s apparent emphasis on holistic education and social change seduced me. In 1970, I left the university to set up the English and creative arts departments of a new C.E.G.E.P., situated in the erstwhile Mother House of the Holy Cross nuns. The state was preempting the Church which had dominated Québec education for three hundred years. Determined to hire "good" people, I interviewed over three hundred candidates for thirty jobs. Despite their excellent qualifications and good will, most of them were to become disaffected by the rigid hierarchical structures which were established within the first three years. The best withdrew their hearts and the worst insinuated themselves into positions of power. Our initial mode of collective decision-making first deteriorated into "consultation," and then into "decrees." How had we allowed this to happen?

The *Rapport Parent*, the "sacred text" of the new educational order, soon was to be dismissed by kindly bureaucratic shrugs and assurances by administrators that while its contents were all very well for the 60s, "times had changed"! In an effort to stem the tide of state control, college teachers affiliated with the province's most powerful trade unions, only to discover in time that union leaders were also unenthusiastic about collective decision-making. Some hopefully fled to other jobs, but most had to stay because options were closing. Besides, by the mid-70s many teachers had children, mortgages, and maybe even a "dacha" in the country. We had a price, and both management and the unions could play upon this. Many radicals of the 60s gave up and privatized themselves, produced erudite and short-lived journals, took superb trips, or followed courses in stained glass making. Then there were those who had prudently never given up *cannabis*, and those who rediscovered alcohol.

I changed colleges, becoming a teacher and then director of an alternative C.E.G.E.P. based on the teachings of humanistic education and psychology as articulated by Maslow and Rogers. The New School of Dawson College, founded in 1973, is a pre-university arts program based on the premise that the best learning develops in response to strong affective needs; the educator's primary job is to help students find appropriate means to fulfill those needs. Education is viewed as a confirming and empowering process, fostering students' talents, interests and autonomy. Our staff and students come from a wide range of social classes and ethnic backgrounds. We struggle for growth and survival each day through a poignantly exacting awareness of the many contradictions inherent in our situation: as 140 individualists striving for community, as English in Québec, and Québecers in North America.

We discuss the "sacred texts" of humanistic education with our students, but always with the addendum of political analysis. The "hierarchy of needs" is usually described outside of the real social context, and we deplore the wide co-optation of humanistic techniques to maintain the existing social order. For a time, inner-city children in North America were treated to self-validating exercises, which carefully evaded the subject of their oppression, becoming agents for the domestication of despair. The application of "I'm O.K., you're O.K." [a vulgarized version of "unconditional positive regard"] is ludicrous applied to the hungry, to children whose noses might be bitten off by rats while they sleep. Many of our students come to school hungry and tired from the part-time jobs needed to help sustain them and their families. Often there is family violence, alcoholism, drug abuse, neglect, breakdown. With few exceptions, the students believe the world is near its end and they will not live to see old age. As educators, we struggle with the contradictions inherent in offering humanistic education in an oppressive social context.

We also are aware of the contradiction that although we are student-centered in our approach, our students do not always share our values. Since 1973, an increasing ethos of social Darwinism has infected our students who ask if our values would truly work "out there," pointing to the Montreal business center which is right outside our windows. "Go and change the out there," we counsel, vexed however by the knowledge that it takes more than individual self-actualization to counter the power of the capitalist state. Yet, without the conviction that personal growth, tempered by social analysis, is an excellent agent for social change, we would have no school and would have folded with so many other alternatives rooted in the 60s. As director of the school, I must ensure our survival in times unsympathetic to alternative education. This sometimes forces me into non-humanistic gestures of politicking, making veiled threats and uneasy alliances, and devising *ad hoc* surprises. Survival depends on being unpredictable, using the loopholes and insisting on the right to define our own reality and get the benefits to be extracted from our society.

"Yes, yes," the doubters always say at this point, "that was all very well in the 60s, but what about the 80s?" I reject the notion that each decade brings with it obligatory rebirth with amnesia. The texts of the 60s gave us the optimistic respect for individual rights: Realpolitik showed us how state power militates against the individual and groups of traditionally oppressed peoples. What we did not produce was a blueprint for surviving the co-optation of the 70s which have led to the present encroachment of world fascism. Too many of our most gifted thinkers became petrified in postures of "political correctness" and "purity." Often we are victimized by our own naivité at accepting the trivializing vision of the media which define and dismiss revolution as an event rather than seeing it as a long and incremental process.

In my own struggles as an educator, living within this spiral of contradiction, I have gained inspiration from the writings of Kozol and Frière. I have also been moved by less eloquent writers: my students who have neither the language nor the metaphors to describe their truncated dreams and impotent rage. Living through these times with them is being true to my own beliefs in the revolution. I am confident that out of this process, texts will emerge that will heighten our retrospective understanding. This is not the time for compulsive big-shots of the revolution to jet about, offering slick and costly speeches to privileged audiences. The most that many of us can do in these days of darkness is to crouch hopefully over our light and scribble. . . as I am doing now. We must stretch out to reach one another in order to overcome our isolation and share our strength, strategies and spirit. The "text" of this era is still to be written; those of us who care must have the courage to improvise it into existence.

Paths to critical theory

ADOLPH REED

I came to politics in the 60s from a black leftist household—Catholic, liberal-left mother and the Party not too far back in my father's past. When I left home for good, in college, he was still conducting a bitter fight through the mail with Sidney Hook, an old professor toward whom he maintained a reciprocated enmity.

Circumstances often had us in situations that made issues of the day alive and tangible: New York, where we lived the Wallace and Marcantonio campaigns; Washington, where we worried about loyalty oaths, wiretaps and witch-hunts in the McCarthy years. Somewhere along the way I remember crying at my mother's explanation of the Rosenbergs' plight; a son was my age. The White House evoked fear as well as awe as I fed squirrels across the street. My father's first teaching job had us forty miles from Little Rock when Central High was integrated; when the 101st Airborne was flown in to protect the integrating students. Black troops weren't allowed to do riot duty and were deposited at an arsenal near us, from which they served as a color guard at my father's college's football games.

My high school years were in New Orleans, where I experienced the revolution in Cuba and its aftermath with an otherwise very conventional grandfather who privately vented his nationalist pride at Castro's victory. With the Missile Crisis the witch-hunting fears returned as we fretted that he might be deported.

One of the first six schools in the city to be integrated was around the corner from my house, and I had to walk past dogs, barricades and police to take the bus to school. Our principal kept us in late to stop us from fighting with hostile Irish and Italian teenagers downtown.

Predictably, therefore, the books that stand out to me from the 60s didn't really shatter illusions about the United States or "our way of life" or capitalism; they structured thinking that was confused and ambivalent between the old left and the new. Identification with Marxism was hardly new; I had thought of myself as a Marxist since deciding against the priesthood in early adolescence—defense of the Soviet Union as the hope of the world's oppressed and all that. (I was well into my twenties before realizing that 1956 in Hungary was not simply the likes of Zsa Zsa Gabor trying to overthrow workers' power.)

When the Black Power storm swept the airwaves, Malcolm X spoke to my spirit and Carmichael captured the rage I felt; I yearned, as did so many others, to spit with him into the faces of power. Black power was murky as a political program, and I waited for a systematic articulation, only to be disappointed when the Carmichael and Hamilton *Black Power* tract finally appeared as very ordinary pluralist claptrap cum rhetorical flourish.

Around this time I discovered Fanon, via a copy of *Wretched of the Earth* that my parents had around the house. Sartre's wild introduction was properly cathartic; however, the famous chapter that all the "militants" were to appropriate (apparently without having read it) for their side of the absurd violence/nonviolence debate struck me as a powerful statement of the dehumanizing effects of oppression. More impressive still was the "Pitfalls of National Consciousness'' chapter that gave new fire to my rejection of the class bias of civil rights—and eventually Black Power—ideology. I read Fanon compulsively and flirted with the colonial analogy.

Other authors come to mind from that period: Cleaver, whose *Ramparts* essays I read with interest, though I didn't quite know what to feel about *Soul on Ice* (I should have known: rape, after all, is simply rape and cannot be dressed up as anything less vile); Laing, whose *Politics of Experience* was perhaps a curious impetus to begin to read Freud through eyes other than Stalin's; Baran & Sweezy, who grounded a critique of American society in empirical political economy and economic history and reinforced what I didn't yet realize was becoming a leaning toward Third Worldism. I believe that I first read *One-Dimensional Man* around that time but didn't really appreciate Marcuse until later; I simply grafted him onto Fanon, Baran & Sweezy and a still orthodox reading of Marx. The hodge-podge of this list reflects both the rapid pace of time and the swirling ambivalence—between old and new lefts, Marxist orthodoxy and nationalism—that lived in my head.

In the midst of this swirl, several months prior to the King assassination I jumped into the Trotskyist movement and became an SWP youth group campus operative. Fittingly, this first new left organizational affiliation was ''new in form, old in essence''. The attraction to Trotskyism signalled, in addition to something like generational rebelliousness, some feeble internalization of my peers' rejection of what Jacoby calls ''conformist Marxism'' as well as a growing desire to act, also characteristic of the time.

The Trotskyist affiliation triggered the first shock of a two-stage paradigm crisis. My old-new left ambivalence left me with strong commitments to the antiwar movement, rigid class analysis and black power nationalism simultaneously; the thoroughly opportunist SWP was the only entity in the black or white lefts that sought to appeal to all three dispositions. Still, the anomaly of advocacy of nationalist organizing from within the white-dominated Trotskyist movement weighed steadily heavier. This burden was exacerbated by the clearly manipulative posture of the organization vis-à-vis racial issues, conflicts over the proper focus of political work, and, God forbid, a silent but no less guilt-inducing reluctance to submit to centralist discipline. My alienation grew, and finally, after an arduous strike of nonacademic university employees, which did not fit the SWP's priority of recruiting antiwar students, I encountered one of the two books of the decade that was both liberating and clarifying: Harold Cruse's *The Crisis of the Negro Intellectual*.

Timing may have had something to do with it. If I had read Cruse a year earlier, I might have glossed his insights. However, his critical reconstruction of the subordinate and manipulated status of black communists within the Party in the pre-World War II years cemented my decision to sever the Trotskyist connection. His critique also crystallized for me much of the recent experience of the left, especially as the Black Panther/SDS nexus had begun to erode the one really important programmatic stance of black power, i.e., the cruciality of autonomous black political organization. Moreover, Cruse's historicized critique of Black Power and his interpretation of Afro-American social thought as a century's debate between nationalist and integrationist tendencies were powerful orienting ideas for many, but not enough, of us then. If one book stands out as seminal in its attempt to locate our efforts in the historical context that we so desperately needed, it is Cruse's *Crisis*. Another volume of equal quality is Lasch's *Agony of the American Left*. Lasch's book did for the left in general what Cruse's did for black radicalism; and in this sense *Agony of the American Left* is a companion piece to the *Crisis*, as Lasch's acknowledgement indicates.

Shortly before reading Cruse, my unstable, ambivalent synthesis received a major jolt from SDS's proclamation of the Black Panther Party (BPP) as the "vanguard of the black liberation struggle." Julius Lester responded in his *Guardian* column, charging SDS with paternalism in designating black vanguards. Kathleen Cleaver replied with what I recall as an outrageous, ad hominem attack on Lester in SDS's *New Left Notes*. At that point the Panthers made clear that they had opted for their tragic style of embodying the nihilistic fantasies of their white leftist allies. No amount of exaltation of and exulting in the imagery of the noble black revolutionary savage (what else was the cult of the "lumpen," which ironically has remained with us in depoliticized form as the suburban racist image of the "bad" ghetto buck ready to kick white ass?) could paper over the condition of clientage that mediated the Panthers' relation to their white patrons. My affinity for the BPP, which I'd hoped would generate an autonomous black Marxism, and their white supporters evaporated. Cruse blew away the residual vapors with his breath of fresh critical air.

Shortly thereafter I left the campus to work on a black GI/community organizing project that was part of the GI Coffeehouse movement. I remember Earl Ofari's *The Myth of Black Capitalism*; James Boggs' various writings, and Robert Allen's ultimately disappointing *Black Awakening in Capitalist America*, along with Lester's work—which I still respect—for opening the dialogue with my co-workers who wore a skin-thin anti-Marxism they inherited from Pan-Africanism. Apart from these writings, I turned increasingly toward the third world, focusing on imperialism.

The final irony in this overly long tale is that as I became ill at ease about Leninism—and felt guilty about these petit-bourgeois doubts—my Pan-Africanist colleagues found Marxism in its most stultifying and dogmatic variety, Marxism-Leninism with Maoist slant. This is the context within which I encountered Korsch's *Marxism and Philosophy*. Leninism's elitism and denigration of consciousness had increasingly troubled me, but I feared I had no recourse without sacrificing a radical theoretical commitment.

Korsch opened an entirely new vista, the "hidden dimension" of Western Marxism, and led to Lukács, a serious reading of Marcuse and eventually the critical theoretical tradition.

Then, as the Ford Foundation broke up our community organizing efforts and the movement dried up around me, I went off, like so many others in similar condition, to the university to try to make sense of what had happened and what to do next. Like most of the others, I've been lurking around there pretty much ever since.

From reich to marcuse

JOEL KOVEL

In 1960 I was a medical student and ardent follower of the recently deceased Wilhelm Reich. In common with other Reichians, I regarded society as at most an impediment to the full expression of the life force, or orgone. Such had been the master's final opinion, forged by the unmerciful repression to which he had been subjected by the U.S. government. In retrospect, Reich's martyrdom was an important element of his appeal. Anybody this far out had to be worth following. It did Reich's radical reputation no end of good, for instance, to have his books actually banned—not to mention burned—in this land of liberty; and I recall the outraged excitement when I had to get my copy of *The Function of the Orgasm* smuggled in by a friend returning from abroad.

However, unlike Reich himself, we who followed him did not have the benefit of a real engagement with society from which to retreat. Our radicalism, therefore, was shallow, romantic, and potentially reactionary. Indeed, Reich's Marxist period had not only been repudiated by him, but was repressed as well by his epigones, so much so that I did not take cognizance of it until 1972, when "What is Class-Consciousness" appeared in *Liberation* Magazine. This revelation, along with Baxandall's edition of the *Sex-Pol Essays*, published a few years later, played a major role in the later direction of my work. But I, too, had changed by 1972; the same works presented to me a decade earlier now elicited only a mild curiosity. What lay between was the 60s and my own discovery of society—a process which placed the course of my own development in the reverse order from that of my youthful hero.

During the 50s my innate radicalism had been pretty well checked by the bourgeois, rabidly anticommunist world that surrounded and nurtured me. As a result, I found myself pushing toward science and medicine (and eventually orgonomy, as the most radical scientific-medical movement I could find). At least in nature things could be made to make sense; there one might look and explore without running into a sheer wall of mystification (a word I did not of course know at the time). Another vicissitude was social-democratic politics. At Yale, in the 50s, to be with Norman Thomas and the League for Industrial Democracy was as far left as could be seen: beyond, one fell off the end of the world into the fathomless hell of communism.

Medical training seemed to have taken me completely outside the realm of sociological thought. Of course this detour was a good thing, since it spared me exposure to much nonsense and left me free to think for myself. But it did delay my development and dictated, moreover, that the pathway I would take toward social theory must pass through the defiles of that portion of medical discourse molded to accommodate itself to the historical world, namely, psychiatry and psychoanalysis.

Thus, when the 60s burst in upon me, which as I best recall came with the murders of Chaney, Goodman, and Schwerner, and the Harlem riots, I met it with the eyes of one trained to look at the mental depths. By 1963, I had pretty much lost interest in orgonomy, which had fallen into a mechanistic cultism, and had commenced a serious study of Freud. For the first half of the decade, the psychoanalytic classics were my intellectual staple, and my proudest moment of possession came with the opening of the carton containing the 23 beautifully bound volumes, complete with pale-blue dust covers, of Freud's Standard Edition (purchased cut-rate from Blackwell's of Oxford, the only bookseller, or commercial establishment of any kind, who ever sent me hand-written Christmas cards).

Psychoanalysis had done more than stir my intellect or provide a framework for a life's work. It had also absorbed into itself my radical energies, drawing them into the comfortable illusion that by carefully tending the subjectivity of a bourgeois individual one was fulfilling some measure of the revolutionary project. The fact that such an individual remained bourgeois for all that did not trouble me then, in the golden age of one-dimensionality. After all, what else was there to be but a bourgeois individual? In any event, psychoanalysis was fast finishing what medical technocracy had well begun, namely, de-politicization, manifested by the near complete loss of any oppositional sense to democratic fascism and imperialism. When the 60s struck me, I was a Kennedy, and then a Johnson man. The idea that "our" motives were anything but well-intentioned in Vietnam struck me as outrageous, for example, as did the insinuation that the liberal state might be less than single-mindedly bent on eliminating racial injustice.

But the negativity of the black experience in America struck deep in my soul. And here a remnant of my discarded Reichianism was stirred forth: an instinctive mistrust of the state. I had become an anarchist despite myself, unconsciously, slowly but inevitably over the years. All that I lacked was a vision of society to be set against the state (Reich having lumped them uncritically together), and a voice to articulate what was growing inside as the true nature of the Indochina War and the depths of American racism dawned on me.

To be sure, this was not a light that came on of its own. It had to be transmitted by others, through the murk emanating from the ideological apparatus—a demon whose existence I only began to suspect then, in the middle of the decade, through the genius and courage of those who dared pierce it. Two names stand forth in the memory of that period: I.F. Stone and Noam Chomsky. To subscribe to *Stone's Weekly* was exhilarating, like snapping an invisible chain that had been binding me without my knowledge. And when he exposed the lies about the Gulf of Tonkin resolution, I began to awaken to my rage and saw myself outside this monster that was sowing death and lies, began, too, to wonder at my previous complicity with it. This continued when I read Chomsky, who was to prove an even greater influence. Stone had been a professional journalist. Here, however, was a man of science with whom I could identify, who had changed his life in response to the war. Chomsky's essay, "On the Responsibility of Intellectuals" (which appeared in a *New York Review of Books* that is no more except in externals), became therefore, a turning point for me. He made me realize that it was not enough to oppose the war abstractly, or to receive criticism of the state from others. One had to proceed from one's place of social reproduction (another term I would not have recognized at the time), taking it on, in other words, from where one had been formed by it. My appetite for the negative had been whetted. I began to read those works which would confirm this negativity: Fanon; Genet's *The Blacks*; *The Autobiography of Malcolm X* (this last especially powerful, in part because of its insight into the Afro-American experience, but chiefly because I had been very much terrorized by the media's image of Malcolm.)

A work was taking shape, molded by practical circumstances no less than by intellectual concerns. We had moved to the west coast, to Seattle, where I was doing obligatory medical duty for the state in the Public Health Service. Scarcely a black face was to be seen. Only the facelessness of bureaucracy and shopping-mall America surrounded me; I, in uniform, spent the day consoling military wives and helping the services get rid of their undesirables through "administrative" means, i.e., finding a mental illness to pin upon them. I decided to write.

After outlining the main argument of *White Racism*, I had to face the fact that I had nothing to put inside those outlines. Ostensibly for the book, but also for the moment of liberation this afforded from my stay in the belly of the beast, I discovered Weber, Karl Polanyi, Hannah Arendt, Sartre, Huizinga and Whitehead. I allowed myself to see literature—Faulkner, Conrad, above all, *Moby Dick*—as critique as well as case study. And I eventually let myself see psychoanalysis itself in the same way, first through Roheim, then Norman O. Brown, and finally, in the culmination of my studies, through the encounter with Marcuse.

One-Dimensional Man had become, then, the counter-revelation. At last, I could see the way between that desire which formed for me the Archimedean point of human experience and the domination whose racist forms I was chasing. More, I could now see how to trace this line "laterally," away from the Father and into the colorless administration of everyday life. I still remember reading the line, "administration is the pure form of domination," then placing exclamation points like flags all over the page. I had found the theoretical structure for my work.

That it was Marcuse rather than Brown who had the greater influence meant that I had better confront that tradition standing behind Marcusean thought, but which I, schooled in bourgeois post-war America, could only approach through intuition: Marxism. This, however, was a job for the next decade.

The left's silent south

JERRY WATTS

Danville, Virginia, contrary to much of the advertising proclaiming a New South, seems to have died decades ago. With only the Dan River Textile Mill in town, most young people have for generations left town seeking employment elsewhere.

Yet in 1963, the "Freedom bug," or whatever one might call the quasi-apocalyptic stirrings that fueled the courage of southern blacks, hit Danville. Black people, primarily the young, without any real sense of those forces that had conspired to deny them opportunities took to the streets. Black ministers, who had heretofore been willing to maintain their intraethnic elite status through an acquiescence clothed in a fundamentalist attire, both instigated and followed the groundswell. From such traditional bastions of Negro servitude as Liberty Hill, Shiloh and Bethal Baptist Churches, and through such unlikely figures as Bishop Campbell of Bibleway Church, International, the masses came forth, not as revolutionaries nor as heroes, but stirred by simple visions of "what is right."

High school and junior high school students, marginally employed dropouts, gas station attendants, janitors, and domestic servants, providing strength for each other merely by being present, marched that mile or so down Mainstreet. Greeted there by city cops, state troopers, and city firemen, the crowd was viciously attacked by billy clubs and water hoses. The jails filled, but more came. Black people acted.

Perhaps even more surprising was the presence of some old folks. My uncle, who had spent 35 years of his adult life filling, emptying, and refilling fire extinguishers at the mill, acted. My grandfather, then in his early seventies, marched. Why this man whose mother had been a slave, and whose income derived largely from his yard work for prominent white families and who seemed resigned to his marginal status, chose to march, I can't explain. Throughout the South, people chose to act, when all that was rational to them demanded that they stay home.

I was last in Danville over the Christmas holidays visiting with my aunts and uncle. My grandfather is no longer alive. My younger brother, now an aspiring student of social theory at Harvard College, and I—true to our post-new left consciousness—would often discuss whether or not the civil rights movement accomplished anything significant. When speaking with Danville relatives, my brother was dumbfounded as to why these people, who have never read a book and who seem to him so simple in character, would take off from work to vote for a dogcatcher if need be. He wondered what it was that would lead people who view it as a major social outing to have lunch "into town" at the Woolworth's on Main Street to take off from work to participate in car pools to help others get to the polls.

When asked about politics in Danville, my uncle reached into his pocket, pulled forth small sheets of mimeographed paper and asked my brother if he wanted to sign up for the NAACP. "It used to be five dollars; now it's gone up to ten." (Needless to say, my brother is too "radical" to belong.) Pointing at the black sportscaster on the local evening news, my uncle proudly proclaimed, "Some people say that nothing has changed, but there didn't use to be no colored on there before." In that short exchange, he had conveyed both the failure and success of the civil rights movement.

When discussing the political events of the 60s with my leftist peers, we usually end up competing over who can present the best macro-theoretical explanation for the failure of the new left. Few of us are ever sufficiently honest to define political success; yet we will expound upon political failure. We accuse ourselves of reformism for expecting too little and political naiveté for expecting too much. Sycophants, we speak in fear of those ever devastating rejoinders, "But what happened *of any significance*?" or "But did this result in systemic change?"

Unfortunately, one of the most enduring and humanly moving results of the political activism of the 60s usually remains silenced by the invocation of the aura of "significance." I am in this sense appealing to us to think about, or better, to think as if we were black and poor in Greene County, Alabama; Farmville, Virginia; or Hattiesburg, Mississippi prior to the emergence of the civil rights movement. Of course many, if not most, of the poor and black in those towns remain that way today. I am asking that we counter that tendency to speak of southern blacks in terms of reified categories without fearing that we will romanticize the lives of blacks in the South, or that we will become partners to the silly celebrations of American political reform which are paraded out every year on Martin Luther King's birthday.

The task is to realize that at some crucial point black individuals who had been subjected to the most intense antiemancipatory socializations in American history, dominated by internalized negative stigma, quagmired in systematically maintained ignorance and self-hatred, victimized by the expected feelings of powerlessness that accompany poverty, and justifiably fearful of the unregulated repressive abuse of the police and court system were able, in however momentary or misdirected way, to *act*.

The act of becoming politicized, of claiming a space and identity, where there had previously been only silence, was, given the historical and social circumstances of southern blacks, as radical an act as occurred in the 60s. The ability of individuals to begin to fight against an abundance of obstacles (both internal and external), never encountered by the antiwar movement or any of its spinoffs, will always remain the source of my deepest emotional attachment to the activism of the 60's. I suspect that it is my understanding of the resilience of the will to become empowered that kindles whatever hope I have for a socialist America in this age of the moral majority.

"Children have no freedom. they are property just like a book."

FINVOLA DRURY

Few will know who said that. Richard Nixon once said that the American people are like the child in the family: they need to be taken by the hand and led. And Tricia Nixon, during her father's Watergate ordeal, suggested that he should be left alone, to rule the people. But it wasn't Nixon, or Nixon's daughter. And it wasn't Governor Rhodes of Ohio, who might have been thinking that when he ordered the fatal presence of the National Guard at Kent State University.

Something like that might have been in the mind and been uttered by the police at Jackson State when they shot and killed two young people shortly after the murders at Kent State. The problem is that many people might have said it, and many agreed with the man who did.

That man was Arville Garland. He was explaining why he walked into an apartment near Wayne State University at two-thirty in the morning of May 8, 1970 and shot and killed his daughter, Sandy Garland, and three others, his daughter's partner, Scott Kabran,and two friends who just happened to have crashed there, Greg Walls and Tony Brown. Shot them FBI style, in their sleep.

Arville Garland went to jail, but there was tremendous sympathy for him. Today he could be the patron saint of the organization calling itself TOUGHLOVE. Back then, the Detroit Free Press account told us that "Many people say that Sandy and Scott and Greg and Tony deserved to be punished for the way they lived." *Deserved to be punished*.

There it is. Why run away from home, make love, take dope? What does it *say*? The measure of Arville Garland's crime is the length he went to demonstrate to the world what his daughter already knew, that someone she had been raised to respect and to love, hated her.

"Father finds slain boy's poems." Scott Kabran left a manuscript. He had told his father he was going to be a poet, the newspaper in front of me, the Detroit News for Tuesday, May 12, 1970 says. Not that he wanted to be a poet, but that *he was going to be one*. I believe as surely as I am sitting here in March, 1983, that Arville Garland got both of them. The child and the book.

One of the things I want to get into these notes about the 60s, something I know a lot about, is the desperate attempt of the younger poets to cut themselves off from a tradition which mandated their destruction, that is, the ruling notion, out of the ruling poet, that the poet destroys himself in the act of creating. The young poets looked around in the 60s and saw nothing but a vocation to which they felt strongly called, but one that was filled with the spectacle of those who had been called before them, in the act of publicly destroying themselves. The history of American poetry contains a long list of suicides, the most notable for the young, of course, being that of Hart Crane, but he wasn't the first, and the death by his own hand of Paul Blackburn, who had himself tried to break away, had a terrible impact on the "new" poets who had taken so much courage from him. When Ginsberg stood up and launched into that immortal first line: "I saw the best minds of my generation. . . ." he, and his listeners, knew whereof he spoke. The poets and their academic trainers, had all bought into the self-destruct system of aesthetics which capitalism and religion had laid down for them, as it had laid down for anybody who works.

So the young saw a steady parade of poets stopping at the podium on their way from the bar to the madhouse, and in that period, the famous suicides, which now dominate literary discussions and are the subjects of many critical and biographical works, either occurred or were in the works. Robert Lowell was willing to exchange almost one third of his life in asylums for the privilege of being first among American poets in his lifetime. Berryman, Sexton, Plath, everybody knows the list. They were important and they were scary as hell. Those coming up after them, the older leaders, Creeley, Duncan, Levertov, and Gary Snyder, represented the hope for a healthier way of life and of letters, and the young wanted to write and to stay sane.

"I am lonely, lonely./I was born to be lonely,/I am best so!"

Kenneth Burke sees in William Carlos Williams' lines an echo to the preamble to the Constitution. To him, Williams' loneliness is as American as . . . the Constitution. It must follow that it is as American as apple pie, and . . . Father, because, the poet ends his dance in front of the mirror, naked asking: "Am I not then, the happy genius of the household?"

The genius of the American household is: loneliness. Then the practice of silence. Williams needed to be alone, needed some respite from his family, from the pressure of his practice to engage in the most real form of pleasure for him, aesthetic pleasure. But once there, the honest doctor was naked once again. Once the gift could be engaged, he was not selfish, speak he must for beauty itself is reduced to a pathological state, "unless the ecstasy be general." Once the self can be reconceived and from this conscious remaking of his own past, the poet is born, the loneliness can end, and Williams tried all his life to end it, the separation from people. But it can go the other way, too, as in the demagogy of Pound and Eliot. And Williams was humbled. Humbled by the sight of bums in the subway; humbled by women in childbed; humbled by what war did to people, his own sons included; humbled by the human condition, that look on a man's face, which a war will not take away; humbled by faith he did not share, but recorded the results of; humbled by his wife's faithfulness; humbled by his physical deterioration. By the reactionary political, academic and critical forces levelled against him, he was never humbled. Confused, saddened, angered, he stayed smart. How remarkable that looks today.

His one hundredth birthday occurs September 17, 1983. In the 60s, campuses throughout the country would have been alive with that news. Students who loved poetry, and many students did, loved those rich, chaste lines, loved the energy in the man, loved the *difference* they discerned in what he was trying to bring to poetry, loved the personal, non-academic, lived flavor of the work. He was a true democrat: he always knew where he was, as Robert Creeley would say. It's the only way you can really survive in this country. Once forget, and you're dead.

In the 60s, American youth started to know where they were, and started to know in great numbers, and they started to know, *openly*, not only could they focus, they could share.

I began these remarks on the revolt of property in the 60s by invoking a piece by John Sinclair in his book of memoirs *The Guitar Army*. I knew John in Detroit in the 60s, all of them. We didn't always see eye to eye. Good for me. If I knew anything I knew that John didn't belong to anybody. In a strange way, and one I recommend, he does now. John and friends started The Artists' Workshop, a modern Renaissance type of support for the arts in Detroit, run on as many shoestrings as they could find. (It wasn't easy, the police kept taking them away.) John became internationally famous when the late John Lennon, who didn't kill himself, wrote a song for him. But the best writing about one of the worst things that happened in Detroit in those years was written by John. And it scares me that I have kept all these years the newspaper account from the aftermath of Arville Garland's crime. I'll tell you why. Because the American confusion over who owns what is back in full force. The easiest thing you can do in our society is to kill your own child, not by abortion, not by withdrawing infant life-support systems, not by euthanasia with the hopelessly ill and suffering, but with a gun.

My own feelings on a similar occurrence I expressed in a poem of that time.

Linda (a true story of the 60's)

Linda Ault
stayed out

too late
one night.

Back at the ranch
her parents lay a-bed

and fornicating
thoughts

jumped
in their head.

Next day
they handed her

a gun:

"For punishment

go out

and shoot
your dog,"

they said.

But she,
being thoroughly

bad
dishonored

them—

went out
and shot

herself
(their dog)

instead.

What is to be done? We can't ask John Lennon, can we? (Do you suppose he's dead because his name reminded them of somebody?)

How about asking each other? Meanwhile, read John Sinclair. He's still with us. He and the song John Lennon wrote about him.

Guitar Army, Street Writings/Prison Writings, A Rainbow Book, distributed by World Publishing Co., 1972, especially the essay, "Slaughter at Stonehead Manor."

More about this see *Middlemarch*, by George Eliot, N.Y. Hurst and Company, 1887, page 131.

On punishment, read "For James Dean," by Frank O'Hara, *The New American Poetry*.
See *Frances*.
Ask to see: *The Jean Seberg Story*.
Re-read the whole of *The Radical Will*: Randolph Bourne.
Form seminars on the post-revolutionary survival of human property.
Read *The Age of Surveillance*, by Frank Donner.
Read the poem, "The Gift," by Phillip Schultz in *Like Wings*.
Read the biographies of John Berryman and Robert Lowell.
Read the poems and letters of Sylvia Plath and Anne Sexton.
Read Louise Brooks' *Lulu in Hollywood* and read Randall Jarrell's *The Lost World*.
Never, never miss a single broadcast or written word of the Rev. Jerry Falwell.
Don't let intellectual snobbery and antipathy to religion keep you a slave to what the right wing is really doing to us forever.
Play a recording of the Weavers made from a soundtrack of the film. Listen to Ronnie Gilbert. Then play a recording of Kate Smith singing "God Bless America," and then write this magazine.
Read the list of the MacArthur Awards. Don't do it if the seconal bottle is loaded.
Look through old *New Yorkers* from the 60s and find the cartoon that has an irascible (that's really pissed) Diogenes holding his lamp up over a tiny figure in a nightie, and saying: "I didn't say I was looking for an honest *kid*." I can't remember the cartoonists' name. Write me care of this magazine.
Read how Tommy Sands got to be called a terrorist. (By Margaret Thatcher)
Look up "moral masochism" somewhere, everywhere. And never be without your pocket edition of Calvin. I mean the theologian, not the designer.

ACKNOWLEDGMENTS

"I have a hard time reading. . ."

ROBERT ROTH

I have an awful hard time reading. I have reader's block. It is almost as hard for me to read as it is for me to write. I have a worse case of writer's block. Maybe one month a year I am relaxed enough to read. As for writing I can only write a short story every other year and only in the summer when it is very hot. This past summer there was one horrible heat wave. But it lasted only a few days, and so it was only a very short story that I was able to write. In truth I can write letters to friends and letters to the editor most of the year round. I now plan to treat my letters as if they were essays, circulate them for people to see and when the occasion arises read an appropriate one in public.

As I've said reading is very difficult for me. My mind blanks out, I day dream, I masturbate, I turn on the TV, I dash out the door, I talk on the phone. Most of my friends though are very well read and love to read. Much of what I know I've learned through them. For example my friend Arnie Sachar, a fine writer and an unusually gifted social critic, reads constantly. He reads *Newsday*, *Fag Rag*, Jimmy Breslin, *Commonweal*. He reads books on philosophy, economics as well as novels and short stories. We talk on the phone a lot and he is always summarizing things that he has just read. He will often read me passages of something that particularly grabs him and on occasion he will read me a whole article. We have been doing this for twenty years. That is except for a three year period when I had forbidden him to read me anything, except maybe something that he had just written.

My stricture was a result of Arnie having read to me for five hours an autobiographical piece in *Working Papers* by Elinor Langer in which she discusses her experiences as a social activist in the 60s. Arnie has a good reading voice and a love for anybody who puts words on paper. And so when he read me Langer's piece I just didn't know when or how to ask him to stop because he was enjoying himself so much. But for the last two hours I could hardly breathe and I didn't want to have that experience ever again.

Still Langer's piece was thoughtful, sensitive and absorbing (if only up to a point). So it saddened me when sometime later Langer wrote a blistering review, in *Ms.*, of Kate Millett's *Flying*. In *Flying* Millett writes about her life in and around the feminist and radical movements after *Sexual Politics* was published. I thought Millett's book was extraordinary in many ways and I could not understand why Langer was so fevered in her attack. Though written in a style much different from her own, I thought Langer would be excited to see a work that covered a similar terrain of feeling and experience. In retrospect I now see Langer's attack as a warning. The Rebel Artist or, as in Langer's case, The Rebel Journalist Political Activist will all too often have a need to obliterate someone as subterranean and deeply subversive as Millett. Particularly if that person is a contemporary. Another thing about Langer's review is that it foreshadowed the mean spirited, punitive social criticism of postvisionary thinkers like Jean Bethke Elshtain and Christopher Back-Lasch. Millett's book was a powerful evocation of pain, confusion, social dislocation as well as explosive sexuality and transcendent vision, and the best Langer could say was that it was self-indulgent and narcissistic. And her fury was unrelenting.

While on the subject. As well as retreating into cultural conservatism many of the postvisionary thinkers (I'm not quite sure where Back-Lasch and Elshtain fit in here) upset with societies such as Cuba and Vietnam, frightened by Soviet power and stories of the Gulag, as they are by the revealed horrors of the Pol Pot regime, have started to sound more and more like the left wing of the State Department. They now, for instance, think it is right to support an armed Europe to protect against Soviet hegemony. So at the same time all too many radicals are still pushing strong support for worldwide authoritarian political movements, our new social democrats are busy proposing elaborate military strategies for the U.S. government. In fact some recent articles in *Telos* sound like Defense Department manuals. Thus from all sides an independent radical movement that speaks deeply to people's yearnings and hopes is made to appear unrealistic and irrelevant.

Works of Introspection, Yearning and Hope (which I have read or which have been read to me):

Though many of the works I am referring to here are very different from each other they have several things in common. They cut through conventional patterns of thought and feeling. They often take very independent positions on delicate moral questions and they open up areas of imagination, sensibility and experience that are often viewed as idiosyncratic or off limits. In essence what puts them all together is a unique measure of passion, courage and integrity.

Some of the authors are well known; others are not. All should be paid attention to.

Oilers and Sweepers by George Dennison; *Women and Dualism* by Lynda Glennon; the *Heresies Sex Issue; The Sweet Trap of Daughterhood* by Lucy Gilbert and Paula Webster; *I Looked over Jordan* by Ernie Brill; "The Bar as Microcosm" by Shulamith Firestone; *A Company of Queens* by Karen Lindsey; Noam Chomsky on the Middle East; "Power, Sexuality, and Intimacy" by Muriel Dimen; *Common Ground* by Gerald Williams, drawings by Ben-Zion Schecter; occasional essays by Igal Roodenko or David McReynolds in the War Resistors' newsletter. *Many Hands*, a gathering of Sephardic songs and proverbs selected and translated by Stephen Levy.

Poetry: Louise Rader, Irving Wexler, Judith Ghinger, Jean Ovitt, Jill Janows, Daniel Berrigan; Social Criticism: Marilyn Kaggen, Gene Brown, Frank Castranova, Sohnya Sayres, Mark Blumberg, Marlene Nadle, Nancy Fraser, Bernard Tuchman, Martin Blatt, James Stoller, Nancy Anderson, Ann Barr Snitow, Connie Peretz, Martin Duberman; Fiction: Norman Alster, Carol Rosenthal, Lynda Schorr, Jane Lazarre, Jim Magnuson, Marilyn Coffey, Carol Ascher, Greta Nemiroff, Kate Ellis, Dexter Guerriere, Joyce Johnson, Alix Kates Shulman, Carey Cammeron; Theory of Sexuality: Pete Wilson, Charles Pitts, Carol Vance, Gayle Rubin, Charlie Shively, Pat Califia, Chantal Bruchez.

Offerings from the multiculture

ERNIE BRILL

There is a great body of literature that grew directly and indirectly out of the 60s, particularly from the civil rights and black liberation movements. This long list of superior writers includes John O. Killens, John A. Williams, Margaret Walker, Alice Walker, Ronald Fair, James Allen McPherson, Ernest Gaines, Ishmael Reed, Toni Cade Bambara, Alice Childress. Many of these writers are not that well known, mainly because they are black and they write fiction. Their fiction reverberates with history and life, using a multitude of styles. Anyone wishing to read 1) plain fine writing, 2) glimpse the black experience in America and obtain (hopefully) a deeper understanding, 3) get a feel of the "period of the 60s"—would do well to read the works of these writers.

Some of the novels deal directly with "struggle." Margaret Walker's *Jubilee* is one of the finest American historical novels about slavery, the Civil War and reconstruction. John A. Williams' *The Man Who Cried I Am*, rivetingly deals with an insidious plot that makes the CIA look like nothing. The Southern civil rights movement (seemingly now historically buried) is beautifully and poignantly explored in such work as Alice Walker's *Meridian*, Ronald Fair's *Many Thousands Gone*, John O. Killen's *Youngblood*, Toni Cade Bambara's *The Salteaters*, and Ernest Gaines' novels *The Autobiography of Miss Jean Pittman*, *In My Father's House*, and William Mahoney's *Black Jacob*. Urban revolt and ghetto rebellion are sharply shown in Ronald Fair's classic *Hog Butcher*, and Henry Dumas' scintillating story "Strike and Fade" in his collection *Ark of Bones*.

Broader than political categories are two of the finest short story collections of the last thirty years—James Allen McPherson's *Hue and Cry* and Toni Cade Bambara's *Gorilla, My Love*. I consider both collections indispensable for any American writer, as well as for anyone wishing to read fresh, startling language.

For a continued assault and rediscovery involving American cultural values, I'd recommend the entire body of work by Ishmael Reed, one of our foremost satirists, particularly *Mumbo Jumbo* (hilarious and devastating), and *Flight To Canada*.

I would also say that the black liberation and civil rights movements spurred publishing to bring out more work by black writers—for sundry reasons including profit (there was a demand), and there might even have been some people in the industry who could recognize good writing when they saw it.

Included in this was the *re*publishing of work by black writers, including three superlative novels dealing with race and class: William Attaway's *Blood on the Forge*, Chester Himes' *If He Hollers Let Him Go*, and Arna Bontemps' *Black Thunder*. In addition, there was reprinted the enormous, stunning *The Negro Caravan*, a one thousand page plus anthology of black fiction, poetry, drama and essays originally put out by the Federal Writers Project, and edited by Arthur P. Davis, Ulysses S. Lee and Sterling A. Brown. Brown himself, one of our country's most unknown and formidable men of letters, had his own out-of-print poetry reprinted—*Southern Road*, an amazing collection of poems (recently included in the *Collected Poems* of Sterling A. Brown).

Between the reprinting and new publishing, a whole spectrum of first rate works grew and circulated, much of it still remaining (a lot of it though is out of print). This includes a multitude of themes and styles: family life (Toni Morrison's *Sula*, Alice Childress' *A Hero Ain't Nothin' But A Sandwich*), womanhood (Gayl Jones' *Corregidora*), manhood (Wesley Brown's *Tragic Magic*), war novels (John A. Williams' *Captain Blackman*, John O. Killens' *And Then We Heard the Thunder*).

II

Other remarkable reading experiences include finding in the mid 60s Carlos Fuentes' *The Death of Artemio Cruz*, and the work of Miguel Angel Asturias, winner of the 1967 Nobel Prize, and author of *El Senor Presidente*, and the Banana Trilogy concerning United Fruit: *The Cyclone (The Strong Wind)*, *The Green Pope*, and *The Eyes of the Interred*.

The 60s helped revive a sense of internationalism, and to an extent, helped bring works of other writers to the American reading public, including such Latin American writers as Fuentes, and Asturias, as well as such African writers as Ousmane Sembene, Chinua Achebe and Dennis Brutus. (Their work can be ordered directly from Heineman African Writers Series, 4 Front St., Exeter, New Hampshire.) There have, since then, also been many excellent anthologies including *Fragments of A Lost Diary: Women of Asia, Africa, and Latin America* edited by Naomi Katz and Nancy Milton; *Political Spider* ed. by Ulli Beier, and *Giant Talk* edited by Quincey Troupe and Rainer Schulte.

The 60s also revived a general interest in "socially relevant" literature. Some fine proletarian 30s literature was republished, including the classic down-and-out novel, *Waiting For Nothing* by Tom Kromer, now out of print and waiting to be picked up by some astute publisher. And when B. Traven passed away, with a typical bizarre American/literary neocrophilia, he was then (safely dead) made into a cult, and republished.

Other writers I consider 60s writers (either they finally got published then, or recognized, or that's when I read 'em) are Phillip Levine (*Not This Pig*), David Henderson (*The Mayor of Harlem, Loweast*) Marge Piercy, Sol Yurick, whose novel *The Bag* remains one of the more ambitious, tumultuous and risky urban novels; and Dan Georakas, author of *Detroit: I Do Mind Dying*.

Lastly there remains those of us profoundly influenced by the civil rights, antiwar, national liberation and student movements. Many of the above writers are still writing. The themes remain (it's not a question here of "decades"). There are many other writers writing in small presses. Some of the best work is yet to arrive.

Anyone would do well to keep an eye out for new work by the following writers: Steve Cannon, Janice Mirikitani, Fay Chang, Robert Roth, Jan Clausen, Wesley Brown, Pedro Pietri.

P.S. Final note: all the novels in the essay are either still in print or available in libraries (to my knowledge). Read them while you still can before the subtle U.S. cultural apartheid deepens further. For anyone interested in reading and pursuing the question of racism in American publishing, they can begin with the following: John A. Williams interview with Chester Himes "My Man Himes" in *Flashbacks* by John A. Williams; "Cultural Hegemony: The Southern White Writer and American Letters" by Addison Gayle in his book *The Black Situation*; Sterling Stuckey's introduction to Sterling A. Brown's *Southern Road*; Ishmael Reed's introduction to the anthology *19 Necromancers From Now*; John A. Williams' latest novel: *Clicksong*.

Women's terms

KAREN LINDSEY

The books that have been most important to me—as a feminist, as a leftist, as a believer in social and spiritual change—have been those that translate the reality we've been handed by generations of male minds into women's terms. Elizabeth Fisher's *Woman's Creation* does this, as does Merlin Stone's *When God Was a Woman*—and though the books contradict each other in ways I find totally confusing, I love them both. I am enormously impressed by the work of two dear friends of mine, Lisa Leghorn and Katherine Parker: their book, *Woman's Worth*, looks at women in cultures around the world and shows that "capitalist," "communist," and "socialist" are words that describe men's lives, and that women's economic lives fall into different categories, systems in which we have "minimal," "token," or "negotiating" power.

This exploration of women's culture, existing apart from the realities of the lives of the men who have lived with us, controlled us, and often literally owned us, is one of the aspects of feminism I find most crucial, and feminist historians are also addressing it. I am excited by the books that have followed in the wake of Carroll Smith Rosenberg's brilliant 1975 essay, "The Female World of Love and Ritual: Relations between Women in Nineteenth Century America"—books that wade through letters and diaries and show us that the myth of superior male bonding is a lie, that women have loved and cherished and supported each other as deeply as any Damon and Pythias or Jonathan and David. I love the feminist biographies that reinterpret the lives of women men have allowed to become famous; I love the reissues of works by women who have been allowed to slip into obscurity. Charlotte Perkins Gilman's *Women and Economics* was reissued in 1966, though the male-dominated left managed to ignore it: again, she redefined economic concepts from a woman-centered viewpoint, and, though she called herself a socialist, hers was a socialism based on a female principle. Similarly, her Utopian novel *Herland* was reprinted in 1975, showing us a mythical all-female world in which violence is unheard of, all women are mothers to all children, and all women do other, important work besides mothering, and in which, when men come into the picture, a form of marriage is introduced which is at once monogamous and nonpossessive.

What I'm most excited about right now is the growing body of feminist literature on spirituality and psychic skills—again involving much reinterpretation of material passed down through male channels. There are books reinterpreting the Tarot, astrology, witchcraft, meditation, psychic healing, all from a feminist perspective—or rather, from a variety of feminist perspectives. Except for the Catholic left, with its male god and its opposition to abortion, I don't see much spirituality, and certainly even less spiritual quest, in the left, which has been dominated by what seems to me an increasingly barren rationalist/materialist vision. Sally Gearhart's *The Wanderground* is a feminist utopian novel that makes an interesting companion piece to *Herland*. Its psychic women are actively engaged in concrete political struggle against the men who live far away, in "the City," and who rape and kill the City's women. She provides an image of the union of political action with spirituality which is often lacking in feminist spirituality. Diane Mariechild's *Motherwit* uses an eclectic and nondogmatic approach to psychic and spiritual skills—it also avoids the separatism which I find a drawback in much feminist spirituality literature.

All these works shift the prism and help us to look at reality in terms of women's experiences. They are major steps toward erasing the universal "he" that has crippled women, and dehumanized men, for so long.

If Ralph Ellison's novel of the 40s, *Invisible Man*, is indicative of black awareness of ourselves as a people not only in the 40s but again in 1983, I would much prefer the 60s' high visibility of *The Autobiography of Malcolm X* or Sam Yette's *The Choice*. I felt more visible in the 60s, not so much to myself, but to others. Much of this visibility came from the literature of the time, it was all in the air; swirling about in the political climate of that decade, you could see it.

I was a teenager in the 60s. Where many of today's kids spend their time in video arcades or in front of the television, I spent mine at civil rights rallies, antiwar demonstrations, or reading. The world of Frantz Fanon, Carlos Castaneda's multiple tales of the sorcerer Don Juan, the African fables of Amos Tutuola, James Ngugi, Alice Walker's *The Third Life of Grange Copeland*, Ismael Reed, Henry Dumas, Toni Morrison's *The Bluest Eye*—I saw myself and my people in these books and countless more; is it any wonder that I was enlightened?

Most definitely the 60s made me a writer, for they taught me the power of the word as well as the sword. My vision was formed by what I saw, experienced, and read. My understanding of the world came as much from reading Garcia Marquez's *100 Years of Solitude*, Leroi Jones's *The Dutchman*, and the poetry of June Jordan and Sonia Sanchez than it did from Marx, Lenin, and Mao. Radical and underground literature of the time had its effect too; I came to learn how to blend fact and rhetoric effectively, and not to be afraid to take risks. We were moving toward a collective vision then—it is sorely missed.

I love Ellison's *Invisible Man* dearly, but I do not want to be him, nor do I want in the 80s to live with him, underground.

Overcoming the memory

PAUL BUHLE

Back in the late 30s, when the communist-based left reached its peak influence amidst the CIO union drive and the popular antifascist sentiment, veteran radicals in *their* thirties and forties experienced a strange mixed feeling. They basically welcomed the renewal of a mass movement such as they had not known in some twenty years. They could at last taste the freedom of opinion when large numbers of workers, intellectuals and ordinary people outside the left ghettoes believed in the doom of capitalism and the need (if not the inevitability) of some cooperative solution. A precious moment, even with the clouds of fascism and war descending in Europe and Asia. Still, it was not the same as 1917. They were older. And the sense of grandeur evident would not return, not as it had been when the Russian Revolution had been fresh, when Western Europeans were seemingly ready to rise up, when the 1919 Seattle General Strike figuratively met the bohemianism of Greenwich Village-style free love, women's emancipation, anarchism and syndicalism.

At the present, this expectation and nostalgia remains the most optimistic meaning of the 60s for the generation shaped by it, and the prime reason for the paucity and poverty of literature about the vivid and almost inexplicable decade. A few years ago, I sent out a hundred or so requests for contributions to a symposium on the Culture of the Sixties and its enduring significance. The results — recorded in *Cultural Correspondence,* #12 (Summer, 1981)—barely scratch the surface of the dark moods, replies I received with disheartening apologies for inability to deal with the source of anxiety. The past weighs like a nightmare upon the present, Marx wrote in *The Eighteenth Brumaire*; it is the pastness of the 60s vision, not only the enduring of the 70s nightmare even into another era which stifles creative response.

Veterans of lost causes incline to see themselves as victims of pitiless fate. The Me Decade inevitably turned expectations, already dwindling, steadily inward. When the smoke had cleared from the final fires of resistance, individuals began to measure themselves for personal survival, continuity, self-definition of worthwhileness. To be harsh, more than a few began identifying themselves with their vitae. Many took self-satisfaction in finishing a book, or getting tenure so they could continue teaching, or moving toward the top of a local union or social agency structure. What else were they supposed to do? The ultimate goal, revolution, socialism, receded further and further. Their institutions and immediate lives—friends, co-workers, family, lovers—became a lot more real and apparently permanent. I say "apparently" because they never quite lost the feeling of transience, and not only because of the nuclear cloud overhanging every personal gain. They had been exiled from the Aquarian Age and could not help viewing the excesses of the present as telltale signs of a Fool's Paradise. The increasing abstractness of their politically formative years left the most prolific monograph writers in American left history helpless before the task of reconsidering their own lives as part of history.

They also began to doubt their own recollections, and here the historic parallel to the 1910s generation becomes painfully relevant again. That earlier Innocent Age spawned much inchoate nostalgia during the following decades, disputed claims between communists, Trotskyists and aesthetes about the franchise of the legacy, and after a while some rich autobiographical literature. By the 40s the lines had become set. On the one side, popularizers, critics and finally movie-makers came to celebrate the adventure of the era for its own sake, personality development the true result when all the political possibilities had been squeezed out. Warren Beatty has since visualized that interpretation unforgettably. On the other side, sniping scholars follow sectarian political treatment in blaming the same personality for the failure of the vintage radicals to become serious agents of change. As described in *Rebels in Bohemia* (Univ. of N. Carolina Press: 1982) by Leslie Fishbein, intellectuals psychoanalyze reputations, study the retreat of post-1920 lives and come to the conclusion that these talented youngsters after all lacked the stuff to build anything solid for the long haul.

Will this be the fate of the 60s, when the last doddering veterans of political and cultural militants can only whisper a few words into the camera? The possibility is real. But if I do not think so, it is because the evidence of *negation* has become so overwhelming in the last few years; by doing for the 60s what the survivors themselves still cannot, the rebel interpreters reveal the seeds of the past's overcoming.

Let me start back in the beginning, with the insight that a generation possessed and then forgot. I can recall with almost intolerable vividness the spirit of alienation in the cold war late 50s. The guiding determination of the Beats, to write stories and poems *against the world*, possessed a spiritual charm all out of proportion to their political or social significance. Jazz, blues and folkish revivals caught a musical strain, as the then-secret society of campus drugs offered escape from a tedious epoch. Young women from small midwestern towns could be seen in black leotards and long hair; however conformist in their own, neo-bohemian fashion, they had the merit of extreme seriousness as if always prepared to answer Jack Kerouac's question, "What does life mean to you?" Diane DiPrima, whose key volume *Dinners and Nightmares* appeared as late as 1962, spoke for them in a certain way—drawn and repelled from the existing left, drawn and repelled likewise from the male society which ruled beat aesthetics. They would be heard from again. The boys they lived with (I was one) picked up the *Evergreen Review*, read the little left-wing arts magazines like *Streets* and *City Lights Journal* then beginning to be produced if they were lucky enough to live in New York or San Francisco, and considered themselves desperate poets of existence whether they could write a word, play a musical note, actually smoke a joint with pleasure or not.

All this is well-known. But another, subtler element had a role far outside the *avant-garde*. Those of us who had grown up on the auto-critique of popular culture in the early *Mad Comics*, Spike Jones and Bob and Ray grasped hungrily for genius satirist Harvey Kurtzman's final magazine, *Help!* In its pages germinated already the beginnings of the Underground Comix and the underground press generally. College humor magazines, for all their blatant sexism, also had an influence: they too reflected nihilism within the popular vein. Without the vague discontent, less articulated but wider and perhaps also ultimately deeper than the dissipated 50s bohemianism or the small if potent subculture of the red diaper left, the 60s as we know them would never have happened.

The evidence has mostly been mislaid or repressed. The Bell & Howell microfilm series of underground papers is atrociously unselective, but contains some of the most interesting material of the 60s available nevertheless. *The Rag* (from Austin), *East Village Other* (New York), *Connections* (Madison), *Express Times* (San Francisco) and hundreds of others tell us something that no account has yet captured: the explosion of creativity at the local level, poetry, graphics and layout overwhelming the prose message with a popular art form, sold on the street, as near to a manifestation of the local constituency's state of mind as any journalism will ever be. The shattering of the apparent consensus on such issues as the war, student power, drugs, black power, etc., made the earlier civil rights crusade—but also small-scale bohemianism and politically inchoate wildcat strikes—all a prelude for conflict across the society. To look deeper than the existing, institutional histories of the new left is to seek the subjectivity which embraced the various aspects of dissent. I believe it to be the search for an America the diverse rebels could call their own. Serious and lazy, politicos and hippies, the searched turned up more than could be possibly absorbed: from the forgotten radicalisms of the national past to Native American soothsayers, neighborhood bar life of the working class (first seen as forbidden territory, with some of the excitement ghetto nightlife had a decade earlier) to the agrarian-communal promise, hardly a well could be found deep enough where they failed to catch a glimpse of a family visage looking up at them.

At least that is the conclusion I drew at the time. My *Radical America 15th Anniversary Anthology* (May–June, 1982) recalls the attempt to press upon a diffuse and explosive movement the importance of grasping tradition, not just instinctually but self-consciously and with the wisdom only hard thought can provide. No doubt we had too little maturity ourselves for the necessary reflection. In any case, time ran out.

And yet something remained. The women's movement carried forward, for a few years at least, the quintessence of the insight that transformation meant a basic change in cultural attitudes and personal relationships. (Mari Jo Buhle's annotated bibliography, *Women and the American Left, a Guide to Sources*, G.K. Hall, 1983, covers the field of analysis, poetry, fiction, etc., for the period up to 1982). And in the obverse image of commercial popular culture, as David Marc says in the *Cultural Correspondence* issue cited above, Norman Lear emerged as the Emile Zola of the small screen precisely upon the legacy of the vanished decade. We learn as much about the implications of the 60s by looking at vintage *All in the Family*, *M*A*S*H*, or even *Mork and Mindy* as at television documentaries of social unrest in the Vietnam footage years. The same could be said for *Cutter's Way* or for Ursula Le Guinn's anthropological-feminist novels like *The Dispossessed* or *The Left Hand of Darkness*: the familiar American themes of uncertain utopia, of bitter disillusionment and berserk individualist revenge upon the corrupters had found new reverberations, along with the quasi-isolationist connection of war with big government and the vague hope for a pluralist democratic order.

The rapidly aging new left militants saw this spectre of neo-commercialism—when they could stand to see it at all—with a confused sense of accomplishment and loss. The generation coming on would be less equivocal. As the high factotum of the Church of the Sub-Genius says:

> The Sixties didn't work at *all*. They were just a kind of decoy to make us think everything would get *solved* eventually. Sure, they made everyone "hip". . . . Why, by 1975, a majority of Americans and Europeans were, if not totally "groovy," at least enough so that most men could shake hands without wiping the inferior germs off on their pant-legs. We had a whole new breed of "Moderately Long Haired People" in the '70s, a white-washed promiscuous breed that reduced the boiling-point of the Sixties down to simmer . . . a simmer which, thanks to the conspiracy that had those soon-to-be disco beatniks under control *from the word go*, will soon lurch forward again . . . it isn't the pressure of NOW that's responsible, it's our own past negligence: it's because those PINKS buried their heads in the narco-sand of the Seventies and procrastinated coping with a *hostile environment* that won't *slow down and stop changing*. . . .
>
> [from *The Stark Fist of Removal,* Spring, 1982]

This a slightly satirical way of stating the obvious. While erstwhile cultural revolutionaries moved on in their lives and careers, 70s graduates understandably looked upon mainstream radicaliberalism with a jaundiced, drug-reddened eye. *Their* explorations for alternatives to academic socialism and vanguard factionalism had to deny the illusions of the 60s, to leap over the decade or consciously negate it.

Paradoxical as it may seem, the compulsion of a younger group for a definitive (and not merely abstract) negation brought their artists further into the subjective logic of the beast, not the grand imperial schemes the new left scholars charted but the reflexive, almost dream-state creation and sales of commodities, the hidden links of manipulated sex and military symbols, the stark raving lunacy which the 60s never totally confronted. Reading free punk throwaway tabloids like Berkeley's *Twisted Times*, plug-zines like *Inside Joke*, and morbid-humor creations by 60s carryovers like R. Crumb (*Weirdo*) and Art Spiegelmann (*RAW Magazine*) offers a distinctly different, and necessary, way of re-examining the ultimate meaning of the lost decade. [See Crumb's "I Remember the Sixties," *Weirdo* #4].

"That there is no longer a folk does not mean . . . as the romantics propagated, that the masses are worse," Theodore Adorno wrote in *Minima Moralia*. "Rather, it is precisely in the new, radically alienated form of society that the untruth of the old is first being revealed." Truly an apt insight for us today. But the proposition can be turned around, too. Grappling with the many-times-removed, corrupted but vital descendants of folk culture amongst the tangled vines of our era allows a way back to hidden roots, and from there to begin the revolutionary project anew.

Murray kempton

GENE BROWN

In the 1960s, when I would see *New York Post* columnist Murray Kempton at political demonstrations, I was struck by what seemed to be his perpetual expression of mild bewilderment and incredulity, as if everything he saw gave him cause to wonder. In retrospect that was perhaps not a bad way for a writer to look.

Kempton's was a unique voice. He combined the perspective of Karl Marx with a knowledge of the social role and moral significance of character and manners that would have pleased Jane Austen. Of the conservative white middle class support for an independent candidate in a New York City mayoralty election, he wrote: "Most of them are small homeowners and they are shabby and no longer young, the defeated people who work hard for a living."

I think my love for Kempton's writing redeemed my early politics; to this day it allays some embarrassment I feel about my younger self. I was in college from 1960 to 1964. In those years English professors, still possessed by the new criticism, were mining texts for symbols as anteaters poke for food; social scientists and historians were already substituting models and statistics for critical thought. Early on I learned to play their game, although my heart wasn't in it; similarly, my politics were conventionally liberal—unconnected to any immediate feelings I had about the way I lived. But my mind was skewed and quirky enough to be stirred (and often stunned) by Kempton.

Kempton was briefly a member of the National Maritime Union and his early writing often focused on labor issues. In *Part of Our Time: Some Ruins and Monuments of the Thirties* (1955), actually a "series of novellas" about radicals who became communists and others who didn't, there are some beautiful passages and acute observations about the kind of people who "set out to be redeemers and end up either policemen or the targets of policemen." Kempton rued his own dalliance with the party (his first public act was to resign), and the book has, in retrospect, perhaps too much of the confessional and breast-beating tone of *The God That Failed*—although in all parts it is more interesting, if only because of Kempton's extraordinary prose.

Murray Kempton left the *Post* for a brief stint on *The New Republic* in the early 1960's, returning to the paper in the middle of the decade. *America Comes of Middle Age* (1963) is a collection of his earlier *Post* columns. In *The Briar Patch: The People of the State of New York v. Lumumba Shakur Et Al.,* Kempton wrote a sensitive and much-acclaimed account of the Panther 21 trial. In recent years he has appeared often in *The*

New York Review of Books and regularly in *Newsday*, the Long Island newspaper.

Looking at the yellowed clippings of his old *Post* columns, it occurs to me that what was striking in his writing was not any one idea or position but rather a willingness to observe and take in with every faculty, scrutinize every statement and stance and delicately balance irony and objectivity with engagement. When he had it all working he wrote with the passion of Gene Debs in the style of Dr. Johnson and Edmund Burke. It made for a marvelous tension. You had to read his pieces slowly because his singular angle of vision hardly ever focused on what you thought it would; besides, you wanted to savor the words.

"He is not a man I cherish," Kempton once wrote of Richard Nixon, "but there is in the sight of him the painful recognition that something human somewhere is being cruelly violated and humiliated." After such a perception, is our knowledge of Nixon's other attributes complete without this essential truth? Some have confused this almost compulsive need to look for the humanity in our more repulsive public figures with sentimentality. But it is, I think, a proper concern of those who would preserve their own humanity. Regular, attentive contact with such a sensibility, as with the reading of great literature, helps raise one's level of awareness. Kempton was not likely to get you to like Richard Nixon (you had no reason to); but you were also less likely, having read Kempton, to acquiesce in the future in reeducation camps or get sappy over "people's" democracies.

Doris lessing

SUSAN OSBORN

When I was sixteen, I was hostile, aggressive, resentful. I was working on a paper titled " A Loss of Touch with Reality: The Biochemical Etiology of Schizophrenia" and keeping a journal. It was in the 60s, when I was sixteen, that someone who knew me rather well suggested that I read *The Golden Notebook*. He said it was the work of an exile.

I was not familiar with Doris Lessing and had not read any of her novels (*The Grass is Singing, The Children of Violence*), or her stories (*The Habit of Loving, A Man and Two Women, African Stories*), or her autobiographical documentary (*In Pursuit of the English*). But—did I neglect to mention?—it was in the late 60s, when I was sixteen, that I was feeling somewhat confused, and struggling to make some sense of my life. Reading had already been established as a solace to me.

When I opened the covers of Lessing's titanic volume, I found Anna Wulf, a writer with a block, a woman who was unable to shape her experience into a whole. By writing four different notebooks (the black about her past in Southern Rhodesia, the red about her involvement with the Communist Party, the yellow in which she tries to understand her former relationship with Michael through the fictionalized personae of Ella and Paul, and the blue in which she details the facts of her everyday experiences), Anna tries to see herself from various points of view, and by so doing, to find a way of bringing the disparate parts of her self together. She is attempting, through a highly intellectualized compartmentalization to find a way of ordering her personal identity. On a deeper level, Anna is trying to decipher the relation between fiction, fact and truth.

But as Anna discovers, the more she writes, the more she dichotomizes, the more the truth of her experience eludes her written words: it eludes the reconstituted past of the black notebook, the political analyses of the red, the fiction of the yellow, and the everyday account of the blue. Anna's mental dissolution begins when she realizes that her "facts" as well as her "fictions" are "failures."

"Words mean nothing. They have become, *when I think*, not the form into which experience is shaped, but a series of meaningless sounds, like nursery talk. . . . It occurs to me that what is happening is a breakdown of me. . . . For words are form, and if I am at a pitch where shape, form, expression are nothing, then I am nothing, for it has become clear to me, reading the notebooks, that I remain Anna because of a certain kind of intelligence. This intelligence is dissolving and I am very frightened."

It is only after Anna's collapse that she realizes that words (her "intelligence") are inadequate to capture her total experience—she cannot "cage truth." As Lessing wrote in her preface (published ten years after *The Golden Notebook*), Anna's "crack-up" is her way of "dismissing" the "false dichotomies" she has tried to impose on herself. It is only after her journey into formlessness that Anna can, to some extent, allow her experience to go beyond her ability to verbalize, and by the final pages of the book, Anna accepts, to a certain degree, the shapelessness of her experience.

(It was only upon rereading *The Golden Notebook* a decade later that I understood that Lessing's form deliberately blurs the distinctions between fiction, fact and truth. *The Golden Notebook* is actually about three writers: Lessing the author is writing about a novelist Anna who in turn is writing about a writer named Ella. Ella's facts are Anna's fictions, just as Anna's facts are Lessing's fictions. Although the book is compartmentalized, full comprehension is dependent upon recognition of the merging of various kinds of experience, of the obfuscating of boundaries, of, in effect, the indivisibility of experience. It does not now seem strange to me that when Anna's block dissolves, she feels that she can best express her own feelings and experience through her fiction writing.)

While I continue to question the transcendence through disintegration paradigm presaged in *The Golden Notebook* and explored in *The Four-Gated City, The Summer Before the Dark, The Memoirs of a Survivor,* and *Briefing for a Descent Into Hell*), this—for Lessing—invariably systematic if Sufistic reintegration and renewal that may be consummated in the *Canopus in Argos: Archives* series (*Shikasta* et. al.), it was Doris Lessing who made it easier for me, as a girl of sixteen and a woman of thirty, to accept the enormity of my own need for form and meaning. For that, I will always be indebted.

Thomas pynchon

JOHN KRAFFT

Cultural historians of the 1960s have, so far, largely ignored the works of Thomas Pynchon. This fact may say something about Pynchon, but I think it says something about current scholarship instead. Pynchon's novels—*V.* (1963), *The Crying of Lot 49* (1966), and *Gravity's Rainbow* (1973)—are hybrids which do not fit neatly into familiar critical categories. Some critics, overwhelmed, puzzled, and/or bored by the novels, dismiss them as "sports." Updike and Bellow on the one hand, Gass and Barthelme on the other, seem much more decorous and manageable. But Pynchon's work is neither mere realism nor pure formalism; it might be called experimental historical fiction.

During the past six or seven years, critics have begun to appreciate the centrality of Pynchon's concern with twentieth-century and all of American history. One rarely nowadays hears the shibboleth, "All those black-humorists think history is bunk," which used to forestall serious inquiry into Pynchon's historical interests. But few critics have directly engaged Pynchon's passionate engagement with the 60s, an engagement which is not public, like Mailer's, nor as flamboyant perhaps, but which is no less provocative. Of course, history aside, Pynchon's works are complex, erudite and allusive enough to occupy generations of those Pynchon calls explicators and masturbators, who have indeed been hard at it discussing thermodynamics, information theory, calculus, alchemy, plastics, movies, Rilke, Pavlov, and God. Much of this scholarship is fascinating and useful, but much of it is self-limiting, trite, or just plain bad criticism, often on account of too myopic a concentration on content.

Formalist criticism has proven to be indispensable to an adequate understanding of Pynchon's work, but it does not get at all there is to Pynchon. Certainly his language is one of his subjects, the informing one, but only one of them. Thus, it is not, after all, so much simple history which concerns Pynchon as it is historiography, which is both a subject and a strategy of his novels. Pynchon's novels do not present mere canned history; they present characters who must discover and make their own histories in order not to remain somnolent victims of, for example, others' political/commerical versions of history and the dissolution or annihilation these threaten. The characters' history-making resembles Pynchon's fiction-making; both may be somewhat idiosyncratic, but are not solipsistic.

Consider *The Crying of Lot 49*. The heroine, Oedipa Maas, begins as a Tupperware-party-goer and Young Republican, rather passive and self-absorbed. But she is impelled on a literary/historical quest in the process of executing a will. Having "undergone her . . . educating at a time of nerves, blandness and retreat" in the 50s, "mothered over" in "her so temperate youth" by "dear, daft numina" like Dulles and McCarthy, she is "unfit, perhaps, for marches and sit-ins, but just a whiz at pursuing strange words in Jacobean texts." She is warned that she could waste her life in arid scholarship "and never touch the truth," and perhaps she heeds the warning: perhaps not. Intermittently at least, the word she seeks seems to be "the cry that might abolish the night"—the night of the contemporary American nightmare of paranoia, alienation, betrayal, waste and death. "This is America. You live in it. You let it happen. . . ." Yet "how had it ever happened here, with the chances once so good for diversity?" Though she gains profound, poignantly lyrical insight into the problem, Oedipa is not sure she can find a remedy, or even an escape. She is also given to hesitation about, if not retreat from, her insight, for she knows that words are both "a thrust at truth and a lie," and cannot be sure whether she is apprehending *the* world or projecting *a* world. Her insight may be the product of true vision, or it may be that of self-delusion or hoax; Oedipa is too tough-minded (as is Pynchon) to settle for a merely hypothetical insight, though "if there was just America, then it seemed the only way she could continue and manage to be at all relevant to it was as an alien, unfurrowed, assumed full circle into some paranoia"—"the orbiting ecstasy of a true paranoia." At the end of the novel, she is still poised, waiting. The fact remains, however, that in doing literary history, Oedipa has been compelled to do European and American history, and has been enabled thereby to re-envision and perhaps also actually to reinherit America. The rest of us, too, might do far worse than to risk reinheriting America by doing literary history.

The following list of Pynchon criticism is highly selective. Limitations of scope and space here require some regrettable, nonjudgmental omissions. (Thorough current bibliographies appear regularly in *Pynchon Notes*.) 0-3 asterisk annotations roughly indicate the works' relative importance or usefulness for the study of Pynchon's novels from a variety of critical perspectives.

BOOKS

***Levine, George, and David Leverenz, eds. *Mindful Pleasures: Essays on Thomas Pynchon*. Boston: Little, Brown, 1976.

**Mendelson, Edward, ed. *Pynchon: A Collection of Critical Essays*. Englewood Cliffs, NJ: Prentice-Hall, 1978.

**Pearce, Richard, ed. *Critical Essays on Thomas Pynchon*. Boston: G.K. Hall, 1981.

***Schaub, Thomas H. *Pynchon: The Voice of Ambiguity*. Urbana: Univ. of Illinois Press, 1981.

**Ames, Sanford S. "Pynchon and Visible Language: Ecriture." *International Fiction Review*, 4 (1977), 170–73.

**Baxter, Charles. "De-faced America: *The Great Gatsby* and *The Crying of Lot 49*." *Pynchon Notes*, 7 (1981), 22–37.

***Black, Joel D. "Probing a Post-Romantic Paleontology: Thomas Pynchon's *Gravity's Rainbow*." *Boundary 2*, 8, No. 2 (1980), 229–54.

**Braudy, Leo. "Providence, Paranoia, and the Novel." *ELH*, 48, No. 3 (1981), 619–37. (619, 625, 627, 629–37)

**Cowart, David. "Cinematic Auguries of the Third Reich in *Gravity's Rainbow*." *Literature/Film Quarterly*, 6, No. 4 (1978), 364–70.

**Davidson, Cathy N. "Oedipa as Androgyne in Thomas Pynchon's *The Crying of Lot 49*." *Contemporary Literature*, 18, No. 1 (1977), 38–50.

Dickstein, Morris. "Black Humor and History: The Early Sixties." In *Gates of Eden: American Culture in the Sixties*. New York: Basic Books, 1977, 91–127. (passim)

***Duyfhuizen, Bernard. "Starry-Eyed Semiotics: Learning to Read Slothrop's Map and *Gravity's Rainbow*." *Pynchon Notes*, 6 (1981), 5–33.

**Gilbert-Rolfe, Jeremy, and John Johnston. "*Gravity's Rainbow* and the *Spiral Jetty*." Part 1: *October,* 1 (1976), 65–85; Part 2: *October,* 2 (1976), 71–90; Part 3; *October*, 3 (1977), 90–102.

**Greenburg, Alvin. "The Underground Woman: An Excursion into the V-ness of Thomas Pynchon." *Chelsea*, 27 (1969), 58–65.

**Greiner, Donald J. "Fiction as History, History as Fiction: The Reader and Thomas Pynchon's *V.*" *South Carolina Review*, 10, No. 1 (1977), 4–18.

**Hollander, Charles. "Pynchon's Inferno." *Cornell Alumni News*, Nov. 1978, 24–30.

**Kermode, Frank. "Decoding the Trystero." Rpt. in Mendelson, ed., above, 162–66.

*Kolodny, Annette, and Daniel James Peters. "Pynchon's *The Crying of Lot 49*: The Novel as Subversive Experience." *Modern Fiction Studies*, 19, No. 1 (1973), 79–87.

*Levine, George, "Risking the Moment: Anarchy and Possibility in Pychon's Fiction." In Levine and Leverenz, eds., above, 113–36.

***Mackey, Louis. "Paranoia, Pynchon, and Preterition." *Sub-Stance*, 30 (1981), 16–30.

*McConnell, Frank D. "Thomas Pynchon and the Abreaction of the Lord of Night." In *Four Postwar American Novelists: Bellow, Mailer, Barth, and Pynchon*. Chicago: Univ. of Chicago Press, 1977, 159–97.

***McHale, Brian. "Modernist Reading, Post-Modern Text: The Case of *Gravity's Rainbow*." *Poetics Today*, 1, Nos. 1–2 (1979), 85–110.

***Mendelson, Edward. "Gravity's Encyclopedia." In Levine and Leverenz, eds., above, 161–95.

**________. "Introduction." In Mendelson, ed., above 1–15.

**________. "The Sacred, the Profane, and *The Crying of Lot 49*." Rpt. in Mendelson, ed., above, 112–46.

**Patteson, Richard. "What Stencil Knew: Structure and Certitude in Pynchon's *V.*" Rpt. in Pearce, ed., above, 20–31.

*Pearce, Richard. "Where're They At, Where They Going? Thomas Pynchon and the American Novel in Motion." Rpt. in Peace, ed., above, 213–29.

*Punter, David. "Modern Perceptions of the Barbaric." In *The Literature of Terror: A History of Gothic Fiction from 1765 to the Present Day*. London: Longman, 1980, 373–401. (passim)

***Pütz, Manfred. "Thomas Pynchon: History, Self, and the Narrative Discourse." In *The Story of Identity: American Fiction of the Sixties*. Stuttgart: Metzler, 1979, 130–57.

Sanders, Scott. "Pynchon's Paranoid History." Rpt. in Levine and Leverenz, eds., above, 139–59.

**Schmitz, Neil. "Describing the Demon: The Appeal of Thomas Pynchon." *Partisan Review*, 42, No. 1 (1975), 112–25.

**Seidel, Michael. "The Satiric Plots of *Gravity's Rainbow*." In Mendelson, ed., above, 193–212.

**Slade, Joseph W. "Thomas Pynchon, Postindustrial Humanist." *Technology and Culture*, 23, No. 1 (1982), 53–72.

***Smith, Marcus, and Khachig Tölölyan. "The New Jeremiad: *Gravity's Rainbow.*" In Pearce, ed., above 169–86.

**Stimpson, Catharine R. "Pre-Apocalyptic Atavism: Thomas Pynchon's Early Fiction." In Levine and Leverenz, eds., above, 31–47.

**Tanner, Tony. "*V.*" In *Thomas Pynchon*. London: Methuen, 1982, 40–55.

***Tölölyan, Khachig. "Criticism as Symptom: Thomas Pynchon and the Crisis of the Humanities." *New Orleans Review*, 5, No. 4 (1977–78), 314–18.

*Wagner, Linda W. "A Note on Oedipa the Roadrunner." *Journal of Narrative Technique*, 4, No. 2 (1974), 155–61.

**Weinstein, Mark A. "The Creative Imagination in Fiction and History." *Genre*, 9, No. 3 (1976), 263–77. (273–76)

**Weisenburger, Steven. "The End of History? Thomas Pynchon and the Uses of the Past." Rpt. in Pearce, ed., above, 140–56.

**Wolfley, Lawrence C. "Repression's Rainbow: The Presence of Norman O. Brown in Pynchon's Big Novel." Rpt. in Pearce, ed., above, 99–123.

Noam chomsky

MARTY BLATT

Noam Chomsky has had an extraordinary impact on me and on an entire generation of men and women who came of age politically in the 60s. Why is this so? For one thing, Chomsky is probably the most eloquent, coherent critic of United States foreign policy. What is especially appealing about Chomsky is his ferocious commitment to honesty, principled positions, and resistance to injustice and illegitimate authority. Combined with this commitment, Chomsky is blessed with a superb intellectual ability and a memory that is breathtaking to see demonstrated at his talks. Chomsky is totally dedicated to rational discourse. In his talks, Chomsky listens with seriousness and great attention to any questioner. Thus, he truly responds to questions that are raised rather than not listening to questioners, something that happens with great regularity at political talks.

In his collection *American Power and the New Mandarins*, Chomsky writes in one essay:

> It is the responsibility of intellectuals to speak the truth and to expose lies. This, at least, may seem enough of a truism to pass without comment. Not so, however. For the modern intellectual, it is not at all obvious.

For several years, Chomsky has hammered away at the subservience of most American intellectuals to capital and the state. I first learned about radical history and politics during the anti-Vietnam war movement from people like Chomsky. Many of us in the new left were politically active on college campuses; I attended Tufts University in the Boston area in the late 60s and early 70s and thus had the opportunity to hear Chomsky speak several times. In his speeches and essays, Chomsky not only critiqued the capitalist system and the state apparatus, but also focused much of his scathing attack on academics and intellectuals who helped to prop up the U.S. imperial system. Chomsky's approach was not narrow. He denounced the mendacity and brutal exercise of power of American leaders rather than simply discussing their economic interests. His sense of moral outrage appealed greatly to those of us in the new left who were indignant and aghast at what was being done in the name of the United States.

Since the 60s, Chomsky has continued to write and speak forcefully against the role of the United States in terrorizing and exploiting much of the so-called free world. Since Chomsky's critical approach calls for radical change, he did not fall silent after the end of the Vietnam war as did many liberal opponents. These liberals saw Vietnam as a national tragedy, an aberration, a blot on an otherwise decent international record. Chomsky has exposed this argument for the sham that it is while also challenging the recent efforts to reassert U.S. power and domination across the globe. With Edward Herman, he co-authored an exhaustive two-volume study, *The Political Economy of Human Rights*, which debunks the mythology that American policy has ever valued civil rights over the maintenance of power and investment/raw material opportunities in developing countries. Most recently, in his collection of essays, *Towards a New Cold War*, Chomsky explores the dynamics of the cold war. He argues persuasively that the cold war system has been highly functional and useful for the two major antagonists. Each side is able to use the threat of the other to repress dissent in its respective sphere as well as to stifle challenges to authority on the domestic front. Chomsky warns of the great dangers we all face from Reagan's wishes to overcome the "Vietnam Syndrome" and aggressively push American interests and military power worldwide.

Chomsky helped propel me in the direction of anarchist philosophy and history. He quoted the Russian anarchist Michael Bakunin in introducing his collection, *For Reasons of State*. The words truly inspired and moved me.

> There is no horror, no cruelty, sacrilege, or perjury, no imposture, no infamous transaction, no cynical robbery, no bold plunder or shabby betrayal that has not been or is not daily being perpetrated by the representatives of the states, under no other pretext than those elastic words, so convenient and yet so terrible: *"for reasons of state."*

Reading this introductory quote from Bakunin and the subsequent essays gave me the motivation to read Bakunin.

Chomsky was one of very few antiwar activists who was willing to speak clearly about the ruthless, authoritarian nature of the Vietnamese communists. He did this while focusing the bulk of his discourse on the U.S. program in Vietnam, feeling it is always much easier for U.S. intellectuals to attack communist oppressiveness than it is to take on U.S.-backed repression. In his essay, "Notes on Anarchism," Chomsky introduced me to the anarchist Rudolf Rocker, who argued that *socialism will be free or it will not be at all.*" Also, in a very important essay, "Objectivity and Liberal Scholarship," I learned from Chomsky that accounts of the Spanish Civil War by both liberal historians and many Marxists cannot be trusted. He documented the communist betrayal of the Spanish anarchists and consequent betrayal of the Spanish revolutionary project itself. It was this essay which propelled me to study the Spanish anarchists and begin to look at the many other ways that communists in the U.S. and abroad have subverted rather than supported revolutionary efforts.

As an American Jew, I have had to confront the political reality and moral implications of Zionism and the State of Israel. Again, Chomsky's essays and speeches have been an immense aid. The mainstream of the Zionist project, he has argued, has basically sought a privileged position for Jews in Palestine or *Eretz Israel*. This domination had to come at the expense of the indigenous people, the Palestinians. In his introduction to a book I coedited (Martin Blatt, Uri Davis, Paul Kleinbaum, *Dissent and Ideology in Israel: Resistance to the Draft, 1948–1973*), Chomsky declared:

> Israel, as a Jewish State, can no more adopt the principle of equal rights for its citizens than can a Moslem State or a Christian State or a White State. The conflict of just demands of Israeli Jews and Palestinian Arabs will be amicably settled, or terror and violence will continue and disaster will never be far removed.

Written in 1975, those words still ring depressingly true today.

Perhaps the most important movement in the United States and Europe today is the drive to curtail the threat of nuclear war. Characteristically, Chomsky has written and spoken about this movement and his ideas have helped me to refine my own thinking. Essentially, he believes that this disarmament movement can go in one of two directions, either taking a narrow, arms control approach or a more thorough, radical approach. He agrees with many liberal activists that the movement should concern itself with limiting the proliferation of nuclear weapons, but he believes that this approach is limited. A thorough disarmament movement should move to halt the huge shipments of U.S. weapons to other countries, weapons whose destructiveness are not far below that of nuclear weapons. In addition, he points out that

> there are other issues that cannot be dissociated from this complex and that are in many respects even more crucial: the domestic factors that drive the arms race, the dynamics of the Cold War and its impact on many millions of people, the extraordinary dangers (and horrors) of superpower intervention, the policies that contribute to maintaining or enflaming conflicts and tensions throughout the world, which, apart from the costs to the victims, are the most likely cause of a potential final holocaust.

Once again, Chomsky's call to action is clear, consistent, radical, and urgent. He remains in the forefront of radical intellectuals.

John dewey

TIMOTHY V. KAUFMAN-OSBORN

In 1927, at the age of sixty-eight, John Dewey published his most systematic treatise on politics, *The Public and Its Problems*. In 1969, at the age of sixteen, I discovered this work on a bookshelf in the home of my parents, pressed between John Calvin's "On Civil Government" and Sigmund Freud's *Civilization and Its Discontents*. I read each of these, but it was Dewey who spoke most directly to my everyday experience; and, fourteen years later, it is Dewey with whom I struggle today.

In his analysis of American political life (which is further elaborated in *Individualism Old and New*, *Liberalism and Social Action*, and *Freedom and Culture*), Dewey argued that the progress of an industrial economy had dislocated the ordinary citizen from the delicate web of customary relationships which, in the nineteenth century, had grounded the politics of democracy in the experience of parochial communities. In its place, there had arisen new networks of regional, national, and even international interdependence, networks whose root causes most could not fathom and whose extended consequences they could not trace. Thus, Dewey insisted, although the nation was now joined together by the division of labor into an interdependent whole, this society was no community; for the vast majority of men and women, the democratic public, could neither appreciate nor comprehend the ties which bound them to their fellow citizens. Unable to apprehend its shared stake in effective control over the rapidly shifting determinants of modern collective life, this unorganized and inarticulate public was unable to prevent capture of the arenas of significant political and economic action by those groups which were best organized to achieve their private ends. The problem of the democratic public was that its political institutions were no longer its own.

I first read this analysis of American politics at a moment when the citizenry of the United States appeared unable to bring to a halt a war whose initiation it had only tacitly condoned and which it now sought to end. The parallel between this situation and that which had stimulated Dewey's analysis of the 1920s was acute and provocative; for it suggested that now, as then, the future of democratic politics turns upon the ability of the democratic public to restore to itself its capacity for autonomous action. In the effort to relearn this lesson, those who are committed to the extension of such politics in the 1980s may still profit from the writings of John Dewey.

Paul goodman

ARNOLD KRUPAT

As the 60s opened, I was midway through my undergraduate education at NYU's Washington Square College of Arts and Science. My parents were Russian and Lithuanian-Russian immigrants—but not of the progressive, educated class Tillie Olsen, Sol Yurick, or Grace Paley can tell about. Rather, their parents, who had brought them, were like thousands of other new arrivals with no collective vision but only the individual hope to make a better life by hard work, sacrifice, and some wary shrewd dealing. My mother's mother could not read or write any language, and no one close to my family had ever been to college. My parents thought their gifted, full-scholarship, first son should get ahead as an engineer, then said to be well-paid and in demand. Law seemed also a possibility, for their image of lawyers was of swayers of juries, great persuaders; and I was thought to have a facile, if not often docile, tongue.

I made my way to Washington Square, taking the crosstown bus from the low income Jacob Riis Housing Project where we lived, across Avenue A, where the "good" neighborhoods began, past Second Avenue, still home to some remnant of Jewish theater and high dining, to the mysteries of the Village. By '61 or '62, I had pretty well decided on the study of literature; I became an English major in preparation for the secret dream of a career as a novelist. At NYU I took classes with William Barrett, a regular member of the philosophy department, and with William Phillips, visiting in English. I had only in the most general way heard of *Partisan Review*; I didn't know these men knew each other; and, if they stood for something in relation to literature or politics, they gave no hint that I ever picked up. To my unbelievably innocent eyes, Barrett and Phillips were simply very handsome whitehaired men intensely interested in the women students in their classes and in getting through their teaching—which I usually enjoyed —with as little effort as possible.

It was a professor of religion, curiously enough, who first mentioned Paul Goodman's *Growing Up Absurd* to me. I didn't read it, however, until I got to the Columbia University graduate school in 1963. (I stayed at Columbia long enough to get my doctorate in 1967, but—to continue this chronicle of innocence—without ever laying eyes on Trilling or Barzun, without—the confession seems barely believable—discovering that either of them stood for something in literature and politics either.) *Growing Up Absurd* was my introduction to the intersection of politics and art, to—as I see it now—an interdisciplinary method that was my first glimpse of sophisticated reading outside the confines of the New Critical-autonomous text paradigm. (Barrett, and most particularly Phillips—who was very kind and helpful to me later on, to the point of getting me my first teaching job—taught almost entirely through the narration of anecdotes. Said, whom I would name as major bibliographic influence on me in the 70s, was at Columbia while I was there—and I did actually see him—but he hadn't yet discovered or begun to proclaim—or, maybe I missed it—his own "worldliness," to use his term.)

So to begin with *Growing Up Absurd* and then to go on to *The Empire City*, to the stories that would make *Making Do*, to the poems I began to look for everywhere (I had learned, at long last, that there were quarterlies!), then, further, to *The Function of Literature*, was an ongoing revelation. I could not have begun, then, to evaluate Goodman's politics, and this is not now the place to comment on their obvious limitations. Yet the combination he presented of artist, literary critic, social and political commentator was something that—I can only once more invoke the particular boundaries of my own personal and class background—I never even remotely imagined. When I read Kerouac's *On the Road*—a book whose effect on me was primarily to make me ashamed of my Jewish, stay-near-home timidity in regard to the big, wide, gentile world—I realized I'd already forgotten that Goodman had published on it, too, and included his review as an Appendix to *Growing Up Absurd*. I mean that even Kerouac—who was, then, important to me — brought me back to Goodman as not only someone who'd already been every place intellectually, but as one who made real to me intellectual terrain I hadn't even guessed was there. Columbia graduate school taught the same damned autonomous text as NYU's English department had, and it was only Goodman, in those years, who kept the context, kept history and the present-as-history, alive to me.

The ceremony—appropriately unceremonious—memorializing Goodman's death, fell, as it happened, on my twenty-sixth birthday. By then—just double *bar mitzvah* age—I thought I was finally a *man*, for I was already divorced (no one in my family had ever been there, either), and I had read Marcuse and Fanon—authors, it was clear, who would carry me far beyond the now-comfortable dimensions of Goodman's thought. But for whatever I had begun to know, it seemed to me that I had only Paul Goodman to thank. I hadn't been acquainted with him, as the others who spoke and read for him at that memorial had, but his books in some central and deeply important way put an end to my innocence. Goodman opened my eyes.

Paul goodman

ARNOLD SACHAR

Reading Paul Goodman was not only dealing in the realm of ideas. It brought me well beyond abstractions. Goodman approached one on the concrete, animal level. In reading him one had to consider the weight and meaning of lived experience. He spoke of sitting in the classroom being graded and tested to death from age six on, of the awkward feeling of growing up with a future that could bring one no satisfaction, of the social environment crushing immediate wish and need. One had from him an active sense of the tension between the superficial and fraudulent world around and the vision of a humane and sensible life.

Goodman's work was, at bottom, cathartic and liberating. It savagely ridiculed pretension and pomposity. It confirmed one's right to recall and dignify one's most embarrassed hopes and dreams. His style is deceptively simple and low-key. There are few grand abstractions or apocalyptic indictments. The terror of daily life is evoked by a seemingly modest observation of casual facts. He could refer to a child day-dreaming in a dull regimented classroom, a man having to spend his time every day writing soap commercials, or the anxious faces of people on city streets. Such realities, on the whole, do not seem especially horrendous. They are, in fact, what were taken for many years as a given of either social existence or the human condition. But gradually the images creep up on one's consciousness and form a grotesque, chilling pattern. When as youngsters we are cheated and betrayed by the world we cry and shout. As we grow older we make relevant compromises and accommodations. Goodman's work compels our attentive recollection of an earlier state. His specific proposals and subjects are ultimately beside the point. What matters is his disruptive existential urgency, his passionate refusal of the second-best. For me it offers an animating insight and vision that I live with daily. The impact on me is to never forget my own yearning or grief. I will not be ashamed of supposedly crazy states of consciousness. I am, as if, conditioned by Goodman to expect a great deal. I thus cherish magnanimity, straightforwardness, and good sense. I will not accept a politics of limited perspectives and short-range goals. I will not bottle up primary feelings and wishes.

This puts me in an ambivalent relationship to contemporary radical politics. One impulse in such politics is toward a kind of hard-edged authoritarianism. There is an obsessive preoccupation with world-wide revolutionary movements and an intense excitement over bloody and militant struggles. Often enough there is implicit contempt here for personal autonomy. One's individuality is utterly expendable in the context of mass-action. And if the supposedly socialist society that emerges afterwards rides rough-shod over the delicate fabric of human personality, this has no significance. All my basic reasons for being a political person to begin with are diminished within the framework of this gestalt. In the late 60s Goodman noticed in his book *New Reformation* the gradual takeover of SDS by an authoritarian, Leninist outlook. He felt increasingly isolated from a movement he personally did so much to galvinize and inspire. As a result, I think, he became too bitter and removed. His work took on a spiteful and churlish turn. But if he were not so smugly patronized and ignored by the movement, we would have been helped by him to discover much of the awful truth about ourselves we, perhaps, learned too late.

Another troubling impulse on the left is social democracy or progressivism. We see it in such movements as DSA and in such publications as the *Nation, Socialist Review*, and *In These Times*. It is a pathetic holding action. It restricts one's concerns to only bread and butter questions. These questions are important but in no way constitute the basis for a radical, visionary politics. Both implicitly and explicitly Goodman spoke up against a politics that ignored or belittled our profound claims upon experience. At this level much that was significant in the counterculture, and the gay and feminist movements, movements which at their best probe the deepest recesses of consciousness and personality, was foreshadowed in his work.

In a recent article in the *New York Times Magazine* Irving Howe retrospectively lamented the authoritarianism and violence of the new left in the 60s. On this matter Goodman more or less agreed with him. But what Howe conveniently omits or fails to recall was his own mean-spirited response to those aspects of the movement that articulated transcendent pas-sions and yearnings. On questions of social justice and human liberty Howe is impressively decent and personal. Beyond that point he is narrow and thin. Against the forces of reactionary brutality he is quite effective. Beyond that his outlook is as good a reflection as any of the present torpid mood on the left.

(RE)TAKES

The strange relation between sex and reproduction

MURIEL DIMEN

When I was 18, I had a boyfriend with whom I was very much in love and of whom I was very much in awe, two not unconnected facts. At that time, he and his friends were in love with a book, *The Ginger Man* by J.P. Donleavy. So naturally I thought I should be in love with it too. I tried. But, somehow, it was very hard for me to see myself as the free-wheeling, woman-served, and woman-leaving main character, a great individualist who loved planting his seed, but didn't like kids or wives. No doubt I took things too literally, too personally. Perhaps, I thought, I should identify not with the character but with the spirit he represents.

This was not the first time I had difficulty with literature which portrayed the wonderful life of adult freedom in male terms. In high school, I wanted to be a beatnik. I too wanted to go on the road, but I could never figure out what would happen if, on the road in Mexico in 1958, I got my period. Were you supposed to carry a supply of Kotex with you? How many could you carry? If you took all you needed, there wouldn't be any room for all those nice jugs of wine in Jack Kerouac's car. The only beatnik I know who even considered this question was Diane diPrima, in her one pornographic novel, *Memoirs of a Beatnik* (1969 Olympia Press). She describes her first big orgy, the one with the works, including Allen Ginsberg. As she takes a deep breath and decides to plunge in, so to speak, she pulls out her Tampax and flings it across the room where somehow it gets irretrievably lost.

A grand moment, that. Do I hear you thinking, How gross? Or, How irrelevant? Gross, yes; irrelevant, no. And that's the point. Having to worry about the gross mess becomes a part of life from puberty on. A nagging, stupid worry becomes a fact of life, not quite as unnoticeable as one's skin. The same nagging worry included wondering whether they had any contraceptive jelly in Mexico, just when in the seduction I was going to put my diaphragm in, once it was in whether it would stay in, and, when it was time to take it out, where I would find the water to wash it.

Feminism and teen romance: 1966–1983

SHARON THOMPSON

For those early second-wave feminists who formed their sexual politics outside liberal feminism where the romantic ideal was the two-V.I.P. family, the sexual quest was for freedom. Tempered and sharpened by a critique of the double-standard and a sexual revolution designed for male pleasure only, the claim to female sexual territory informed most of the classics of the late 1960s and early 1970s women's liberation literature—for example, Shulamith Firestone's *The Dialectic of Sex* and Kate Millet's *Sexual Politics* (both 1970); a number of works of fiction [the most notorious are probably Erica Jong's *Fear of Flying* (1975) and Rita Mae Brown's *Rubyfruit Jungle* (1973)]; as well as many essays and articles collected in such volumes as *Sisterhood is Powerful* (1970); *Out of the Closets* (1972); and *Beginning to See the Light* (1981).

Women's liberation activists generally assumed that teenage girls and feminists shared the same interests and history. This assumption led to a defense of teenage sexual freedom and reproductive rights on the conviction that teenage girls, like all women, had the right to control their own bodies. Recent personal experience made activists keenly aware of the harshness with which the rules of sex and gender affected teenage girls. Coming of age sexually was seen as an initiation into objecthood and oppression, the time when the gender divide opened (as Freud had pointed out) and girls fell into the tender trap. Sexuality beckoned in adolescence but following its lure, activists knew, could have terrible consequences. Many feminists had gone through illegal abortions as teenagers or been shunted off to homes for unwed mothers. The social humiliation of being labeled a slut remained fresh, and there was indignant recognition that for some girls simply being sexual brought institutionalization. [A key reference here was Gisela Konopka's *The Adolescent Girl in Conflict* (1966); *Seizing Our Bodies* (1978) contains a number of pre-1973 abortion stories.] At adolescence, girls became candidates for feminism.

By the late 1970s, history was separating the teenaged from those who made the nervy opening bids of second-wave feminism. Partly because of the gains of the women's movement—the right to abortion and contraception, in particular — feminism no longer seemed a natural conclusion of adolescent experience. At the same time, the right wing was moving against teenage girls as it had moved against poor women, in an effort to pare reproductive rights down to nothing by dividing and conquering. Feminists responded to these shifts in a number of ways. The reproductive rights movement continued to include teenagers among all "all women" in its defense of the right to abortion. But others began to talk about teenage sex and romance chiefly in terms of exploitation, false consciousness, and violence. This rising sense that younger women needed protection instead of liberation was related to a more general tendency in feminism, described by Alice Echols in "The New Feminism of Yin and Yang," *Powers of Desire* (1983) to describe sex as a source of victimization rather than of pleasure. Initially this discussion was a concrete response to the work with battered women and rape victims, but gradually distinctions between the concrete, the similar, and the metaphoric dissolved in the face of a propensity to argue that the concrete and the like were general, universal, the same for everyone. Illustrative here is a comment of Susan Griffin's, cited in Florence Rush's *The Best Kept Secret* (1980) that her forced sexual initiation was "typical," that every woman "has similar stories to tell."

Other work addressed the problem of the transmission of feminism to a younger generation through developing feminist young adult books on sex and relationship—e.g., Andrea Eagan's *Why Am I So Miserable If These Are the Best Years of My Life* (1976) and *Changing Bodies, Changing Minds* (1980). Hybrids of feminism and sexology, these books slipped into the mainstream publishing niche of advice books for young people—a checkered tradition of serving up-to-the-minute commonsense about growing bodies and minds to teens, by proscribing or prescribing certain key symbolic acts, such as cold showers or masturbation. [What mixture of material conditions and fantasy, resistance and cooptation, vision and submission oxygenates this stuff has not been adequately explained, but a useful bibliographic review is Patricia Campbell's *Sex Education Books for Young Adults 1892–1979* (1979).]

Miserable and *Changing* are decent books that stand firmly and benevolently behind teenagers' rights to sex and bodily autonomy, but they seem period pieces in the 80s. Part of the problem is genre. In spite of bravely progressive intentions, these books cannot overcome the condescending and simplifying effect of the *sine que nons* of the advice book, for example, the second-person singular and the optimistic, panacean imperative. For example, from Eagan:

> Make a list of everything you like about yourself and know you can do well. Then make a list of everything that's wrong with the relationship. Then, whenever you think about him, try to think of something positive about yourself and something negative about the relationship. It may take a while, but you should eventually get to the point where he no longer seems desirable.

Advice books typically describe the speedy resolution of hypothetical problems, a narrative technique more suited to satire than good counsel. The feminist rendition draws on the cheer of early second-wave feminism to propose that the wrinkles in sex and gender relations can be easily ironed out, with plenty of brisk self-respect, several thousand hours of sincere communication, responsible contraception, and equal amounts of fair play and foreplay.

A little positive thinking probably never hurt anyone much, but unlike romantic fantasy, which seems stimulated by its antithesis, the glow of falsely optimistic advice wears off rapidly when it doesn't work. Romance is a wet dream. When you wish upon a star, you don't wait around for the wish to come true. You just think about it and pulsate. Advice—whether from Heloise or Ruth Bell—is an applied science. Particularly if the underlying intent is the conversion of the advisees to feminism, it damned well better work. Unfortunately, as those who have tried to live feminism for almost fifteen years know too well, feminism has few quicky solutions to the contemporary problems of relationship. We have a diagnosis regarding the sources of these problems in gender socialization and inequity, and we have long-term strategies for change and short-term tactics for making the best of a bad situation. But that is about it.

Few feminists would dare to serve up the advice in books of this kind to friends in the 80s, and it is no more appropriate for teenage girls, who arrive at the problem of sex and romance from a different historical experience but with no less complexity. Adolescence is a crunch point in gender divergence. Teenage girls need to know what they are up against. To suggest that their difficulties can be resolved simply, for instance, by a girl calling a boy, or to set a girl off on the Sisyphean task of trying to "communicate" with a boy who is fleeing into macho anomie as part of separating from infancy and mother seriously understates the problem. One can imagine the gods setting up such a plot, but it is self-defeating for feminism to do it. We are not in this, after all, for a few sardonic laughs.

The most recent entry into American feminist literature on teen romance is the July 1983 issue of *Ms.*, which takes off from the provoking assumption that feminists are mothers, that all their teenage daughters are heterosexual, and that the job of feminist mothers is to help their daughters avoid the pitfalls of "too much, too soon" by setting rules. Masturbation is recommended as an enlightened replacement for sex on the ground that it teaches orgasm, no small point, but the inclination to advertise it as an exclusive alternative, which arose earlier in the work of Atkinson and Densmore (Dodson is more eclectic), peculiarly overlooks the extent to which sex is social and turns sex into a metaphor for individuality rather than for collectivity, for transcending the self. Other suspicions arise as well, for example: Does masturbation seem preferable because it keeps girlish sex clean, out of the mess of passion and exudation? Is it a new change on the old theme of encouraging girls to turn inward? If pregnancy is the pitfall that masturbation avoids, why isn't lesbianism another alternative? Why isn't it a choice in itself?

As to feminism joining the conservative hue about "too much, too soon," it's clearly a far cry from the first rowdy, impetuous demands of women's liberation for teenage sexual freedom. Yet I have to admit that in gathering life histories about teenage sexual and romantic experience, the idea of rules has occurred to me more than once as a means of alleviating the sexual pressure and romantic agony with which the histories are rife. But even if rulemaking were an effective parental option, it would not be so for feminism, which is not parental.

The pain and frustration that heterosexual girls feel stems, largely, from the futility of trying to blindly strike the old bargain of sex for love under changed material and social conditions. Only a return to the primal rule—the shotgun connection of sex, reproduction, and marriage—can make that bargain work and women would no more endure that rule now than we would fifteen years ago, nor is the economy in any condition to support it. Unless we are prepared to rule out feminism and pay all the consequences, we must take a different route. We must acknowledge and explicate the difficulty of transforming the relation between the genders and speak to why that transformation is worth the pain of change. We must level with teenage girls and open up channels for them to level with feminism, to shape the course of the movement so that it resonates for them as it has for so many of us for nearly the past two decades.

Movements never die

CHARLIE SHIVELY

Numerology of decades leads to obfuscation and confusion. History should be seen as a process, not as a meaningless clicking off of birthdays of "Our

Lord's Years" (Anno Domini). Among the eschatalogists, the number six looms large: thus 1666 was thought to be the end of the world as the sixth seal was broken in preparation for the seventh. You could invert two of the sixes and get 1969: the date of the Stonewall Rebellion, but such exercises would not get you very far.

Because virtually everything that happened between December 31, 1959 and January 1, 1970 has both a past and a future. Many examples could be given from black, third world, working class, counterculture, drug, music and other histories. Here I want to consider only two histories: that of architecture and of faggots.

In two wonderful books—*Seven American Utopias: The Architecture of Communitarian Socialism, 1790–1975* (1976) and *The Grand Domestic Revolution: A History of Feminist Designs for American Homes, Neighborhoods, and Cities* (1981) both MIT paperbacks—Dolores Hayden recovers and articulates a past, which will not allow us to ignore the material reality of our lives. In the *Seven Utopias* the living experiments of communitarians have been rescued from the slanderous "utopian" label, and while their mistakes have not been slighted their contribution has been recovered. The communards attempted to put ideas into practice, to test them by experience and then offer them to others who would join. In *The Grand Domestic Revolution*, Hayden explains that "The Marxists lost sight of the necessary labor of one half of the population: the feminists lost sight of class structure under capitalism and addressed most of their demands to the state. Only the small group of material feminists . . . carried on campaigns to end the economic exploitation of household labor, holding, ever so precariously, to the belief that women's labor in the household must be the key issue in campaigns for women's autonomy," (p. 7) The corporate capitalists no less than the Marxist-Leninists were surprised by the 60s because they had taken such pains to suppress communitarian and feminist ideas.

Among the faggots likewise one can find a continuous stream of experiments and material activities which belie and oppose the compulsive heterosexist norms. Arthur Evans' *Witchcraft and the Gay Counter Culture: A Radical View of Western Civilization and Some of the People It Has Tried to Destroy* (Boston, 1978) concludes: "We are casting aside the shackles of the industrial patriarchy. Like butterflies, we are emerging from the shells of our past restricted existence. We are rediscovering the ancient magic that was once the birthright of all human beings. We are re-learning how to talk to the worms and the stars. We are taking flight on the wings of self-determination." Larry Mitchell's *Faggots and Their Friends Between the Revolution* (New York, 1977) and the *Fag Rag Twelfth Anniversary Issue* (Boston, 1982) demonstrate that the propaganda about the 60s being dead is not a description of history but a prayer by the uptight who never approved of it and are continuously running around pronouncing it dead. But those writing out of the material/sexual activities of faggots come closer to a political understanding of revolution than those who know only the abstractions of dialectics.

My own forthcoming *Cocksucking As an Act of Revolution* will develop some of these experiences further. In the meantime, let those who say "The 60s are dead" rephrase their sentiments: what they mean to say is, "I want to kill revolutionary change."

On recurring debates

ELLIOT LINZER

Have you ever noticed how some political and ideological debates seem to go on year after year, generation after generation, with the same arguments being raised and often with the same participants, each time seemingly as if the issues were new?

Some of these debates, such as the one over the existence of god, have gone on for millennia with nothing really new being said. An example of this is the debate on pornography and "politically correct" sex, which is part of a larger discussion over the general issue of "the personal is political."

The slogan "the personal is political" became popular among feminists around 1970. At its most elementary level, this doctrine simply means that one's behavior should not contradict one's political ideology. As such, that is just a proscription against hypocrisy and not a prescription to engage in any specific acts or thoughts.

This doctrine, while closely identified with modern feminism, had its origins prior to and outside the rebirth of the feminist movement. The cultural radicals of the 1960s, especially the Amsterdam Provos and the Youth International Party (Yippies) had a slogan "live as if the Revolution had already happened," a direct precursor of "the personal is political." Other antecedents include actions as simple as boycotting lettuce and grapes in support of striking farmworkers.

In my own life, reading Henry David Thoreau's "On Civil Disobedience," Martin Luther King, Jr.'s "Letter from a Birmingham Jail," Albert Camus' "Neither Victims Nor Executioners" and various essays by A.J. Muste (usually in *Liberation*) opened me up to the importance of closely tying individual actions with political belief. I became a draft resister, a tax resister and a participant in many civil disobedience actions. Accepting the feminist implications of this came easy, at least intellectually.

I must confess that during the 60s I was hopelessly naive, confused, inexperienced and embarrassed about anything that had to do with sex. The resistance had a slogan "girls say yes to boys who say no." I never knew if this was true about the sex lives of other draft resisters, but it certainly was not true about mine. That sexist slogan was one factor which led to the creation of women's caucus within the resistance in 1968, one of the first manifestations of feminism in the movement.

In the mid-60s I fervently read Herbert Marcuse's *Eros and Civilization* with a dictionary and a popularization of Freud next to me so that I could look up all the words I did not understand, and there were many I had to look up. The ideas of Marcuse, Paul Goodman and the sexual liberationists were in the air around me. I read what I could and comprehended what I could, in spite of my naiveté.

The sexual revolution was on. The most pressing idea of the moment was that there were nearly an infinite variety of sexualities to choose from, all of which were regarded as equally valid. The main targets of this revolution were both the sexual repression within mass culture we all bore witness to and the capitalist-consumption-oriented view of sex which appeared in *Playboy* (*Playboy* was never a voice for sexual liberation, in spite of claims to the contrary.)

In early 1970 a group of women staff members took over the newspaper *RAT*, published on New York's Lower East Side, a hotbed of revolutionary activity. I knew some of the original staff of *RAT*. I believe that several later joined or were close to the Weather Underground. They took their apocalyptic fantasies with them wherever they went. They *really believed* that if they bombed enough banks and corporate offices the masses would rise up and accept their leadership in the coming revolutionary struggle.

The women who took over *RAT* had lost their patience with the obnoxious male leftists who maintained their romantic fantasies of being New York-intellectual versions of Chê Guevara. The women were justified. They firmly believed in "the personal is political." Unfortunately, they shared many of the same revolutionary delusions of their male counterparts.

I remember some of the articles the women published in *RAT* after the takeover. My memory could be distorting and exaggerating some of this, but these were the essentials. In the first issue after the takeover there was an article about male sexism in the movement. I read it and agreed with it. In the following issue there was an article about the sexism of homosexual males. It seemed consistent with what I saw of the time. The third issue contained an article condemning masturbation by heterosexual males because they had to objectify women in their fantasies.

My reading of these articles brought sexual politics to a place it had not been before. Taken together they seem to say (1) If you are a male radical, you must be a sexist. (2) If you are gay, you are probably engaging in role-playing or sadomasochism, in which the dominance relationships of the sexist society are extended. (3) If you are a heterosexual male and you masturbate, you objectify women in your fantasies and probably in your external life. (4) If you are a male in a relationship with a woman, you must be benefiting from the sexual oppression she is suffering under. Undoubtedly she would be better off without you. The only "politically correct" thing for a male to do would be to disappear. Of course, the *RAT* articles were not typical but did represent one position on sexual politics.

So the debate on "politically correct" sex re-emerged. It was not new to this period. From at least the 50s the parties of the old left, Communist and Socialist Workers, had a political line on sex: their members *must* be heterosexual and, if living together, *must* be married.

In February 1970, the same time as the takeover at *RAT*, I joined a men's consciousness-raising group. The movement of men supporting feminism suffered from sharp differences in political vision from its very beginning. It was never able to congeal into a stable organization nor did it ever focus its energies on any issue other than whether it should exist.

One faction did insist on talking about the issues of oppression when other men became caught up in "personal growth." This group formed around someone who had been a close friend of mine in the late 60s, Kenneth Pitchford. The group was first called Flaming Faggots and later changed its name to Radical Effeminists. They believed that the only way to end patriarchal oppression was to subsume all political activities by males into organization led by females. They opposed masochism, sadism and male transvestitism. I had very mixed feelings toward this group. On one hand, they were alone in the "men's movement" in having a political analysis. On the other hand, something about their analysis rubbed me the wrong way. At that time I was unable to articulate what it was.

Throughout the remainder the 70s sexuality waned as a subject of political controversy in both the feminist and gay communities. By 1980 this began to change. In New York, Women Against Pornography sought to become the voice of the women's movement on all issues relating to sexuality. They redefined "pornography" to include all depictions of violence against women (somehow this new definition still included gay male pornography) and then expanded the definition of violence to include all objectification of women. Anyone who disagreed with them, especially other feminists, became subject to the most bitter verbal attacks. The members of WAP had the habit of lumping together all their opponents, calling them sadomasochists, and then subjecting their alleged sexual fantasies to public ridicule. On occasion they resorted to libeling their opponents. By 1981 sexuality again became a topic of political debate.

As I said in the first paragraph, have you ever noticed how some political and ideological debates seem to go on year after year . . .

I still firmly believe that the personal is political. The social relations which constrain our behavior in economic and political institutions are reflected in our relations with each other. It is not possible to struggle against oppression in the abstract without it profoundly changing our day-to-day lives, including our sexual lives. But, we must pause briefly and remember just what it is that we are struggling for. Once we gain an end to all war, economic security for everyone in the world and the elimination of imperialism, we get to the real hard job, insuring the personal autonomy of each individual. What is the point of fighting for freedom if that freedom is nothing more than the freedom to think alike? To me, human diversity is something to relish and defend, not something to feel threatened by. That includes the right to have "counter-revolutionary" ideas, including those of "politically incorrect" sex.

What was wrong with the Communist Party, *RAT*, the Radical Effeminists and Women Against Pornography is that they each put blinders on their imaginations and they wish to put those same blinders on everyone else's imaginations. Our fantasies, sexual and otherwise, are our own, and nobody should be forced to defend their fantasies as a ticket of admission to a political debate.

The other side

SOL YURICK

As I write this, *The New Criterion*, edited by Hilton Kramer, blames what has gone wrong in the 60s with its destruction of standards. He seems loath to blame the mass media and its ability to market anything and everything. The *Rolling Stone* does a stupid, sensationalizing piece on the Weatherman, of the drugs, sex and violence type. Floating in a vacuum, the article never mentions that drugs, alcoholism, indiscriminate sex and violence are a commonplace way of life among the ruling elite. Nothing that Bernadine Dohrn allegedly did is foreign to Plato's Retreat or to, from what I can gather, Mary Cunningham, late of Bendix. Irving Howe laments the failure of politics in the 60s decade in the *New York Times* magazine section of September 19, '82. He, among other things, takes issue with one young student's statement that a revolution was about to happen. (Fact of the matter is that it did happen—a revolution answered by a counter-revolution from the top. Only this revolution didn't turn out to look the way a number of people thought it would look like. Look around. Nothing is as it was.) The

Times "Week in Review" (Sep. 26, '82) devotes a full page to a symposium on the American left, which, lest you should forget, is titled "Radicals, Reformers and Bank Robbers." Of course, the "bank robbers" are not interviewed nor are their political opinions solicited. Once again we are in one of those "end of an era" modes. Let me recommend two theme songs as an accompaniment, "The Eve of Destruction" and "Desolation Row." Remember those? They should be the theme songs, not of the movement, but of the multinational banks and corporations.

How many of us have had discussions of the "mistakes of the. . ." variety? Intense reviews, movements of the past assailed, dissections, probes into the failure of tactics and strategies of the communists, the socialists, the Trotskyists, the narodniks, the populists, the social revolutionaries, the sects and cults of the 19th and 20th century, the IWW, the union movements, the Bolsheviks, the Mensheviks, the anarchists, the nihilists (still a favorite), the third world, women's and gays' liberation. . . all under the keen, penetrating eye of those who were not there. Done it myself. Most of the histories of the movements (if they are not outright attacks) are of this variety. Kirkpatrick Sale's history of SDS targets the principal destroyers of the movement: Weatherman. For him the promise of the era ends with the explosion in the townhouse on 11th street. But this was premature endism; the lid is still to be placed on top of the coffin with the trial of the Nyack activists.

No one seems to ask: while reform or revolution was on an agenda, expressed as a movement, while people were challenging *all* institutions, while something wild, vast, amorphous, chaotic, uncontainable in any political or cultural category emerged in just about every country in the west (and China), what was the "other side" doing? Surely they didn't passively watch the disruptive process developing and sit bemused waiting for the inevitable divisions, interior acrimonies, unresolvable conflicts to arise of themselves and fragment the movement? The massive student uprisings, the ghetto rebellions, the thousands of bombings (those the "other side" didn't do itself in order to prove a revolution was happening), the rise of urban, rural and cultural guerrilla activity, all certainly frightened "them."

Surely "they" took it upon themselves to act to insure that the dissolution and repression would take place. The Trilateral Commission's *Crisis of Democracy* (mostly put together by Samuel Huntington) should alert us to their fears: people are asking for too much—there are not enough material goods, democracy, energy. Democracy is entropy. Entropy is chaos.

Social historians seem loath to confront the historic role of "police" in maintaining a "state"; to ask what kind of actions could have been, should have been, anticipated. I'm using the word "police" broadly, to include police agencies, properly speaking, and intelligence agencies and their bureaucratized voyeurism, the promulgation of counter-intelligence—

which would also include the production of an ideological fog (cf. Sun Tzu on *The Art of War*) in which the instrumentalities and personalities of rule conceal themselves. No history is complete without a consideration of such agencies of order. None. Surprising how much of Yvonne Kapp's *Eleanor Marx* depended on the police files of various countries. Old Marx's every move was monitored.

Who this "other side" is would require a massive book and this is only a sketch. Certainly E.P. Thompson's *Making of the English Working Class* gives us a glimpse. The "other side" is a fluctuating entity. But we can say this much. They evince two kinds of police activity. The overtly repressive and the covert. The covert attempts to maintain proper cultural climates: white and black propaganda, disinformation, control of the popular media, news, culture. In the west there is no *one* agenda. Todd Gitlin, Stuart Ewen have written about this. Although not perfectly distinguishable, the non-ideological covert involves intelligence and counter-intelligence operations, spying, provocation, penetration, deception, the use of fronts and cut-outs, the creation of disruptive splinter groups, seizing control of leadership positions, and so on.

In the 60s a vast army of such agents was deployed, like psychologists and sociologists who defined the upsurge as a mass infantile manifestation. After all, social analysis can come in the form of spying. And we should remember the beatings, the murders—Malcolm X, Fred Hampton, Kent State—to remember the repression was by no means ideological only.

Where does it begin? One would have to go back to the ancient Egyptians and Chinese and take notes forward to the modern states with their visible or amorphous ministries of culture. In the United States the age of the police state begins with the Civil War (the Pinkertons), takes a leap during the First World War, and a quantum leap into a new order during and after the Second World War. The Manichean *causus belli* was the cold war—the devil, the Soviet Union. One should refer to Gabriel Kolko's *The Politics of War*, or if you can get it, the *National Security Memorandum,* '68. (In 1947 the CIA and the National Security Council were set up—the FBI and the Treasury agents were already in place—and 1952 saw the National Security Agency.) But the major business enterprises already had their intelligence operations.

The opening of our eyes should have begun with the publication of Wise and Ross's *The Invisible Government* in 1964. If "they" did it abroad, did "they" do it at home? The Big Leap Forward in consciousness came with the 1966–67 revelations about the CIA (*Ramparts, New York Times*, articles in the *Nation, New York Review of Books* and elsewhere): funding of the National Student Association, the planting of articles in newspapers, the penetration in the literary establishments and organized labor (see Ron Radosh), the buying and selling of name communists in Europe, Latin America, Africa: coups, attempted assassinations, torture, mass murder—

surveillance and provocation in a hundred ways. And even more: grisly psychological experiments (*In Search of the Manchurian Candidate* by John Marks) in which we learn, among other things, that mind liberating LSD was developed first as a tool of control by the CIA. And what did LSD, and all the other drugs, do to the movement?

What picture could we put together from the discoveries under the Freedom of Information Act, the deluge of books and periodicals devoted to the exposure of such activity? Massive penetration and surveillance of any and all dissident-to-revolutionary tendencies. By whom and how? The local police departments and their political sections: red squads. The State police. To this add the activities of the FBI and their armies of agents and part-time informers and include the CIA, the Defense Intelligence Agency, State Department Intelligence, Army and Naval Intelligence, the Secret Service, the Drug Enforcement Agency and perhaps the most important and biggest of all, the National Security Agency with its massive electronic surveillance capabilities (James Bamford: *The Puzzle Palace*). For instance, the NSA's mail-opening operations: code-named Minaret and Shamrock. The common carriers delivered copies of all international traffic to the NSA. What did they do domestically under the rubric of the present danger?

We remember such events as Operation Chaos (the destabilization of the movement; how did it work?) Cointelpro, the Huston Plan, and so forth. We saw us turn against ourselves. We saw the destruction of the underground press (*UnAmerican Activities* by Geoff Rips).

But what would a state not do in order to preserve itself? To expect otherwise is naive. But it should be said that even if this was a police state it was not totalitarian. The killings were selective. If we were in a totalitarian state, we would have all been dead.

I do not pretend that without the intervention of these forces that all would have been sweetness, light, and unity of movement. A provocateur cannot heighten tensions and divisions if he or she cannot strike a respondent chord, appeal to desire, political agenda, ambition. The confidence man can only succeed on an appeal to greed. There are always the opportunists, the trimmers, the psychological double agents, the self-centered, the crazies, as well as the principled. (The ruling elite has the same range—from Walter Wriston to a Bernie Cornfield to the different insanities of a Howard Hughes, Alexander Haig, Henry Kissinger.) But they can afford the sniffing of a hundred flowers up to the point where the system becomes totally disruptive and unproductive, and beyond.

We can speculate. What would the communist parties of the world have looked like without the intervention of the repressive forces of the west on the one hand, and the destruction of these parties by Stalin on the other hand? And to what extent did pressure from the outside contribute to the making of a Stalin? Certainly one response to the FBI's efforts in the Communist Party and the various Trotskyist sects was rigidification. Let us not forget that history of the state's refusal to give ground to the most moderate demands in the past. Let's not forget that Dupont and others wanted to mount a coup against Roosevelt.

The movement, in all of its manifestations, was the sign by which many began to perceive that there was something fundamentally wrong with our society, capitalism considered not merely as an economic system, but as a cultural system. The whole of an entity we can provisionally call Western Civilization was threatened. This Western Civilization, with its hierarchies of structure, its long trajectory of culture, its arrangements, its implicit standards was threatened. Even a cultural critique implicitly threatened consumption patterns. So remember the strength, the vitality, the breadth of the movement in all its directions, the totality of the culture, both high and low, it investigated and challenged, the depth of the changes it recommended and fought for, in spite of all forms of repression. It succeeded in leaving, as it was destroyed/destroyed itself, a permanent distrust for the way life is lived in this modern, internationalized bottom-lined society. And that's why the 60s, like some compulsive recurrent nightmare still persists in the consciousness of the ruling elites. They must exorcise and reexorcise it, demand acts of contrition, to ask of its adherents that they confess that they were possessed by the devil. And perhaps the signal for that self-exorcism is the trial of the BLA and the Weatherman remnants. We are asked to admit, once and for all, they (which also means me) were wrong, to make penance and obeisance, to hypostasize those sins into those devils now on trial.

All the news . . .

NANCY ANDERSON

What specifically pushed me to the movement, I now remember, was an editorial by James Reston in 1963 or 64 condemning the nascent antiwar movement. According to Reston, antiwar protesters were mistaken on two counts. First, Hanoi and the Viet Cong were characterized as agents of just another totalitarian communist regime, a regime with no respect for such cherished ideals as freedom of speech, assembly or press. Second, if antiwar protesters were sincerely concerned with ending the war's devastation, their actions could only serve to prolong the fighting by giving encouragement to the North Vietnamese when they caught wind of domestic

American dissent. Therefore the antiwar protesters should stop protesting.

In 1963 or 64 I had no particular views on the nature of the North Vietnamese government and wasn't prepared to agree with or reject Reston's editorial on that score. But, like many of my generation, the combination of a liberal family background and a liberal education had instilled in me the belief that civil liberties were of great value and should be honored not just in theory. I began to smell a rat. How could Reston, and by extension the *Times* itself, castigate the *act* of dissent against government policy? Didn't this deny people, in practice, the very civil liberties that presumably characterized democracy in the U.S. and made it so superior to North Vietnam? Was the only difference that the good American citizen should silence her/himself while in a communist country the government had to step in to silence its citizens' protests?

However inadequate or "merely liberal" this equation now appears, still, Reston's editorial was a catalyst. It led me to the antiwar movement, the new left and, after a time, to the writings of Marx and all those basic to my understanding of my times.

One last point: I still read the *Times*, even if with little trust in what I find there. Don't you?

Why you will never read the novel you might like to

JAY BOYER

You have asked me about those of us who came of age in the 60s, about the war in Vietnam, about the writing it has produced. Let me answer you in this way.

I have yet to read a novel about the war which seems to be about the war I knew. For a long time I thought that was because the war was at once too public and too private, but I'm coming to think there's more to it than that. I'm coming to think that those of us most schooled to write about the war came to the war least equipped to understand it.

Even when I come across a novel that seems to me to be particularly right, a novel so well written that it could not have been written better, I never feel as though it does what all of us were taught a novel could do.

I never feel as if it has explained anything, brought things into focus, found the proper tongue.

Of the short story, the books of nonfiction, of the poems, I can say that there are lines, sometimes. There's one in *Obscenities*, a book of poems by Michael Casey. *If you have a farm in Vietnam and a home in hell, sell your farm and go home*. Or something like that. And every now and again there are lines that seem to work only because of the way one line leads to another. What's that passage by Michael Herr? *The patrol went up the mountain. Only one guy came back. He died before he could tell us what happened.*

All of which is to say, There is no way to say it.

Perhaps this has less to do with the possibilities of writing than with the nature of language itself. I think those of us who'd spent so long in school, the lot of us, those of us who were trained in the magic of words, came back from the war with nothing to say, and worse. We came back distrusting the very notion of tongues.

Somewhere, packed away in a box somewhere, I have a picture—you know, a snapshot. I think I took it in Bangkok, but it doesn't make much difference. It's a street scene. The traffic is jammed—though the traffic is only in the middle distance, you can make out cyclos, lambrettos, a boy on a Vespa in a cheap nylon shirt—it is bumper to bumper traffic.

In the foreground, there's an American. He is looking right at the camera. He is my age, maybe, I don't know, maybe he's younger. But he's an American and he's looking right at the camera.

He is wearing a sandwich board. It says something about Luckies or Levis.

He does not seem to be embarrassed about having his picture taken, there is nothing to suggest that he'd like to turn away, but neither is there any suggestion that he is posing for the camera. There is nothing to suggest, in fact, that there's been any communication between us at all. You neither have the sense that you are looking at a boy in a sandwich board nor that a boy in a sandwich board is looking at you. Rather it's as if someone, sometime, took a snapshot, and then again, maybe he didn't, the snapshot you hold in your hand notwithstanding.

Have you ever ridden a train with your back to the forward motion? That is the way it makes you feel.

When I come across a few lines that seem to touch something within me, as in the case of Casey, lines which seem to take on physical properties—height, weight, mass, those sorts of properties—or a paragraph that seems to, like Herr's, I feel the way I feel when I look at that picture.

I would send you that picture if I could find it, but I probably can't. I'm not sure where to look. And then, too, it's not the sort of photograph that prints very easily.

The same to you

KATE ELLIS

Soledad Brother is out of print. On the thinned out shelves of Black Studies one can still see Malcolm X and *Manchild in the Promised Land* but no George Jackson. I gave copies away freely when I first discovered this book in 1970. It only cost $1.50. I even made it required reading in my freshman comp class at Columbia. And what I want to write about is the aspirations that accompanied what would now seem to be a predictable disaster. But obviously I didn't think it would be a disaster when I put in my book order at the Columbia bookstore, nor did I assess the class that way after I, a white graduate student and recent convert to Marxism and anti-imperialism, had introduced twenty-five male students to George Jackson.

I was a graduate student in English, so the introduction by Jean Genet made a necessary bridge between Jackson's militant politics and the subject I was allegedly teaching. "Every authentic writer," Genet announces, "discovers not only a new style but a narrative form which is his alone." I had attended a class in the alternative university that had flourished during the strike of 1968 and read, in Franz Fanon's *The Wretched of the Earth*, of the historical moment in which the colonial native "turns himself into an awakener of the people; hence comes a fighting literature, a revolutionary literature, and a national literature." Fanon continues:

> During this phase a great many men and women who up till then would never have thought of producing a literary work, now that they find themselves in exceptional circumstances—in prison, with the Maquis, or on the eve of their execution—feel the need to speak to their nation, to compose the sentence that expresses the heart of the people, and to become the mouthpiece of a new reality in action.

Armed with this vision, we, the subset of English graduate students who had been arrested (or wished they had) on a night in May that was the closest most of us had ever come to actual violence, began to deconstruct, as we now say, the literary canon and add to it books like *Soledad Brother*.

It is easy to adopt an ironic tone in talking about the person I was then, new to the left and infatuated with the Black Panther Party, whose newspaper was now seen regularly on our thrift shop coffee tables in there with the books we were reading for our orals. The nice girl that I was once collided on the phone with this highly intimidating organization to which we all felt inferior. I was arranging for a couple of Panther leaders to come to speak at a teach-in that a group of us were setting up on the Columbia campus. "Power to the people," said the male voice from the Panther office on Lenox Avenue and 124th Street. "The same to you," I said. I knew perfectly well that you were supposed to repeat the phrase but I just couldn't do it. Now, with a stronger sense that it's okay to be white and a Columbia student, it seems no sillier than repeating the phrase that signalled membership in a culture in which I did not really have a valid place.

It is Jackson's autobiographical introduction to his letters that I now read with the most widely divided consciousness. All crimes in Jackson's eyes are crimes against "the man," against a system one sees, and shoots at, from a distance. It's not a safe distance, of course. "Blackmen born in the US and fortunate enough to live past the age of eighteen are conditioned to accept the inevitability of prison." This is certainly as true now as it was when Jackson wrote it. But I have a much more complicated reaction now than I did when I first read it. I read about black and hispanic teenagers, a roving army 150,000 strong, raping and killing old women, of children killed in the crossfire of gang warfare. And I read these headlines as one who came close to death, having been shot by two such teenagers, armed with a .38. Both shorter than me and younger than my son, they do not even know (or, I suspect, care) if they killed me or not.

But back then, on the far side of "the Gates of Eden," I took the statement about blackmen, which announces the theme of the book as a whole, as an indictment of a "system" that was also waging war against orientals. Then the enemies of this system in Vietnam were heroic even though they were killing people. The people they were killing were not our lovers or husbands, who had deferments. The coffins unloaded on the West Coast were filled with the bodies of boys who believed in killing "Charlie." Their deaths might be sad but they were not unjust. Americans, agents of the system we hated, were responsible for those other bodies we saw on the news, riddled with American bullets and pineapple bombs. The Vietnamese, and by extension the militant blackmen for whom Jackson is speaking, were avenging the crimes of our oppressor. They would never turn against us.

Then the war was brought back home, though not by us, and it's hard to put oneself in a frame of mind that would see this as a way to bring a better world into being. I have looked down the barrel of the gun of a young man who was probably a lot like Jackson at the same age (14) and what came out was not politics but terror and a close brush with death. Two voices speak simultaneously of this experience. One tells me I have now made my descent into the lowest part of the underworld. I have paid my dues for being white and sheltered from violence most of my life. This is my voice from the late 60s, calling forth an imaginary obliteration of difference. The other voice demands death for all those kids who are fascinated by guns, who collect them, as Jackson did, and use them, and who might say with Jackson, "All my life I've done exactly what I wanted to do, no more, perhaps less sometimes, but never any more, which explains why I had to be jailed."

The letters in *Soledad Brother* become increasingly passionate and compassionate, a fact that prompts Genet to comment:

> . . . at the same moment he was living his life (a kind of death or higher life), without his realizing it, by letters and certain notations in his letters, he was also writing a legend, that is, he was giving us, without intending to, a mythical image of himself and his life . . .

This image is one of a visionary intent on throwing off the white oppressor, who is at the same time a loving son and brother. What makes Jackson's ideas so easy to take in at an emotional level is that they are expressed within a domestic context. He was jailed several times prior to the one-year-to-life sentence that had kept him behind bars from 1960 to the time of his death ten years later. Indeterminate sentencing allows authorities to keep a prisoner in jail until they deem it unlikely that he will repeat his offense. Jackson's idea, which many of us on the left shared, is that a corrupt system has no right to try or jail people, that not only he but all blackmen are political prisoners.

Now I try to hold two truths in my head at the same time: the system condemns the poor, and especially black youth, to a life of servitude in or out of jail, but it is equally unjust that I and the gas station attendant Jackson robbed at gunpoint in 1960 should bear the brunt of that inequity. Seeing the movie *Brothers*, released by Warner Brothers in the mid-70s, brought home to me the difficulty of the task. The movie stars Bernie Casey as a beautifully muscular George Jackson surrounded by equally good looking black prisoners (who were actors) and scruffy white men who were actual prisoners. They were all in for rape, armed robbery, and murder, but the blacks were just the nicest guys you could possibly meet. I walked home late at night after the movie, my heart pounding when I heard steps behind me.

If the movie sentimentalized Jackson along the lines of the new left that I remember, he himself did not. He developed a loving side to himself in jail that, by his own admission, was absent when he was roaming the streets, armed and extremely dangerous and proud to be that way. George Jackson published *Soledad Brother* for people like himself. What an irony that it is now out of print.

Blacks in the 60s: a centennial reprise

CARL JORGENSON

As the 60s began, I did not know and no one really knew if, when and to what degree significant change would occur. Blacks had been demonstrating, boycotting, legally appealing and otherwise protesting segregation and antiblack terrorism since the fall of Reconstruction with only very moderate success. By the end of the decade legislatively-mandated racial segregation was ended, barriers to black enfranchisement broken, opportunities for employment improved, political representation increased.

Yet, it is difficult to rejoice overmuch about the gains of the 60s. One hundred years before, the Thirteenth Amendment abolished slavery. The Fourteenth guaranteed equal protection under the law. The Fifteenth guaranteed the right to vote. The 1875 Civil Rights Act guaranteed equal access to public accommodations and public facilities. In large measure the Civil Rights Bills, Executive Orders and Supreme Court decisions of the 50s and 60s were merely the partial realization of rights blacks and their white supporters thought they had won in the 1860s and 1870s: enfranchisement, equal protection under the law, the end of legal segregation and a partial opening of the doors to equality in education and employment. These legal guarantees were voided in the segregationist fervor that closed Reconstruction.

In 1983, the battle for equal protection under the law is still in progress. The struggle against the brutal suppression of civil rights protests by southern law enforcement may have been won. The struggle against police excessive use of force against blacks and unnecessary "justified" killings of black suspects continues. The differential political and legal response to the Nixon administration's subversion of the moderate wing of the Democratic party in Watergate and the FBI's and Justice Department's subversion of the civil rights and antiwar movements demonstrated that the protection of the law which extended to middle-of-the-road Democrats did not necessarily extend to more liberal reformers or radicals. Since an acknowledged goal of this repression was prevention of the election of the candidates supported by black Americans, these actions were a successful partial disenfranchisement of black America. (See Nelson Blackstock, *Cointelpro: The FBI's Secret War on Political Freedom* [Random House, 1976], and Roger Rappaport, "Meet America's Meanest Dirty Trickster," *Mother Jones*, April, 1977, for examples of the various forms of sabotage, falsified testimony, forgery, theft and other subversions which pervaded these campaigns.)

I personally have no doubt that these tactics were effective in diminishing public support for aspects of the civil rights movement and antiwar movement. Although as a left-liberal I prided myself on being aware of government manipulations, I now know I was repeatedly deceived by effective government subversion. I falsely believed the shoot-out between Karenga's US and the Black Panther Party demonstrated only destructive competitiveness, never suspecting government manipulation. I considered the local police to be enemies of the civil rights movement. Nonetheless, when I purchased *The Black Panther Coloring Book*, I was disgusted by the dehumanized degrading portrayal of police and lowered my opinion of the Panthers. I never suspected government forgery.

In the thirty-nine months between February 20, 1965 and June 17, 1968 assassins murdered Martin Luther King, Malcolm X, and Robert F. Kennedy. None of these men was a member of the left, but each was strongly supported by the black community and none was effectively replaced. The deaths were defeats for the liberal civil rights movement, victories for the right and additional partial disenfranchisements of black voters.

The economic gains of the 60s were also partial. They are not secure. Education is no guarantee of equal opportunity. In Herbert Hill's study of inner city youth the unemployment rate of blacks with some college education exceeded that of whites who were high school dropouts (See Robert Hill, "The Illusion of Black Progress," *The Black Scholar*, Vol. 10, No. 2. October 1978, pp. 18–52. This is an extract from a longer report also entitled "The Illusion of Black Progress," published by the National Urban League, Research Department, 733 Fifteenth Street, N.W., Suite 1020, Washington, D.C. 20005.) With a neo-conservative movement declaiming that the battle against racial discrimination against blacks is almost won and a presidential administration committed to lessening pressures for affirmative action, working-class and middle-class gains in employment may be lost.

There were unexpected gains in the 60s. The primary unforeseen gain was the identification and rejection of much of the self-degrading idealization of whiteness in favor of a rising black consciousness. As a Harvard undergraduate, Peace Corps volunteer, and University of Michigan graduate student during the 60s, I continuously resented the pathological depiction of black culture and society in the social science literature. Several white faculty members and one black faculty member I knew during this period were knowledgeable of criticisms of racism in social science, and very helpful and supportive of my interest in dissecting it. Nonetheless, to the best of my memory, my combined education in these two most elite institutions included one assigned reading by one black author, Kenneth Clark's *Dark Ghetto*.

The black and white scholars whose "consciousness had been raised" rejected long-standing "scientific" theories that black culture was pathological and could become healthy only by assimilation of white culture. They declaimed that the black family was not matriarchal but equalitarian, that black vernacular was not just broken down standard English, but rather an African influenced dialect with the same degree of grammatical structure as other organized dialects, that blacks did not lack intelligence, intelligence tests lacked intelligence. The attribution of failure of blacks to achieve in school was taken from the home and moved to the school.

This was one of the most positive outcomes of the 60s. The struggle in which I felt I was alone became a collective one. If, from the perspective of the 80s, some of these scholars attacked white racism and defended black culture to such a degree that they romanticized black culture and ignored defects within it, the college or graduate student studying race relations or black culture today is, nonetheless, in an incredibly advantaged position compared to my situation as a black student, merely nineteen years ago.

Now the intellectual trends are reversing. In the 80s the two most prominently discussed black intellectuals are Thomas Sowell (*Black Education: Myths and Tragedies*) and William J. Wilson (*The Declining Significance of Race: Blacks and Changing American Institutions*). Thomas Sowell proclaims that affirmative action hinders rather than helps blacks and radical/liberal racism rather than conservative racism is the major enemy of black advancement. William J. Wilson speaks out for radical social change to assist the black poor, but in a way which repudiates much of the ideology of the 60s. To Wilson the problem of the black poor is simply the structural dislocation caused by advancement in capitalist technology such that low-skilled black workers are no longer needed. But in the process of making this analysis Wilson argues that race no longer has a significant influence on the employment opportunities of either the black middle class, the black working class or the black poor, an unwarranted conclusion supported by citations which misrepresent the work of others. Neoconservatives hostile to the continuation of governmental affirmative action efforts in support of a tenuously situated black middle class and working class are quite pleased.

A second additional gain was even more surprising. According to the 50s' social science belief as emphasized in *The American Dilemma*, Blacks were most likely to obtain first, what whites opposed least, an end to occupational discrimination. Blacks were least likely to quickly attain what was a low priority for blacks and highly opposed by whites, interracial social association, interracial sex and intermarriage. In 1983 numerous individuals remain hostile to interracial social association and/or intermarriage but organized resistance has largely dissipated, while the battles over economic equality remain fierce: demonstrating the pitfalls of 50s liberal social science's emphasis on group ideology rather than structural economics.

The 80s have not in any sense brought the intensity of racist reversal experienced in the 1880s, but they have brought reconsiderations which may either assist or impede the integration of the black middle-class and the black working class, while no trend yet provides hope for the black poor. As Harold Cruse and Christopher Lasch point out, the social reformism of the civil rights movement poses a problem for radicals. (Christopher Lasch, *The Agony of the American Left* [New York: Alfred A. Knopf, 1969]; Harold Cruse *The Crisis of the Negro Intellectuals* [New York: William Morrow,

1967]. Harold Cruse, "Behind the Black Power Slogan," in Harold Cruse *Rebellion or Revolution* [New York: William Morrow, 1968]). On the one hand racial oppression is unjust and must be opposed. On the other hand, most of the civil rights movement fought for inclusion of blacks in American capitalism, not a restructuring of the American economic order towards elimination of class inequalities. If the intellectual liberals of the 40s and 50s overemphasized the importance of ideology in race relations and underestimated the influence of economics, a similar problem faces radical theorists of today. It is easy indeed to fall into the trap Wilson fell into and by underplaying the existence of racial inequality in arguing for radical redress of economic inequality make the continuing struggle for liberal racial reform more difficult, without necessarily advancing the cause of radical reform. In the 60s, Cruse and Lasch warned activists who tried to be effectively radical were failing to do so because they were insufficiently critical in applying European Marxist principles to black American realities. The charge still stands.

From "(re)sublimating the 60s"

HERB BLAU

With an imperiousness worthy of Norman Mailer and an apocalyptic sealing of the envelope, I had just written President Johnson a letter advising him not do so, when it was announced that the United States was mining the rivers of North Vietnam. The President admitted the possibility of error—the land might be flooded and people starved—but he stressed (publicly, not to me) the terrible loneliness of decision-making and the earnest consciousness behind it. He quoted Truman: "The buck stops here." He quoted Lincoln: "a band of eagles swearing" wouldn't prove him right if he was wrong. He was acting out of a combination, in a single figure, of modernism and populism: an inviolate self, autonomous in its ambiguities and paradoxes, yet guided by consensus and analysis. . . .

Every such act seemed to narrow the chance of exemption from the horrors we were, in the ecology of slaughter, storing up for ourselves and which—like grain in the other silos, filled to overflowing—are still pending. The President was convinced he was teaching aggression a lesson. The aggression of the 60s was to teach the President a lesson. But does aggression ever learn? On either side of such instruction? The seeds of confusion

**Selections from a paper delivered at the 1982 MLA Convention.*

scatter the dead, and the living seem to grow more violent or more paralyzed, more exacerbated and more powerless every day—and that continues, the only supply-side theory that really works, depending as it does on chance. The rest is outrage. It is the outrage which gets our attention in literature, as it was the outrage which got our attention in the 60s.

If the connection between politics and ontology still seems vague, we are still very good at diagnosing—through the ethos of suspicion which is the major heritage of modernism—the concealed and exposed horrors of our collective lives. It is one of the means, ironically, of psychically perpetuating them. It was conspiracy theory which dominated perception in the 60s, for good reason or wrong, almost more on the left than the right. It was made of *paranoia*, as in *The Crying of Lot 49*, the psychological condition of the human condition and, by a kind of homeopathic magic occulted for the time, a therapeutic cure as well.

For there is a determinism in perception, a seeing which (psychically) kills and which, having drawn blood in exposure, always demands more. Having discovered, for instance, the rationalizing instincts of aggression, we almost take pride in its manifestations. The tradition extends in modern literature from Dostoyevsky on Raskolnikov to Mailer on the White Negro and Gary Gilmore. The 60s gave us a literature that tried in exhaustion or ebullience or gratuitous play—in writers from Kesey and Vonnegut to Coover and Barth—to pull away from the unregenerate demonic of the doubly crippled oedipal tradition. Some never really believed it could be done, though they were not untouched by the dissidence and desire: Robert Lowell, for one, whose personal demons confirmed the "mortmain" of history, even as he brought a lumbering grace to the scene in which they were going to levitate the Pentagon; or John Hawkes, who forced the brutality into the psychopathology of every glamorizing dreamscape of his prose. What beasts, we say, ethologically, and then—enforcing that aboriginal nature—what *holy* beasts, like the phallocratic thug in *The Lime Twig* who tends a war-wrecked Shadow like an angel of mercy and slits elegantly an innocent wrist. . . .

As we go on living, however, in the armed madhouse, which extends its dominion by "staying the course," it's hard not to think of the 60s without being tempted to misrepresent it—that singular period of communal desire—by overstressing its spectacular excesses along with the unnegotiable demands. There were obvious examples, from the earliest sitdowns on, of quiet valor and waiting dissent—the energizing passivity of which, the negative capability, was anticipated by *Waiting for Godot*, by no design whatever, but still, the most important *political* drama of the 50s. But so far as literature is concerned—which doesn't necessarily seek its models in forbearance, unless it is extremist too—it is the *theatricalizing consciousness* of the 60s which has kept it memorably before us and, whatever it does or doesn't do for politics, provides the ongoing momentum for the literature of the postmodern. As for what became *canonical* in the 60s—with its desire for an uninterrupted present wanting the future in the instant—it was not so much in literature as in *performance*, or literature *imitating* performance, which has the virtue of a repetitiveness which rehearses itself away: the canon to end all canons. If carried theoretically far enough, that includes the canonical weapons of a devious and invisible power—which was maybe the reason the Pentagon *couldn't* be levitated. For it is not by any means a "dense pack" which can be thwarted in Congress but, to use a favorite word of deconstructionist theory, an *occultation* of power, which can't quite be located.

The repetitiveness which disappears into rehearsal has become the model for the cyclical behavior of postmodern forms. The doxology of the recursive without closure is not meant, however—as in the older drama or psychoanalysis or the "retrospective hypothesis" which Beckett saw in Proust—to bring repetition into *remembrance*. It is, looked at askance, essentially the doctrine of the 60s that when a work enters the canon it is already, or "always already," reflecting a lost cause. "No more masterpieces," said Artaud, one of the tutelary deities of the 60s, who was studied not only by Grotowski and Peter Brook but by Derrida and Roland Barthes. Derrida wrote two essays on Artaud during the 60s, when Artaud brought to the theater that "integrity of flesh" which sought "the unpolluted body" in "a body without a work," which is the excrement of a mind which imposes *separation* and is always already defiled. . . .

There was, as we remember, a liberating energy in the libidinal thinking body which—seeking a "body without organs" or instituted power—subverted the repressive text and disrupted, along with education, the institutions of literature and theater. They, too, were exposed in their collusion with other instruments and agencies of power. What I am suggesting, too, is that when the radical activism of the 60s abated or went underground, it surfaced again in *theory* as a new erotics of discourse. The lifestyle desires and polymorphous perversity which were celebrated at Woodstock and seemed to be savaged at Altamont also went under, retreating across the Atlantic, and entered the high intellectual traditions of continental thought, given the *ideology* they were charged with *not* having in the 60s, and are being recycled, biodegradably, as an assault on the phallologocentric structure of bourgeois power, with its invisible ideology.

The "desublimated sexuality" described by Marcuse has been (re)sublimated, then, in both senses of the word, moving from lifestyle into thought, reified in repression. What we see, too, in poststructuralism and the schizo-analytical aftermath of Lacanian feminist and homosexual thought is a further reification of performance in the quest of *jouissance*. The model here is not Goffman's presentation of the self in everyday life—since the self is a delusion of bad acting theory—but Artaud's truer theater, the naked sonorous streaming realization he believed Plato had perceived in the Orphic Mysteries.

If you ask, then, of literary theory what Stanislavski asked of actors who were building a character or Freud asked of women who were eluding ego psychology: *what does theory want?*—it wants, at the simple level of living (the *dis*-semination of the oedipal text momentarily aside) what the students used to want, or thought they wanted. . . .

For nobody was adequate to the 60s which, for any thinking person, was a period of noble aspiration and apocalyptic dimensions built into a double bind. It is that double bind, with its universal paranoia and ethos of performance, which is reflected in certain talismanic works of the period, from the anonymous legions of the Trystero to the clamorous armies of the night. If one was moved by the ardor of the period and caught up in the memory of its radical objectives, there was the reserve Catch-22 in the derision of law and order which insisted upon due process, in the disruption of the very courtroom, to keep the revolutionary spirit alive. . . .

It is not the aesthetic minimalism but the political reductivism of the 60s that one regrets, although I suppose one was in fear of the other, the falsifying afflatus of a mind-blowing consciousness. It's one thing to say it's possible, as Robert Frost once did, to wish a reality into being, and quite another for those who have not experienced much reality to do the wishing (and Frost's luck ran out of gas with the New Frontier). . . .

Power was never seriously threatened by the movement, as it is not now by the politics of deconstruction. Long before literature caught up with the dispersion of its authorizing Text, the exchange mechanisms of bourgeois capitalism had grown immensely diversified and multinational, so that the invisible network of power which Foucault taught us to recognize may be theorized but not contained.

Meanwhile, if power corrupts, so does naiveté about power, so far as it is encoded in language. That was the major lesson, I think, of the manic aggressiveness of the 60s, which is now in danger of encoding itself in the alluring discourse of desire. *But:* this danger is no warrant for those who know nothing of that discourse—the most engaging we have around—to continue what was business as usual even before the 60s began.

What distresses me most about the 60s is that what I do best in the daily work of higher education owes so much to the students of those days while they themselves don't have jobs. Not long ago I was on a panel made up of aging "experimental" educators from those times. While we extolled the opening up of learning and hoped for its prevailing against reactionary efforts to restore the core curriculum, there in the audience sat one of our best graduates, unable through the preceding decade to get a full-time faculty appointment. They just won't hire anybody who went to school in the 60s except on a piecemeal, "part-time" basis.

Partly, it's a failure of the older faculty to respond, directly that is. What these so-called "anarchistic hedonists" did was to put the Text in solution. This was revolutionary and is now at work in criticism, philosophy, and literature. What liberal authoritarian faculty members continued to do, then and subsequently, was to look for "answers"; what was needed was response.

Once there is an opening in human matters, however, the energies continue; sometimes, as we have suggested, unacknowledged and under other names. What follows delineates the legacy in education itself; it is that which persists whenever in the place between coherence and difference there is enacted education as appropriateness.

HIGHER EDUCATION

McKeon, Richard P. "Philosophy of Communication and the Arts," in *Perspectives in Education, Religion and the Arts* ("Contemporary Philosophic Thought: The International Philosophy Year Conferences at Brockport."). Edited by Howard E. Kiefer and Milton K. Munitz. Albany: State University of New York Press, 1970. pp. 329–350.

A good place to start. Although McKeon is always difficult reading, his discussion of rhetorical "demonstration" as meaning "manifestation" and "presentation" rather than deductive "proof" or logical "inquiry" is important for an understanding of how "the wheelies and the feelies" (as Philip Margolis once classified students in the 60s) might be brought together conceptually. McKeon says: "A position or a policy is established by manifestation or assertion of oneself and of what one is saying or doing, of what has been said and done by others, and of what will be said and done . . ." (p. 341)

Riesman, David, Gusfield, Joseph, and Gamson, Zelda. *Academic Values and Mass Education: The Early Years of Oakland and Monteith*. Garden City, NY: Doubleday and Company, Inc., 1970.

Believing that "Everybody counts," we went in 1959 (after I had finished my studies with McKeon) to Detroit, to help found Monteith College at Wayne State University. Riesman and associates study this founding and that of Oakland University, mostly by considering the faculties. At Oakland the faculty reverted to (or continued) academic standards and disciplinary connections. The Monteith faculty pulled away, experimentally, from these as customarily understood; but to, or towards, what? The book suggests "personalism" as a name for this destination.

Cassidy, Sally W., and Others. *Impact of a High-Demand College in a Large University on Working Class Youth* (Final Report to the U.S. Office of Education for Project No. 5–0818). Detroit: 1968.

Here Monteith College is studied in terms of student interaction (the students being distributed in sociologically significant groups) and faculty-student interaction ("faculty salience"). This discrimination of interactions in an educational subculture during the early 60s is invaluable for opening the way for a less objective conception of the student than that which makes of him or her someone who passes the examinations on curricular subject matters. The student as learner begins to emerge.

Hamlin, Wilfred. "Fission and Fusion," in *Contemporary Educational Psychology: Selected Essays*. Edited by Richard M. Jones. New York: Harper and Row, 1966. pp. 76–95.

Is the "student as learner" to be conceived of as "the epistemological subject" (Piaget) or as someone creatively using "preconscious symbolization" (Kubie)? The demonstrative power of standing up and refusing to be held to inapplicable alternatives proposed to you is illustrated in the exchange between "the poet and teacher of poetry [and quondam student leader, Finvola Drury]" and Dr. Kubie. She cites "the creative relationship between the unexpressed and the work which is going to come into being, that every poet knows" (p. 263), in this account of The Goddard College conference on Psychoanalytic Concepts and Education in 1964.

Cohn-Bendit, Daniel, and Sartre, Jean-Paul, "Daniel Cohn-Bendit Interviewed by Jean-Paul Sartre," in *The French Student Revolt: The Leaders Speak*. Presented by Hervé Bourges; translated from the French by B.R. Brewster. New York: Hill and Wang, 1968.

If the student concretely is more than what is covered by the psychologists' dichotomy, what is the student *vis-à-vis* social classification? Daniel Cohn-Bendit, one of the leaders of Mai 68, replies to Sartre that students "do not constitute a class. Workers and peasants form social classes and have objective interests. Their demands are clear and they are addressed to the management and to the government of the bourgeoisie. But the students? Who are their 'oppressors,' if not the system as a whole?" (p. 82)

Chickering, Arthur W. *Education and Identity*. San Francisco, Jossey-Bass Inc., 1969. This important work approaches the social aspect of studenthood from the side of psychological research on student development. It explores the development of the student's identity ("the accrued confidence that one's ability to maintain inner sameness and continuity is matched by the sameness and continuity of one's meaning for others," (as Erikson says) among six major dimensions of change, viz. developing competence, managing emotions, developing autonomy, freeing interpersonal relationships, finding purpose, and developing integrity.

Sayres, Sohnya, Review of Morris, Dickstein. *Gates of Eden: American Culture in the Sixties*, in *Telos*, XXXVI (Summer, 1978), pp. 235–249. This excellent review and the work itself should be read as dialogic reflections on the 60s by two who were students in that time. The topic is the literature of the decade; the reflections most relevant to our subject concern the author's worry about the disconnection of protest politics with the preceding implicational politics of literary modernism and the reviewer's wondering about the assumption which many seemed to make in the 60s "that auto-biography made history." (p. 236). Reflection, however, can separate what was together in demonstrative experience; it also makes a place for what McKeon calls grammar—"the art of recovery" (*op. supra cit.*, p. 344)—to come into play. The dimension in the political which the student experience attained at the level of deep structure was that in which mystique, as Péguy calls it in *Notre Jeunesse*, can be engendered or attached. The sensibility probed by students and other young people at the time turned out at its deepest to be, not individualistic or even hedonistic, but communal. Both the politics and the sensibility were meant to count on everybody; to have brought this in view with regard to both is, to change our metaphor, to have established a high-water mark.

Seabury, Paul (ed.) *Universities in the Western World*. New York: The Free Press, 1975. Essays, mostly originating as papers at a conference held by the International Council on the Future of the University in Venice in 1973, (Charles Frankel cites a writer in *Le Monde* to the effect that this meeting presented the paradox of assembling so many scholars who were liberals in politics and conservatives in education [p. 473]), which converge on the theme: Austerity and smaller numbers of students bode well for higher education since too many concerns and people who didn't belong got in — and look what happened. Rhetorical amplification will always bring on these logical reductionists. It is a tribute to the strength of what shook higher education in the 60s that it took them so long to make a start on the come-back trail.

South of your border

JEAN FRANCO

There were two Latin American 60s. The first started in Cuba in 1969; for ten years Cuba became the pacemaker of both revolutionary literature and politics on the continent. In "Words for the North Americans," in 1963, Carlos Fuentes wrote,

"South of your border, my North American friends, lies a continent in revolutionary ferment—a continent that possesses immense wealth and nevertheless lives in a misery and a desolation that you have never known and barely imagine." For Sartre, the Cuban revolution was "la rêvolution qui n'enmerde pas," a revolution to a samba rhythm. Susan Sontag wrote an introduction to a book on Cuban posters, Ché Guevara spoke of a society powered by "non-material incentives" in his *Profile of Man and Socialism in Cuba*; Régis Debray raised the experience of the Cuban guerrilla movement that toppled Batista to the level of a generally applicable theory—"foquismo," that depended on a militant vanguard sparking of the latent revolutionary potential of the peasantry. In the first rural guerrilla movements in the early 60s, poets like Otto René Castillo of Guatemala and Javier Herrero of Peru were martyrs.

Cuba became a cultural center which attracted the best young writers of the continent. Novels like *The Death of Artemio Cruz* by Carlos Fuentes, *The Time of the Heroes* by Mario Vargas Llosa, *Hopscotch* by Julio Córtazar spoke directly to an iconoclastic youth for whom social change was a matter of urgency and for whom the violence of the past, dramatically described in Eduardo Galeano's *The Open Veins of Latin America*, was an evil that only immediate action could overcome.

All the while, however, another revolution was going on—the silent revolution of multinational corporations and their allies—the conservative and the miitary. The death of Che Guevara in 1967, the imprisonment of Régis Debray, the military coup in Brazil which brought the first news of tortured priests to the notice of the world came like a cold shock.

1968 was the crisis point for both revolutions. The Cuban-inspired rural guerrilla movements faded out after the death of Che Guevara and gave way to the spectacular urban guerrilla movements of Marighela in Brazil, the Tupamaros in Uruguay and the Montoneros in Argentina. Against these, a war to the death would be unleashed.

Meanwhile the U.S. (and the CIA in particular) had launched their own effort to influence the cultural allegiances of Latin American writers. There was direct subsidizing of books favorable to the North American image; and revelations of CIA involvement in literary publications such as *Mundo*

Nuevo. Most serious of all, in Mexico, a pro-Cuban demonstration on July 26, 1968 escalated into a confrontation with the government whose sole concern seemed to be keeping Mexico orderly for the Olympic games. The Mexican student movement was primarily a youth rebellion against the rigidity of morals and ideas, against the failure of the government to live up to its rhetoric but it was also a movement that defended a basic freedom of Latin America, the autonomy of the University. That autonomy was shattered in October 1968 when army tanks moved in. On October 2, 1968, several hundred students were slaughtered in a demonstration, an event that was recorded in Elena Poniatowska's *The Night of Tlatelolco*.

After 1968, the war became overt rather than covert. The social revolution promised in the early 60s not only did not materialize but the old types of civil society in which a modicum of political action had become possible begin to disappear. The destruction of Chile after the overthrow of Allende in 1973 definitively marked the end of the decade.

Despite the Bay of Pigs, Cuba stubbornly kept its independence. But culturally it was harmed by the blockade. Edmundo Des Noes' *Memories of Underdevelopment* is still probably the best account of this society caught at its most dynamic and heroic moment. But the great literature of the 60s did not come from Cuba—it was the work of middle-class writers many of them living in voluntary exile from their own societies and projecting the vision of a violently anomalous Latin America: Garcia Mârquez's *One Hundred Years of Solitude,* Vargas Llosa's *The Green House* and Josê Donoso's *The Obscene Bird of Night* bear witness to a Latin America that was already slipping away even as these novels were published. The old order which these novels displayed would however come to seem benign beside the new authoritarianism that would put Latin America back on the tracks for capitalism.

Thinking back on those last years of the 60s, I remember vividly how many like myself were caught in an either/or situation in which both extremes were impossible and there was no middle. You were either for the revolution or against it, when it was impossible to be against a revolution that meant not only socialism in Latin America but, for the first time in the history of the Caribbean (and after Grenada still the only time), self-determination. But equally, it was impossible to be for certain aspects of the revolution, particularly the machismo, the persecution of homosexuals, the system of personal rule, the rigid cultural policy.

Confrontation politics which inhibited the development of Cuban revolution turned the island into a fortress (the same thing is happening in Nicaragua) but it also meant the struggle for democratic socialism became more than a Cuban problem. The U.S. was helping to determine the meaning of the Cuban revolution. It stigmatized it as socialism without individual freedom, austerity as against capitalist freedom. We have to remember that in Latin America capitalism has never brought into being any freedom other than the freedom of the very rich based on the genocide of the poor. The Cuban revolution is an ongoing process: we can contribute to it by attacking the confrontation politics that stall progress and that encourage militarization and paranoia.

60s feminism

RACHEL BOWLBY

Among the earlier books taken up at the end of the decade when the new feminist movement took off were Simone de Beauvoir's *The Second Sex* (1947) on the ideologies and forms of feminine passivity in western culture; Betty Friedan's *The Feminine Mystique* (1963), a primer for middle-class feminists on women's oppression as consumers and housewives; and Doris Lessing's *The Golden Notebook* (1962), an autobiographical novel which became a model for the problems and possibilities of linking a feminist awareness with left-wing politics. Two useful anthologies of writings from this period are Robin Morgan, ed., *Sisterhood is Powerful* (1970) and Leslie B. Tanner, ed., *Voices from Women's Liberation* (1970).

The years from 1969 on produced a spate of programmatic and ground-laying political publications—Shulamith Firestone's *The Dialectic of Sex* (1970), Germaine Greer's *The Female Eunuch* (1970), Kate Millett's *Sexual Politics* (1970), Juliet Mitchell's *Woman's Estate* (1971), the Boston Women's Health Collective's *Our Bodies, Ourselves* (1971), and influential manifestoes by radical groups like Redstockings and SCUM.

The institutionalization of women's studies and of feminist perspectives in the humanities generally has meant a continued expansion through the 70s of academic approaches to feminist questions—coupled, however, with a progressive loss of directly political impetus common to other movements of the 60s. Theoretical and sociological studies of women in contemporary society, along with reinterpretations of history, literature and other cultural practices in light of the women excluded, repressed and resisting within their conventional forms have appeared in great number. There has also been an ongoing recuperative effort to republish works by earlier feminists and women writers in general. These are too many and too diffuse to summarize. What follows is a brief list of works from the first group: *The*

Feminist Papers from Adams to de Beauvoir (ed. Alice S. Rossi, 1973) is a good basic anthology.

Nancy F. Cott and Elizabeth H. Pleck, eds. *A Heritage of Her Own: Towards A Social History of American Women* (1979)
Susan Brownmiller *Against Our Will: Men, Women and Rape* (1975)
Phyllis Chessler *Women and Madness* (1972)
Ellen Frankfurt *Vaginal Politics* (1972)
Vivian Gornick and Barbara K. Moran, eds. *Woman in Sexist Society* (1971)
Bell Hooks *Aint' I A Woman: Black Women and Feminism* (1981)
Juliet Mitchell *Psychoanalysis and Feminism* (1974)
Ann Oakley *Sociology of Housework* (1974)
Rayna Reiter, ed. *Towards an Anthropology of Women* (1975)
Michelle Zimbalist Rosaldo and Louise Lampere, eds. *Woman, Culture and Society* (1974)
Sheila Rowbotham *Woman's Consciousness, Man's World* (1973)
Lydia Sargent, ed., *Women and Revolution* (1981)

An excellent overview of developments in feminist theory and attempts to link it to Marxist perspectives is Michele Barrett's *Women's Oppression Today* (1979). Recently, however, feminist work has moved in a conservative direction in keeping with other ideological trends and the general depoliticization of its practice. "Cultural feminists" like Mary Daly (*Gyn/ecology*, 1977) and Dorothy Dinnerstein (*The Mermaid and the Minotaur*, 1977) take on the traditional notions of feminity unmasked as male constructions by the writers of a decade ago, and adopt them as positive, timeless values that women should not attempt to give up. Betty Friedan in *The Second Stage* (1981) came up with an unfitting footnote to 60s feminism, offering a defense of traditional values perfectly accommodated to the familial ideology of Reaganism.

Rock music

MIKE DENNING

The criticism of perhaps the central cultural form of the 60s, rock music, remains largely undeveloped, the result both of the occasional nature of record and concert reviews and of the anti-interpretative tenor of the rock aesthetic. So most of the best early rock criticism appeared in the pages of the rock journals and underground press of the 60s: *Rolling Stone, Cheetah, Crawdaddy, Creem,* the *Village Voice*. The work of some of the best of these critics and reviewers has been collected: see Ellen Willis' *Beginning to See the Light* (1981), Robert Christgau's *Any Old Way You Choose It* (1973), and Greil Marcus' *Rock and Roll Will Stand!* (1969). Two indispensable collections of early pieces on rock were edited by Jonathan Eisen as *The Age of Rock*, Vol. 1 & 2, (1969, 1970). The best early history was Nik Cohn's *Rock from the Beginning* (1969); it can now be supplemented by the encyclopedic *Rolling Stone Illustrated History of Rock & Roll* (1976, revised 1980). Two early attempts to construct a rock aesthetic are worth looking at: Richard Meltzer's pretentious, unreadable, but symptomatic *The Aesthetics of Rock* (1970), and Paul Williams' *Outlaw Blues* (1969).

Perhaps the most ambitious American book on rock thus far, Greil Marcus' *Mystery Train: Images of America in Rock 'n' Roll* (1976), argues that rock, far from being a counterculture or oppositional culture, is in the mainstream of American culture. Marcus uses the American Studies rhetoric of myths, symbols, and archetypes to recognize in figures as diverse as Robert Johnson, Elvis Presley, and Randy Newman, the "unities in the American imagination" and finds in the tension between community and self-reliance the roots of rock as a "democratic art."

Surprisingly, the new left paid little careful attention to rock music. Considerations on rock in such journals as *Studies on the Left, Socialist Review, Radical America*, and *Cultural Correspondence* are few and far between. At this point the best contribution by left critics has been Steve Chapple and Reebee Garofalo's *Rock 'n' Roll is Here to Pay: The History and Politics of the Music Industry* (1977), the most thorough account of the rock industry. The British left has made more interesting and extensive contributions, beginning with Dave Laing's *The Sound of Our Time* (1970) and the exchange between Andrew Chester, Richard Merton and Michael Parsons in *New Left Review* (1969–1970).

But the principal British debates have centered around the relation of rock music to youth subcultures, and this work can be found in the publications of the Centre for Contemporary Cultural Studies (particularly *Resistance through Rituals*), in the pages of *Screen Education* in the late 70s, and in Simon Frith's excellent *Sound Effects: Youth, Leisure, and the Politics of Rock 'n' Roll* (1981). Frith (who also has a fine and up-to-date bibliographic essay) looks at the processes of production and consumption of rock—rock as mass culture and rock as youth culture—in order to argue that "rock is a mass-produced music that carries a critique of its own means of production."

Economics

RICK WOLFF

The 60s was in many ways both the high point and the turning point of liberal, mainstream economics in the U.S. It was the highpoint in terms of the nearly universal acclaim and respect accorded the modern synthesis of the neo-classical tradition in economic theory and the Keynesian prescriptions of state intervention to cure the periodic ills of the capitalist business cycle. Epitomized in the works and the personality of MIT economics professor Paul A. Samuelson, advisor to President Kennedy, liberal bourgeois economics had reached a pinnacle of influence and acceptance: capitalism, it demonstrated, was optimally efficient in meeting consumers' needs and perfectly manageable in its oscillations by properly administered doses of fiscal and monetary policies at the national level.

Yet, as if to mock bourgeois economics at its historical moment of supremacy, the 60s also saw the rise of three major currents of direct criticism of the economics establishment. The first current was most evidently inaugurated by Michael Harrington in 1962 with the publication of *The Other America*. It undermined notions of capitalism's efficiency in solving the age-old problem of mass poverty and it challenged the ability of national policy makers to solve the problem as well. It ushered in a literal flood of books and articles on the problems of poverty in America, its resistance to eradication, and on the theoretical implications for capitalism's ability to secure the welfare of those living with it. Connected issues of racial, regional, sexual aspects of American poverty became major objects of study and debate among those interested in economics and impatient (and often angry) with bourgeois economics' disregard of the entire issue.

A second current of criticism of what came to be called the economics of celebration (of capitalism's near-perfection) was inaugurated by Paul A. Baran and Paul M. Sweezy's book, *Monopoly Capital: An Essay on the American Economic and Social Order*, published in 1966. Building both on these authors' important earlier books and on the continuing economic analysis of the *Monthly Review* magazine, *Monopoly Capital* did much to put an explicitly Marxian economic analysis back on the intellectual map of Americans rapidly being radicalized by the civil rights and anti-Vietnam war movements. The growing list of Marxist economic analyses published in book form by the *Monthly Review* in the late 60s accelerated this development: notably Andre Gunder Frank's *Capitalism and Underdevelopment in Latin America* (1967); Ernest Mandel's two-volume *Marxist Economic Theory* (1968); and Harry Magdoff's *The Age of Imperialism* (1969).

The works of Frank and Magdoff particularly inserted a specifically Marxist set of theorizations offering answers to the big question of why the U.S. found itself involved in increasingly costly global imperialist operations.

The third current began outside the U.S. and had its impact more narrowly contained within the circles of students and teachers of economics. Its originator was Piero Sraffa in Cambridge, England, whose 1960 *Production of Commodities by Means of Commodities* shook some basic theoretical foundations of the Samuelson-type neo-classical synthesis in economics while also lending itself to a reformulation of Marxist economics whose mathematical rigors and apparent direct applicability to current economic discussions generally gained it wide attention. It began to seem that Marxist theory had made quantum leaps toward respectability in economics just as neo-classical economics was in theoretical trouble and under heavy fire for having nothing interesting to say about poverty, imperialism and other burning social issues of the day.

Out of these three intertwined and mutually effective currents emerged some key developments of importance within economics by the end of the 60s. Young economists—mostly graduate students and junior faculty—formed a successful counter organization to the dominant American Economic Association. Called the Union for Radical Political Economics, it commenced its own journal of economics and a lively program of meetings, debates and mutual assistance in the finding and retaining of academic positions for critical economists. Albeit with many setbacks, enormous progress was made in opening up academic positions for radical economists thereby bringing such orientations to wide college audiences and thereby bringing commercial publishers into the market for radical economics literature which had become profitably saleable. Marxist theory, while still deeply suspect, nonetheless became a topic of growing interest to the young radicals so that the 70s would see the beginning of a serious grappling with that theory—or rather with the variety of theories within that tradition—and the slow formation of a genuine Marxist economics tradition in the United States.

A matter of influence

KIRKPATRICK SALE

I have one long shelf of books in my apartment devoted to books from and about the 60s. It occupies a central place in the entranceway, and it contains works for which I feel a good deal of, the word comes to me, affection. But I almost never look at it or take a book from it.

On the other hand, on the shelf over my desk, I have a quite diverse collection of books that I consult often and occasionally reread with pleasure. As I look across them now, I can find only one—*The Last Horizon*, a somber book about environmental folly by Raymond Dasmann —that was written between 1960 and 1970.

And yet, there is not one book on that second shelf, I think, that could have been conceived or written without the sequence of events, feelings, insights, connections, and associations known as the 60s—and I mean of course the ideological, political, psychological, philosophical reorientations that a small number of people provoked at that time within a great many millions.

Hazel Henderson's *Politics of the Solar Age*, for example, building on economic and feminist breakthroughs of the 60s; David DeLeon's *The American as Anarchist*, stemming from the new populism as well as the antiauthoritarianism of the era; and Michael Zwerin's *The Case for the Balkanization of Practically Everyone*, Jane Jacobs' *The Question of Separatism*. William Catton's *Overshoot*, Martin Carnoy and Derek Shearer's *Economic Democracy*, Ivan Illich's *Gender*, the various *Whole Earth Catalogues, The Book of the New Alchemists*. These are all books, though written in the 70s or 80s, which would have been almost unimaginable without the intellectual and attitudinal substructure provided by what transpired in the 60s.

One recent, for me surprising, example.

A few weeks ago, while researching a new project, I began to read a small university press book with the appropriately academic title, *Territory and Function: The Evolution of Regional Planning*, written principally by a professor of planning at UCLA, John Friedmann. I knew of Friedmann's work slightly, because in doing previous work on my *Human Scale* book I had come across a text on regional planning he put out with the conservative William Alonso in 1975, and I didn't much like the stuffy and hidebound way they presented conventional wisdoms. But I persevered.

Imagine my surprise, halfway through the book, to discover that *Territory and Function*, for all its academic disguise, was a wonderfully imaginative and quite unorthodox argument in favor of what Friedmann calls "agropolitan districts," autonomous and largely self-sufficient divisions of the nation into areas that combine country and city, agriculture and urbanity: "Each agropolitan district is a self-governing unit [with] authority over its own productive and residentiary activities." It was a vision, fully matching my own, almost totally at odds with what one would have expected from a proper professor of planning.

Well, I went back to the library to read the rest of what the fellow had written and, sure enough, it was clear that something had happened to John Friedmann sometime along there in the late 60s and early 70s. I don't know the man and he never makes his epiphany explicit, but as near as I can tell, it was the movement in the U.S., coupled with news of Chinese rural development and the shocking tidings from the Club of Rome, that made him rethink and resee his professional and political ideas. It seems clear that he began to question the assumptions on which he had based his careful career and started exploring new and unusual pathways, starting to understand things in new ways and imagining life in wholly different patterns. And he concluded, as so many others did around the same time, that the gigantic scale of American industrial and political life was intolerable and that one had to struggle for a new polity whose aims may be said to be "that the individual share in those social decisions determining the quality and direction of his life" and "that society be organized to encourage independence in men and provide the media for their common participation." To borrow a phrase.

Of course what I am saying is that, whatever mainstream re-revisionists may argue, the process called "the 60s" profoundly changed basic American attitudes to the world. In fact, I'd be prepared to say that no decade of this century, not even the 30s, produced such radical alterations in American society, not merely in those who in fact "became radicalized" (letting that phrase stand for a lot of things) but in those many others whose lives today would have been literally unthinkable fifteen years ago. One has only, for starters, to reflect on how much has changed throughout society in attitudes toward sex, health, food, dress, parenting, central government, women's identity, local politics, environment, technology, and race.

Which is, you understand, not to claim great victories for all the politics of the 60s, not to argue that most of the dreams were realized, most of the hopes fulfilled. Only to reflect that it was given to that time, to not a few among us, to express a thoroughly American vision of democratic and libertarian possibilities, a long-neglected declaration of Ought, that resonated throughout America then and in many ways reverberates today.

From mommy's womb and daddy's jism to nuclear doom and anarchism

RICHARD METZ & ALEX JEAVINS

This is about consumption and our various reactions to the culture we consumed in the 60s. We, Studabaker and Otto, were children and young adolescents during the heyday of the counterculture. As suburban kids we were fed on images of reaction and revolt, and we enjoyed it. It sounded, tasted, and looked very appetizing. Gilligan's Island and the Weather Underground were presented as exotica for our consumption, and we were, in some sense, left to decide.

Sexism was rampant in the mid-60s. Our gender consciousness was strongly reinforced by Dick, Jane, and to a lesser degree, Spot.

60s animated cartoons gave us conflicting messages. The small prey usually could defeat their larger predators by use of cunning and cooperation. On the other hand, it seemed to end up as "survival of the cutest."

My friends and I built plastic fighter planes and reenacted the glory and fun of war. I found out later that my two favorite jets were used extensively in Vietnam.

We didn't play war much on my block, mostly we played noncompetitive games (hop scotch, mother may I, jumprope) and went off in secret to undress together.

Lots of radicals our age were deeply affected by the counterculture of the 60s. *Life* and *Look* magazines inadvertently presented us with images and alternatives that were otherwise inaccessible and alluringly forbidden. By

the time we left home most of the hippies had become stockbrokers (i.e. advocates of the dominant culture).

Science Fiction was a lot of fun. At its best, it offered visions of radically different societies, an affirmation of possibility, and the idealism necessary to work toward anarchist futures. Combining imagination and reality, sci-fi gave us a medium to explore our fantasies and our sexual and social non-conformity.

The shape of our lives has been deeply affected by the 60s movement. We enjoy the struggle against the limitations society has placed on our relationships. We experience the pain and frustration of trying to achieve something together and the difficulty of integrating collective effort and intimate relationships. We try to trust each other enough to be very honest, supportive, and critical when necessary. We were never taught how to talk to each other or change ourselves.

What we learned from the 60s movement was a passion for revolt and the belief in the possibility of radical change. But we must create new forms of personal/political action which suit the situation. The process of doing this article, the excitement and joy of exploring our past together and having long arguments about our personal lives, has been just as important as the completed essay.

Questionable cartoons

TULI KUPFERBERG

THE MYSTERIOUS LONGHAIR

LEFTOVER HIPPIE?	BUM?	PUNK WHO FORGOT TO TAKE A HAIRCUT?
GALLOPING GURU?	LEADER OF THE GREEN PARTY?	"WITH IT" STOCKBROKER?
TRAVELLING TRANSVESTITE?	NARC?	JESUS CHRIST?

WHO IS HE?

HONOR OUR VIETNAM VETS

DANIEL BERRIGAN	JOHN LENNON
PHIL BERRIGAN	DA LEVY
MARSHALL BLOOM	HOWARD LEVY
H. RAP BROWN	SAM LOVEJOY
MIKE BROWN	MALCOLM X
LENNY BRUCE	RUSSELL MEANS
CESAR CHAVEZ	SAM MELVILLE
MARK CLARK	DAVID MILLER
DAVID DELLINGER	JEFFREY MILLER
BERNARDINE DOHRN	RICHARD NEVILLE
DANIEL ELLSBERG	PHIL OCHS
JIM FOURATT	DIANA OUGHTON
ALLEN GINSBERG	GRACE PALEY
TED GOLD	JIM PECK
FRED HAMPTON	GUS REICHBACH
TOM HAYDEN	TOM ROBBINS
ABBIE HOFFMAN	SANDRA LEE SCHEUER
GEORGE JACKSON	WILLIAM K. SCHROEDER
DEAN JOHNSON	BOBBY SEALE
MARTIN LUTHER KING	JOHN SINCLAIR
ALLISON KRAUSE	BENJAMIN SPOCK
SHARON KREBS	ALLEN TOBIAS

ETC. ETC. ETC. ETC. ETC. ETC. ETC. ETC. ETC.

HEY...REMEMBER WHEN WE WERE YOUNG AND STUPID?
YEAH!
?
NOW WE'RE OLD AND, STUPID.
"ROTC...ON THE COMEBACK TRAIL— the govt. now provides scholarships to abt. 25% of the cadets... the promise of receiving early assignments to leadership positions is an added attraction. As another senior cadet at Chris. Newport College, 22-yr-old Eric Cipriano, sees it: "I'll be making management decisions as soon as I graduate. How many businesses give you the same chance right out of school?" ..."
U.S. NEWS & WORLD REPORT, May 16, 1983
LET'S SEE— Shall I just Kill adult men today... OR Shall I Kill women & children too?
AIR FARCE

Putting feminism back on its feet

SILVIA FEDERICI

Almost fourteen years have passed since I became involved with the women's movement. At first it was with a certain distance. I would go to some meetings but with reservations, since to a "politico" like I was it seemed difficult to reconcile feminism with a "class perspective." Or this at least was the rationale. More likely I was unwilling to accept my identity as a woman after having for years pinned all my hopes on my ability to pass for a man. Two experiences were crucial in my becoming a committed feminist. First my living with Ruth Geller, who has since become a writer and recorded in her *Seed of a Woman* the beginning of the movement, and who in the typical feminist fashion of the time would continually scorn my enslavement to men. And then my reading Mariarosa Dalla Costa's *The Power of Women and the Subversion of the Community* (1970), a pamphlet that was to become one of the most controversial feminist documents. At the last page I knew that I had found my home, my tribe and my own self, as a woman and a feminist. From that also stemmed my involvement in the Wages for Housework campaign that women like Dalla Costa and Selma James were organizing in Italy and Britain, and my decision to start, in 1972, Wages for Housework groups also in this country.

Of all the positions that developed in the women's movement, Wages for Housework was likely the most controversial and often the most antagonized. I think that marginalizing the struggle for wages for housework was a serious mistake that weakened the movement. It seems to me now, more than ever, that if the women's movement is to regain its momentum and not be reduced to yet another pillar of the meritocracy system, it must confront the material condition of women's lives.

Today our choices are more defined because we can measure what we have achieved and see more clearly the limits and possibilities of the strategies adopted in the past. For example, can we still campaign for "equal pay for equal work" when wage differentials are being introduced in what have been traditionally the strongholds of male working class power? Or can we afford to be confused as to "who is the enemy," when the attack on male workers, by technological unemployment and wage cuts, is used to contain our demands as well? And can we believe that liberation begins with "getting a job and joining the union," when the jobs we get are at the minimum wage and the unions seem only capable of bargaining over the terms of our defeat?

Conducted in New York City, summer 1983, by S. Sayres. Questions have been deleted.

When the women's movement started in the late 60s we believed it was up to us women to turn the world upside down. Sisterhood was a call to build a society free from power relations where we would learn to cooperate and share on an equal basis the wealth our work and the work of other generations before us have produced. Sisterhood also expressed a massive refusal to be housewives, a position that, we all realized, is the first cause of the discrimination against us. Like other feminists before us we discovered that the kitchen is our slaveship, our plantation, and if we want to liberate ourselves we first have to break with our identification with housework and, in Marge Piercy's words, refuse to be a "grand coolie damn." We wanted to gain control over our bodies and our sexuality, to put an end to the slavery of the nuclear family and of our dependence on men, and explore what kind of human beings we would want to be once we free ourselves from the scars centuries of exploitations have left on us. These, despite emerging political differences, were the goals of the women's movement and to achieve them we gave battle on every front. No movement, however, can sustain itself and grow unless it develops a strategic perspective unifying its struggles and mediating its long term objectives with the possibilities open in the present. This sense of strategy is what has been missing in the women's movement, which has continually shifted between a utopian dimension posing the need for a total change and a day to day practice that assumed the unchangeability of the institutional system.

One of the main shortcomings of the women's movement has been its tendency to overemphasize the role of consciousness in the context of social change, as if enslavement were a mental condition and liberation could be achieved by an act of will. Presumably, if we wanted, we could stop being exploited by men and employers, raise our children according to our standards, come out and, starting from the present, revolutionize our day to day life. Undoubtedly some women already had the power to take these steps, so that changing their lives could actually appear as an act of will. But for millions these recommendations could only turn into an imputation of guilt, short of building the material conditions that would make them possible. And when the question of the material conditions was posed, the choice of the movement was to fight for what seemed compatible with the structure of the economic system, rather than for what would expand our social basis and provide a new level of power for *all* women.

Though the "utopian" moment was never completely lost, increasingly, feminism has operated in a framework in which the system—its goals, its priorities, its productivity deals—is not questioned and sexual discrimination can appear as the malfunctioning of an otherwise perfectible institution. Feminism has become equated with gaining equal opportunity in the labor market, from the factory to the corporate room, gaining equal status with men and transforming our lives and personalities to fit our new productive tasks. That "leaving the home" and "going to work" is a precondition for our liberation is something few feminists, already in the early 70s, ever questioned. For the liberals the job was coated in the glamor of the career, for the socialists it meant that women would "join the class struggle" and benefit from the experience of performing "socially useful, productive labor." In both cases, what for women was an economic necessity was elevated into a strategy whereby work itself seemed to be a moment of liberation. The strategic importance attributed to women's "entering the work-place" can be measured by the widespread opposition to our campaign for wages for housework, which was accused of being economistic and institutionalizing women in the home. Yet, the demand for wages for housework was crucial from many viewpoints. First it recognized that *housework is work*—the work of producing and reproducing the work force—and in this way it exposed the enormous amount of unpaid labor that goes on unchallenged and unseen in this society. It also recognized that housework is the one problem all of us have in common, thus providing the possibility of uniting women around a common objective and fighting on the terrain where our forces are strongest. Finally it seemed to us that posing "getting a job" as the main condition to becoming independent of men would alienate those women who do not want to work outside the home because they work hard enough taking care of their families and if they "go to work" do it because they need the money and not because they consider it a liberating experience, particularly since "having a job" never frees you from housework.

We believed that the women's movement should not set models to which women would have to conform, but rather devise strategies to expand our possibilities. For once getting a job is considered necessary to our liberation the woman who refuses to exchange her work in a kitchen for work in a factory is inevitably branded as backward and, beside being ignored, her problems are turned into her own fault. It is likely that many women who were later mobilized by the New Moral Majority could have been won to the movement if it had addressed their needs. Often when an article appeared about our campaign, or we were invited to talk on a radio program, we received dozens of letters by women who would tell us about their lives or at times would simply write: "Dear Sir, tell me what I have to do to get wages for housework." Their stories were always the same. They worked like slaves with no time left and no money of their own. And there were older women starving on Supplementary Security Income (SSI) who would ask us whether they could keep a cat, because they were afraid that if the social worker found out their benefits would be cut. What did the women's movement have to offer to these women? Go out and get a job so that you can join the struggles of the working class? But their problem was that they already worked too much, and eight hours at a cash register or on an assembly line is hardly an enticing proposition when you have to juggle it with a husband and kids at home. As we so often repeated, what we need is more time, more money, not more work. And we need daycare centers, but not just to be liberated for more work, but to be able to take a walk, talk to our friends or go to a women's meeting.

Wages for housework meant opening a struggle directly on the question of reproduction, and establishing that raising children and taking care of people is a social responsibility. In a future society free from exploitation we will decide how this social responsibility is best absolved and shared among us. In this society where money governs all our relations, to ask for social responsibility is to ask that those who benefit from housework (business and the state as the "collective capitalist") pay for it. Otherwise we subscribe to the myth—so costly for us women—that raising children and servicing those who work is a private, individual matter and that only "male culture" is to blame for the stifling ways in which we live, love and congregate with each other. Unfortunately the women's movement has largely ignored the question of reproduction, or offered only individual solutions, like sharing the housework, which do not provide an alternative to the isolated battles many of us have already been waging. Even during the struggle for abortion most feminists fought just for the *right not to have children*, though this is only one side of control over our bodies and reproductive choice. What if we want to have children but cannot afford to raise them, except at the price of not having any time for ourselves and being continuously plagued by financial worries? For as long as housework goes unpaid, there will be no incentives to provide the social services necessary to reduce our work, as proved by the fact that, despite a strong women's movement, subsidized day care has been steadily reduced through the 70s. I should add that wages for housework never meant simply a paycheck. It also meant more social services and *free social services.*

Was this a utopian dream? Many women seemed to think so. I know, however, that in Italy, as a result of the student movement, in several cities during the hours when students go to school, buses are free; and in Athens, until 9 A.M., during the time when most people go to work, you do not pay on the subway. And these are not rich countries. Why, then, in the United States, where more wealth is accumulated than in the rest of the world, should it be unrealistic to demand that, e.g., women with children be entitled to free transportation, since everybody knows that at $3 a trip, no matter how high your consciousness is raised, you are inevitably confined to the home. Wages for housework was a reappropriation strategy, expanding the famous "pie" to which workers in this country are considered entitled. It would have meant a major redistribution of wealth from the rich in favor of women and male workers as well, since nothing would so quickly de-sexualize housework as a paycheck for it. But there was a time when money was a dirty word for many feminists.

One of the consequences of the rejection of wages for housework is that almost no attempt was made to mobilize against the attack on welfare benefits that unfolded since the beginning of the 70s and that the struggles of welfare mothers were undermined. For if it is true that housework should not be paid, then women on ADC (Aid to Dependent Children) are not entitled to the money they receive, and the state is right in trying to "make them work" for their checks. Most feminists had towards women on welfare the same attitude many have towards "the poor": compassion at best, but not identification with their condition, though it was generally agreed that we are all "a husband away from a welfare line."

Another example of the divisions fostered by the politics of the movement is the history of the Coalition of Labor Union Women. Feminists mobilized when CLUW was formed in 1974, and by the hundreds participated in the founding conference held in Chicago in March of that year. But when a group of welfare mothers led by Beulah Sanders and the wives of the miners on strike at Harlan County asked to participate, claiming they too were workers, they were turned down (with the promise, however, of a "solidarity dinner" on that Saturday) because, they were told, the conference was reserved to card carrying union members.

The history of the last five years has shown the limits of these politics. As everybody admits, "women" has become synonymous with "poverty," as women's wages have been continuously falling both in absolute terms and relative to male wages (72% of full-time working women make less than $14,000, the majority averaging $9,000–$10,000, while women with two children on welfare make $5,000 at best). Moreover, we have lost most subsidized forms of child care and many women work on a cottage-industry basis, at piece work rates, often below the minimum wage, because it is the only possibility they have to earn some money and take care of their children at the same time.

Feminists charged that wages for housework would isolate women in the home. But are you less isolated when you are forced to moonlight and have no money to go any place, not to mention the time to do political work? Isolation is also being forced to compete with other women for the same jobs, so that we see each other as competitors on the labor market rather than as sisters in a struggle. And isolation is competing with a black or a white man over who should be fired first. This is not to suggest that we should not fight to keep our jobs. But a movement that purports to struggle for liberation should have a broader perspective, particularly in a country like the United States, where the level of accumulated wealth and technological development make utopia a concrete possibility.

The women's movement must realize that work is no liberation; work in the present system is exploitation and there is no pleasure, pride or creativity in being exploited. Even the career is an illusion as far as self-fulfillment is concerned. What is rarely acknowledged is that most career-type jobs require that you exert power over other people, often other women and this deepens the divisions between us. We try to escape blue collar or clerical ghettos in order to have more time and hopefully more satisfaction only to discover that the price we pay for advancing is the distance that intervenes between us and other women. Moreover, there is no discipline we impose on others that we do not at the same time impose on ourselves, which means that in performing these jobs we actually undermine our own struggles.

Even holding a position in the academic world is not a road to becoming more fulfilled or more creative. In the absence of a strong women's movement working in academia can be stifling, because you have to meet standards you do not have the power to determine and soon begin to speak a language that is not your own. And from this point of view it does not make a difference whether you teach Euclidean geometry or women's history; though women's studies still provide an enclave that, relatively speaking, allows us to be "more free." But little islands are not enough. It is our relation to intellectual work and academic institutions that needs to be changed. Women's Studies are reserved to those who can pay or are willing to make a sacrifice, adding a school day to the workday in continuing education courses. But all women should have free access to school, for as long as studying is a commodity we have to pay for, or a step in the famous "job hunt" our relation to intellectual work is nearly impossible.

In Italy in 1973 the metalmechanic workers won as part of their contract 150 hours of school on paid work-time and shortly after many other workers began to appropriate this possibility, even if it was not in their contract. More recently in France a school reform proposed by the Mitterand government opened access to the university to women, independently of any qualifications. Why hasn't the women's movement posed the question of liberalizing the university, not simply in terms of what subjects should be studied, but in terms of eliminating the financial cost of studying?

I am interested in building a society where *creativity is a mass condition* and not a gift reserved to the happy few, even if half of them are women. Our story at present is that of thousands of women who are agonizing over the book, the painting or the music they can never finish, or cannot even begin, because they have neither the time nor money. We must also broaden our conception of what it means to be creative. At its best, one of the most creative activities is being involved in a struggle with other people, breaking out of our isolation, seeing our relations with others change, discovering new dimensions in our lives. I will never forget the first time I found myself in a room with 500 other women, on New Year's Eve 1970, watching a feminist theatre group: it was a leap in consciousness few books had ever produced. In the women's movement this was a mass experience. Women who had been unable to say a word in public would learn to give speeches, others who were convinced they had no artistic skills would make songs, design banners and posters. It was a powerful collective experience. Overcoming our sense of powerlessness is indispensable for creative work. It is truism that you cannot produce anything worthwhile unless you speak to what matters in your life and are excited about what you write or draw. Brecht used to say that whatever is produced in boredom can only generate boredom and he was right. But in order to translate our pains and pleasures into a page or a song we must have a sense of power, enough to believe that our words will be heard. This is why the women's movement saw a true explosion of creativity. Think of journals from the early 70s like *Notes from the First Year*, (1970), *No More Fun and Games*, (1970), or the *Furies*, (1971), such powerful language, almost all of a sudden, after we had been mute for so long.

It is power—not power over others but against those who oppress us —that expands our consciousness, not vice versa as it is mistakenly assumed. I have often said that our consciousness is very different depending on whether we are with 10,000 women in the streets, or in small groups or alone in our bedrooms. This was the strength the women's movement gave to us. Women who ten years earlier may perhaps have been subdued suburban housewives called themselves Witches and sabotaged bridal fairs, dared to be blasphemous, proposing, as in the *SCUM Manifesto* (1967), suicidal centers for men, and from the vantage point of our position at the bottom declared that we had to shake the entire social system off its foundations. But it is the moderate soul of the movement that has prevailed. Feminism now is winning the ERA, as if the objective of women's struggles were the universalization of the male condition. Let me emphasize, since criticism of the ERA is usually taken as a betrayal of the movement, that I am not against a legislative act stating we are equal to men. I am against concentrating our energies around a law that at best can have a limited effect on our lives. We should also decide *in what respect we want to be equal to men*, unless we assume that men are already liberated. One type of equality we should refuse is equality in the military, i.e. women's right to have a combat role. This is a goal organizations like NOW have campaigned for for years, so much so that the defeat of Carter's proposal to draft women could be represented as a feminist defeat. But if this is feminism I am not a feminist, because I don't want to assist the U.S. imperialistic politics and perhaps die in the process. To fight for equal rights in this case undermines the struggle men are waging to refuse the draft. For how can you legitimize your struggle when what you refuse is presumably considered a privilege by the other half of the population? Another example is protective legislation. There is no doubt that protective legislations were always instituted with the sole purpose of excluding women from certain jobs and certain unions, and not out of concern for our well-being. But we cannot simply demand that protective legislation be struck down in a country where every year 14,000 people on an average die in work-related accidents, not to mention those who remain maimed or die slowly of cancer or chemical intoxication. Otherwise the equality we gain is the equality of black lungs, the equal right to die in a mine, as women miners have already done. We need to change working conditions *for both women and men*, so that everybody is protected. The ERA, moreover, does not even begin to address the question of housework and childraising, though as long as they are our responsibility, any notion of equality is doomed to remain an illusion.

I am convinced these are the issues the women's movement must confront if it wants to be an autonomous political force. Certainly there is now a widespread awareness of feminist issues. But feminism risks becoming an institution. There is hardly a politician who dares not to profess eternal devotion to women's rights, and wisely so, since what they have in mind is our "right to work," for our cheap labor is a true cornucopia for the system. Meanwhile feminist heroines are no longer Emma Goldman or Mother Jones, but Sally Ride, the first woman in space, the ideal symbol of the self-reliant, highly skilled woman capable of conquering the most secluded male territories, and Mrs. Wilson, the head of the National Caucus who, despite her pregnancy, decided to run for a second term.

It is also a sign of the crisis in the women's movement that at the time when this country is witnessing the most intense attack on working people since the Depression and a militarization foreboding another world war, the main debate among feminists is about the vices and virtues of sado-masochism.

Glorifying sado-masochism seems to me a step back with respect to the "woman-loving-woman" relations we wanted to build in the movement. I also think that sado-masochistic desires are the product of a society where sexuality is so emmeshed with power relations that sexual pleasure and violence, either suffered or inflicted, are difficult to separate. It is good that we stop feeling guilty for our "perversions," and what perversion, by the way, compared with what is daily carried on by this government as the highest example of morality. Sticking pins in each other's breasts is an act of great civilization compared with what takes place daily at the White House. It is also good that we play out our fantasies at a time when we are continuously asked to center our lives around church, work, and the heterosexual couple. But is practising sado-masochism liberating our sexuality? It may have a therapeutic effect to admit to our secret desires and cease to be ashamed of what we are. But liberation is being able to fully determine when, under what conditions, with whom we make love, outside of any exploitative relation.

The truth of the matter is our sexual lives have become quite boring because the possibility of experimenting with new social relations has been drastically reduced. In fact we have become quite boring to each other, for when we are not on the move we have little to offer our friends except mutual complaints, hardly a recipe for sexual excitement. So we prick our sensibility, find new ways of stimulating ourselves. Actually they are old ways, what is new is that now women are openly practising them. This is a new area of equality we are opening up, it is like getting a job as a construction worker. But liberation is being able to go beyond both.

There are signs today that the paralysis the women's movement has suffered from may be coming to an end. A turning point has been the organization of the Seneca Women's Encampment, which has meant the beginning of a *feminist-lesbian antiwar movement.* With this our experiences are coming full circle. The first feminist groups were formed by women who had been active in antiwar organizations but had discovered that their "revolutionary brothers" so sensitive to the needs of the exploited of the world would blatantly ignore theirs, unless they took their struggle into their own hands. Now, fourteen years later, women are building *their* antiwar movement and starting directly from *their* needs.

Today the revolt of women against all types of wars is visible all over the world: from Greenham Common to Seneca Falls, from Argentina, where the mothers of the *desparecidos* have been in the forefront of the resistance to military repression to Ethiopia, where this summer women have taken to the streets to reclaim their children the government has drafted. A women's antiwar movement is particularly crucial in a country which seems bent on asserting, by the power of its bombers, its domination over the planet.

In the 60s we were inspired by the struggles of the Vietnamese women, who showed to us we too can fight and change the course of the world. Today we should be warned by the despair we see on women's faces cast every night on our screens as they crowd into refugee camps, or wander with their children among the wrecks of their homes destroyed by the bombs our wage cuts have paid for. For unless we regain our impulse to change this society from the bottom up, the agony they presently suffer may soon be our own.

"It's damn slick out there"

FLO KENNEDY

I'm old and forgetful. I don't remember the 60s, though I guess I wrote my book *Abortion Rap* in the 60s and I guess every concern we had in the 60s, we still have. But we've also got payoffs. When I see black people working in banks, in TV and Madison Avenue, I see a payoff. § Things take a long

**Conducted in New York City, summer 1983, by S. Sayres. Finvola Drury deserves special thanks for her help in preparing this manuscript. Questions have been deleted.*

time to change. In a society that has 34 million to waste on a motion picture, a penniless, virtually unfunded struggle shouldn't have been surprised at how little has changed. We on the left, though I don't know anybody who's on the left and I'd hesitate to use the word *progressive*, but none of the people on what's called the left, seem to take socialism seriously. And most of my socialist friends don't seem to realize that the media is important. Any so-called socialist who doesn't use cable TV is retrograde and reactionary. No poverty-stricken, grass-roots constituency buys books. Teaching reaches only those in the classrooms. We call ourselves progressive, but we've never mounted a decent consumer fight against the pigocrats who control this society. And it would be *very* easy. § Whether we're joking or serious, I think the 60s woke a lot of us up. We may be lying in bed, but we're lying in bed awake, and planning and talking occasionally to one another. I'm proud to be a part of that dialogue. § Maybe it ought to be off the record, but I don't like increasing the horizontal hostility already obtaining between antiestablishment people, social advocates, whomever. I'm delighted to work with anybody on this side, even if I'm sure they are CIA. I can't check people's political credentials and naturally, if they are CIA, their political credentials are impeccable. I try to work with who comes along and hope that if they are CIA they get my message straight when they report back to the establishment. § Most of my ideas now, although I still work on them, I had at the outset. I said back in 1931 that marriage was for the birds and that if you didn't have webbed feet and feathers, you shouldn't get into it. For me the 60s was a continuation of what I did in my twenties in Kansas City, Missouri, like boycotting Coca-Cola for refusing to hire black drivers. In 1967 I was after Proctor & Gamble complaining about the lily-white soap operas and game shows they sponsored. In those days Proctor & Gamble used up 245 million dollars in their annual advertising budget; last time I checked, it was 775 million. So I still advocate that we follow our dollars and see what business, government and the media are doing with them. § I'm no original thinker, but I'm very smart about picking up ideas from people who have an original thought of a political nature. In some cases, I'm slightly ahead of progressive people; in other cases, I'm ready for them. I'm proud to say that there haven't been any progressive ideas that the establishment has ignored that I didn't love. § So, as a black woman, I never bought the idea that blacks and women, both and each, should be twice as good as men. Looking at the people at the top, I should be able to get twice as far on half my energy, and I'm always working at half-speed. I'm lazy and I have poor health and my eating habits are irregular. When I don't eat so well, I say to myself, if I ever have to go to jail, at least I won't have to complain about the food. I consider myself first concerned with finances and fun. I expect politics to be fun. If it gets difficult, I don't bother to do it. I'm not much of a leader; on the other hand, I'm not much of a follower, either. I'm too impatient. When they want to go in one direction and not the other, I don't hesitate to split. § Last week, for example, I was interested in opposing certain feminists who were picketing the Playboy Club when Christie Hefner was handing out first amendment awards to a Kentucky publisher for a brave stance he had taken against mine owners. It didn't seem the time to picket when *Playboy* was doing something half decent. Most of the establishment which would not offend Women Against Pornography, nevertheless offends women. The *Ladies Home Journal* and other jockocratic periodicals do more harm to women with their Can-This-Marriage-Be-Saved drives and pseudo-panic they add every time we think about the USSR. § So I am not an orthodox feminist, but I may be quite orthodox in my thinking about the antinuclear movement. I'm terribly upset with the pro-freeze Democrats' compromises, in their ridiculous prescriptions and emphasis on verification. I know that some black people are upset with me for the importance I give to this issue. I know that they are also upset with *me*—for one thing, for my liberal use of the word nigger, for another, because I deal with a lot of white people. They may grow fonder of me because I advocate a black ticket which white people worry will help to re-elect Ronald Reagan. My answer to white people is if they can't get the Democrats to respond to what black people are demanding, then I'm right: the Democratic Party is a wimp, certainly not good enough for me at my age and in my condition, since I've so overstayed my time. With the time I have left I need to do what is basic. And what is absolutely essential now is for black people in America, and for white people who have their heads on right, to get in back of Jesse Jackson and see that if he can't become the first black president, he can at least achieve the kind of power base which will force the Democratic Party to pay attention to the needs of black people and others whom their neglect over the years has virtually disenfranchised in this country. It isn't just the Republicans who are to blame for the kind of cruel and corrupt society we live in. It's high time the Democrats saw the light. And with a strong voter registration campaign and real discussion of the issues, for once, we'll get somewhere. By the way, if you are talking first in terms of time and numbers, nonwhites are first world. § I don't know how anyone can be anti-establishment in this country and not be pro-socialist and pro-communist; it just has to be part of the dialogue. I'm not interested in joining the CP because I'm not interested in European crossfire. I'd probably get frostbite in the Soviet Union and I'm not that much interested in travel, not even to Africa. I'd give money to the CP, though, if I had any. § The 60s reinforced my antiestablishmentarism. I don't recall drawing back from any position I've taken since 1932. I've had to disavow alliances when somebody turned out to be a CIA agent but not my allegiances. § You know, what made me unhappy about the so-called left in the 60s is the way they always seemed so scruffy and dumpy, their work places so shabby, like the Alternate U was. Perhaps because blacks are on the defensive about keeping clean, perhaps because poor people are awful snobs, I think that anyone trying to appeal politically to the poor should keep as attractive a place as possible. Most poor people are not reassured by poverty. I don't practice what I preach—you're sitting in the dirty room and the other room I call the filthy room—but it always made me wonder, what was the innocence, ignorance, incompetence and impotence that kept the left from raising enough money for comfortable enough surroundings that would make poor people believe that this social change group would actually know what to do. The less urban peasants have, the more they dream, and I think it's a mistake for the pimps to outshine the politicoes. § I don't see the little we did in the 30s and the 60s as more than a splinter under someone's fingernail. The establishment whines so loud we tend to believe them. Yet I haven't found any struggle embarrassing. For instance, if non-feminist women are dissatisfied with what the women's movement has not done, has not been able to do yet, they shouldn't be blaming the feminists, but they should be talking about banks and insurance companies and the courts and the church. Why is it we always whip the people trying to make changes against all odds? We accuse weak people, instead of examining what harm the powerful enemy has done. If women have been unfairly treated, consider what the media and government delinquents did with the millions they made. If you want to fix blame, take the strongest person or institution in the establishment, and work your way down. § I blame myself for what is lacking in the feminist movement, not sombody over there. Those people are urging their issues, why shouldn't we urge ours? The cultural fare served up to me tells me that women are the chief consumers in this consumer society. Many even buy their husbands' underwear. Women need to organize their dollar power into political power. § One of my favorite stories that I will be certain to tell at one point is the story on which the Testicular Concept is based. The idea is that there is this woman in a dental chair, and she is a black woman, or maybe we should call her a colored lady, because she is not at all political. She is as I would be if I were normal. And she is in the dentist's chair, and he has her back in the position dentists like to put you in. And he has sliced her gum on the inside. And that seemed kind of bad to her. But she rinses and spits. And then he slices her gum again. And she rinses and spits again. And then (he is hung-over, it is about eleven-thirty on a Monday morning and he has been drinking all weekend) he carelessly cuts her tongue. And that seems more than enough. Next thing he knows—she has a pressure—she has a grip—on his testicles. Now he has gone to a very good college, a dental college of the first quality, but they haven't told him what to do if the patient grabs your balls. So, when she does this, he is naturally upset and asks her, "What's this?" Giving an additional squeeze, she says, "We're not going to hurt each other any more, are we doctor?" Now this is my way of saying, however much you may feel helpless, however the establishment seems to have you in an awkward position—and there is hardly a more awkward position than that of a patient at the dentists's because even at the gynecologist's or the urologist's, they don't have all those sharp instruments they go at you with —my message is that when you are vulnerable yourself, if you put pressure on the balls, you very often find that the hearts and minds follow. So when I refer to a "testicular approach," I mean place your pressure on the money scene or on the publicity scene, or in some way hurt them so that they will respect your wishes, not because they love you, but because they know that you know how to hurt them. § I'm interested in seeing that women have a choice whether or not to serve a twenty-year-to-life sentence in raising children they didn't want for a pittance, or for nothing at all, whether or not they can refuse to raise children for the penitentiary or for cannonfodder, and whether they can help bring about socialist ideals. Women have everything at stake in this struggle. Their working conditions are deplorable. The import of the death of Karen Silkwood is tragically underestimated. It all goes together to mean that women should absolutely take over the leadership of the nuclear disarmament movement, because everything they have is involved in the winning of that struggle. Women just have not found where to put the pressure, where the most tender spot is. Overall, though, I'm not disappointed in the feminist movement. I'm an inclusionist, a coalition kind of person. § You have to remember that the media have taken the spotlight off the movement, so we tend to think it's not there. But that's just not true. I speak on campuses all the time, and honey, they are ready to go. I can remember one of those Ofay Today type persons broadcasting from the Columbia campus talking about apathy on the campus and somebody comes along and throws coffee all over her skirt and she keeps right on talking. We might have shrunk, but I suspect we are at least like the termites. There are so many of us, with Hispanics and native American Indians and all, that one day they are going to step out on the platform and it will collapse. Look what happened in Chicago. That "Johannesburg-on-the-Lake," as a young Chicago poet, George Drury, calls it. Jane Byrne steps out on the platform, and it has been termited away! § Some people complain about being tired, but I think that anybody who is smart enough to have fun with their politics is not going to get burnt out. The Feminist Party has dwindled, due to lack of time and money. I think one of my weaknesses is that there isn't much depth to my commitments, though I don't care if that's true. What can I say? I enjoy politics. What do people do that they like if it isn't politics? I know that I get a kick out of everything that I do. When I hear about the first amendment attempt to remove the Playboy Club channel from cable TV, I'm all reinvigorated. § My father, back in a white-trash neighborhood in Kansas in the 20s, faced off maybe fifteen Klansmen who told him he had to get out. My father said, "Wait a minute," and went back inside and came out with a shotgun and said, "The first man who steps on my porch I kill, and you can decide who can kill me." So we were never bothered after that. Of course, they never spoke to us. I guess I'm the way I am because of my father, which is to say that I am the way I am because I'm interested in living the good life, the best life I know how at my age and condition. I'm earning my living off my politics and I'm having fun. § I think that most people when they made their first struggle felt they were in over their heads, so immediately they crawled back into their shells to start to think as they had done. Then they were embarrassed and ashamed and didn't feel good about themselves and so became very resentful when another group came to center stage. That's why I say that coalition is so important. It's crucial that we all join the struggle and stay in it *together*. And, too, if you don't build on your initial success, you get embarrassed. Some of the people we've been talking about did one great thing and shot their wad. I've never done that; I keep doing things over and over. § You see, the way my sisters and I were brought up, we were given the idea that life was not supposed to have any pain at all. Outside, imposed pain, yes, but there was no pain inside my family. So no one inflicts pain on me, never. I don't accommodate to pain. In the same vein, I don't do any volunteer work, except to disrupt. I'm still having the best time of my life, except that I wish I were dead. Only, I'm not dead. § I feel everybody has to fight. Fucking has its place in this world. One of the reasons I haven't practiced fucking is that the fucking line is so long half the fuckers don't even get to the fuckee. You could be all ready to kiss ass and there is such a line sucking up ahead of you, you can't even get there. If I'm angry, I'd rather be biting than sucking and I've always found that the biting line is so much shorter, you can walk right in and bite. And it's immediate in its results: it may not have the total effect you're looking for, but it's far more satisfying. I've seen women on the sucking line for twelve years who can't get up to the Congressman to ask about the Equal Rights Amendment. § When I lecture, I usually make a speech which is so raucous and crazy and crude and my reputation is such, that people are usually afraid to ask me any questions, so I don't really have a way of gauging what they are thinking about feminism that might not be political. But I don't spend that much time talking about feminism, over say, international relations. Crotch control, I call it. To give a whole speech about crotch control doesn't make any sense to me. I can't stay on the subject, because it doesn't go anywhere and I guess I've been of the opinion that you cannot nonviolently change a violent society. One of my basic concepts is the right to violence. When I talk about women and realize some of their total commitment to nonviolence, then I realize that I can't stay on the subject, because the things that interest me will most probably result in violence. So, if I'm questioned, I can talk about the feminist movement, but my mind is more like a skating rink than a race track, I'm the world's worst speaker in terms of staying on the track and so I have a disdainful attitude towards a lot of things other people hold sacred.

§ I think the country is now more serious, more political. I know black people are different. The only thing I'm disappointed in is the lack of use of cable television. In terms of electoral politics, the black people are so wonderful, in Sioux City, in Houston, in Chicago, so when people talk about apathy, I don't know what they're talking about. But then as I said before, I am naturally invigorated by these developments. I pick up on things. There's this so-called Nighttalk on Radio WWRL. I've never heard white people on it. Political calls come in from New Orleans, St. Louis, Detroit, Philadelphia, and honey, there is a lot of bullshit spoken, to be sure, but the ones who got this program together and most of the people who call in are so fabulous. I gave a series of four talks on the use of the dollar––one hour raps—and the extent to which black people have the right to demand their dollar power from the Democratic Party, from Proctor & Gamble and General Foods. And let me tell you: these people are hot to trot. We're about to suggest that people return packages of food, soap, whatever, to these companies; they can't wait. § You can't let the pathology you see all around you, the bad people out front doing the rest of the people in, discourage you and obscure your vision. You've got to get past that, past *them* and deal with the general situation. When I do this, I'm almost never disappointed. When I hear people say there's apathy, there's lack of empathy, that the counry's moving inevitably to the right, I say: I don't believe it. And I sort of believe what makes me feel best. But analyse it. Some fish are really delicious and have terrible bones. I never talk about the bones. I don't tend to evaluate worthwhile movements by what's wrong with them. I suppose it's perfectly true that the feminist movement and other movements are now more like those tiny, boney smelt than bluefish, but personally, I love smelt. So, I don't contradict people who say the movements are tasteless or bloated or whatever other things they call them because I'm thrilled to death with sardines. So, if you're eating your fill of sardines and smelts and porgies, you don't get upset when there's no swordfish on the table. I don't know where the swordfish went—maybe there is apathy—I know people now are different: they don't accept niggerization. § I never had to separate myself as a feminist from the Black Movement. When a white woman would say something to a black man in the audience who had said something about chicks, I would go crazy. I'd go bananas. Don't talk to no black man like that in my presence. I wrote a letter to Bella Abzug when she ran against Percy Sutton because I thought she shouldn't be doing that. Feminist or no feminist, black people started this revolution and for a white woman to get ahead of me in this line I thought was bad manners. Of course, in the end, they both lost. Now Bella Abzug is not bitter. She sent me a check to help out with my cable show and I'm happy that she did it. I wish we didn't have these horizontal hostilities in electoral politics, because they work against us, but until everybody gets a fair share in elections, I know we'll have them. § I was married to a

Welshman; my sister is married to an Irishman. Some of my favorite people are white. More of my best friends are white. I could never be a separatist because my property and everything else is tied up with whites. But I'm very supportive of black separatism, very supportive. Personally, in my personal, intimate life, I'm very close to white people. When it comes to politics, I go with the blacks. § I raised money for the Panthers; I worked on Rapp Brown's case with Billy Kunstler; at one point I raised money for Angela Davis. Yet I'm not sure I can think of one serious black politician who would trust *me* that much, except those people who are working for Jesse Jackson. But I did a segment on the *60 Minutes* show some years ago which might have gotten more black people interested in me. My college presentations until very recently were to whites. Various organizations would get blacks in there because they wanted us in their coalition. but it was the feminist community who got me visible. Most blacks don't or didn't know who I am. § When I try to see what I'm radical about, all I can say is that most people follow authoritative lines. I just wonder why people don't feel pretty much the way I do. If it were a strain for someone to think alone with establishmentarian authority, then it would seem radical because it would weary them. I would be weary if I tried to accept establishmentarism. I guess I'm political because it's the best game in town. It's the most fun; it's authentic, not phoney. Running around and falling down over a ball and all these jockocratic ways of having fun to me are artificial. Why do you want to be artificially excited when you can be genuinely excited? If you want to be in danger, why would you ski down a mountainside, when you can carry picket signs? § I have never bought America's political line. I never learned to ride a bicycle—I probably fell a few times—and I never learned to skate because I probably fell a few times and asked myself, who the hell needs this shit? I don't do anything that is difficult. I always do what is fun. But the artificial, the jockocratic, is not my idea of fun. It's a red herring, a turn off, some form of distraction; a turnacide. § If you're disappointed, it's because you expect too much. I've had a couple of really serious illnesses. I tend to be in such a good mood when I get well, though I'm not completely well. I spend a lot of attention of learning how to live and not be unhappy. While people learn to do things—ballet dance, make pots, write clearly or read logically—I've learned to minimize unhappiness. How to distinguish between pain and suffering, things like that. One of the reasons I'm so free in politics is because nobody ever hurts me. I'm persuaded that society never recommends anything that is politically healthy, that will improve the social order. So if society says that marriage is good, fucking is fine, balls in holes are important, then I know that isn't for me. What this society is trying to accomplish through its use of people does not interest me. § I'm rarely disappointed in people because I tend to judge them pretty much where they tend to end, in their innocence, for example. Innocence is the way some people justify their pain, justify their setbacks. Some people are proud of their ignorance/innocence. There's an innocence that means free of guilt and there's an innocence that means free of knowledge, and therefore, free of responsibility. There are several more types, and they are all the good peoples' out. Good people have pathological qualities in a pathological society. I once described good peoples' pathology, by the way, in a book that never got published called *The Pathology of Oppression*. Good people have to be pathological or you would never have the pathology of oppression to the extent that you have it. I, incidentally, have a way of categorizing oppression—four different varieties: personal, private, public and political. Many people, especially in the feminist community, are hip to personal oppression: "my husband beats me." But you see, personal oppression becomes private oppression on the job. It becomes public when there is a law against it. It becomes political when you not only challenge the law, but you try to change the structure of the institution within which the law obtains. These four kinds are important to keep in mind, because you can give a lecture and someone will say, "My wife never cooks," or "my wife has to ask me for money" or something like that; and the second thing I like to talk about is power: body power, vote power and dollar power. § Now smart people are people who can manipulate their environment to their advantage. If their environment is barren, and in the case of black people I mean barren of money, then people become skewed. Black people are unsmart to the extent that their motivation to manipulate their environment has gotten diluted. There was a joke someone told about an ice-skating contest. These contestants come out before the judges and do all sorts of cascades and squats and jumps and leaps. One did all this wonderful stuff and got a nine or a twelve or something, and another got a ten. Then somebody came out crashing across the floor, knocking the judge's table down, and running a skate through the judge's ankle. And the judge looks up and says, "It's damn slick out there." In other words, it takes a special category of skill to manipulate this society. Now I don't think it's fair to say people are inept when they can't make it in an event as specialized as that. That's why, when someone comes along and cuts my ankle, or knocks my table down, I look out and say, "Its damn slick out there." It's hard to judge the leaders of an untreasured people. It's very, very slick out there. § It doesn't take much maneuvering, cajoling, persuading or swiftness of foot to get on an empty bus. When we talk about smart or unsmart, we're talking about people who are on a very full bus. You might stand in front of a white person and think he's going to get off before Harlem and find out he owns a fish store in Harlem. What's thought smart is what happens to be selling in a pathological, prostitute society. Naturally, if blow jobs are paying, being on the blow-job line is the smart thing to do. Now if blow-jobs were bad for your teeth or your tongue or your neck, I don't know, then being smart might mean not being on the blow-job line, even if being there secured you the coin of the realm. § I mean, if a baby bites his mother's tit, the mother doesn't exactly get angry. I think most people are inferior to me, I really do, in the sense that they could never hurt me. Not inferior intellectually, financially, or even analytically; they just can't insult me. I understand me too well. Other people seem so less capable of coping. I avoid horizontal hostility, but there is no limit to how I will fight. I will positively wreck someone—ah, maybe once in ten years, this time it may have been five—if he or she is out to hurt me. I'm very lazy, I'm weak, I'm not well. I don't think that I have the physical strength to picket again in this life, though if I really wanted to, I guess I'd go and just lean on somebody. Anyone who stays in bed as much as I do would think of themselves as an invalid, I guess that has allowed me to distinguish between suffering and pain. If you rise up and hit your head on the back of the door, that's pain. But if a friend hits you with the same amount of force, you suffer from the fact that you trusted this person and then they turned on you. I rarely tried to do things I can't do, and I rarely think I'm wrong. § I really don't understand why people get burned out politically. I should think that if they really believed in what they are doing, they would know that they have the best thing going for them. And I don't understand how anybody who reads the newspapers can limit themselves to a specialty, like Women Against Pornography or the Nuclear Freeze. § I loathe the church, but I was so set forward by the pastoral letter of the American bishops that I just think it's one of the most wonderful things in the world. On abortion, they're just as sick as a dog. The Pope is as much a CIA agent as he is a Catholic. I know about racism; I know about sexism. And I'm so glad when the Commission on Human Rights, if that's what it's called, opposes racism and sexism and doctrinaire bigotry, and the ideological bullshit of Reagan, that I don't feel I've lost anything in responding this way. But then again, I think I know how the state works. That's where my conceit lies. In other words, I refuse to regard it as a personal defeat if something I was working on for social change didn't develop, when if I analyzed the society right in the first place, there was just no way for change to prevail. If it does prevail, I'm set forward; if it doesn't, I say, uhah, that proves that I'm right. That's what I mean when I say you've got to minimize the suffering though you can't avoid the pain. § Now if someone comes along and says, look Flo, you've wrapped yourself in individualism and you wouldn't be so free if you lived in South Africa where you have to make choices and a commitment, I'd answer, "Well, I would say that, but I'd be much freer too if I was blue-eyed, blond and living in Denmark." I'm not going to be nailed into any place where I'm unlucky. That's bullshit. It's like saying you're lying on the ground with a car on your ankle and someone comes along and says, "You think you've got it bad, wait until a Mack truck comes along." A car on your ankle will immobilize you as much as a Mack truck, although it's true, a truck is harder to get off than a

Volkswagen. § In 1968, I was on a platform with the Congress for New Politics, and Martin Luther King, Jr. was there, along with Dick Gregory and Dr. Spock. That was the beginning of the feminist movement, in a way. There was a black caucus and a women's caucus, about what women expect from the new politics. I met people on the various panels though I really don't know that many people. I don't expect Jesse Jackson will call me to ask what to have for dinner. But I believe Jesse Jackson will make the best presidential candidate for the black ticket. He's organizing a lot of voter drives, and will control some of the delegates, and because he's the most politically sophisticated of the contenders. Although my personal favorite, in terms of how he talks, would be Ron Dellums. I'd probably back Ron Dellums, because I know the establishment would like to get his ass, though the one who deserves the nomination most is Jesse Jackson. § All the black leaders are favorites of mine. They're all really, really wonderful. I don't know one I don't like, except maybe Eldridge Cleaver. I regard him as a person who may well have at one time been political, but who made, in extricating himself from exile, a lot of commitments to religion. I'm very hostile to religion, so I don't have any respect for him. And he also talks about the correctness of disciplining your wife, for which reason he beats up his wife. And he also is a bit of a traitor, it seems to me, in that he seduced and romanced this white lawyer who got him out of prison, then he became very black and he didn't want any white women anywhere near him. I regard him as exploitative, as unreliable, as turncoaty. I don't trust people who can switch back and forth like that. And I don't like the direction in which he switches. § In the first place, he was a prisoner and a rapist. Now I got very angry when Susan Brownmiller was on the Donahue Show with Cleaver and accused him of being a rapist and a scourge to white women. Black women have been raped by white men throughout the ages. I almost went bananas. You see to me the rape-syndrome centering on white women is racist or has a racist overcoating because it seems to imply that non-white men are after white women a lot. And it is true that white women are very often raped by black men. But the number of non-white, first world women who have been raped by white men far exceeds any attack on white women by non-white men. One of the reasons white women are so sensitive to rape is that their husbands and brothers and fathers were raping native Americans and African slaves. But by keeping white women from fucking non-white men, they would make this fucking a terrible thing for white women. So the sensitivity of women in the feminist community to rape—and rape *is* horrible, don't get me wrong—is exaggerated compared to their sensitivity to raising cannonfodder. To my knowledge, there is still no movement to resist raising cannonfodder. There are peace groups and mothers' marches, talking about war as immoral and racist, everything. But with all that, the theoretical discussion is in my opinion, very low key. I don't know of any writing that tells women how to say before they get married, "now we are going to have two children, but I want you to know I'm not raising any cannon-fodder." That kind of dialogue is not in existence. Women have been active in noncompliance with the war effort, that's clear, but the specific dialectic of refusing to raise children for war, that dialogue is nonexistent. § Black people are more politically aware, generally, than other oppressed groups in this country, whether they are Hispanics, or women. And most of these people pattern their resistance after blacks. That's one of the reasons I get mad, when, for example, a black man runs for president that white women understand it's appropriate that the woman runs for vice-president, particularly since blacks struggled first, struggled more, struggled harder. Women are very wimpy. Now I don't expect women to be any better. I'm not tired. I'm not disappointed. They picket. They do all sorts of nonviolent things. They may be steady in some cases, but they are extremely cowardly. They simply don't even think of poisoning people, though I'm sure they do it on an individual level. In fact, I've often said, partly in jest, that since men do the battering and women do the cooking, it may be that it's not high cholesterol that makes women outlive men. And I'm only half joking. I mean I think women should be mistresses, I guess you'd say, of poisoning, because that would have to be the way they would do it—they'd have to be sneaky and nervous. The feminist movement has never suggested poisoning as a way to change society. Every man who tells a woman to go get coffee should be afraid that she would poison him and that he would fall over dead in his tracks. Well, I mean it's a thought! Every man who batters his wife should be afraid of a poisoned casserole. These things aren't even brought up for discussion, let alone application. § I don't think that women have created a feminist politics. Women have made a tremendous change in this society, at every level; at least no woman is the same. I hardly think there is any woman in any city of any size who doesn't know that if she wants to she can terminate her pregnancy. That is women's politics. Women are learning carpentry, engineering. Sally Ride is women's politics. But you see, it's sort of like drinking the Atlantic Ocean. I think the model of sexism in our society is in those proportions. Every woman may have a cup of ocean water that she didn't have before. The change in the level of the Atlantic Ocean is not noticeable. There is not one single feminist program on TV; not one. There are many, many more women on TV. § Let me tell you something. There was a creepy editorial recently in *Newsweek*, the thrust of which, excuse the expression, is that Jackson has to be careful, because if he goes in with delegates and the white candidate is nominated without him, then black people will be in trouble. Do you see how racist that is? In other words, the only reason we'll treat you decently is that we're counting on your votes. If a farm group doesn't support us, are we going to cut down on the farmers? Certainly not. But if the niggers don't support us, they're out: out-voted, out of the money, out of everything. Well, if that's the way it is, then it's more important than ever that we get our shit together. If the only reason that we have some power is that we have votes, we should pull out now. One of the analogies I like to use is the appendectomy. After surgery for a while, you may be sicker than when you had the appendicitis, but then you are rid of the cause of the illness. You may be worse off after your struggle, but you are getting better. Well, the black ticket to me is just sacred. Just sacred. Mandatory. I have no problem with it at all. And white women need to get on, right up there behind us. § You know, Reagan and the New Right are "goosing" us—as we say colloquially—into action. We are spurred to act the way you'd spur a horse. So I predict in the next five years you will see some widening of action. I think that there will have to be a further letting of socialism out of the closet. § I like to ask things like: Can feminism be trusted to use the media? Some women are not involved in feminism any more because feminists can't be trusted, cannot be trusted, for instance, to use our understanding of government to hurt government and make things better for women. And I think the feminists generally are not aware of the value of black men to the feminist community. This is a general problem with all oppressed peoples. They won't get together. But I think there needs to be a coalition of black men and black women with white women. § I think one of the reasons we don't fundraise well is that we don't push our ideology. Now that the ideology and the straight line is so good, we need to *push*!

APPENDIX

Photomontage by Fina Bathrick

LEXICON OF FOLK-ETYMOLOGY

RALPH LARKIN & DANIEL FOSS

One of the three mutually reinforcing characteristics of a social movement (the other two being the disruption of the instrumentalities of domination and the redefinition of the self) is the reinterpretation of social reality. At the height of a social movement, this reinterpretation of reality becomes a totality, wherein conventional reality—including the "hegemonic ideology," thought-forms and imputations of intentionality—is redefined by dissidents as either totally meaningless or part of a vast and malign conspiracy. In the place of conventional reality emerges an oppositional reality which renders the former problematical. Even linguistic structure and semantics can be undermined by the movement (e.g., the women's movement and linguistic gender bias).

Now, more than 15 years after the middle class youth movement created in 1968, it is easy to forget just how radical it became. Former middle class youth movement activists form one of the basic constituencies from which the post-60s left draws its recruits. The cultural radicalism has been largely dismissed by the left as childish self-indulgence. White middle class radicals who, in the mid-60s believed that sex, drugs and hair (self-repression and cultural monism) were issues as important as the war in Vietnam and oppression of minorities, now have redefined the middle class youth movement of the 60s as the "student movement," or the "antiwar movement," neither of which covers the gamut of dissidence manifested within that social category during that period.

This lexicon of folk-etymology of the 60s is a reminder that the youth movement was not merely against racism, the war or school administrations, but against the *totality of bourgeois social relations*. It is easy to forget in the 80s that many took drugs not to ease the pain of reality, but to experience a reality that superseded and opposed bourgeois reality. Dissident youth had visions and lived myths. The lexicon gives a hint—and only a hint—of the thought-forms which were an inextricable part of the youth movement of the 60s.

**Selections from a forthcoming book from Bergin & Harvey publishers.*

bullshitting. *n.* or *v.* Routine conversation in everyday life; could carry a negative loading if the speaker was frustrated by contrast between humdrum quotidian activities like going to classes and more grandiose visions of what SHOULD have been happening "instead of us just sitting around here bullshitting." **Ants.:** HEAVY RAP; really laying it down, man; MEANINGFUL COMMUNICATION; going out and making the revolution.

trip. *n.* or *v.* (*der.:* LSD use) An idiosyncratic or small-group response at variance with "WHEREIT'SAT." (*q.v.*) E.g., "Well, that's your trip, man." (In this sense, vaguely analogous to "Right-opportunist deviation" in Marxist jargon.)

tripping on our heads. Backhanded admiration for extremely clever deception by representatives of the System.

a trip-and-a-half. **a**) Quite satisfactory. **b**) Very bad.

tripping out. Retirement from the movement or at least a prolonged vacation or hiatus in participation. Alternatively, idiosyncratic behavior not necessarily disruptive of collective action, but at least distracting attention from it. Not quite as negative as "EGO TRIP." Alternatively, vulgar hedonism disgracing the movement as opposed to the species of hedonism currently thought to foster the development of the movement. All these meanings indicated that the person who was tripping out was still defined as a participant in the movement subculture, which, e.g., COPPING OUT did not.

guilt trip. *n.* **a)** An inhibition preventing one from "getting into the experience of one's own oppression" because of the existence of other social categories more oppressed than one's own. **b)** The behavioral disturbance manifested by individual or collective political passivity deriving from such inhibition.

guilt trip. *v.t.* **a)** To maneuver politically to paralyze one's opposition by making them aware of their socially-privileged status and immunity from retribution. **b)** To reduce one's friends or lovers in everyday life to subjection by continually reiterating to them the extent of one's benevolence or munificence relative to their just deserts at the hands of others or alternatively the extent of one's suffering on their behalf.

bum trip. *n. Der.:* In LSD use, a process whereby a pattern recognized in the external environment or intrapsychically or in combination, perhaps initially conducive to joyous or even transcendent feelings, subtly shifts to induce panic. **a)** Anything which induces suffering or depression for over thirty seconds. **b)** Disappointment. **c)** Political defeat. **d)** Harassment by bureaucracy, e.g. low grades, getting drafted, hostile action by police from drug bust to traffic ticket. *Alt:* BUMMER. Semantically, BUM TRIP is more serious than HASSLE but not as bad as FREAKOUT.

bum trip. *v.t.* To induce, usu. deliberately, depression or aggravation in others.

head trip. (*Der.:* Allusion to the capacity of LSD to stimulate or induce any psychic state, sensation, or process, including abstract reasoning. An example of a "head trip" on LSD would be Foss' first in 1967. While waiting for the so-called "hallucinations" to commence, which they never did, he got extremely bored. As the night was very long, he picked up a novel by Robbe-Grillet he had previously found incomprehensible. On this night, though, he breezed right through it and found it a simple straightforward story albeit on the morrow he found it as incomprehensible as before.) In terms of standards prevailing with the subculture, an excessive preoccupation with, indulgence in or proclivity for abstractions, ideas, theories, or other variants of intellectualization. **Ants.:** BODY TRIP, GETTING OFF.

"Head trip" and synonymous

usages such as "intellectual bullshit" portended to outsiders a wave of "anti-intellectualism" among college students, even or especially among the "brightest" of them. What transpired may more accurately be characterized as the breakdown of the bourgeois cultural / hegemonic-ideological paradigm without its replacement then or since. Bourgeois society has of course since persisted and even flourished by dint of the constraints dictated by structure; not least of these are constraints which coerce the manufacture of "knowledge" and which purchase the manufacture of "high culture" and the arts, all in ever-swelling mass. The suspension of the hegemonic-ideological structure in the 60s nevertheless facilitated the filling-in of what had been previously excluded from the cultural paradigm given the development of "antistructure" by the social movements of the period; and with the liquidation of the politically and socially subversive developments, we still retain: body-awareness, the foundation of the physical fitness, amateur athletics, natural foods, "holistic health," and kindred industries; sexual awareness, inevitably a big seller; "consciousness"-awareness, the cornerstone of the humanistic therapy and spirituality industries; black-awareness, with innumerable new products developed for the market deriving therefrom; woman-awareness, representing not only a new market but—possibly even more important—a formidable and hitherto largely untapped source of new talent to be recruited into the ranks of the bourgeoisie (whose resourcefulness in drawing new blood to itself was noted by Marx in Volume III of CAPITAL [1867]); and Gay-awareness, for which the latter holds also. Each and every one of these fillings-in of the paradigm brings with it its own theoreticians, professional practitioners, and "knowledge"-manufacturers whose work—however obstructed by lingering obstacles and prejudices—daily swells the volume of "intellectual" output in the USA.

The understanding of the 1960s "youth" culture as "anti-intellectual" is possibly as superficial as a naive acceptance of the self-description of the 1950s Beats as "intellectuals" opposed to conventional philistine "anti-intellectualism."

reality trip. Characterization of temporary or reluctant concessions to bourgeois social relations such as writing term papers, studying for exams, accepting a job when alternative sources of funds failed, or making some compromise necessary to stay out of the military. Alternatively, in the new left, a course of action said to be dictated by "realism," but seemingly amounting in substance to conservatism or passivity. Alternatively (*Late*.), whatever one was doing in the 1970s.

death trip. A course of action believed by the speaker to eventuate in catastrophe (such as a head-bashing mass bust or, expulsion from school) with no counterbalancing gain (like media coverage or "radicalization" of the whole student body) to show for it. Vaguely analogous to "Left-adventurist deviation" in Marxist jargon. (Obviously, a proposed "action" dreaded as a "death trip" before-hand might easily prove afterward to have been "where it was really at" all along.) Alternatively, any policy of the Johnson or Nixon Administrations. Example of usage was a warning issued August 1968 by a Chicago group to "kids" lured thence by Yippie promises of a music festival: "Stay away from Chicago if you are expecting a Festival of Light and Love. The Chicago Convention will be a death trip."

ego trip. An exercise in self-promotion or self-aggrandizement at the expense of the collective interest, often associated with advocacy of a "death trip." Alternatively an epithet impugning the motives and character of a movement personage evidently relishing the attentions of the media. Alternatively, a mental disorder said to afflict an individual wielding a species of autocratic dominion over the local movement participants, even if the latter should not oppose this or even actively encourage it. Alternatively, a disorder said to characterize any idiosyncratic behavior, usually of an attention-getting nature, which disrupted the harmony of the local movement participants or distracted their attention from more pressing matters.

media trip. Collective action, symbolic gestures, granting of interviews, or general outlandishness perpetrated for the sole or paramount purpose of eliciting coverage by the "establishment media" as opposed to what was understood to be "real."

real, to be. *v.i.* **a)** To care, that is really really care, for one's lover or friend. Somewhat stronger in emotional loading than 1970s therapy-talk successor "to be there," as in "I want you to be there for me." **b)** To be brave, courageous, tough; e.g., "That guy's REAL, man." Alt. form, "to be for real." **c)** Being what one became upon rejection of the conventions inculcated by the parental generation, which from one's current perspective are understood as having amounted to "lies," "bullshit," "brainwashing," or "a phony mindfuck," etc. **d)** To be excessively dangerous, e.g., "Things are really gettin' too fuckin' REAL around here, man; let's split." Reflective of the underlying conviction that objective reality in the USA was a mere generalization of South Vietnam and Watts, that is, violent and perilous, with the outbreak of civil war imminent.

unreal. *v.i.* **a)** "real" in sense **(d)** above. **b)** Disorientingly or outlandishly disconcerting, as when minions of the establishment pull a fast one; E.g., say a bunch of freaks is passing joints around in a circle, but one of them is an undercover NARK, so there is a mass bust; someone is sure to say, "Man, this is like just too fucking' unreal." (Note: In the preceding, "bunch of freaks" properly took the singular "is." In the 60s grammatical usage could be crucial in distinguishing between authentic freaks and "pseudos." Thus, in Michelangelo Antonioni's movie *Zabriskie Point* the female lead—played by Deborah Halperin, subsequently a disciple of Mel Lyman, a pretender to Divinity in Boston—was made to say, "I don't dig to do it." As we left the theater we heard an indignant customer mutter to his companion, " 'Dig' does not take an infinitive.") **c)** By extension, any surprise or unanticipated event: "You in from Minneapolis? Fuckin' UNREAL, man!

really. *particle* or *prefix*. E.g., **syn.** with "Mmmmm" for purpose of seeming to respond to someone else's monologue; poss. der. from example of "nondirective" therapy talk. Could be used to begin or end a sentence or both ("Really, you know, that's bullshit, really") or as intensifier, often in serial repetition, to indicate that the speaker is "not bullshitting." ("Like, that's really really fucked, I'm serious.") The semantic impact of the redundant usage of "really" was the communication — or intersubcultural fortification—of a sense of nebulosity, that is, the uncertainty as to just what "really" was or wasn't whose deepening ambiguity was brilliantly captured by the Beatles in their 1968 song "Strawberry Fields": Recall the gentle idyllic mindset created initially, the stoned-out refrain "Nothing is real/Nothing to get hung about," and the devastating dissonantly hideous conclusion: a sonic evocation—perhaps—of the incursion of an armored division into the complacent pastoral paradise suggested earlier. To this extent the maxim of Jack (Werner Erhard) Rosenberg, "What is, is; what aint, aint," represents not only "a blow struck for the Other Side in the struggle for the control of "reality" itself, but also *eo ipso* was symptomatic by reason of time and place — 1971 on the Bay Bridge between the Holy City and Political Capital of the movement from the Beat Generation/anti-HUAC riot period down to People's Park and beyond—of the triumphant reassertion—somewhat updated to be sure—of the conventional "reality/hegemonic ideology" in society as a whole.

A crucial empirical datum is not available to us and is not known by us to exist: This would involve a quantitative sociolinguistic content analysis comparing the incidence of the usage of "really" of the sort described here —and there were/are numerous others it should go without saying—in common speech as taped in contexts approaching its everyday milieu as between, say ca. 1968–70 and a decade later among persons of comparable ages and social origins.

whereit'sat. *n.* der.: Black speech. **a)** Objective reality, as distinct from the appearance of social relations, and as conceptualized in terms of the subjectivist ideology. Its delineation was collectively arrived at within the movement by endless discussions of and searches for patterns in the configuration of microevents, that is, in everyday life, and macroevents, that is, of movement-wide or national or even international scope. **Ant.:** BULLSHIT. **Syn.** (*SDS*): CORRECT ANALYSIS **b)** A particular aspect of objective reality of specific, personal, or immediate concern; e.g., to lover: "Like, what I want to know is, I mean, whereitsreallyat between us." **c)** Divergence in opinion reflecting individual differences: in that subjectivist ideology was collectively developed via the intensification of individual feeling-states or "experiences," whether in isolation, in small-group settings (most commonly), or in crowds, and in that the ideology was superimposed upon existing individual differences, non-standardization was the rule rather than the exception. Hence: "That may be whereitsat for you, but it aint whereitsat for me."

happening. *adj.* **whuzhappening**. *n.* der.: Black speech. **a)** Fashionable, somewhat avant-garde; replaced HIP. **b)** Conformist, faddish, superficial; the doings of the multitude as viewed from the perspective of someone who knows whereitsat. E.g., the following actual conversation, which transpired in a restaurant as a rock song with an overtly political message was playing: Q. "Is that whereitsat?" A. "No, that's where it was at six months ago. It's only happening now." **Syn.** (*SDS*): CORRECT LINE.

down. There are two "families" of "down" words. The first is derived from Black speech; the second is derived from drug use. They will be presented here in that order. The etymological distinction is very important.

I. Black-derived "down" words:

put-down. *n.* Insult to one's dissident social category as defined by the victim. Most commonly the perpetrator of the put-down was oblivious of putting anybody down until this was pointed out: E.g., in 1970 we observed a man utter the word "chick" (obs. and taboo after 1969) to another man; this was overheard by a woman who accused him of committing a "put-down of all women." When the perpetrator of a put-down was additionally accused of knowingly putting down the victim, this took the usage of DELIBERATE PUT-DOWN.

The importance of "put-down" in subjectivist ideology lay in that the more "consciousness" was "expanded" or "raised," the more "awareness" was "heightened" or "developed," the more one was "radicalized" or "got into" (*q.v.*) one's "experience," the more such loadings one spotted and consequently the more deeply one became convinced of the genetically warped, pervasively inimical, and fundamentally-irreconcilable character of those, previously one's opponents, who are now one's deadly enemies (it went without saying in some quarters at certain times that one was ready to die.); and the more evident it became (*q.v.* PARANOIA) that not only had the enemy invented the language for the explicit purpose of one's own subjugation (*q.v.* BRAINWASHING) but was furthermore backed by the armed might of a stupendous "power structure" of global scope.

We should now underscore that in the end it is out of the question to attempt to communicate in English or any other language without adventitiously, gratuitously, fortuitously, or unconsciously embodying in one's message connotations of racist, sexist, bourgeois, homophobic, etc., etc., ideology. This alone set finite limits to the critiques of "put-downs" in that the critiques themselves were necessarily articulated in speech or print.

As the 60s witnessed the emergence of an unprecedented conception of the "personal" with which the conception of the "political" was fused, it became correspondingly difficult or impossible to make any statement regarding the seemingly-idiosyncratic somatic or psychic trait of a member of another dissident social category/social-movement collectively without being charged with a put-down.

If there was no probability whatever of critiquing the insult on any political pretext [for example: The TRUTH of the statement in question was irrelevant if the credentials of the individual who uttered it were challenged. Thus, if a white man said that a black woman was ugly, this was **a)** racist on grounds that white esthetic standards were irrelevant to black people, who were all Beautiful; and **b)** sexist, on grounds that men only consider women as sex objects. If he said she was Beautiful, this was still **a)** racist on grounds of "the well-known sex thing about our women"; and **b)** sexist on the same grounds as before.], the specific form PERSONAL PUT-DOWN was used.

going down. **a)** Philosophically, the general thrust and motion of objective reality, WHEREITSAT, beneath the flux of the appearances of things, WHUZHAPPENING. E.g., "What's going down in the Movement?" **b)** Oral sex. **c)** To happen or occur. E.g., "What went down at your house last night?" (The loading of GOING DOWN in sense (a) was normally neutral or somewhat negative.)

coming down. **a)** Philosophically, deriving a sense of the future as threatening, portending doom, or at least challenging. E.g., "I can see some very heavy shit coming down on us."

laid down. (Poss. akin to commonplace with usage, "laid down the law.") Pronounced authoritatively; articulated forcefully; dictated ex cathedra. Example: "laid down a heavy rap."

get down or **git down**. (*Late*. Supplemented and partially replaced GET IT ON, of somewhat similar meanings. Der.: Black pimp subculture, which is suffused with metaphors self-consciously mocking the conventional business world; this is due to pimps' quite justifiable understanding of prostitution as a prototype of a "service industry" organized on capitalist lines (cf. Milner and Milner, BLACK PLAYERS, 1972): Thus "git-down time" is the hour at which the labor force **a)** gets down to work, **b)** gets down on the street, and **c)** gets down on their backs. This done, the pimps take care of business, meaning that they engage in conspicuous consumption and other aspects of keeping up "respectable" appearances; compete invidiously for prestige conferred by women, money, luxury products, cocaine, etc., with said prestige upheld by violence if necessary, whence the political usage; and undertake the recruitment or discharge—hiring / firing — of personnel and, of course, the supervision and disciplining of the existing staff of the enterprise.) **a)** Sexual intercourse. **b)** Philosophically, to engage in or to prepare oneself psychically for an event of some moment, frequently sexual or violent in character, for which the prognosis is favorable. **Syn**.: GET IT ON. **Ant**.: COMING DOWN. Example: "This is revolution, y'unnderstan', and revolution, like Chairman Mao says, is war! (cheers); An' we gotta go beyond bein prepared to die! That's what the Black people found out! (cheers) What th' Vietnamese people, the Cuban people, the Chinese Red Guards, all Third World people found out! (hysteria) So we gonna get DOWN, we gonna get our shit TOGETHER, y'unnerstan', we gonna get it ON and that means by any means NECESSARY! 'Cause we're tired of it coming down on us an' from now on it coming down on THEM! (pandemonium)" (This is a slight—but only slight — exaggeration of Weatherman and 70s neo-Leninist rhetoric. Here is the real thing: "We will say, I'd rather die than live another day like this. We're gonna go out and say, Let's not only die, but kill to make revolution. . . ." This is taken from a 1979 poster of the Revolutionary Communist Party/USA quoting its Central Committee Chairman Bob Avakian (autocratic leader since the inception of the party in 1969 as the Bay Area Revolutionary Union, or shortly thereafter). No date for the quotation is given and none is necessary as the rhetoric has not changed.

II. Drug-culture derived "down" words:

coming down. The wearing off of a HIGH, especially that from an LSD trip. By extension the subsiding of any "up" feeling, sensation, or "experience," especially one which altered one's definitions of, and hence expectations from, "reality." As it was precisely the coordinates of the latter which were in question during the 60s, it was only too easy during the post-movement post-mortems of the early 70s for many former participants to become convinced that the entire movement had been a "trip" from which "coming down" to "face reality" had been immanently inevitable. This in turn induced some to obliterate memories of past dissidence and others to adopt the perspective of the old leftists and neo-Leninists.

bring-down. In LSD use, the unanticipated and precipitous termination of the high, normally due to extrinsic rather than intrapsychic factors, and its conversion into a BUMMER; occasionally, an antidote—e.g., a tranquilizer—used deliberately to effect this. By extension, any rude shock, such as a "repressive" act by the "Establishment," being rejected sexually, getting an unanticipated low grade, etc., which terminated an otherwise pleasant interlude.

down, downer. A central nervous system depressant like a tranquilizer or sedative. By extension, anything depressing, boring, or stupefying. (Replaced DRAG.) Adverbialized to denote a psychically-depressed state: "I'm down." Note: while metaphors of much the same tenor were common prior to the advent of sophisticated pill-popping, they commonly required additional verbiage, e.g., "down in the dumps.")

down trip. An activity or course of action which was predicably boring or psychically depressing and was thus to be avoided on principle.

down head. (Poss. der. from early-60s, that is, pre-"psychedelic" drug-culture by analogy with POT-HEAD, marijuana smoker; A-HEAD, amphetamine user; or GARBAGE-HEAD, person who says, "These pills are pretty! Lemme take a few." Later a distinction was drawn between the category of those persons regarded within the youth culture as excessively preoccupied with certain drugs and the category of those who were not; whence SPEED-FREAK, amphetamine addict; of DOWNER-FREAK, barbiturate addict; as distinct from POT-HEAD, to the extent that marijuana use is self-limiting by reason of boredom; and ACID-HEAD, to the extent that the same is true of LSD because of BUMMERS, and THE CHANGES.) An individual who has become obnoxious by reason of such chronic and conspicuous depression that it contaminates the social environment by inevitably "bringing down" everybody else. More odious in California than in Northeast Corridor variant. This concept illustrates a major shift which had occurred in the youth culture from the time of the beat generation subculture of the late 50s. In the earlier period, a well-cultivated depression had been a mark of respectability among the bohemian element: The word BEAT, whose ambivalence, multiple derivation, and self-mockery foreshadowed some of the principles of categorization which came to flower in the late 60s, itself evoked not only the obligatory affinity for jazz; but also the word BEATEN. The Beats couldn't stand it all, had no idea why, couldn't care less, and were certain that nothing could be done about any of it. Optimism was the face of the enemy; otherwise respectable people went out of their way to wallow in filth and despondency, as these were the outward signs of philosophical depth. While Beats shared with later "freak"-radicals the disgust with conventional social relations, as in, e.g., Gregory Corso's "Abomunist Manifesto" (1960), they were politically in substance a variant of the conservatism of the period, as they imputed a repository of moral and spiritual purity to the most victimized in society which in the urban context meant the sub-proletarian blacks (cf. Norman Mailer, "The White Negro," in ADVERTISEMENTS FOR MYSELF (1959), for examples of some of the most amazing racist stereotyping outside Mississippi at the time.). Ten years later, say 1969, optimism was still the face of the enemy, specifically the optimism of corporate managerialism as practiced by McNamara and Kissinger and as extolled by Daniel Bell and Zbigniew Brzezinski (the latter getting his chance to practice it later); but it was opposed by dissidents whose own optimism in many instances detected boundless possibilities for demolishing the optimistic Establishment. But on this dimension alone both sides lost: After another ten years had passed (1979) pessimism had become the faith of the majority to the extent that the President of the USA felt obliged to denounce it in an address to the nation. **Syn.**: *NEGATIVITY.*

downed out. Incapacitated by a depressed psychic state. (*q.v.* OUT)

out. (*Der.*: Standard English usages of "out" suggesting absence, as from work, school, or other situation where presence is obligatory; also kindred usages such as "out of commission," "out of order," "out of service," and "out" in baseball. Further developed in Black musicians' argot, e.g., OUT TO LUNCH, mentally deranged or playing in a relaxed and inspired fashion; OUT OF IT, culturally retrograde or stoned; WAY OUT, avant-garde or unacceptably deviant within the standards of the subculture, loathsome, disagreeable; etc.) Usually, a suffix denoting a psychic state which renders someone incapacitated, especially for "economic" or other "action" in the Richardian-Weberian-Parsonian universe. Loading may vary from positive to negative depending on the degree of incapacity and its desirability in the particular context.

spaced out. Originally Black musicians' usage denoting the effects of marijuana whereby in seemingly "slowing down time" it renders each musical note more discretely perceptible in that the notes and passages seem to be stretched or spread—hence "spaced" — over longer time-spans with longer intervals between. Acquired additional connotations in 60s thanks to the simultaneous popularity in the youth culture of LSD—whose effects upon musical perception are similar, only more so—and science-fiction; these connotations are well-illustrated by the Rolling Stones' "2,000 Light Years From Home" on THEIR SATANIC MAJESTIES REQUEST (1967). Thus: **a)** Stoned or tripping. **b)** Behaving as if one were stoned or tripping. **c)** By extension, anything only someone stoned or tripping could appreciate. **d)** By further extension: (*Late.*) chaotic, disorganized, inefficient, inept.

tripped out. Tripping on LSD in such a way as to annoy, disconcert, or be of no practical utility to others. By analogy, any sort of selfish individualistic behavior. (*q.v.* above for overtly-political meaning).

wiped out. (From California surfer subculture, originally meaning "to get capsized by a stupendous wave," the latter known as a "wipeout.") **a)** So stoned as to be reduced to a state of complete conceptual collapse; incapable of abstract thought or perception mediated by culturally-implanted "conceptual frameworks"; in an "altered state of consciousness." **Syn**.: BLOWN ONE'S MIND, BLOWN OUT, BLOWN AWAY, all derived from conventional colloquialism, "blown (it)," meaning malfunction of fire, fuse, etc., or having failed in a competitive struggle; also BOMBED OUT, WASTED. **b)** Too overjoyed for words, suggestive of "peak experience" e.g., an expression of pleasure following orgasm: "I'm wiped out." **c)** Shocked speechless: "That wipes me out."

farout. **a)** Nice. **b)** Satisfactory. **c)** Quite so. (Words in this particular niche in the linguistic structure were frequently recycled: Thus, FAROUT replaced OUTTASIGHT, which replaced GROOVY, which replaced HIP OF I'M HIP; and was itself supplanted by RIGHTON.) For emphasis FAROUT took the intensifier FUCKIN' to make FARFUCKINOUT.

freak out. (Up to about 1966, an episode occurring during an LSD trip which combined **a)** panic with **b)** total loss of self-control; the ensemble appearing to resemble a psychotic episode, whence "psychotomimetic drug." The semantic picture then became complicated by a growing tendency for the users of LSD to designate themselves as cultural mutants and manifest this by such devices as inordinate quantities of hair or prophesying in public whilst attired in sheets; these called themselves "freaks." Things were still further complicated within the emergent "freak" culture by the linguistic borrowing of "freak," possibly from the prostitution subculture, where it meant — Xaviera Hollander, *The Happy Hooker* (1973)—a person defined even in that context as outlandishly perverted and whose tastes, e.g., S&M, B&D, required the services of a "specialist" within the profession for satisfaction: The "freak" culture early on idealized emancipation from repetitive routine activity, "living by the clock," "preprogrammed" careers, keeping up appearances subsuming the conventional practice of incessant cleaning and the consumption of countless products marketed for this purpose with the intention of maintaining living quarters and personal appearance—or odor—in perpetual readiness for inspection by impersonal outsiders, and other activities which might be covered by stretching the term "compulsive." As this idealized emancipation developed, they applied "freak" in the prostitution sense to those deviant in terms of the "freak" culture itself who displayed tendencies to narrow focusing upon strictly limited sources of gratification and so were analogous to S&M and suchlike "freaks" whose sexual activity was quite narrowly circumscribed by rituals, costumes, and props. This might explain the use of "freak" to designate deviance WITHIN the subculture of the "compulsive" sort: Hence those dangerous to themselves and others by reason of drug addiction, e.g., SMACK-FREAK, SPEED-FREAK, DOWNER-FREAK, etc.: proto-terrorists and bullies were VIOLENCE FREAKS, and advocates of rigidly bureaucratic political organizing were STRUCTURE-FREAKS. "Compulsiveness" external to the "freak" culture was stigmatized by other lingo, such as UPTIGHT, borrowed from black speech and originally alluding to the retraction of the testicles when anxious or to close friendship, but infused with additional connotations associated with the white's postural rigidity and their proclivity to anal metaphors, e.g., "keep a tight asshole"; and STRAIGHT, replacing SQUARE, developed by Black musicians to allude to white managerial-bureaucratic phallicism, then diffused to the homosexual subculture which was not yet the gay movement, as well as to white drug-culturists when the latter were devotees of black jazz artists. Of course, given the proclivity of the dissident youth culture to multiple derivations, ambivalence, and ambiguity, there were obviously herein the makings of confounding and confusion or original meanings and the synthesis and proliferation of wholly new conceptual categories.) **a)** Insane, deranged, out of control; originally stronger than FLIPPED OUT or WIGGED OUT, words also current in the 60s and borrowed from the black musician subculture. **b)** In a rage; lost one's temper. **c)** Shocked, aghast. **d)** (Late.) Irritated, possibly to the extent of raising one's voice, but not necessarily. **e)** With "of,": Suddenly blasted from one interpretation of social reality into another, e.g., "freaked out of the way I was brought up and into the movement." **Syn**.: RADICALIZED. **f)** A party attended by a bunch of freaks whereat the speaker had a great time: "Wow, whatta freakout, man." **g)** Chaos, disorder, rioting; if successfully provoked by the movement, e.g., during a "confrontation," then a glorious victory, provided that bodily injury was minimal and nobody was thrown out of school who had not planned to drop out. If a FREAK OUT in this sense was forestalled by a massive show of force by the police, then this was a FREAK

SHOW or FREAK SCENE; the same terms applied to movement meetings where incomprehensible jargon was used. **Variants**: FREAKY. *adj*. **a)** Weird, incomprehensible. **b)** Very fine; interesting. FREAKED ON. **a)** addicted, as to a drug, to the extent that self-control is impossible. **b)** Obsessed with one's hobby, pastime, or THING to an extent which arouses the concern of one's friends, TRIBE, AFFINITY GROUP, or COLLECTIVE. **c)** Madly in love, perhaps to the point of monogamy.

burned out. **a)** A psychic state, simulating that of the cabbage, brought on by prolonged excessive use of LSD or central nervous system stimulants. **b)** By extension, a person once active in the early stage of the movement, but now too senile to appreciate that 19-year-olds calling themselves the "Action Faction" are best suited to understand WHEREITSAT. **c)** (*Late*.) The state or condition of having never recovered emotionally from the end of the movement and to have spent the ensuing years either seeking salvation by exotic means in strange places, e.g., India, or whiling away the epoch plodding away in a trancelike state at one's job. In the latter variant it is to be noted that not only can one not get burned out without drugs, but also that it becomes progressively more difficult to tell the burned out from those in whom nothing has ever been lit.

sold out, sell out. (*Der*.: conventional speech.) **a)** Betrayal, usually of a political character. As "the personal" was "political," accusations of being a SELL-OUT, that is, deficient in militancy, could not be avoided short of incurring the danger of bodily injury. Even in the early 60s the old left (1930s) conception of "support action" whereby dissidents demonstrated in physically safe places, propagandized, raised funds, wielded political influence, or otherwise "supported" those on strike, fighting in Spain, etc., was somewhat contemptible. Thus in 1963 we heard a black radical-integrationist tell a crowd in the South: They [northern white liberals] say they are with us ... But I say to them: WHERE is your body?!" (By 1966 this individual was an executive of a Federal agency.) **b)** The cultural radicalization of the mid-60s, associated with the drug culture and the near-hegemonic influence in youth-culture ideology of Dr. Timothy Leary's slogan "Turn on, tune in, drop out!" an alternative and somewhat contradictory ideal of movement participation was counterposed to the first: the maximum feasible renunciation of the totality of bourgeois social relations, beginning with school and "gainful employment." The catch was, obviously, that as there was a war on, male dissidents who were neither II-S (in school) or II-A (in jobs "vital to national security") were liable to military service; hence the exacerbation of the contradiction between the "political" and "economic" thrusts of the movement—noted earlier—following the resurgence of overtly-political action in 1967. With the further intensification of both thrusts of the movement, those who had dropped out could accuse those still in school—however reluctantly—of "selling out by bullshitting their lives away," while the latter in turn could taunt the former for "selling out by not putting their asses on the line in the anti-racist and anti-imperialist struggle." Yet even these drew the line in rejecting "preprogrammed careers in the corporate-liberal establishment." (Whence the slogan: "Work! Study! Get ahead! Kill!") Yet the movement sputtered out ca. 1970–71 (excepting the feminist and gay spinoffs), thus entailing the simultaneous liquidation of overtly-political "confrontation" and DROPPING OUT. There consequently arose, especially for heterosexual men, a third sense of SELLING OUT: **c)** (*Late.*) Renunciation of the ideal of DROPPING OUT in favor of mere vulgar careerism, by contrast to the speaker, who is "working for change within the system," "radicalizing students," "using my skills and movement consciousness in a position where I can do some good for the betterment of humanity," etc., etc., any variant of which being, from the standpoint of someone still a DROP OUT, a COP OUT, to rationalize SELLING OUT.

cop out. **a)** An act of cowardice. **b)** A euphemism for, or lesser degree of SELLING OUT. **c)** A self-serving rationalization or LAME-ASS EXCUSE whereby one evaded DEALING WITH (*q.v.*) WHEREITSAT with oneself, which subsumed, say, one's persistent failure to put one's ASS ON THE LINE; one's intrapsychic HANG-UPS; one's victimizing of others; one's political backwardness, e.g., in refusing to engage in SHARP STRUGGLE (*q.v.*) on grounds that it was "boring"; etc.

strung out. (*Der.*: junkie subculture; shorthand metaphorical allusion for one's habit having one in leading strings and bringing one UPTIGHT if one fails to get off.) **a)** Hopelessly addicted to a drug; stronger than FREAKED ON. **b)** By extension, a state or condition of preoccupation to grotesque excess with one's own THING, TRIP, or RAP, e.g., "strung out on one's own rhetoric." c) Exhausted, as after completing a term paper or partying for an entire week. **d)** Terminally bored, as to be "strung out on revolutionary rhetoric" in general.

zonked out, zonked. (*Der.*: California drug culture. Obs. after 1966 but used as archaism.) **Syn.**: BOMBED (OUT); BLOWN (OUT); WRECKED; WASTED; TOTALLED (OUT); BLASTED; way, way, OUT there.

●

Subcult: Lingo Politico

communism with a small c. Declared by Bernardine Dohrn, leader of the National Office (NO) faction of SDS, 1968–69, as the objective of SDS, but never defined by her.

communism. **a)** A mental disorder whose symptoms included: delusions to the effect that the Mongolian People's Republic was a real country and that its admission to the United Nations was an issue of pressing national concern; that Alexander Dubcek acted alone; or that USA college students would involve themselves in anything from which the benefits would at earliest accrue to their grandchildren. Example: Irwin Silber declared in 1969, in a post-mortem on the disintegrated SDS, that "the revolution may take 50 years." **b)** A word whose use was a sure-fire indication that the ESTABLISHMENT was REDBAITING either oneself or the LIBERATION FORCES in the THIRD WORLD (foreign or domestic). The latter were always innocent lambs forced to PICK UP THE GUN to fight IMPERIALISM (or RACISM) and were sufficiently busy hiding water buffalos from helicopter gunships that they could be presumed to have as little use for theory as oneself.

liberate. *v.t.* (*Der.*: French Revolution. Originally meaning "to conquer and loot a place or country on the pretext — often sincerely believed at the outset — of delivering the populace from an odious political regime." In 1792 the Girondin regime in France, confronted with economic disaster of its own creation, social polarization, and the rise of the Jacobin opposition, cast a beady eye upon an aristocratic exile army training across the border in Prussia; the Girondins then jumped the gun and declared war on most of the European powers, vowing to LIBERATE the peoples thereof from their "tyrants." The first place LIBERATED was the Austrian Netherlands, which was picked clean before being lost, along with a large chunk of France. The Girondins were thereupon overthrown (May 31–June 2, 1793) by the Jacobins, but their adherents revolted and held out in the city of Lyons for a couple of months. When the city fell, the Jacobins commenced what became known to history as the "reign of terror," killing hundreds in Lyons by firing squad. The Jacobins were unable to obey the order to level Lyons to the ground, as the explosives ran out after the demolition of a few blocks of downtown, but they renamed the place Ville Affranchie, or LIBERATED CITY.) **a)** To forcibly occupy, as by a crowd, especially in defiance of regulations, and to remain in the premises until the BUST, the latter being ensured, where necessary, by a LIST OF NON-NEGOTIABLE DEMANDS. E.g., "We liberated X Hall." **b)** Removal of papers, subsequently known as LIBERATED DOCUMENTS, from the files of a minion of the CORPORATE-LIBERAL ESTABLISHMENT, commonly the university president, which established his ties to the MILITARY-INDUSTRIAL COMPLEX. If it transpired that the papers failed to turn up any personal preoccupation with the development of a new nerve gas or pathogenic bacilus, then correspondence with bankers speculating in real estate inhabited by racial minorities sufficed. **c)** Any other appropriation of the possessions of PIGS, the latter term where necessary applicable to those dissidents considered insufficiently to the left (not to speak of anyone to the right of them). Notable instances: The LIBERATION in 1968 of the printing press of the Liberation News Service by new leftists who regarded the staff as too hippieistic; and the liberation in 1969 of the premises of the GUARDIAN by new leftists who regarded it as too old leftist, thereupon named—need we tell you—THE LIBERATED GUARDIAN. **Syn.**: (from either side) RIP OFF. A place once LIBERATED becomes a LIBERATED AREA.

liberated area. (*Der.*: Chinese Revolution.) A place forcibly occupied by dissidents, which they were prepared to forcibly defend against efforts at expulsion by the PIGS, at least to the extent—as at Columbia University (1968)—of barricading the entrances to somewhat retard the progress of the BUST. By extension, the following graffito we saw in a college classroom building in New York City ca. 1970: "THE SPOT ON WHICH YOU STAND IS A LIBERATED AREA. DEFEND IT." The implication of the graffito was plain: Any individual attempting for any reason to victimize or intimidate the reader of the message was to be identified with the PIGS and was to be resisted or subjected to retaliation in kind.

liberated, to be. *v.i.* **a)** (Behavioral) Accolade for conformity to whatever was GOING DOWN (*q.v.*) at the time. Thus, a woman was said to be liberated in 1967 if she said Yes and in 1969 if she said No. **b)** Purified of HANGUPS, which were periodically redefined in accordance with shifting understandings of WHEREITSAT. **c)** (Obs. or vulgar) An allusion to a member of the women's movement. The term WOMEN'S LIBERATION was proudly borne by participants when actually engaged in social conflict both within and without the "male-dominated left." This connoted something more conservative than what was designated by RADICAL FEMINISM. These expressions have dropped out of use by the women's movement, as they patently lack what is commonly called "class." Worse, those days are now something of an embarrassment, in that Phyllis Schlafly has in recent times been horrifying the church ladies in Iowa by merely reprinting the 1973 Program of the National Organization of Women (NOW) verbatim. An analogous process has led to the restyling of GAY LIBERATION as the gay movement.

manipulative elitist. Derogatory designation of an individual accused of reproducing within the movement the executive-managerialist attitudes, if not the actual behavior, encouraged within the bureaucracies to which the movement was understood to be opposed. The term was transmitted by heredity from the new left to women's liberation. Like other lingo, this term was also situational and relativistic in its applicability. For obvious reasons one was likelier to use it in condemnation of one's opponents than of one's allies. The temporal context also mattered: In the early 60s, when the use of form and ritual in meetings was not unknown, the individual who knew who was out of order and under what circumstances a motion could be amended, and used such knowledge to advance or oppose a particular line of policy was an obvious target of resentment, as is customary in any organization. As time went on—that is, as people began to "hang loose"—attention shifted to sins of omission: If, say, the local "scene" of movement participants was dominated by a single forceful personality whose talents, eloquence, physical bravery, and propagandist ability were incomparably superior to those of any other participant, this person might still be targeted—absent or present — as a "manipulative elitist" for failure to make extraordinary efforts to develop the potential of others; yet, and we have seen this, when something simply had to get done, the critics would nevertheless say, "We can't start the meeting: X isn't here." Other vices which might be adduced to substantiate the charge included: failure to hold meetings in a circle, preferably on the floor; talking too much, even if nobody else had anything to say even if it wasn't worth saying; failure ca. 1969–70 to ensure that the predominance of remarks in discussions (in a group comprising both sexes) were made by women; ensuring the same but for sneaky reasons; practicing polygyny (1968–69); practicing monogamy (Weather Underground); putting people down; not submitting to criticism-self-criticism (putting oneself down, with help from the group); promoting a division of labor along lines of amount of education, specialized training, gender, ability, etc., or promoting it at all; insistence upon the priority of the individual over the "collective"; stifling individuality in the name of the "collective" etc., etc.

heavy. (*Der*.: Black speech.) *adj*. **a)** Grave or serious in content; e.g., "laid down a heavy rap." **b)** Dangerous, risky; e.g., "This trip is gonna get heavy when the real shit comes down." **c)** Psychically troublesome; e.g., "going through some heavy changes." *n*. (*Der*.: Metaphorical depiction of an individual in the psychic state of "weightiness.") **a)** An individual regarded with respect and whose views or actions were emulated within the local dissident "scene." A person of this kind was normally but not always a "leader—the latter having been a dirty word designating something which should not have existed within the movement but did anyway, such that one was, if a leader, obliged to deny that one was one or at minimum that one desired to be one, in the vain hope of evading charges of MANIPULATIVE ELITISM—and if so was not always designated by a formal title. **b)** By extension, a celebrity within the movement, especially if of more than local significance. A HEAVY in this sense was either conspicuously under surveillance by the FBI or local Red Squad; or was ASSUMED (*q.v.* PARANOIA) to be watched anyway. A known HEAVY would be sought out by the ESTABLISHMENT MEDIA for purposes of DISTORTION. **c)** (1969) One of "a bunch of people who think they're the whole movement and only talk to each other so they can spout Marxist bullshit." **d)** (*Late.*) Any crazy or dangerous person. E.g., "You're too heavy."

structure-freak. (obs. after ca. 1968) A person suffering from a psychic malady symptomatized by anxiety states brought on by a deficiency of bureaucracy or formal procedure. Outward manifestations included insistence upon or excessive knowledge of parliamentary procedure in meetings; excessively neat or expensive clothing; punctuality; or relative absence of hair in males. The disease was often associated with efforts by the victims to take over or infiltrate what they hallucinated as an "organization," but this was not universal: They may have, say, arrived with the friendliest intentions of "forming a united front" with others supposedly on the left, only to get bewildered by an absence of office, files, membership lists and cards, dues, etc.; and finding instead a mysterious maze of NETWORKS, AFFINITY GROUPS, TELEPHONE TREES, COMMUNES, COLLECTIVES, and DEALERS, whose purposes, especially that of the latter, were incomprehensible. Yet withal, the structure-freaks had a place in the scheme of things if given tasks appropriate to their peculiar talents, which could range from the "mobilization" of half a million people in Washington for a few hours of speeches on down: Thayer, the *The Farther Shores of Politics* (1967), reported asking Jerry Rubin about the presence of communists in the Vietnam Day Committee (VDC) in Berkeley: "Of course we have communists working here. They're the only ones who show up on time. We couldn't run the mimeograph machines without them."

With the growing popularity of PARANOIA in the late 60s, however, the presence of a manifest structure-freak in the vicinity became a cause of grave concern, as it was implicitly understood that this person was a NARK, a PIG (FBI or local Red Squad), or, worst of all, a member of the Progressive Labor Party (PL), as this betokened endlessly stupefying SHARP STRUGGLE.

During 1968–69 the term STRUCTURE-FREAK vanished altogether, in that anyone who pretended to status or even respectability in the movement necessarily paid lip-service to the VANGUARD even if not knowing or caring what this meant or implied.

sharp struggle. (*Der.:* Early Communism, "To browbeat with dogmatic rhetoric." E.g., 1924 Communist Youth International directive ordering "SHARP AND RELENTLESS STRUGGLE AGAINST RIGHT-OPPORTUNIST DEVIATIONS AND SOCIAL—DEMOCRATIC VESTIGES." Emphasis in original.) The disputations between the NO and PL factions within SDS, leading to the contest over "control" of that "organization" in June 1969 followed by its swift disappearance. SHARP STRUGGLE was mostly confined to the occasional Regional Conferences (RC) and quarterly National Conferences (NC), to which only HEAVIES were (informally) invited or self-invited. For this reason we only heard this term because Foss was the next-door neighbor of the Syracuse University SDS chapter president. (On the eve of departure to attend an RC he yawned, "Sharp struggle. . . ." to a woman present. "Yea, sharp struggle," she yawned back.) There was nothing implausible or historically unprecedented about a tiny disciplined minority like PL infiltrating and taking over a mass-organizational "structure," e.g., a trade-union or special-interest group, but if we use "structure" as our metaphorical yardstick, then SDS was a tub of Jello or chocolate pudding: While perhaps 100,000 people participated regularly in the activities of local chapters at the height of SDS ca. Fall 1968, there were never more than 5,000 paid-up "national members," while the NO in Chicago had only the vaguest idea as to the number of chapters and their location (cf. Sale, 1973). It was thus a simple matter for PL to "take over" SDS via the mechanics of taking over small chapters (thanks to the soporific properties of Marxism administered in large doses), soliciting proxies from chapters wherein nobody was interested in going to the National Convention in Chicago, or inventing chapters whose nonexistence could not be verified by the NO, thereby managing to outvote the NO partisans at the Convention; but this merely opened the drain through which the pudding — melted by the heat of the strife—just leaked away.

paranoia, paranoid. (*Der.:* psychotherapy) **a)** In the drug culture, an allusion to the effects of marijuana and LSD attributable to the lateralization of the pattern-recognition function in the right cerebral hemisphere. There is speculation to the effect that marijuana acts by depressing the functions—including abstract reasoning—of the normally-dominant left hemisphere; and that LSD stimulates the functioning of both hemispheres such that neither is dominant but thereby entailing a species of relative "upward mobility" for the normally-subordinate right hemisphere. As patterns thus recognized may be rendered vividly malevolent by slight extrinsic or intra-psychic perturbations, these may induce psychic states in which fear or anxiety predominate, these moreover accompanied in LSD use by roller-coaster ride called GOING THROUGH THE CHANGES, the usage of PARANOIA became well-nigh universal among users of these drugs during the 60s. **b)** In the practice of overt politics, the term PARANOIA was applied when fear and anxiety analogous to that encountered in drug use were manifested intrapsychically. The usage would otherwise seem silly, as one was indeed followed, infiltrated, entrapped, monitored electronically, harassed legally and illegally, and subjected to official and unofficial discrimination. Though fear of what was designated under the general rubric of REPRESSION was extreme and was attributed by some movement participants to excessive use of drugs by the most fearful, subsequent revelations which emerged during and after the period (1973–74) of the Watergate scandal of the extent of the surveillance and harassment operations of the Johnson and Nixon Administrations, as well as of the multiplicity of secret-service bureaucracies not under the *de facto* control of the Head of State, indicate that the worst fears of even those allegedly crazed by drugs were if anything understated.

repression. Something which in the late 60s the PARANOID person sat home and patiently awaited as for the coming of the Messiah and when it came did nothing to scare away; but which the TOGETHER person went out to actively provoke, until, thus annoyed, it finally CAME DOWN.

relevant. In the early 60s, something which an avowed radical said or did in hopes that someone in the Kennedy Administration would notice. In the late 60s, something done expensively by a member of the Johnson Administration in hopes of appeasing some bunch of avowed revolutionaries; or, alternatively, something done by the administration or faculty of a college or university in response to a LIST OF NON-NEGOTIABLE DEMANDS.

nigger. This was a manifestation of the Law of Emergent Contradiction among white dissidents in the 60s in that the usage indicated the emergence of a newly self-defined "oppressed" social category, that is, one whose members had begun to "get into their own oppression" as opposed to vicariously "getting off" on the struggles of others. The usage of NIGGER was dictated by its connotations of "invisibility" and "powerlessness," these words having also been conspicuous in the socio-political vocabulary of the period. Examples: **a)** From 1964 incipient Black Nationalism in what was then called the Civil Rights Movement resulted in the progressive extrusion of young whites from participation alongside young black students and intellectuals even while the objectives of the latter were still nominally "integrationist." The whites were told to "go organize your own communities," a euphemism for "get lost." Some white students thereupon concluded, however reluctantly, that the movement had something to do with themselves, as became manifest in the Free Speech Movement at Berkeley (1964–65), though even here blacks served as the initial pretext. A document prominently associated with the FSM upheaval was a pamphlet—subsequently published as a book—by Jerry Farber entitled *The Student as Nigger* (1969). White radicals remained committed to the understanding of students as an oppressed category until they were GUILT-TRIPPED at the end of the decade by the concept of WHITE SKIN-PRIVILEGE. **b)** Following this precedent, the women of the Cornell University SDS chapter in early 1968 wrote a mimeographed document entitled "The 'Chick' as Nigger."

masturbation. a) Up to ca. 1969, in general terms anything which did not foreseeably eventuate in CONFRONTATION. The latter term denoted a situation fraught with at minimum the possibility and preferably the probability of physical conflict with PIGS, however defined. Thus, mere talk was MASTURBATION, protracted talk was BULLSHIT MASTURBATION, and abstract rhetoric was INTELLECTUAL MASTURBATION. In 1969 black students at Cornell University, conspicuously if perhaps only symbolically armed, occupied the student union, Willard Straight Hall, while students held a mass meeting in their support and militant rhetoric flew thick and fast, but no riot eventuated immediately. Overnight, though, the trick was turned by the SDS chapter, which in the morning circulated a flyer headed "MASTURBATION? OR INTERCOURSE!" **b)** This sort of usage became taboo shortly thereafter as radical feminists understood it as sexist: Masturbation, to some radical feminists, was considered a progressive step for women in that it freed them from sexual dependency upon men; there was, of course, a school of thought which condemned this, in that it stopped short of lesbianism, as SELLING OUT. This period witnessed the popularity of Anna Koedt's "The Myth of the Vaginal Orgasm" (1973).

Black Loan Words

thing. Self-expression, personal bent or inclination, hobby or preoccupation, event, celebration, collective enterprise.

into. Preoccupied, absorbed, or involved, at least for the time being, especially as with a THING, TRIP, BAG, or HANGUP. HEAVY INTO designated a greater degree of INTO.

do. a) Take a drug. *b)* Be involved as with a THING; replaced by INTO.

shit. a) drugs. **b)** Weapons, as in "get our SHIT together, y'unnerstan? y'know what I mean?"

dig. a) Understand. **b)** Like. **c)** Accept.

like. Particle employed to establish an informality of tone. Usable for beginning, ending, or punctuating sentences, provided that the speaker was sufficiently "compulsive" to retain discernible sentence structure.

man. Particle frequently coupled with LIKE. In some periods or places, acceptable for use by man in addressing woman but not vice-versa. Correct when used by man in addressing another man during pre-feminist period; subsequently avoided in same situation by man seeking to show that he was DEALING WITH his sexism.

with. Indicative of ongoing sexual relations between two people, with implications of monogamy; otherwise indicated that a woman was accompanied to a party or such-like event by her lover.

gone. a) Exaltedly stoned. **b)** Insane. **c)** Quite good. **d)** BURNED OUT.

rap. Derived from black prison argot as a shortened form of "rapport" and meaning, "speak gravely on weighty matters." In the black original therefore, HEAVY RAP was a redundancy; this did not apply to white usage. Common meanings: **a)** Speech under the influence of drugs which sounded like senseless babble to others whatever their "state of consciousness." **b)** By extension, any monologue. **c)** Any monologue repeated by the same individual on numerous occasions: "so-and-so's usual RAP, you've heard it a million times I'm sure." **Var.:** RAP TO. Address a monologue to an audience. RAP WITH. Converse with another person without monologues. **Syn.:** MEANINGFUL COMMUNICATION; RELATE TO; ESTABLISH DIALOGUE.

REFERENCES

Corso, Gregory
1960, "Abomunist Manifesto." In *The Happy Birthday of Death*. New York: New Directions.

Farber, Jerry
1969, *The Student as Nigger*. New York: Pocket.

Hollander, Xaviera
1973, *The Happy Hooker*. Paris: J.C. Lattes.

Koedt, Anna
1973, "The Myth of the Vaginal Orgasm." In Anna Koedt, Ellen Levine and Anita Rapone. *Radical Feminism*. New York: Quadrangle.

Marx, Karl
1967, *Capital*, Vol. III. New York: International.

Mailer, Norman
1959, *Advertisements for Myself*. New York: Putnam

Milner, Richard and Christine Milner
1972, *Black Players*. Boston: Little, Brown.

Sale, Kirkpatrick
1973, *SDS*. New York: Vintage.

Thayer, George
1967, *The Farther Shores of Politics*. New York: Simon & Schuster.

CONTRIBUTORS' NOTES

PAULA GUNN ALLEN
a Laguna Pueblo Indian, teaches native American Studies at Berkeley; her new novel is *The Woman Who Owned the Shadows* (Spinster's Ink, 1984). She has written 5 books of poetry and edited a MLA volume *Studies in American Indian Literature, 1983*.

NANCY ANDERSON
lives in NYC; she is a contributing editor to *Social Text*.

DAVID APTER
is professor of Comparative Development at Yale University and the author of several books, among them *Against the State* (Harvard University Press, forthcoming.)

STANLEY ARONOWITZ
is professor of sociology at The Graduate Center City University of New York and The Center for Worker Education, City College. He is the author of four books, the most recent of which is *Working Class Hero, A New Strategy For Labor* (Pilgrim Press, 1983). His articles have appeared in *The Nation*, *Social Policy*, *The Village Voice Literary Supplement*, and the *Los Angeles Times*, as well as numerous academic journals.

MARTIN BLATT
writes for Pacific Street Films (Brooklyn). He has worked with Noam Chomsky since 1968 on numerous projects. Recently he has completed a biography of Ezra Heywood, a 19th century free love anarchist.

HERBERT BLAU
is the author of *The Impossible Theater; A Manifesto*, about his early theater work, and of two new books *Take Up the Bodies: Theater at the Vanishing Point*, which derives a theory of theater from the work of KRAKEN, and *Blooded Thought: Occasions of Theater*, a series of theoretical essays on postmodern performance. He teaches English at University of Wisconsin, Milwaukee.

MURRAY BOOKCHIN
an old radical from the 30s and a CIO labor organizer in his youth, is now a retired professor of social theory and environmental studies. He lives in (socialist) Burlington, Vermont, where he is very active in the peace movement. He is author of *Our Synthetic Environment*, (1962), *Post-scarcity Anarchism*, (1970), *The Limits of the City* (1973), and most recently *The Ecology of Freedom*, (1982).

CONTRIBUTORS' NOTES

RACHEL BOWLBY
studies at Yale and is working on "Commerce and Culture in Dreiser, Gissing, and Zola."

JAY BOYER
teaches at Arizona State University. His work has appeared in a wide variety of periodicals, including *The Nation* and *The Paris Review*. "As Far Away As China," a longer consideration of the 60s and the war in Vietnam than that which appears in this volume, will be included in *Perspectives*, edited by John Clark Pratt, which will be published by Viking-Penguin later this year.

ERNIE BRILL
is a fiction writer and the author of *I Looked Over Jordan, and Other Stories* (South End, 1980).

GENE BROWN
is a freelance writer based in Brooklyn. His published work has included social criticism, popular science, and humor.

PAUL BUHLE
directs The Oral History of the American Left at Taminent Library, New York University, and is editor of *Free Spirits*, City Lights Annual. The Buhles' Derrwar Bookstore, 107½ Hope Street, Providence, Rhode Island 02906, carry most of the works mentioned here.

MARILYN COFFEY
writes poetry and prose, fiction and nonfiction. Her nonfiction has been published in *Atlantic Monthly*, *Natural History*, purchased by *American Heritage*, and nationally syndicated by Associated Press. An assistant professor of English and Humanities, she teaches at Pratt Institute in Brooklyn.

MIKE DENNING
teaches at Columbia University's Center for American Culture Studies and is the author of *Cover Stories: Narrative and Ideology in the British Spy Thriller*. (Routledge & Kegan Paul, forthcoming).

MURIEL DIMEN
is associate professor of anthropology Lehman College and a psychoanalyst. The author of *The Anthropological Imagination* (McGraw-Hill, 1977), she has written on sexuality, ethnicity, feminism, and social theory. She is currently working on *Sexual Contradictions* (MacMillan, forthcoming).

GEORGE DRURY
is a philosopher. He has taught at Loyola University (Chicago), Wayne State University (Monteith College) and is presently on the faculty of Empire State College (SUNY) in Rochester, New York.

FINVOLA DRURY
is a poet and writer. Her work has appeared in *Poetry* (Chicago) and has been published by *The Alternative Press*, Grindstone, Michigan. She now lives in Rochester, N.Y.

MARTIN BAUML DUBERMAN
teaches at CUNY, Lehman College. He is the author of nine books among which is *Black Mountain: An Exploration in Community*. Currently he is writing a life and times of Paul Robeson (Knopf) and has been commissioned to do a play on Paul Goodman.

KATE ELLIS
teaches English at Rutgers University. She contributes to *In These Times* and is presently working on a book-length feminist analysis of gothic novels.

SILVIA FEDERICI
is the founder of the New York Wages for Housework Committee (1973) and spokeswoman for the Wages for Housework campaign in the US. She has written on various feminist issues, her latest work including a book on women and reproduction in the transition from feudalism to capitalism.

A. BELDEN FIELDS
teaches political science at the University of Illinois at Urbana. He is the author of *Student Politics in France* (Basic Books, 1970) and *Trotskyism and Maoism: Studies of Theory and Practice in France and the United States*, to be published by Praeger/Autonomedia, 1984. The essay collected here, in slightly altered form, comprises a portion of it.

DANIEL FOSS
is the author of *Freak Culture* (Dutton 1973) on the youth culture of the 60s, and "The World View of Talcott Parsons" in *Sociology on Trial* by Arthur Vidick and Maurice Stein. He has coauthored numerous articles on contemporary social movements with Ralph Larkin, with whom he has recently completed a book on the same (Bergin and Garvey, forthcoming). He is presently working on a study of attention-interruption syndrome.

JEAN FRANCO
teaches at Columbia University in the Department of Spanish and Portuguese. She writes social and literary criticism on Latin America. Among her works are *The Modern Culture of Latin America*, and *Cêasar Vallejo: The Dialectics of Poetry and Silence*.

SIMON FRITH
is Senior Lecturer in Sociology at the University of Warwick, rock critic at the London *Sunday Times*, and the author of *Sound Effects* (Pantheon, 1981).

JAMES GILBERT
grew up in a Republican enclave outside Chicago and attended Carleton College in the late 50s. Then he went on to graduate school in history at the University of Wisconsin. While there, he became an editor of *Studies On The Left* until it moved to New York. Since the late 60s he has been Professor of History at the University of Maryland.

COLIN GREER
taught social history at CUNY and was the editor of *Social Policy*. He is now the vice-president of the New World Foundation which awards grants in such areas as civil rights and nuclear disarmament. He is the author of *The Great School Legend* (Basic Books, 1972) and *The Divided Society* (Basic Books, 1974). He is co-editor of

What Reagan is Doing to Us (Harper and Row, 1982) and of a forthcoming book, *After Reagan* (Harper and Row).

FREDRIC JAMESON
is Professor of French and the History of Consciousness at University of California at Santa Cruz. His most recent book is *The Political Unconscious* (Cornel U.P. 1980). He is currently writing a book on postmodernism.

CARL JORGENSON
is associate professor of sociology at UC Davis. His areas of interest are black personality and achievement, affirmative action and race relations, and Afro-American studies.

TIMOTHY V. KAUFMAN-OSBORN
teaches political theory at Whitman College. He is currently working on a study of the relationship between science and politics in the thought of John Dewey, Emile Durkheim, and Max Weber.

FLORYNCE KENNEDY,
a lawyer and feminist activist, is the author of *Abortion Rap* (with Diane Shulder), *Color Me Flo*, and most recently *Sex Discrimination in Employment* (Mickie-Bobbs-Merrill). She can be seen on *The Flo Kennedy Show*: Manhattan Cable and Group W, Channel C. She is the national director of VAC-PAC (Voters, Artists, Anti-Nuclear Activists and Consumers for Political Action and Communications Coalition).

JOEL KOVEL
's most recent books are *The Age of Desire* (Pantheon, 1982) and *Against the State of Nuclear Terror* (South End, forthcoming).

JOHN M. KRAFFT
teaches English at Suffolk County Community College. He edits Pynchon Notes with Kaachig Tölölyan.

ARNOLD KRUPAT
is the co-editor of *Native American Autobiographics Series* by University of Nebraska Press. He teaches literature at Sarah Lawrence College.

TULI KUPFERBERG,
a renaissance man, was a founder of, and songwriter and performer in the Fugs, the notorious satirical radrock group of the 60s. Poet, peasant and pamphleteer, he is also director of The Revolting Theater and a singing cartoonist. His latest book is *Was it Good For You, Too?* Vanity Press, 1983.

RALPH LARKIN
is the author of *Suburban Youth and Cultural Crisis* (Oxford U.P., 1979); he has a book forthcoming with Daniel Foss from Bergin and Garvey entitled *Revolution of Order, Order of Revolution* on social movements. At present he is working as a social science research consultant with special interest in the effects of intensified interpersonal competition.

KAREN LINDSEY
is a poet and teaches at Emerson College: she writes on women's issues, spirituality, and other stuff.

ELLIOT LINZER
earns his living as a freelance indexer: he has been active in radical politics since 1961.

RICHARD METZ and **ALEX JEAVINS** (Otto Nomia and Studabaker Evans) were born and grew up in suburban Philadelphia. Both are middle children in large families with patios and animals. These amusing ex-art students live and work with people they love in Philadelphia. Otto feels he is the living reincarnation of Plato, and Studabaker experiences himself as part Moose.

JILL NELSON
is a freelance writer based in Harlem and a Charles H. Revson Fellow at Columbia for 1983–84.

GRETA HOFMANN NEMIROFF
is Director of the New School of Dawson College in Montreal. She is a member of various feminist organizations and has written and published widely on women's issues. The author of several published stories and a completed novel (so far unpublished). She is married and mother to three children.

SUSAN E. OSBORN,
a freelance writer and reviewer, is books editor of the *Vassar Quarterly*.

FRED PFEIL
is co-editor of *Minnesota Review* and a writer whose fiction has appeared in *Plowshares*, *The Sewanee Review*, *The Georgia Review*, and *Boundary II*, among other places. He is also a member of DSA.

HERMAN RAPAPORT
teaches English at Loyola University of Chicago and is the author of *Milton and the Postmodern* (Nebraska University Press, 1983).

ADOLPH REED JR.
teaches political science and Afro-American studies at Yale. He is also a contributing editor of *Telos*.

ROBERT ROTH
writes fiction and social criticism. His work has appeared in the *St. John's Review*, *Social Text*, and *Cultural Correspondences*. In the late 60s he edited *Park Row*.

ARNOLD SACHAR,
essayist and social critic, has written for *Liberation* and the *Village Voice* and has broadcast over WBAI.

SHARON THOMPSON
is co-editor of *Powers of Desire: The Politics of Sexuality* (New Feminist Library, Monthly Review Press, 1983). Her stories and articles have appeared in a number of publications, including *Feminist Studies* and *Heresies*, and she is currently working on a book of life histories about teenage sexuality and romance.

KIRKPATRICK SALE
is the author of *Human Scale* (1980) and *Power Shift* (1975), as well as a history of the 60s and the Students for a Democratic Society, *SDS* (1973).

SOHNYA SAYRES
teaches humanities at The Cooper Union and New York University. She is presently completing a book entitled *Susan Sontag and the Practice of Modernism* (Bergin and Garvey, 1984).

CHARLEY SHIVELY,
a member of the Fag Rag Collective, is a professor of law and justice at the University of Massachusetts, Boston.

ALIX KATES SHULMAN
is an essayist and novelist. Her novels include *Memoirs of an Ex-Prom Queen*, *Burning Questions*, and *On The Stroll*. She has taught fiction at The New School for Social Research, Yale, and NYU. She has been an active feminist since 1967. Her contribution in this volume is from her novel on the 60s, *Burning Questions*.

ANDERS STEPHANSON
is managing editor of *ST*, and is at present writing on George F. Kennan, art and foreign policy.

JERRY WATTS
teaches political theory and Afro-American politics at UC Davis. He is presently completing a book on the politics of Black and Jewish intellectuals since the 30s.

IRVING WEXLER
is an artist-writer whose work has been published in *Poetry Magazine*, *Dublin Review*, *Cultural Correspondence* and various anthologies. A number of his plays have been produced off-off Broadway, and his artwork has been exhibited in Soho and elsewhere.

CORNEL WEST
teaches philosophy at Union Theological Seminary, New York City and is the author of *Prophesy Deliverance! An Afro-American Revolutionary Christianity* (Philadelphia: Westminster Press, 1982). In the fall 1984, he will become Associate Professor of Philosophy of Religion at the Divinity School of Yale University.

ELLEN WILLIS
is a senior editor at the *Village Voice*. She is the author of *Beginning to See the Light*, a book of essays on culture and politics, and a long-time feminist.

RICK WOLFF
is professor of economics at University of Massachusetts at Amherst. He is presently completing a book with Steven Resnick on Marxist theory.

SOL YURICK
is a novelist. Among his works are *The Warriors*, *The Bag*, and *Richard A*. This last is available in Avon paperback. He lives in New York.

Courtesy of Paul Buhle.

INDEX

The editors of *The 60s, Without Apology* are all members of the *Social Text* collective. **Sohnya Sayres** teaches humanities at New York University and Cooper Union; **Anders Stephanson** is managing editor of *Social Text*; **Stanley Aronowitz** is professor of sociology at CUNY Graduate Center; and **Fredric Jameson** is professor of French literature and history of consciousness at the University of California, Santa Cruz.

Library of Congress Cataloging in Publication Data

Main entry under title:

The Sixties, without apology.

1. United States—Civilization—1945- —Addresses, essays, lectures. 2. Intellectuals—United States—Biography—Addresses, essays, lectures. 3. Intellectuals—United States—Books and reading—Addresses, essays, lectures. 4. United States—Intellectual life—20th century—Addresses, essays, lectures. I. Sayres, Sohnya. II. Title: 60s, without apology.
E169.12.S524 1984 973.92 84-2274
ISBN 0-8166-1336-2
ISBN 0-8166-1337-0 (pbk.)